SENIOR
SERVICE

SENIOR SERVICE

Carlo Feltrinelli

Translated by Alastair McEwen

Granta Books
London

Granta Publications, 2/3 Hanover Yard, London N1 8BE

First published in Great Britain by Granta Books 2001
Published in Italian by Feltrinelli

A CIP catalogue record for this book
is available from the British Library.

1 3 5 7 9 10 8 6 4 2

ISBN 1 86207 456 9

Typeset in Imprint by M Rules

Printed and bound in Great Britain
by Mackays of Chatham plc

1

Austria, Christmas 1967. We came to the edge of the wood in Indian file; the man with the rifle in the lead, a long trail of footsteps in our wake. Mine spoiled the symmetry. Sometimes we walked in the footprints left by those in front, to save effort. I remember the slow, hesitant, mechanical movement of boots sinking too deep in the snow.

When we got to the barn, we had to open it, and it fell to me to fill the bucket with oats and sesame. Carrying the bucket was my job. The others loaded the hay.

Then came the turnips, gigantic turnips, so sweet-smelling that you felt like peeling away the rind to reveal the hard flesh beneath. The turnips had to be scattered around. I hurled them as though I were an Olympic shot putter. When I threw them at the tree they burst into mush.

And in fact we all found ourselves up in that very tree, squatting down hidden and silent, screened only by four pieces of wood nailed to the branches. We were sitting on a creaky plank, forbidden to move. Even I, the least experienced of the three, had brought along two pairs of thick socks, remembered my gloves, and was wearing the right type of pants. In the vacuum flask there was mulled wine, but only a mouthful for me.

My father lit up an untipped Virginia cigarette; now it was a matter of waiting, the minutes stretching into quarter-hours, at least until something made a move up there on the crest of the hill: they usually came down into the gully from the left-hand slope.

The herd never arrived in a compact group. First came a reconnaissance party of three or four that I never managed to spot. (I am shortsighted like my father.) And when I finally did spot them, there were already ten or twenty head, maybe more. How many of them were there? They were almost on top of our hiding place.

The man with the rifle (he did not need it that day, but he always carried it) was the forest ranger. That evening he seemed satisfied because lots of deer had come, even big Walter with ten kilos of bony antlers on his head. The season, announced the ranger, had gone better than they thought: fewer head shot, no epidemics of eye disease, no animals fallen down the crevasse. And for the winter some new arrivals had come from the neighbouring valley.

Every so often, muzzles would be raised from the troughs to observe our camouflaged tree. They knew we were there, they smelled it and thought it and sensed it; but it's all right, they seemed to say, we'll play along. As if it were all perfectly natural.

Watching the deer coming down from the Fütterung, I associated their tics and gestures with those of humans. Where had I seen that face before? The first to come forward seemed to be the courageous ones, smarter or prouder than the rest, while the last were diffident, fearful, or perhaps simply more prudent. Just like people. I could not manage to banish the childish thought that I had already seen all these looks before. Human expressions on animal faces and vice versa.

But now darkness was falling and the raking nails of the wind ruffled the waters of the mountain stream. The big buck stationed on the left emitted a throaty rumble; a dry branch snapped, all the vague gestures became a single movement: the herd was gone, having suddenly darted off, for no reason. We remained motionless.

After a few moments, my father nodded to me. We could get the ladder, climb back down, and go back the way we had come. Ingelein would be waiting for us with dinner, wanting to hear what we'd been doing in the local dialect.

The man with the rifle continued watching over his mountains for another thirty years. One day, he surprised me by saying: 'Your father had a real feeling for the mountains, just like Hemingway.' I can't say if he was right, if he had really known Giangiacomo Feltrinelli, or even if he really knew anything about Ernest Hemingway.

* * *

My grandfather, who was called Carlo like me, may perhaps have seen and heard the same things on the summit of the Hochsitz, and who knows if one day my children will want to don those heavy green jackets with the horn buttons. They were born 122 and 125 years after him, but it's still a good idea to remember the heavy green jacket when going out after deer.

I believe that the person who chose the valley as the family's holiday home was Maria von Pretz, my Austrian great-grandmother. The twentieth century had barely begun when she bought the only hunting lodge in the area. It had been built in 1880 for one of Queen Victoria's grandchildren. After the Great War, Maria's children, middle-aged by that time, added a new wing to the residence, whose furnishings were inspired by the Wiener Werkstätten. The new wing was the work of thirty men who lived in the valley; my grandfather provided their sons with two pairs of shoes, complete summer outfits and the necessary winter clothing.

Carlo Feltrinelli was of average height, with a prematurely bald but well-shaped head, an aquiline nose and one of those slim moustaches that were in vogue at the time. He was an important man.

Left fatherless at the age of fifteen (Giovanni Feltrinelli died in 1896), Carlo was the eldest of four brothers. Maria, his mother, was helped by Giacomo Feltrinelli, Giovanni's uncle, who made the family leave Bolzano and move to central Milan. Uncle Giacomo, who had no children, acted as a father to the four boys, a task he carried out with generous and responsible affection. His wish was that the boys, once they reached adulthood, should maintain the place in society that their father had earned for himself.

German was spoken at home and discipline was strict. A set of family rules accepted by adults and children alike prescribed standards of behaviour, with a system of fines and incentives: those who went into the kitchen for no reason were fined ten cents (article 3), and there was a similar fine for those who dared to speak in Italian more than three times over lunch (article 5); then there was a twenty-cent fine for anyone caught touching the women (article 9), a 2 cent fine for anyone who bit his fingernails (article 10), and a 20 cent fine for those who did not switch off the electric light when the light was not needed. But there's more to life than punishments and so, conversely, arriving at breakfast in the correct order (by age) meant a five-cent tip, a whole day without a reprimand was worth ten, and a minimum of three As on the weekly school report brought in a good thirty cents.

All the boys studied. Carlo, for example, was sent to the Rosmini college in Domodossola in 1895. It was a hard life, with only a few decidedly spartan privileges. He was good at maths, but found Latin more difficult.

Shortly after Giovanni's death, Giacomo Feltrinelli took his nephew Carlo on a European tour. They spent time in a variety of places, including a two-week spell in Carlsbad, where Carlo's uncle took the waters once a year. During lunch in the hotel restaurant, Carlo was asked what he would like. 'A chicken breast,' he replied timidly. The waiters brought a whole chicken and, after Giacomo had finished serving himself, he let Carlo do the same, adding only: 'It's all paid for, now you have to finish it.'

Carlo did not dare disobey and the rest of the chicken was forced down with remarkable difficulty, an episode he never forgot.

This brief educational trip also included Munich, Zurich and I don't know how many other places; but, before returning to Milan, they stopped over in the family villa on Lake Garda. Carlo's uncle taught him how to snare birds on Mount Gargnano, using all kinds of traps and decoys. During that period Giacomo wrote down a comment on his young great-nephew, which he sent to the boy's mother. He is good company, he told her, although shy and still very much a child. But if he learns to travel, for it is of paramount importance to know how to travel, then for all I know he may even make something of himself.

A few years later, Giacomo came to appreciate Carlo's level-headed ways, his reserved intelligence and his capacity for study and work. In him he saw the main hope for the continuation of the family's business enterprises.

According to Giannalisa (who is my paternal grandmother), the founder of the Feltrinelli family was a certain Piero da Feltre, who lived around 1500: as the town of Feltre has walls dating from the 1500s, then they must have been built by him. This, at least, is grandmother's version.

At any rate, the people in the Garda area who earn a living from timber have always said they were 'Feltrinéi' (hailing from Feltre), which may not be entirely true; expert carpenters, tradition has it that they came to Garda to construct merchant vessels and warships, as well as fortifications.

I know Giacomo Feltrinelli's face very well because in the park at Gargnano there is a heavy life-size bust of him, mounted on an overly tall pedestal that was not made for the bust in question. We stuck a basketball basket under his chin. Perhaps this was somewhat disrespectful on our part, but at least I can say I know the face of my great-grandfather's uncle.

Giacomo was born in 1829, the youngest of thirteen. That the family was a poor one is clear from the fact that at twelve years of age he used to wander the streets of Gargnano selling 'three of a kind', which was a mixture of yellow flour, white flour and rice. Later he was to go into the charcoal business.

In 1846, when Pius IX was elected pope and when the people of the Lombardy–Veneto region, still a part of the Hapsburg empire, were dreaming of a federal Italy, the first Feltrinelli timber yard was opened.

At first, the timber came from the woods behind the house, whence it was transported down the lake to Desenzano, where the yard was situated. But soon supplies were also coming in from the Trent area, and from there all the way up to Val Pusteria. When Giacomo joined the family firm full-time, his presence gave the business a decided boost. Joking, my father used to say that the secret lay in selling 'heavy' timber, that is to say lumber that had been soaked with water in order to increase the weight.

A more plausible reason for Uncle Giacomo's meteoric success in business was that those were boom years for both the construction industry and the railroads. Industrial expansion, especially in the Milan area, was leading to a growing demand for timber: wood for scaffolding, wood for cross-ties, wood, wood, wood: it seemed that all people wanted was wood, and especially deal, the speciality of the Feltrinelli firm.

By 1870, the national rail network was three times bigger than it had been a decade before. But, because of the limited size of Italian forests (which were also hard to exploit), the production of resiniferous trees was still insufficient.

The firm moved to Milan in 1857 and over the following decade its clientele grew remarkably, even though the business was still a semi-regional one. It is hard to be precise, but from the early 1880s things changed radically: Feltrinelli timber was expanded with the addition of fifteen branches in Italy, while various commercial agencies within the Austro-Hungarian empire and in the Balkans were also opened. The strategy was to ensure direct control of the sources of supply, to have a hand in processing timber and, in certain cases, its installation. This was the reason for investments like the purchase of whole forests in Carinthia or the firm's participation in the construction of railroads in Vienna, Salonika, Sicily and Calabria.

Things went so well that it became necessary to diversify: in 1889 Uncle Giacomo created the Banca Feltrinelli. One of the bank's first moves was to finance the work of the engineer Giuseppe Colombo, the founder of Italy's first electrical company. This was the Milan-based Edison concern, named after Thomas Alva Edison, with whom Colombo had been in contact since 1881. With this operation (1896) the bank managed to ward off a massive take-over bid by German financiers, thereby welding the future destiny of the Edison Company to that of the Feltrinelli family.

In those same years, the business branched out into other sectors: textiles, with the establishment of the Feltrinelli & Co. Cotton Mill; and transport, with a stake in the company that ran the boat service on Lake Garda.

At the beginning of the twentieth century, while the timber company was supplying half the world with wood, the construction–real estate branch had attained at least equal importance within the group. This can be deduced from the establishment of some historic companies involved in building, construction, and real estate.* One of the first moves made by the real-estate company was to purchase twenty-four lots for a total of 115 thousand square meters in the Testaccio, the working-class district of Rome. At that time the Feltrinelli group also held other properties in Rome, such as the semicircle around Piazza Esedra. The entire block had been picked up for 271,000 lire following the failure of the Banca Tiberina.

By that time one of the leading lights of the entrepreneurial bourgeoisie, Giacomo Feltrinelli apparently was the kind of man who always knew where to find real Bardolino,[†] and how to decant, transport and drink it. And the same held true for pressing olives or growing lemons.

Looking at him face to face before taking a free throw at the

* These were Compagnia per imprese e costruzioni; Edilizia per il centro di Milano; and the Società italiana per il commercio degli immobili. All footnotes are by the translator unless otherwise specified.
† A famous red wine from the Garda area.

basket, I used to imagine him as authoritative, with the proud gaze and the frown of the wise man. I would say that this was also the image of himself that he left his great-nephews when he died in 1913. The newspapers, in their obituaries, spoke of him as a 'singular example of a self-made man', and in defining him as 'the wealthiest man in Milan' they estimated his personal assets at 60 million lire. This, at least, was the view of *L'Illustrazione italiana* of 9 March 1913.

I imagine that Giannalisa had also waited in silence for the herd to come, getting her ration of cold up there at the top of the tree. Or maybe not; she, less contemplative, was not partial to waiting, although she definitely was partial to hunting. She boasted of her 'distinguished career as a huntress'.

One day, so the story goes, she was obliged to wait at a level crossing at the mouth of the valley. Giannalisa was in her Rolls (she never went out without a Rolls in all her life). The train was late and, as she waited, she noticed that a hundred metres away a roe deer had come too far down the mountainside to graze. Repressing a start of surprise, she calculated that the animal was perfectly visible, ten paces beyond the edge of the wood. She picked up the brand-new rifle she had with her, steadied it against the copper-coloured window frame of the car door, and took aim. Three shots. The chauffeur, terrified, nearly lost his eardrums. One thing has to be said straight off: she was not the kind of woman you forget.

Family bonds never allow for indifference: for Giannalisa I felt sincere affection and serene detachment, the way it is with every good grandchild. She gave me strange presents, almost always with no appeal for a young boy: one of the last was an umbrella stand; perhaps not devoid of value, but an umbrella stand none the less. I feel now that it would be too complicated to explain why she gave me an umbrella stand and so it would be better to recall one of her more charming gestures. Like the time I asked her to bring me the American edition of *Blonde On Blonde* from New York. I wanted it because of the photo of Claudia Cardinale on the inside cover: the European version of the album did not have the photo. She made a note. And she made a visit to a record store on Fifth Avenue just for me.

* * *

On the death of Giacomo Feltrinelli, of the four heirs it was Carlo who intuited the exact state of affairs. Merely managing the assets would not be enough. Much better to try to broaden the company's prospects, step by step, maybe even within a Europe exhausted by the Great War. Since international business was the most important aspect of Carlo Feltrinelli's career as an industrialist and financier, I would be tempted to say he was a kind of pioneer, were it not for the fact that the term is too frequently used to mean adventurer, something he definitely was not.

Little is known, however, about my grandfather. He lived and had his personal offices in via Andegari, next to the La Scala opera house. There are no biographies or profiles of him; a few newspaper articles at most. In the economic yearbooks there are pieces on eminent names who were perhaps less important at the time, but only a few terse lines on him. He was said to be a reserved man who demanded privacy about his personal life.

In commemorating him on his death (in 1935), the attorney Edoardo Majno described him as a man 'of few words, but one sustained by sound studies and profound experience, thoughtful, and accustomed to approaching problems calmly in order to subject them to thorough examination'. Aristocratic in spirit, he was a man of few words, and definitely was not brilliant when it came to expressing his thoughts, 'but how pithy, how prudent, how profound!'. And, Majno added: 'He really was a man of good counsel, of prudent counsel, in the full Latin sense of the word.' And he defined Carlo as a 'simple and melancholy' man, whose industriousness was felt and professed 'as a technical activity, to which he devoted himself out of ingrained duty and a lofty awareness of its social function and

importance'. But, he concluded, 'without expecting to get anything out of it and, unfortunately, without gaining any joy for
himself. With that temperament of his, he was left, as it were,
on the outside of things, wrapped in the cloistered modesty of
his life and in a constant and serene bitterness.'

On the subject of timber, it is only right to point out that
with Carlo the fame of the Società Fratelli Feltrinelli grew
even more thanks to a massive importation programme. Deal,
beech and oak from Europe; pitch pine, Douglas fir, and iroko
from North America; teak from Asia; and costly mahogany
from Africa. Carlo Feltrinelli also acquired Austria's biggest
lumber company, and in 1932 he signed agreements of decisive
importance with the Russian trade delegation (Feltrinelli
became the exclusive importers for Italy), while from the
United States he obtained one of the first licenses granted by
the Masonite Corporation for the production of hardboard
panels.

The family's forestry company, the Società forestale
Feltrinelli, based in Fiume, invested heavily in Transylvania.
The photos are around somewhere. They show factories,
cableways, railroad networks, workers' houses, all specially
built. It was the first Italian undertaking of this kind and it
provided employment for about three thousand people. From
here, lumber was sent off to Bulgaria, Greece, Turkey, Egypt
and Syria.

In the thirties, warehouses, depots and sawmills were also set
up in numerous locations in East Africa while European deal
for urban construction work was sent to Eritrea and Ethiopia.

Some think that Carlo was overly involved in his work, forever driven by the idea of increasing the firm's assets. Others,
less agreeably, thought him a miser, unresponsive to the
promptings of the heart. To all he replied: 'The management
of our assets is a necessity; am I supposed to work toward
diminishing them, to make deals in order to lose?'

From the early years of the century, through the Banca
Feltrinelli, my grandfather helped finance the Acciaierie fer-
riere lombarde, the steel concern run by the Falck family. Carlo

was a man to whom everyone listened with respect. Giorgio Falck described him as 'an eclectic and shrewd man'.

The list of companies in which he was involved was a very long one indeed. In Italy alone, there were dozens and dozens of companies in fields like construction, land reclamation, chemicals, textiles and building. But he also ran companies in Calcutta, the Italian Far Eastern Company, the Bank of Italy and Egypt, and electrical companies in Latin America.

Towards the end of the twenties, at the peak of his career, he became chairman of the Edison Company, the most important in Italy, as well as chairman of Italy's second largest bank, the Credito Italiano. The controlling shareholder in both institutions, through them he was able to obtain the right to exploit the hydroelectric resources of the Styria region, thereby illuminating, or so the legend would have it, half of Austria. The *Times* estimated his personal fortune at eight hundred million lire.

Before her death, my grandmother set down her recollections in a text intended exclusively for family members. Only a few pages were devoted to her husband Carlo and practically all the rest dealt with the immediate consequences of their first meeting. The interesting thing about this document is what it *doesn't* say. But while grandmother's account arouses rather than satisfies one's curiosity, there wouldn't be much sense in expecting anything else.

I came to know more about Carlo through Teresa, the trusty, faithful, long-lived secretary I shared with him. Teresa first arrived in the office in Via Andegari at just over twenty years of age and she did not decide it was time to retire until fifty years later, when I was nearly twenty.

So yes, grandfather was withdrawn by nature, a reserved gentleman and a tireless worker. I gather he had little time for himself. He married when he was past forty and nothing is known about his other female friendships, except, perhaps, for a noblewoman of Russian origins, Ljuba Aleksandrovna, with whom he shared a passion for classical music.

As for the pleasures of the arts, the family pictures (including an Antonello da Messina donated to the Brera Museum) are fine but very sombre; and there was literature, certainly: what could be better than a good book after a frugal meal in his austere country house? But he was not a literary man in the real sense of the term; according to Giacinto Motta,* 'he was devoid of lyricism'. His only real passion seems to have been music, the piano being his favourite instrument.

Apart from that, it is worth mentioning his continuous promotion and protection, as a benefactor, of the Scuola industriale Giacomo Feltrinelli in Milan, a school still active today in the technical–scientific field. While he had no inclination toward ordinary charitable works, he was true to the family's public spirit and contributed toward the foundation, on the Gargnano estate, of a hospital, a nursery school and an old folks' home.

'Grandfather Carlo had two brothers, Bepi and Tonino': Giannalisa's handwriting is recognizable on the envelope with some family photos inside. Now, come on, Grandmother! Weren't there three brothers? Pietro, the missing one, born in 1885, committed suicide at twenty-eight for love of a Romanian dancer. He was in charge of the lumber reserves at Sibiu and his life was so short that Giannalisa must have thought it wiser to have him disappear altogether.

For Giuseppe, known as Bepi, things did not go that much better, even though he did live through the last splendours of the Austro-Hungarian Empire. The division of family labour assigned him the Eastern European side of the business, which is why he lived between Vienna and Villaco and oversaw the importation of lumber into Italy.

He spent his free time hunting wolves, grouse, foxes, roebuck, red deer and mouflons. Bepi's hunting exploits are documented in a precious album of photos in which he

---

* (1870–1943). Engineer, professor at the Milan Polytechnic, business man, managing director and CEO of Edison during the Fascist period.

appears together with all his trophies, including a group of zebras dispatched on an expedition to the African savannah. But his career as an obsessive hunter is also documented by some hundreds of horns and a bizarre variety of stuffed animals: from an eagle shot just as it was sinking its talons into a white hare (both of them ended up stuffed), to the bust of an enormous wild boar felled on the Hungarian estate of Prince Andràzy, who my mother claims was Empress Sissy's lover.

Every time Bepi returned to Italy, he lived the glittering life of a wealthy man about town and he made sure he was seen with the most beautiful women (including the celebrated Mazzolenis sisters), but he had no real interest in culture. They say that, once, at the railway station in Rome, the conductor of the train came puffing up, all hot and bothered, to ask him if he would please be so good as to let the renowned poet Gabriele D'Annunzio have a seat in his compartment (or maybe it was his own personal train). 'Never heard of him,' he is said to have replied.

The life of Giuseppe Feltrinelli took a dramatic turn the day he decided to look after a bear cub, probably found in Valle dei Cervi. Perhaps the cub had lost its mother – who knows? The fact is that Giuseppe wanted to keep it, in the garden of his home.

As the cub grew, he really became fond of Giuseppe. To the point that, one evening, on seeing his master return after a long trip, he greeted him with such exuberance that he gave him a bad wound on the shoulder. Bepi took morphine for the pain of the deep slashes left by the bear's claws, until he could no longer do without it. He died in Rome in 1918 after a last injection. He was thirty-five.

Antonio Feltrinelli, called Tonino, survived his three brothers and ended his life holed up on the shores of Lake Garda. Tonino enjoyed painting in oils. Married to the Countess Luisa Doria, he frequently clashed with Carlo's widow and, being childless, out of spite he left a large part of his estate (including a majority stake in Fratelli Feltrinelli lumber) to the Accademia dei Lincei.* The rich prize that bears his name is still awarded to outstanding international figures from the worlds of letters, the physical sciences, mathematics, history and medicine.

Antonio died in 1942. He was hit by an army truck near Brescia and fractured a number of ribs. The doctors prescribed pepper poultices to ease the pain. Septicaemia set in within the week. When Tonino was laid in his coffin, or so they say in Gargnano, his body burst in two, full of worms.

* * *

In early 1925, on behalf of the Italian government, Carlo Feltrinelli was nominated a board member of the Reichsbank, within the terms of the agreement between the Allies and Germany.

In Milan, it was rumoured that he wanted to take a wife and start a family: it's a thought that tends to crop up at a certain point in life.

One evening, on visiting Mino Gianzana's box at the La Scala theatre (Gianzana had started out as a clerk with the Banca Commerciale, of which he became the chief executive officer), Carlo's eye fell on one of his daughters, a faun-like twenty-two-year-old by the name of Giannalisa. Wasn't she the little girl that had gone swimming with them six years before, at Forte dei Marmi?† That summer, Carlo had rented Villa Hildebrandt for his mother, Maria. At that time Giannalisa was still in high school (she went to school with Dino Buzzati)‡ and her swimming costume was almost laughably chaste. How she had grown in the meantime! Now, Carlo felt she had become quite another person.

A reception during Carnival at the Esterle home served to renew the acquaintance. The girl was enchanting. Then came

---

* Academia dei Lincei: An academy of Science founded in 1603 by a small group of noblemen. Galileo was one of its earliest members.
† The upper-class seaside vacation resort in Tuscany.
‡ The author of the *Tartar Steppe*, one of the great Italian novels of the last century.

the announcement to her parents, smelling salts, fainting fits, tears and strings of pearls: then the wedding, forty days later.

At the mouth of Valle dei Cervi, a landau drawn by a pair of horses and two hunters wearing light-coloured festive livery awaited the bride and groom for the first stop on their honeymoon journey.

Giannalisa entered the house in Via Andegari with a black pearl in her left earlobe and a white one in the right. Light-blue eyes, long neck, short hair, slim figure: a classic beauty with a hint of something odd about her. She had been very unsettled as a child. Her father, a very strict man, had struggled to tame this rather wild little creature, and her mother's last words on her death bed were: 'Giannalisa, I never understood you enough, forgive me.'

Her sister Josefa was the opposite: less effervescent, less attractive and docile by nature. It ought to be said that the two sisters were about as compatible as the devil and holy water. And when Josefa found a husband in the person of Filippo Sacchi, a young teacher not devoid of charm, Giannalisa did all she could to oppose the marriage and to sow discord between the respective relatives.

The first two years of Giannalisa's marriage with Carlo were punctuated by two forceps-assisted births: Giangiacomo Feltrinelli was born on 19 June 1926, and Antonella on 13 November of the following year.

Then came the long vacations in all the right places for bringing up children, with many nannies and the husband often busy elsewhere. A serene and privileged life spent between Lake Garda, Villa Rosa (the Gianzanas' estate on Lake Como), the Baur du Lac in Zurich, the Excelsior at the Lido, and the Austria hotel in Via Andegari. Sometimes Carlo took Giannalisa with him, and for her those trips were the beginning of a great adventure. From her book of memoirs:

Life picked up again and in mid January 1928 Carlo and I took great joy in going to the landing stage in Genoa to take up residence in our splendid cabin on board the

Esperia. Carlo had to go to Cairo for a meeting of the
Banca Italo-Egiziana, of which he was chairman. Egypt
was still a British protectorate, a system that inculcated
order and discipline. We lodged at the Hotel Semiramis,
perfectly kept red felt and not a white thread to be seen.
On our arrival we found an invitation to dine with King
Fuad at the royal palace. The king had great difficulty in
talking, owing to a bullet that had lodged in his oesopha-
gus during an assassination attempt. Also in Cairo at that
time were His Royal Highness Prince Umberto and
Guidone Visconti di Modrone, who conducted the
orchestra in the theatre of the royal palace. In all my various dinners at court, I will never forget the incredibly
wide staircase, on which, at each side of every step,
Arabs and Negroes in full dress uniform stood motionless with long, burning torches in their hands. The
dinners were served by enormous waiters in sumptuous
full dress uniforms. There were always about a hundred
guests seated around a long, horseshoe-shaped table. The
local dignitaries wore frock coats and tails. Only three
ladies were invited, the Italian ambassadress, the lady in
waiting to the queen, who never appeared in public, and
I, who usually sat opposite the Prince of Piedmont. He
lived in the same hotel as us. His room was above mine
and every morning at eight I used to hear his feet touching the floor when he got up. Our friendship dates from
then. Carlo and I invited the prince to lunch in the desert
under an immense Arab tent, with the élite of the Italian
colony. An Arab equestrian show was planned to enliven
the lunch. I recall saying to the prince: 'Your Royal
Highness, we are eating more dust than they can serve
us.' Another day, we invited him to visit the three pyramids near the Mena House Hotel. I can still see His
Royal Highness climbing the one-metre-high steps all
the way to the top of one of the pyramids. After this
social whirl, Carlo had promised me we would visit the
royal tombs at Luxor and a wagon-lit left us at the Hotel

Palace on the banks of the Nile. The mountains before us housed the royal remains. We took a little boat to cross over to the other side of the Nile, where a camel took us to the foot of the mountains. Our guide, an Arab, warned me not to visit the tomb of Tutankhamen because it would bring me bad luck. But I am not superstitious, even though the pharaoh was still in his tomb all wrapped up, awaiting transportation to London. He had been assassinated at twenty-one. The tomb was small, the objects were all packed in crates. We visited the treasure chamber, the first to be discovered by Carter, financed by Lord Caernarvon. The other tombs were much larger because [their occupants] had lived longer. Luxor too came to an end and on our return to Cairo, fascinated by the Arabs and their abilities, I suggested to Carlo that we take one back to Milan, but with great sweetness Carlo had me understand that our house would soon have been infested with little Arabs. I was enchanted by the work they could do, in Cairo I saw one with a clothes iron attached to his ankle pressing a most delicate blouse with an infinity of pleats on the front. They were Arabs . . .

I suppose it was an unlucky coincidence, but the prophecy of the Arab guide before the tomb of Tutankhamen was to come tragically true in the subsequent pages of her memoirs.

Carlo accepted an invitation to spend a few days hunting at Castello della Mandria, where the guests included the Duke and Duchess of Pistoia and the Prince of Piedmont. On 21 November 1928, with joy, we set off in the car for Mandria, which stands a few kilometres outside Turin. Not far from the castle there was the cottage built for 'la bella Rusin'.* The next morning, we were going to stroll

---

* Rosa Vercellana, called 'la bella Rusin', was the mistress of King Victor Emanuel III.

through the estate to try to take a few hares. It was a damp, drizzly day. I shot one and saw a hint of something tragic in its dying eyes. The pheasant shoot proper was scheduled for the afternoon, with the Duke and Duchess of Pistoia. It was just midday when another guest arrived from Milan. I refuse to write his name, in any case he was the managing director of the Credito Italiano, the Milan bank of which Carlo was the chairman with an 80 per cent stockholding. A quarter of an hour later, Giacomo (our host) said: 'Giannalisa, let's see if we can bag a partridge in the quarter-hour before lunch.' We came to a wide, asphalted road, the coach backed away from the point where it had left us. Giacomo assigned a place to everyone. Carlo was in the vast meadow in front of me. I was on the edge of the road and less than a hundred metres to my right stood the wretched man, also at the edge of the road. At a certain point I heard him call me and as I turned toward him I saw his shotgun trained on a level with my eyes. He fired a shot at my face. I felt an atrocious pain and the blood gushed down my cheeks. I put the safety catch on my gun and put it down before making off as fast as I could towards Carlo, who was running down the meadow toward me, as were Giacomo and Gigetto, who, protected by the trees, had emerged in the meadow. They comforted me, Carlo put his handkerchief over my right eye and I saw a flash of madness in his eyes. In the meantime the guilty party was escaping in his car toward Milan and on the way his chauffeur ran over and seriously injured a man. The hunting party at Castello della Mandria was suspended.

'Child, did you shoot yourself for love?' 'No, Sister, someone shot me.' While in the hospital, she received an affectionate letter from the queen.

We shall never know if the shot was fired in error or if the wretch, a certain Orsi, was inspired by a sudden fit of insane passion. All we know is that the specialist, summoned urgently from Switzerland to save her uninjured eye, had to remove the one struck by the pellets, the right. A sad Christmas awaited the family.

The only alternative to a pirate's patch was a glass eye, but Giannalisa took courage: to disguise the glass better, she opted for a monocle; everything had to remain as it was before. She did not even want to give up hunting. She ordered the sight of her rifle to be realigned for her left eye, so she could still use it. But her husband obliged her to accept one condition: hunting on family land only.

Despite their efforts, the incident at Mandria introduced a note of gloomy ineluctability into their marriage.

'Mister Carlo', already reserved by nature, began to close up like an oyster. But in the professional field, these were the years of his apotheosis as one of the leading lights of Italian capitalism. In 1922 he became Vice-President of Edison, in 1924 he was appointed to the board of the Credito Italiano, while in that same year he was nominated Knight Grand Officer of the Crown of Italy and the government appointed him to the board of the Reichsbank.

Between 1925 and 1926, together with Giovanni Agnelli, Riccardo Gualino, Piero Puricelli, Giovanni Lancia, Piero Pirelli and Silvio Crespi, Feltrinelli was one of the promoters of the S.A. Autostrada Milano–Torino, at the time the longest highway in Italy (125.8 kilometres), and his name was linked more and more with the dynamic side of big business.

In 1928, with Mussolini already in power for six years, the appointment to the chairmanship of the Credito Italiano marked the peak of his career. The lumber business carried on without particular problems for the entire decade.

* * *

I repeat, I have not managed to find out much about my grandfather. My father didn't have enough time to get to know him really well and I didn't have enough time with my father to learn about his father from him. In her frenetic flight from time, Giannalisa managed to lose – goodness only knows where – her husband's most private papers.

Only the reports of the Fascist police, found in the state archives, provide more biographical information on Carlo. For example, there is one very interesting request from the chief of the political police to the Chief of Police in Milan (July 1927) in which the latter was asked to provide 'highly confidential' information on Carlo Feltrinelli, suspected of having expressed 'his strong disapproval of the actions of the National Government'. One of Carlo's employees, in reality an informer, had 'caught' him making ironical remarks to a colleague about the 'merits' of Mussolini's government. The issue was the revaluation of the lira. 'It may be that Mussolini and his gang of toadies are right, but I don't think so,' Carlo Feltrinelli is reported to have remarked, according to the tip-off.

The following year, another black-shirted employee was fired for persistent lateness and he inundated a series of desks – all the way up to those of Starace* and Mussolini – with denunciations of 'serious tax evasion on the part of the Feltrinelli company'. The dossier was sent to the Finance Minister. And there matters ended.

Another report concerned Giannalisa: 'They say that, when Feltrinelli's wife was on vacation last summer, not only did she talk freely of her husband's immense wealth, but also added that he kept a very large amount of Italian capital in England.'

In many confidential reports on my grandfather, reference is made to the 'silk waste affair'. He had been arrested in 1918 (for one night or perhaps a little more) because he was the managing director as well as a stockholder in the Società anonima cascami, a firm dealing in silk waste. The other partners suffered the same fate. During the war, the company had exported seven hundred thousand kilos of yarn and silk waste. The purchaser was a Swiss firm with contacts in German industry. The bottom line was that the consignment ended up

* Achille Starace (1889–1945). A die-hard Fascist who rose to become secretary of the Fascist Party. He was known for his ferocity.

in Germany, where it was used to make the envelopes of Zeppelin airships.

Although the subsequent sentence cleared the Italian producers of all direct responsibility, years later the accusation became a source of suspicion as far as the regime was concerned. This explains the numerous reports on the group's foreign business, all of which began with 'They say that . . .' Carlo's expected nomination to the Senate was quashed and labelled an 'infamous idea' by the highest echelons of the military. No one trusted in his patriotic spirit.

But relations between Feltrinelli and the Fascist government were formally perfect: Carlo was chairman of the Fascist Lumber Industry Federation and he frequently called on the head of government, received awards and what have you. These canonical attestations and signs of respect were necessary to carry on living in peace and working normally. Being pro-government is a predictable option for great industrialists. Feltrinelli, whose politics might be described as liberal, was first and foremost faithful to his work.

In 1930, Carlo Feltrinelli was almost fifty. He was not an old man but he sometimes felt he was. Perhaps this sprang from the continuous burden of responsibility or from the fact he was losing his teeth. The son of his dentist, whom I have met, recalls that Giannalisa (twenty-three years younger than Carlo) never missed a chance to rub salt in the wound: 'You're an old man!', she would say to him.

In the April of 1930, Carlo and Giannalisa travelled to Romania on board the *Orient Express*. They met with the managers of the local branch of the firm, visited Bucharest and, their work done, they stopped over at Sibiu. I think it was in a house or a hotel. But such was Giannalisa's passion for the chase that Carlo could not avoid a hunting party near the mouth of the Danube. Before them lay the Black Sea: she shot at the ibis, but failed to hit any of them.

On his return, Carlo had other things to deal with. The Wall Street Crash was making itself felt. The banks were in crisis

and everything was in turmoil. Although deposits with the
Credito Italiano had slumped by 14% per cent, this was a time
of mergers, incorporations and take-overs. But not every move
met with success, like the attempt to gain control of the Bastogi
group (which meant gaining control of a large part of the electrical sector). The government, the Bank of Italy and Alberto
Beneduce (the government's top man in the public finance
sector and the chairman of Bastogi) all vetoed the ambitions of
Carlo Feltrinelli's bank.

The developing crisis led to the restructuring of the great
'mixed' banks (including the Credito and the Commerciale),
which were saved by state intervention. In 1933, through the
banks, the state came to hold a 40 per cent share in Italy's joint
stock companies. The Iri was created.*

Carlo's problems grew as his control of Edison began to
weaken, because his hold on that company was guaranteed by
the stocks held by the Credito Italiano (which was about to
become a publicly controlled company). The problem was how
to avoid losing power in Foro Bonaparte.† I don't know how
long talks lasted, but in the end Carlo got what he had wanted
so badly: Edison would remain in private hands.

The man he had to deal with was Beneduce, the new chairman
of Iri. The two men had known each other for a long time, and
they respected each other. They were, along with Alberto Pirelli,
Giacinto Motta, Giovanni Agnelli and a few others, the leaders
of the various sectors upon which Italian capitalism depended.

October 1934. The regime boasted of stability while it passed
a law obliging all Italian citizens to declare any assets held outside Italy. Carlo's state of mind is not hard to imagine: electrical
stocks, German, Austrian and American bonds, stock holdings
in lumber companies (a good part of the Feltrinelli portfolio),
all were outside the state. The game was beginning to get

---

* The Institute for Industrial Reconstruction, a state-run industrial con-
glomerate.
† Headquarters of the Edison company.

tough, and he committed himself (the source is Giannalisa's memoirs) to honouring the new obligations. According to Giannalisa, his lead was not followed by his brother Antonio, who was also against declaring the assets held in the name of their mother, Maria von Pretz, by then eighty years of age.

The months that followed were particularly difficult. In 1935 the authorities managed to bribe some employees of the Bankverein in Zurich. They laid hands on the Feltrinelli family dossier and on those of another sixteen people. Checks on Carlo's position seemed to correspond with the statement of his assets. But this was not the case with Antonio and Maria von Pretz.

On 28 October, the national holiday in commemoration of the March on Rome, the Prefect of Milan sent a coded cable-gram to the Ministry of the Interior, intimating that Mussolini had ordered, through the Finance Ministry, the interrogation of some persons resident in Milan. They had to answer for assets held in Switzerland. The list included the name of Maria von Pretz. Three days later, the chief of police stated he had inter-viewed the lady 'concerning the existence of 165 kilograms of gold, as well as foreign stocks to the value of two millions, deposited in her name in the Bank of Switzerland'.

Maria von Pretz said that she didn't know, she couldn't remember. Carlo and Antonio were also summoned. Neither denied the existence of the deposits and they immediately telegraphed for the contents to be transferred to the foreign exchange department of the Bank of Italy. But by then the scandal had broken; the head of a powerful man, who was a source of embarrassment for an autarchic regime, was at stake.

In the following days it was rumoured that Antonio and his mother might be arrested. On 6 November, Carlo went to Rome to seek the eleventh-hour intercession of the governor of the Bank of Italy. He returned to Milan at night, apparently reassured. But he did not know that in those very hours Alberto Beneduce had received a government order requiring Feltrinelli's resignation from all his posts within the Iri group of companies.

The meeting took place on 7 November, at 6 p.m., in the
offices of Bastogi, of which Beneduce was Chairman.
Feltrinelli went there with the managing director of Edison,
Giacinto Motta, his influential partner in many a business venture. The words he heard were pronounced with
understanding, but their meaning was all too clear. Carlo could
not get his breath, his heart rate went through the roof, and
suddenly he collapsed. This, at least, is the story of the event as
reported in a night-time cablegram sent out in code by the chief
of police.

Suffering from this heart attack or embolism, my grandfather was escorted by Motta to Via Andegari. His secretary
Teresa saw him being carried into the bedroom. Giannalisa
called the specialist and told the children not to make a noise:
daddy had a bad headache. By the following evening, Carlo
Feltrinelli was clinically dead; forty-eight hours before that, he
had played the piano for the last time. He was fifty-four.

The propaganda machine immediately talked of suicide. In his
personal dossier there are copies of the confidential ministerial
memos that were circulated in the days immediately after his
death. Unfailingly preceded by the words 'they say', these
sources maintain that Carlo Feltrinelli committed suicide in a
sleeping car, in prison, in his own home, with a hand gun, with
poison, for fear of incarceration, and in any case always for
shame.

He killed himself, they say, after having discovered the extent
of his mother's flagrant guilt, a mother 'in the grip of a special
form of monomania attributable to congenital avarice'. 'What a
dirty business! What a dirty business!' concludes an anonymous informer. And, obviously, it was necessary to root out
possible accomplices: 'they say' that Alberto Pirelli too had
'organized a vast contraband currency ring', and 'they say' that
he and Feltrinelli were aided by the Fascist podestà* Visconti di
Modrone, who was suddenly ousted.

* The equivalent of mayor in the Fascist system.

Lending credence to the suicide-for-shame theory served to counter any attempts to exploit the affair in order to discredit Fascism. In the Paris headquarters of 'Giustizia e Libertà'[*] and in some parts of Italy there were those who ventured a parallel between Feltrinelli's death and the Matteotti[†] murder.

A broken heart or a poison capsule? Giacinto Motta's correspondence does not tell us everything we need to know. Five days after witnessing Carlo's death, Motta wrote to his Neapolitan friend Emma Savi Lopez:

> It was a most harrowing scene [. . .]. We were talking calmly, even though Carlo was troubled in spirit, in the office of a friend, who half an hour before had asked me to join them, when poor Carlo clutched his forehead with his left hand while clamping his right convulsively over his heart, thus arousing in us the gravest apprehension. A few minutes later, while someone had been sent off to call his doctor, two successive cries escaped his lips: what a pain, Giacinto, what a pain in my head; I am dying, Giacinto; I commend my children to you! And he spoke no more.

At a later date, 12 June 1936, in a letter to Majno, Motta alluded to a 'crazy gesture' on the part of Carlo Feltrinelli, without explaining further. This is a strong clue in favour of the suicide theory.

Vinzio, the deliveryman with the *Cantieri milanesi* firm who half-carried Carlo all the way to Via Andegari, is convinced that it was a heart attack, and in all the various ramifications of my family I have never heard any reference or allusion to hidden truths, to things that are known but never mentioned. And furthermore, the few people still able to provide some

---

[*] 'Giustizia e Libertà' was a group of anti-Fascist exiles based in Paris.
[†] Giacomo Matteotti (1885–1924). An Italian politician, member of parliament and secretary of the Socialist Party, Matteotti was an active anti-Fascist. He was murdered by a Fascist action squad in March 1924.

form of direct testimony, like Falck's daughter, Giulia Devoto Falck, flatly deny the suicide hypothesis.

But the doubt remains: what was the 'crazy gesture' that Motta referred to in his letter to Majno?

* * *

Perhaps Giannalisa did not manage to weep even for the grief of widowhood. Sorrow soon gave way to a kind of vertigo. Fate had decreed that, at a mere thirty-two years of age, she was to have an enormous fortune at her complete disposal.

Her father, Mino Gianzana, and Antonio Feltrinelli insisted on taking over the corporate posts left vacant on Carlo's death, but Giannalisa refused; she wanted to do things her way.

Her first move was to dismiss her husband's most faithful colleagues, thus revealing her true nature. This was noticed by Giacinto Motta, who wrote to his friend Majno:

> I only hope, and I trust that this will hold for you too, that I will be forever spared further dealings with a person who has put her own resentment and insane fear of losing the hoped-for profit before her sacred obligations toward children already bereft of their father. [. . .] May God protect those poor children, this is my most ardent wish, to which I add my fond hope that for you too there may soon be an end to the vexations and problems that this family has procured you.

Giannalisa's second move was to request an audience of His Excellency Il Duce: 'In order to explain the difficulties that I now find myself obliged to face on my own', she wrote. Mussolini, in this instance perhaps more sensible of decency than the widow, did not receive her.

No matter, she determined to make it on her own and showed that she was more than capable of doing so: she procured the statements of assets, replaced a few trustees and played her part to perfection.

In the afternoons, every now and then, she lent a hand in an institute run by a renowned Milanese biologist who was researching into tumours. She did this to take her mind off things. Her job was injecting cancer cells into rabbits.

'Bringing up children is a matter of luck.' I don't recall who said this but in any event you have to keep the most extreme instincts at bay. Giannalisa loved her children, this is certain, but she did not realize that she treated them in accordance with the dictates of an ill-considered logic. For she would punish and then repent. First she would mortify them and then shower them with kisses and hugs.

Giangiacomo and Antonella, in the meantime, were transported here, there and everywhere, like monkeys. The metaphor is not a brilliant one, but it is appropriate. An example? In 1936, after a splendid springtime cruise to Rhodes, it was off to New York by ship; but at Gibraltar the sea was rather rough: better to disembark in Lisbon. Whence it seemed like a good idea to make a flying visit to the resort town of Cascais. A car came to pick them up, and clothing and trunks were promptly stowed aboard because now they had to cross France and Switzerland. The new destination was much farther east: welcome to Austria! Attacks of carsickness at every bend.

For Giangiacomo and Antonella, school was out of the question, at most a semester at Milan's Giuseppe Parini high school: this was in 1937 or thereabouts. (According to the recollections of the famous Italian wine expert, Luigi Veronelli, at that time Giangiacomo's classmate). It was then that Giannalisa enrolled her son in the Gioventù italiana del littorio, the Italian Fascist Youth Movement. But the excessive shuttling between the new villa in the exclusive suburb of San Siro and the family's Roman residence on the Aventino persuaded Giannalisa to opt for private coaching. The teacher chosen to give literature lessons was Luciano Anceschi,* the future maestro of the New Italian Avant-garde, whom Giangiacomo, his first pupil, was to

* (1911–95), publicist, literary critic and professor of aesthetics.

encounter again much later. An alumnus of one of the city's
finest high schools was chosen to give the children lessons in
the family's Roman residence. From him, Antonella and her
brother learned the fundamentals of art history. His name was
Jean Piva. Today, he is a retired doctor, and I have met him.

He says he well remembers the yelling in the Feltrinelli
home, so much like a grand hotel, which always smelled of the
wax used to polish the brassware, and where a pair of dirty
hands was enough to set the fur flying. With the excuse of
museum visits, Giangiacomo could occasionally go out. He
almost always avoided the museum, preferring a field belonging
to the family on the Appian Way. Not that it was a special place:
it was a patch of ground, with some crops and a few trees. 'But
you could see that he stayed there willingly, he felt good there,
with a few tools and, thank heaven, a little silence.' Did he have
any friends? He didn't.

By way of compensation, one morning at breakfast there
appeared Luigi Barzini junior, thumb and index finger hooked
into the lapels of a gangster-style bathrobe. He was wearing
plush slippers and a cigarette hung from his fleshy lips: he was
the new fiancé of the richest widow in Italy.

The son of the greatest special correspondent of the early
twentieth century, an adventurous spirit who had reported the
Peking-to-Paris rally, Luigi junior was in his turn a journalist.
A period spent studying in America had provided him with a
lively, modern style that was superior to that of the average
Italian journalist. But he was overly influenced by his father's
aura, he felt he was the crown prince, and his English-style
clothes hung badly on him. His colleagues, perhaps out of envy,
said that he 'dressed like a white man', because he always had
the look of a 'Black' dressed in European clothes. Apart from
that, he was said to be fond of the comfortable life, and not
averse to a few luxuries.

In April 1940, two months before Italy entered the war, the
young man and Giannalisa pronounced the fateful 'I do'. It
happened in Amalfi, in the chapel of Sant'Andrea in the cathedral. The marriage was later to be annulled by the Rota, but the

bride had a clear memory of what she wore that day: 'a navy blue dress with white polka dots and a straw hat in the same colour'. Like his sister, Giangiacomo was dressed in a pageboy's outfit and his task was to toss silver coins in the air when the bride and groom emerged on to the steps. Amazement and pandemonium among the local children.

A few days after the wedding, on the point of leaving for his honeymoon, Gibò, as Barzini was nicknamed, was arrested by the Fascists. It seems that some time previously he had been taken by a hankering to play at espionage: during a spell as the London correspondent of the *Corriere della Sera*, he had passed on useful information to the authorities in Rome. On his return to Italy, in the course of a dinner with some British diplomats, prompted by a desire to show off, he let slip something about the messages in code sent out from their embassy: in short, he gave them to understand that the Italian intelligence service could read the messages with ease. The British checked this out right away: they sent a message quoting what Barzini had said; the Italian secret service, which was in fact listening in, was obliged to collar the newly wed groom.

Thanks to his father's connections, Luigi Barzini was sentenced to confinement right there in Amalfi, in the Hotel dei Cappuccini, together with his wife. A decidedly mild punishment for a crime that was in itself rather a serious one. Giangiacomo and Antonella spent part of the first year of the war there.

The two spouses, in theory, were obliged to present themselves once a week at the police station in Salerno in order to sign the register. But there was no need to enter the station, all they had to do was knock on the window overlooking the promenade in order to receive an 'OK, OK' that did not even interrupt their stroll.

Before this, my grandmother had also been arrested by the authorities: again in the course of a diplomatic dinner, she had been heard to speak badly of Mussolini. She got out of this predicament thanks to the immediate intervention of Enrico Caviglia, a friend she vacationed with who had been a Field

Marshal in the First World War. This minor incident came in handy as proof of her 'anti-Fascism' and she played on it for the rest of her life.

In the meantime, Mussolini's office had received Giannalisa's request that an aristocratic title be conferred upon her son. This happened in 1940 and the affair was brought to a satisfactory conclusion thanks to a substantial cheque. We do not know if the future Marquis of Gargnano had any opinion on the matter.

Again thanks to Barzini senior, who was friendly with the chief of police, Barzini junior was allowed to move to Milan. This was in March 1941. His 'compulsory residence' was the Hotel Continental, via Manzoni, because my grandmother did not want any flatfeet tailing her around the house. But after a few weeks, they were able to savour complete freedom once more and took up permanent residence in Miracielo, their villa in San Siro. But there, six months later, Barzini's swimming-pool was commandeered: they said it had to be converted into an air-raid shelter.

It was at this point that the needle of the compass swung once more toward central Italy, to avoid the worst of the fighting. In October 1942, the Barzini–Feltrinelli family opted for the Argentario, an area on the scenic road to Porto Santo Stefano where, not long before, work had been completed on Giannalisa's dream villa. It stood on top of a promontory, surrounded by thick Mediterranean vegetation: myrtle, lentisk and juniper.

Looking out from the veranda, to the left you can sense the presence of a sheer cliff face, while to the right the coastline shelves inward and you cannot see the beach, which is hidden by the undergrowth. It is a splendid place, but 'for us it was sheer murder', explains Aunt Antonella, then fifteen. 'We were left entirely to our own devices, but like kidnap victims, without ever going beyond the gate, without ever being able to get to know anybody . . .'

In fact, the human scenario was rather unpromising: when

Luigi Barzini was not marching around the estate giving orders (such as ordering sacks to be attached to the backsides of the mules so they couldn't soil anything), he was arguing with everybody. Giannalisa included.

It was no idyll and it was wartime, but in the meantime the family multiplied: Giovanna Ludovica was born in September 1942 and Benedetta came along a year after.

The first-born son, for want of an alternative, talked with the only people prepared to listen to him: the gardener, the son of his old nanny Ester (the gardener's wife), the workmen who came to see to the house, his private maths teacher (there was no hope for it: really pretty and an anti-Fascist into the bargain; she lost her job almost immediately). They listened to him; it mattered little if his talk was simple or if he rambled on as adolescents do. 'My father even gave him a little money so he could sneak out,' mutters the gardener's son in his thick Tuscan dialect.

All this familiarity with the servants and his disregard for the rules stuck in his mother's craw, and, for his part, Giangiacomo hated his stepfather with all his might, a sentiment that was cordially reciprocated. Giannalisa and her husband did not hesitate to inflict humiliating punishments on him, such as locking him up in the cellar for days on bread and water. There are witnesses. He suffered from claustrophobia from then on.

Barzini, later, was to justify himself like this:

I tried to take as much interest as I could in his upbringing, and, at a certain point, to steer him in the right direction with his studies . . . Perhaps I am a very poor teacher, perhaps I didn't even have the stuff of a stepfather, perhaps Giangiacomo was a careless scholar, rebellious and hostile, or perhaps there was no way we could understand each other, as he and I were profoundly dissimilar, the fact is that I don't think I ever taught him anything that stuck.

In the meantime, the war proceeded on its inexorable course.

After the Anzio landings, the Argentario, thought a safe place at first, became a key base for the German supply lines. The bombs rained down almost every day – one hundred and seventy-five air raids in all – and the Barzini–Feltrinelli household was regularly shaken by the blasts. At night-time, Luigi would shriek out the latest news culled from the radio transmitter; Giannalisa would yell 'Moron, moron!' if Antonella woke up the little ones ('but Mummy, shouldn't we run to the air-raid shelter?'); the estate filled up with poor people because the Croce neighborhood had been wiped out and even the church in the town had a hole in its cupola.

At that point, they say, Giangiacomo 'took a powder'. Armed with a pistol, accompanied by the future village butcher, he went into hiding in the maquis at the top of the hill. The only person with any chance of locating him was his friend the gardener, and in fact he found him: 'I'll come back only if you'll put me up for a bit in your place,' Giangiacomo told him. Deal.

One fiery night in May 1944, Giannalisa hid her jewels in a mule's excrement sack, Barzini's latest invention. They had to move fast, abandon the villa immediately, and chauffeur and servants grabbed what they could. At the top of the cliff, they jettisoned seven demijohns of grain; they were too heavy. After a night of bombs, the evacuees were left with a few shards of glass.

Giannalisa took herself and the others off, but it is not clear if she knew where her son was when she was leaving. For he was right there, close at hand, in the servants' quarters just below the citrus orchard.

* * *

The flight of the seventeen-year-old Feltrinelli lasted only a few days; then Giannalisa, who had reached Rome after many adventures, sent the cook (she called him 'the malign hunchback') to bring him home. Giangiacomo appeared beneath the pergola over the gardener's doorway; he came along without making any objections.

His mother was never to forgive him for that first escape. Many years later, on recalling the episode, she attempted to justify herself for having abandoned her son during the bombing: 'My duty was not to take any risks with the lives of the two little girls' – of which there were three (though in the meantime she had quarrelled with Antonella, who had been struck off the list).

Back in the family fold once more, Giangiacomo was sent off to school in the monastery of St John Lateran in Rome, where he spent the middle part of 1944. He struck a deal with his mother: once he got his school-leaving certificate, he would be free to enrol in the struggle against the Germans. 'She never expected me to succeed in this,' he confided in an interview years later, 'but I did.'

As well as Piva, his young tutor, he found another friend in Luigi Aurigemma, a few years older than him. Aurigemma's father, an archaeologist, was curator of the Museo delle Terme, where he lived with his family. Apart from the funereal little parties in the Feltrinelli home, Aurigemma remembers his strolls with Giangiacomo in the courtyard designed by Michelangelo.

Fifty years on, Aurigemma is over seventy and lives in Paris. A psychoanalyst, he has translated the complete works of Jung into Italian. In the evenings, he says, when the museum was free of visitors, they would stroll together 'talking of heaven and earth', and if there was a word that resounded under the arches more often than the others, 'that word was justice . . .' He may well have yielded to nostalgia, but the image is crystal clear.

In the November of 1944, Feltrinelli enrolled in the Legnano combat unit, a volunteer corps seconded to the 5th Army. After a brief spell of training in the Naples area, he made his way back north. He stopped over for a while near Lake Bracciano, where a married couple from Gargnano put him up. By chance, they too were called Feltrinelli, but they were not relatives and so Giangiacomo took an immediate liking to them. One morning, corpses were found lined up along the streets of the village. The couple went to turn them over, one by one. No, the young man they had treated for dysentery the day before was not among them. Perhaps he had already left for Tuscany.

In the area around Siena – where the presence of his division is documented in early March 1945 – the young soldier underwent more military training and joined the Italian Communist Party. From one of his autobiographical notes: 'I was introduced [to the party] by comrade Monti, another member of my unit (an old comrade who had done a year in Civitavecchia [prison] for political reasons) and comrade Ciafrè Vincenzo of the Siena federation.'

They all trooped off to the front, near Bologna, for the days of the Liberation. I have a clear memory of a story about the time when a mortar shell missed him by a whisker. Using his index and middle fingers to mimic the act of digging, he described to me how he poked around in the earth for the shell case.

The few months spent as a soldier in wartime made him more of a free man, with a tendency to act and take his own decisions. Demobilized in the August of 1945, he went back to Rome and enrolled in the polytechnic.

Like a well-disciplined militant, he frequented the local party branch in the evenings, but the officials of the PCI preferred to use him for another kind of task. They wanted to exploit his capacity to gather information, especially in monarchist circles.

But on 28 April 1945 the party newspaper *l'Unità* blew his cover by publishing an overly explicit article in which the Allied intelligence service also took an interest. At that time, the Referendum* campaign was in full swing, and the article contained information that someone in the Feltrinelli household had overheard. Here is a salient passage:

On the basis of information received from an excellent

---

* The Referendum held to decide whether Italy was to remain a monarchy or become a republic (1946).

source we are able to give news of an important meeting
held in the home of a family of big industrial sharks, the
Feltrinellis. The meeting was attended by the Duke
Acquarone, as the direct representative of the House of
Savoy, the president of the outgoing Senate, the Marquis
of Torretta, Senator Bergamini, the Hon. Porzio, and the
well-known slanderer of office workers Epicarmo
Corbino, the Treasury Minister. At this meeting, the discussion centred on the suitability of a great *coup de
théâtre* on the eve of the Constituent Assembly, in order
to restore the virginity of a compromised monarchy: the
abdication of Victor Emmanuel the elder and the subsequent renunciation on the part of Umberto in favor of
Victor Emmanuel the younger. Minister Corbino proposed an even bolder move: the withdrawal of the entire
House of Savoy along the lines of the withdrawal of
Alfonso XIII in Spain . . .

During the meeting, there was also talk of a more precise
coordination of the conservative press, with a major role
reserved for Barzini. By that time, Giannalisa was financing
his activities: he ran the Si press agency and two newspapers, *Il
Globo* and *Libera Stampa*. My grandmother enjoyed this kind
of commitment; she did not lack fighting spirit: on the eve of
the Referendum, she personally distributed pro-monarchy
pamphlets through the streets of Rome. From the Rolls.

Given the climate (and also the foul-up caused by *l'Unità*),
Giangiacomo was obliged to make himself scarce. He opted
for Milan, where, again in the late spring of 1946, something
important happened to him: he met a young militant with the
Socialist Party of Proletarian Unity (PSUP), Bianca Dalle
Nogare.

The piles of snow remained on the streets until April. Milan
was still a great wounded city that no longer stank of burning
debris but was still full of blackened patches where the fires had
been put out and of strange abysses inside apartment blocks
awaiting reconstruction. But life in the city had started up

again, the various social classes and categories were in search of
a new equilibrium, the newspapers were coming out, the the-
atres had reopened and the schools were once more crowded
with a new generation of schoolchildren. Their overcoats were
made from American blankets sold in the markets.

Giangiacomo and Bianca took to each other. At first, theirs was
a platonic relationship. She was a beautiful girl, from a family
that had been fairly wealthy before the war.

But in the aftermath of the slight suffered by her monarchist
friends, Giannalisa seemed horrified by the turn her son's
career had taken, and she was scandalized both by his spells on
the run and by the company he kept. Having a Communist for
a son was tantamount to having a son with the plague. In order
to redress matters, she came up with a diabolical plan. Probably
acting on Barzini's orders, four bogus soldiers in uniform were
to confiscate the couple of firearms her son had brought back
from the front. Following a sham search of the premises in Via
Andegari and a convincing threat of arrest, their brief was to
persuade him to take himself off, perhaps to Spain or to
Portugal, where Antonella was already living. Then there
would be the Referendum and, if the monarchy lost, or so my
grandmother's reasoning went, the entire family would have
taken its leave: crossing the Atlantic from Portugal was the
merest of mere bagatelles.

The plan worked perfectly: frightened by the idea of a sentence for the illegal possession of arms, Giangiacomo left for
Lisbon via Madrid, leaving Bianca without a word.

The account of the immediate aftermath of the Referendum
of 2 June, again taken from my grandmother's recollections, is
a minor masterpiece that explains many of her future moves.

At eleven a.m. of the 4th, His Majesty was expecting me
at the Quirinal but unfortunately I could not go because
a short distance from the palace my little car was struck
and wrecked by a Polish truck on the road that runs
alongside the gardens owned by Prince Aldobrandini.

The passers-by extracted me from the wreckage and laid me on the pavement, offering me handkerchiefs to stem the blood that was flowing from my head, but I did not accept them for fear of infection. I caught a glimpse of a carabiniere and I summoned him with my right hand, begging him to go to the porter's lodge of the Quirinal to leave word that I could not go to His Majesty because a short distance away I had been struck by a foreign truck. Finally a person knelt down at my side and said to me 'I am a doctor, you cannot stay here, allow me to accompany you to the Villa Bianca clinic. I shall stop a car', and we went to the clinic. They took me straight off to the X-ray department and at every plate taken, they came to me announcing in amazement that nothing was broken except for a fracture in the wrist bone at the side of my right hand and that it was natural that I was in pain all over on account of the knock I had taken. [. . .] I was extremely annoyed about being in hospital without a telephone in the room and on the fourth day I begged the doctors to send me home with an ambulance. I was champing at the bit but I managed to gain my bed. Alberto Bergamini visited me many times every day. On the evening of 12 June at 7 o'clock General Graziani called me to say that His Majesty wished to dine with me without other persons present, and I replied that only Bergamini was with me. 'That's perfectly all right, let him stay.' At nine in the evening, Bergamini was at the door of my house to greet His Majesty. He brought the king to my room. The windows gave on to the garden where gently swaying cypress trees screened the Baths of Caracalla. It was a splendid night. His Majesty kissed my hand, the table was at the foot of my bed and at my side there was an armchair for him to sit in after dinner. My absolutely wonderful cook performed miracles and my butler in his tailcoat served them up. The nurse helped me to eat because of the plaster on my wrist. But in everybody's heart a nightmare loomed over this apparent serenity. Gi [Barzini] went to the *Libera Stampa* newspaper offices before eleven and I implored him to phone with any news. After dinner the table was cleared and the four of us sat there waiting for something that no one wanted to talk about, something far worse than anything any of us could imagine. Shortly before one o'clock, the telephone at my side began to ring. De Gasperi* had called an emergency Cabinet meeting to proclaim immediately, without waiting for 18 June as agreed, the results of the Referendum. The monarchy had been defeated. Whiter than the nightdress I was wearing, I turned to the king, saying: 'Majesty, I always told you that De Gasperi was not to be trusted.' Fraud had certainly been committed. The thorny problem in which we were all entangled had become a reality. The advance information we had received seemed almost devoid of sense. The king talked of Queen Maria Pia of Portugal, and said that he would follow Carlo Alberto into exile in Oporto. The king was wearing a grey suit, Bergamini's look held all the horror of what we were going through minute by minute. A millennium of the House of Savoy that had begun with Umberto Biancamano was coming to a close with Umberto II because of the damned corrupt and treacherous politics of the Christian Democrats. With arrogance and injustice, they had demolished a monarchy that had endured for centuries. This sorrowful historic act was unfolding amid dimmed lights and the dark outlines of the cypresses that seemed projected into my room. The words followed one another in a disconnected stream. Every now and then, the king would take a glass of champagne from an antique silver salver and put it to his lips. I tried not to cry, but when he bent over to

* Alcide De Gasperi (1881–1954). Founder of the Partito Popolare (1919), a Catholic-inspired party that was to become the Christian Democratic Party in 1943, De Gasperi was a convinced European and anti-Fascist who served as prime minister on several occasions.

embrace me, my tears fell on his hand. It was four thirty
in the morning of 13 June. What anguish. Alberto
Bergamini accompanied His Majesty to his automobile.
On his return to the room, he paced up and down like a
wounded lion, up and down, unable to talk under the
weight of the destiny that was about to come to pass. 'I
told you De Gasperi was a traitor,' I would explode from
time to time . . .

From then on, Giannalisa could only visit the king in
Cascais; and goodness knows if there is any truth in the story
that she used to take him rounds of Gorgonzola cheese to alle-
viate his homesickness.

In the meantime, her son was holed up in Lisbon following
the charade of the threatened arrest. According to Antonella's
recollections, he was in the worst possible spirits and never
uttered a word. 'He didn't write to me for two months,' recalls
Bianca.

Then I received a packet containing all the letters he had
never sent me. They were letters full of profound
despondency. I replied, telling him to come back, on foot
if necessary, but to come back. He arrived by train trav-
eling third class. He was exhausted, he had bronchitis
and needed looking after. I couldn't put him up in our
house because my mother, my sister and I were all staying with friends. So I asked a socialist comrade to put
him up for a few days.

This was in July 1946, and, in those same weeks, Giannalisa
left Italy for Cascais, along with her two little daughters by her
second marriage. She was entirely unaware of her son's intentions. She telephoned the hotel where she thought he was
waiting for her. They told her he was not there, and that he had
gone back home. Infuriated, she decided to enlist the aid of
the Italian minister in Lisbon with a view to having
Giangiacomo arrested at the frontier. Nothing doing. Leaving

daughters and nannies at Cascais, she boarded a plane for Italy and, after shuttling between Rome and Milan seventeen times, she finally found him. Face to face. There were no reproofs. She merely told him that she intended to leave Italy in the very near future. That was all. It was one of those moments in which you just stand there looking at each other, without saying anything.

A few months later, Giannalisa took herself and the family silver off to Rio de Janeiro. It must have struck her as a place that was as far from any kind of Communism as it was possible to get. The only concession to the enemy was the broker they hired in New York: his name was Charlie Marx. As Lacan says, the signifier never lets you go.

2

Milan, late summer 1946, the end of the long break, and the return to his city. Giangiacomo still mumbled incomprehensibly, like many shy people, but he seemed more relaxed when he met convivial characters of his own age that might be considered friends. It wasn't a bad feeling. And from somewhere or other the first girlfriend appeared (I know who she is; she now lives a quiet life in the provinces).

A tall, thin, bespectacled twenty-year-old, who walked with his head held high and his toes turned slightly outwards, he became a familiar sight in the Milan branch offices of the party. Some turned up their noses at his pedigree, but others took a liking to him right away. Most people had other things to worry about.

During this period, Giangiacomo got to know Bianca better. In the meantime she had joined the PCI and he felt he might impress her by showing up in the suburb of Sesto early in the morning to accompany her to the office. But, wearing that strange blue suit, made up by a refined tailor and cutter hired years ago by his mother, the admirer–militant turned up at night-time, too: with Bianca and her sister, he had to organize the wall newspaper for the following day. Giangiacomo's suit hung off him; perhaps they found him a bit ridiculous.

At that time they made frequent evening visits to the house of a young Communist Party official, Armando Cossutta.* His mother used to welcome them with platefuls of pasta and beans, apparently delicious.

After a sheltered childhood, in the strict sense of the term, Giangiacomo now encountered the misfortunes of a more normal life. He suffered belated attacks of measles, German measles and scarlet fever, but these were only minor impediments.

In the July of 1947 he married Bianca Dalle Nogare. Neither Giannalisa – who thought Bianca was a 'Muscovite Pasionaria' – nor Barzini went to the wedding. But Giannalisa's father, Mino Gianzano, was present. 'It was a civil wedding,' recalls the bride, 'extremely rapid and entirely nonconformist, without invitations and without photographers. We said I do, and then we said goodbye right afterwards. I went back home to my mother; Giangiacomo went back to his place. We did not meet again until the next day, when we set off on our honeymoon.' The destination was Prague. They set off in a smoky-blue Buick convertible, and they took along their dog, a German shepherd by the name of Gisa. 'Gisa', I imagine, was an abbreviation for 'Giannalisa'.

Prague was the venue of the world youth festival, an event that was not restricted to young Communists: the representative of the Italian federation of young Republicans, for example, was Alberto Ronchey (the future famous journalist, the inventor of the K factor[†] and later a government minister).

---

* Born in Milan in 1926, Armando Cossutta became a great leader of the PCI. In 1991 he founded Rifondazione Communista and in 1998 he founded the party of Italian Communists.

† 'The K factor': an element in a political equation that, according to Ronchey, made any swing to the left impossible because of fears aroused by the strong links between the Italian and the Soviet communist parties. The Soviet connection effectively delegitimized the PCI's claims to recognition as a political governing party.

Probably Giangiacomo began to realise what was important once he got back from his honeymoon. For not only had he married, he was also over twenty-one; in other words, he was no longer a minor, and this brought him rights and obligations the effects of which were hard to foresee at the time. And while it is true that he wanted to study engineering, and possibly earn a living through a good profession, he was still the sole male heir to Giacomo, Giovanni and Carlo, to the Feltrinellis who counted: everything they had left in the world was now in need of good management.

Of course, as the Italian saying goes, this is better than grazing goats on someone else's land. But it is also like riding a very special, souped-up roller coaster, on which first you pick up speed before you throw up, go off the rails, and if necessary even jump off. This is an experience common to many men who wound up rich but did not have the faintest idea of how to handle money. It would not have been surprising, therefore, if the same thing happened to the Feltrinelli heir, who was forever in conflict with his mother, as she shuttled continuously between Italy and the world.

As soon as his sister Antonella came of age, she married almost immediately and went to seek a new life in France (with André D'Ormesson, the son of the French ambassador to the Vatican). From Paris she brought a suit against Giannalisa, accusing her of allotting her daughter an incorrect share of the inheritance. Giangiacomo, who was as much an injured party as his sister, did not feel like taking the whole family to court. He let the matter drop.

Given this climate, given these conditions, Giangiacomo must have seriously considered getting rid of the damned money and 'handing it all over to Togliatti'.* He was heard to

* Palmiro Togliatti (1893–1964). The leader of the Italian Communist Party from 1926 to 1964. Close to Stalin, he wielded considerable influence in the Kremlin during the Comintern period. From the 20th Congress 1956 onward, he favoured pluralism in the Communist world. He had a genuine interest in culture – which explains, at least in part, his privileged relations with Feltrinelli.

say this by several people. In a personal profile written for the party, with regard to his 'extensive fortune', he wrote that the inheritance came to 'weigh on my shoulders'. What's more, 'until he was twenty he didn't even know what a bank cheque looked like', as his wife Bianca recalled in an interview. And it was thanks to her that he became a more thoughtful thinking man. He threw himself into the study of economics and gradually began to find his feet in business matters.

But while he had no inclination to 'play the rich man' and while he was looking for his own road to follow, even managing to act like a good Communist in the meantime, he was still a rich man. A rich man in search of a strange equilibrium, one not easy to understand, precarious and apparently unattainable. According to the usual stereotypes, he ought to have been a spendthrift or a zealous philanthropist, or a businessman bent over his accounts. But he turned out to be none of these things.

The outcome of the elections of 18 April 1948, which resulted in an outright majority for the Christian Democratic Party and confined the Popular Front* to the opposition, corresponded to the logic of Yalta. So much the better (because the alternative would have involved a serious risk of political instability). This was also what Palmiro Togliatti must have thought. Thus began Italy's long post-war period, the eternal aftermath of Fascism with its reconstruction and stagnation. Those tempted by the idea of a Fascist revival were energetically opposed by an already mature public opinion: the war of Liberation, the Referendum and the Constitution all amounted to a new order. But there were moments in which the slightest thing could have brought the whole house of cards tumbling down.

'I was eating, I must have come back home about one, when I heard someone calling me from the yard of my house, in via Paolo Sarpi. I looked down, Feltrinelli was searching for me: "Get down here, come on, Togliatti's been shot".' It was 14

* The Popular Front was an electoral coalition of the parties making up the Italian left.

July 1948. Silvano Giuntini has very clear recollections of dashing first to the offices of the Federation and then to the local branch office of the party, where all the party members had to be sent home because they were too steamed up and above all because they were steamed up and armed.

Giuntini, who was to become a commercial specialist with a renowned Milanese publishing house, was in charge of propaganda at the party's via Cantù office, a big branch with about one thousand five hundred members, in the heart of the city. He met Feltrinelli when the latter invited him to his home in San Babila, where they spent the night listening to Yugoslav folk music. A few years before, Giuntini had taken a call from Alberganti, the secretary to the Federation, announcing the arrival in the local branch office of a 'particular' comrade.

In the course of musical evenings, snacks prior to visits to the branch office, and a lot of political work, Giuntini and Feltrinelli began to associate with each other. In the immediate aftermath of the attempt on Togliatti's life, they probably shared the same sense of chaos and confusion, which was common to everybody because no one had a clear idea of what to do. The only certain news was that the CGIL labour union had called a general strike.

The national political scene was in a feverish state: the party line was 'take it easy', but in Genoa, Turin, Venice and Livorno, groups of militants occupied whole districts. Seven thousand people were either arrested or investigated.

In Milan, where things were not that much calmer, four or five young men from the 'Duomo' party office went out one night to stick up placards. This was fairly minor militancy, but Feltrinelli was with them. 'About four in the morning, in via Meravigli, the police caught us with the placards in our hands. They took us to police headquarters and then to San Vittore [prison] on the following morning, for five or six days.' Comrade Sergio Monti, now in retirement after a long career in the cooperative movement, has a clear memory: 'It wasn't so bad, our misfortune put us in a good humour, and what's more, I was living high on the hog in prison because I had a share of the food parcels that Bianca brought in every day. We were always hungry in those days . . .'

Revolution, the armed variety, was not on. The conditions were not right. In the days following the wounding of Togliatti, who was soon declared out of danger, this fact became clearer. Insurrectionary tensions began to abate.

While the PCI was a powerful advocate of a different, alternative world, it had opted for electoral methods and moderation three years before, when its increased share of the vote was considered 'the principal instrument with which to shift the balance of power in parliament and consequently in the country'. This is the view of a modern historian, Paul Ginsborg.* Palmiro Togliatti, moreover, had had to accept De Gasperi's manoeuvre of May 1947 that led to the Communist leader's exclusion from the government: the real challenge, therefore, was to take on the Christian Democrats in the battle for votes.

The notion that between compliance and insurrection there lay a 'middle way' (as Pietro Secchia† called it) that might exploit the spirit and the moral fervour of the popular base of the Resistance movement was a hypothesis more talked about than tested, and served only to complicate the problem. And the problem was in fact far from being resolved.

Events followed one another unpredictably and rapidly. If the wind of the people is driving us forward, what cannot be done today is merely put off until tomorrow. We have come a long way, we will go a long way.

Sergio Monti also became a good friend of my father's and they carried on selling *l'Unità* and sticking up placards together ('Feltrinelli did not feel himself above these tasks in any way'), often using the smoky-blue Buick. 'People were scandalized when they saw us coming to do those things in a car like that,

---

* An English historian, a specialist in contemporary Italian politics, who teaches at the University of Florence.
† (1903–72). A leading figure of the PCI, Secchia was a hard line Communist, member of parliament, and senator.

but at the time Feltrinelli didn't give a damn. It was a good car, but windshield defrosters hadn't been invented yet and I recall coming back from a meeting near Lodi (it was a cold, foggy night), when we had to take turns at hopping on to the bonnet and taking a leak on the windscreen to defrost it.'

In 1948, Monti attended a summer camp organized by Feltrinelli and a group of young party members. They went to the villa at Gargnano on Lake Garda, the residence and emblem of the Feltrinelli family: 'a kind of Bavarian mausoleum', according to the description of a writer friend. Half of the time indoors, half in the park, the group of fifteen lived it up for two weeks. There was also the painter Giovanni Fumagalli, known to everyone as 'Fuma', who was the secretary of the 'Duomo' branch office and an advocate of socialist realism in the polemic about contemporary art that had just begun. His convictions were probably highly debatable but it wasn't the campers' aesthetic preferences that upset the parish priest so much. It was the idea of all those Communists using the villa as their meeting-place that rankled: too much, altogether too much! The priest wasn't going to stand for it, the master of the house had to be discredited: hence the stream of official complaints, denunciations from the pulpit and posters on the walls. The posters spoke of his marriage: he had gone through a mere civil ceremony, not a church wedding!

But if my hunch is right, organizing the summer camp was more than just a provocation. It meant several things, even on an unconscious level. Especially if you consider that, in the October of 1943, villa Feltrinelli had been commandeered to serve as Benito Mussolini's personal residence. After he had been dramatically rescued from the Gran Sasso by German paratroops who enabled him to set up the short-lived Republic of Salò, Mussolini, who detested lakes ('a hybrid of rivers and the sea'), had to live isolated in our home under the protection of the crack troops of his ally and master. When he left this blind alley, it really was the end.

But while Fascism had been defeated, six hundred thousand amnestied supporters of the Republic of Salò had to go somewhere. Some sang party anthems in the slums and hoped to return one day for the 'reckoning'. But many of them had already returned, some as shirt-sleeved bureaucrats full of scorn for 'goddam democracy', others masquerading as right-thinking folk who affected starched collars out of caste arrogance. In the courts there were judges who took great pains to do what damage they could to ex-partisans, turning trials on their heads the way a cheese maker turns a churn: on the other hand, of course, there was the Volante rossa.*

This explains the extravagant gesture, the campsite set up in the grounds of the villa that had once been Mussolini's. It was a deliberately arrogant move and a clear warning to the Fascists: try to come back, and you'll get yours.

This summer camp was to become a talking point the following year, in 1949, when people in Milan were getting worked up about the 'Ciappina gang', also known as the 'everywhere gang'. Ugo Ciappina, who was little more than a boy, but dangerous, and the Armenian Colust Megherian, both members of the Carrobbio cell, had made themselves a reputation for the improper use of arms that had been kept hidden even after 25 April. But this was not politics, merely armed robbery. They had recruited half a dozen shady characters and two of them, when they were arrested, stated they had opted for a life of crime in the summer camp on Lake Garda. Perhaps the parish priest hadn't been so far wrong.

Feltrinelli was arrested once more, again in Milan. It was the work of the political office of the city police: 'Have you heard? We've taken in your pal the millionaire!' said one cop to a reporter with *Milano Sera*. But it seems that Feltrinelli had absolutely nothing to do with the affair: because at that time he was a party 'regular', disciplined in his work and offering total adherence to the party line.

But the misunderstanding cost him a day in the cells and the

---

* A 'hard-line' Resistance group that did not lay down its arms upon the cessation of hostilities.

first worried comments began to appear in the conservative press. For the first time, they began to talk of 'Giangi the millionaire'. The political office also sent the following note to the Ministry of the Interior: 'Feltrinelli (a major financer of the party) was arrested and then freed. He was suspected of having financed the well known 'everywhere gang'. [. . .] Feltrinelli is an activist and his wife Bianca Dalle Nogare is a madwoman in the service of the "terrorist" organization of the PCI (inoperative for now).'

Following his second arrest, Feltrinelli had to give up his normal activities at the branch office (he had recently replaced Giuntini as the press and propaganda officer). It was proposed that he become a member of a working group at the Milan offices of the Federation. The party wanted to look after him better. They appointed a former partisan to serve as his chauffeur, factotum and bodyguard. A kind of guardian angel for the most valuable party card* in Italy.

* * *

But, at that time, what did it really mean to be a militant, be it Communist, socialist, grass-roots Catholic, or even Christian Democratic? Comrade Monti said it was necessary above all to 'get things done', maybe a kindergarten, a school, Female Comrade's Week, Communion, or a gesture of working-class solidarity. It was a militancy some today might describe as politically incorrect, but there's no denying that it was socially useful.

A political struggle! Obsessive hypercommunism, fanatical anti-Communism, extreme clericalism, there was something for everybody, but after a war like that a scrap of passion is needed to keep the flag flying; Red or White. But there was no middle way, in the sense that the lay-reformist–liberal-socialist

* Party members paid their dues on a discretionary basis. On receipt of the yearly payment, which was a conspicuous sum in Feltrinelli's case, a stamp was stuck in the party card.

current, the truly democratic impulse, could not find a suitable channel between the colossi of the two 'churches' of Catholicism and Communism. The state? It was chronically weak, needless to say.

'We lived through some damn tough times, but, if nothing else, they were constructive times, you understand?' Giuntini and Monti, members of the Duomo branch in those days, greeted me in unison with these words. They told me that Feltrinelli wanted to make a summer camp out of the former Fascist village near Canzo, that he wanted to make a film about the rice-weeders in Lomellina or, possibly, to establish a local library.

But, apropos of 'getting things done', in March 1992 *l'Unità* published a fine article on the subject by the journalist Anna Del Bo Boffino. I barely got to know Anna before her death, but I knew about her because she had been married to the man I used to call Uncle Sergio and other people knew as Professor Del Bo.

> In '49 we were two newlywed couples: Giangiacomo with his first wife, the girl from Sesto San Giovanni, as beautiful as a Tanagra figurine, I with Del Bo, who was six years older than us and always acted as our big brother. All of us had been involved with the Resistance, and we were all members of the PCI. Together, we were looking for a space between the dogmatism of the party and the hypocrisy of bourgeois culture. At twenty years of age, one has many dreams, and the desire to be the 'new men' is a powerful one. And we were no different. But those were the days of commitment, when the model of the 'organic intellectual' was the only model one could adopt with honesty. They were also hard times: during demonstrations, we were the ones who had to run from the batons of the riot cops. Communists had no access to the world of newspapers or of publishing. And all-out strikes were weakening the proletariat, bringing it to near starvation. We knew about an extremely prolonged strike

on the part of the agricultural labourers in the lower Po
valley, and we really needed to show our solidarity. We
did this with words, but Giangiacomo could do more. In
Gargnano, where his family came from, he owned half
the town: he had a part of the old folks' home cleared
(there were only a very few old folks there at the time)
and it became possible to take in about thirty children,
who arrived from one day to the next. We, the two
women, were detailed to look after them, and for a few
weeks we fed, clothed and took them out and about. A
little blond boy, all skin and bones, with a dazzling smile,
had head lice and all the other kids caught them from
him. We cleaned them up, and I would have fed them ten
times a day just to see them put a little meat on their
bones. So that's how it was: we had dreams, and we kept
them locked away. Giangiacomo could make them come
true, and it seemed miraculous to have him on our side.

It is not easy to deal with someone one thinks 'miraculous'.
Even the best of intentions are always counterbalanced by the
difficulties that can arise in interpersonal relations. I had just
enough time to return to this issue with Anna Del Bo Boffino in
the summer of '95: 'Coexisting with Giangiacomo, who had
huge possibilities, was very difficult for all of us. He could just
turn around and decide to do anything he wanted. All relations
with him had this dual aspect.'
    In the meantime, his marriage with Bianca was on the rocks.

'Uncle Sergio', Anna's husband, was in reality named
Giuseppe, Giuseppe Del Bo. Milanese, born in 1919, he had
studied theology at the Gregorian University in Rome. He was
a priest. During the war he enlisted as an army chaplain and
was imprisoned in Tunisia. He managed to get back home at
the time of the liberation of Naples, after which he made his
way back up the peninsula with the Allies, calling himself
'Sergio'. It was his *nom de guerre*. At the end of the war, in
Milan once more, he picked up his studies again. He enrolled in

the philosophy faculty of the Università Statale, where he met Antonio Banfi, who was teaching and advocating a new and universal culture. Banfi waived two years' worth of exams and introduced him to Anna.

At the end of 1946, Del Bo went through his toughest existential crisis. In love with a woman, attracted by Marxism: it was his moment of truth. The bishop of Como had him recalled to the seminary, but it was to be the last time. By 1948 the story was over, all dilemmas resolved, and Sergio decided to marry Anna.

The man of whom it was said that he had been able to maintain relations with the Vatican and Palmiro Togliatti at the same time found his first job in the Cantoni bookshop in corso Vittorio Emanuele. But he soon went to work for the ex-partisan Vando Androvandi, in the Einaudi bookshop in via Filodrammatici. The journalist Alberto Cavallari recalls having met him there, 'while he was transporting packets of books on his bicycle'.

Giangiacomo also met him in the back of that bookshop. There was nothing strange about this: cultural life, the first House of Culture, the meetings of the magazine Politecnico,* the encounters among the bookshelves with writers like Vittorini, Pavese and Fortini: this was the place where it was all happening. Nearby, the dairy run by the Pirolini sisters and an eating house called 'Il soldato d'Italia' in via Fiori Chiari offered the luxury of a good cheap meal. The publisher Giulio Einaudi† recalled that 'Feltrinelli came to the meetings out of curiosity, to listen. I remember that he would sit on the floor, good as gold, listening . . .' Feltrinelli financed his activities, lending money that sooner or later Einaudi would pay back. The PCI had asked Feltrinelli to do this.

Palmiro Togliatti always dined at the Brasera Meneghina on his fleeting visits to Milan. It reminded him of when he was the

---

* Founded by the writer Elio Vittorini in Milan in 1945, it was a lively forum for political and cultural debate.
† (1912–99). The head of one of Italy's most important publishing houses.

editor of *l'Unità*, in the mid-twenties. They always brought him his favorite dish, *ossobuco con risotto* (shin of veal with risotto). According to Cossutta's reconstruction, it was in this very restaurant that Togliatti and Feltrinelli met one evening. And this was apparently the occasion on which the party leader encouraged Feltrinelli, offering him his support, to undertake an extremely special task: the construction of a library devoted to the history of the workers of the world. Apparently Feltrinelli got the idea from a priest.

But before describing what Feltrinelli and Del Bo engineered together, we must first take a look at an important document. In order to take part in the courses held by the party's regional school, Giangiacomo, who was twenty-four at the time, had to write down an autobiographical profile. It reappeared many years later in the basement of the former offices of the Federation. It is worth much more than a simple resumé.

The date was early 1950:

To the Cell Office of the Milan Federation of the P.C.I.
Re: PROFILE
Giangiacomo Feltrinelli, son of the late Carlo and of
Giannalisa Gianzana, born on 19/6/1926 in Milan, and
therein resident in Piazza S. Babila 4/b. My father was
one of the most outstanding figures in the world of
finance between 1927 and 1935. The Chairman of the
Credito Italiano and of Edison, as well as of other companies in which he held the majority stockholding, he
was a classic example of how financial capital can be
merged with industrial capital. He died in 1935.
    My mother, a banker's daughter, is still alive; in 1940
she remarried with Luigi Barzini junior, from whom she
is now separated. She lives in Rome.
    I was brought up in a manner that, from a bourgeois
point of view, was as orthodox as can be, with nannies,
comforts, travel, etc., and I was always kept apart from
children of my own age. Until 1942 I never attended

school and was privately tutored. I thus grew up practically without friends.

Given this situation, how did it happen that I came first to join the PCI and then to serve as an activist within its ranks? What were the elements that orientated me decisively and led me to understand the necessity and the importance of my joining the PCI to aid the organized vanguard of the working class in the struggle against capitalism, in the cause of socialism?

A first important element was, I believe, the following: in '36 my mother acquired a large garden, which, over a period of years, was constructed by workers, labourers, and farmhands. I very soon made friends with these workers and labourers and so for the first time I came to know another world, which was not the glittering one in which I lived; from accounts and from discussion, I came to understand about the straitened lives that the workers were obliged to lead, the efforts they had to make to keep their families, the inadequacy of their wages, and the constant threat of unemployment that loomed over every one of them. I thus realized that there were two different and quite distinct social classes. Later, in '38–39, amid the bitter debate on international events, war became a grave threat that impinged upon the already hard lives led by the workers. I realized that it was not the students, the gentlemen who were calling vociferously for war, who would have gone off to fight. On the contrary, I saw that business people could hope to gain from a war while the sacrifices would have to be made by the workers.

In 1940 I made the acquaintance of a worker from Erba, Augusto Sala. It was from his accounts, and from discussions I had with him that I first came to know the details of the people's struggle against the Fascists in '21. For the first time I learned of the existence of other parties and in particular of the socialists and the Communists. The account of the heroic episodes in the people's struggle against the Fascists and their action squads, financed and backed by the industrialists, filled me with enthusiasm. Obviously my parents were worried by the direction I was taking. They posed as anti-Fascists, especially after my stepfather was confined to Amalfi as a consequence of his excessive fondness for double-dealing between the English and the Fascists.

I was still a mass of contradictions: I was a member of the GIL, the Fascist youth organization, and I was glad when the war was going well and the Fascist armies were advancing; at the same time I was listening to Radio London, I was against the Germans, and could see no good coming of the war. I hoped that the monarchy would grasp the first opportunity to get rid of the Fascists.

In the meantime, the war continued and by the end of '42 the situation was becoming tragic: the first bombing raids on the cities, the arrival of the first Germans in Italy. In this situation I realized that the overthrow of Fascism and the cessation of the conflict were two tasks requiring urgent action that could not be brought to completion without an effort, without a struggle in which everyone had to give something. It was at that time that I met Renzo Negri, resident in via Melzi d'Eril n° 22, who was in contact with the Resistance. It was the end of 1942. I only had occasional contact with him because I had to move to Tuscany with my family. Nevertheless, it was through him that I had news of the heroic strike of March '43. It was then that I contributed one hundred lire to a clandestine newspaper. This and other episodes, even though insignificant, contributed to the development of a closer and closer bond between me and all those who, even if I did not know them personally, were fighting against Fascism, that is to say the working class.

During that period I read *The History of Italian Literature* by Concetto Marchesi, which helped me make a qualitative leap and to put in perspective for the first time those events, those feelings, those ideas of justice that had developed in me and that had led me to be against the Fascists and the bosses.

In fact I was particularly struck by the essay on the struggle of the Gracchi in Ancient Rome. Marchesi took his cue from that event to demonstrate the existence of two social classes fighting each other: patricians and plebeians, the exploiters and the exploited. This scheme of things, which holds to this day, fitted in with my experience, and political events, Fascism and the war took on a new social content.

I subsequently studied what little historical material was at my disposal. In particular, I recall reading Croce's *History of the Risorgimento*, which told me, albeit in a harshly critical tone, something about the international socialist movement. I also read a book by Bissolati on the history of the Italian labour movement. From these books I learned about the men, the parties and the events of Italian political history; I learned about the labour unions, the strikes, etc. The opportunism and the compromise that oozes from every line of Bissolati had only a slight momentary influence on me. The very situation, current at that time, of bitter struggle, the proof of the pudding that is, provided evidence of the bankruptcy of all reformist ideas that was superior to any reasoned argument.

After the liberation of Rome, where I found myself on 4 June 1944, I had the good fortune to read immediately two works of particular importance and topicality: the *Communist Manifesto* and Lenin's *State and Revolution*. In the *Manifesto*, as had previously been the case with Marchesi's book, I was impressed by the analysis of society and its division into classes locked in continuous struggle with one another, while historical materialism taught me the reasons for the development of society, thus giving me a new method for understanding history.

In the November of '44 I enlisted as a volunteer in the Legnano combat unit that was attached to the American

5th Army, not without having first listened to the views of a comrade, Trombadori I think, who was introduced to me by a young comrade of my acquaintance.

Armed with this admittedly limited theoretical background, I joined the party in early March '45 while we were in training with the division in the province of Siena. I was introduced to Comrade Masotti, who was also in my company (he was an old comrade who had spent a year in Civitavecchia prison for political reasons) and to comrade Vincenzo Ciafré of the Siena Federation. Shortly afterwards the division was sent to the Bologna front and in the August of '45 I was demobilized.

I returned to Rome, where I picked up my studies once more (I attended the Rome Polytechnic). Until the April of '46 I carried out no political activities inasmuch as comrade Fulvio Iacchia of the Rome Federation preferred to use me to gather information in milieus hostile to the party. My cover was blown in April '46 when, as a result of an error, *L'Unità* printed a detailed report of a monarchist meeting that had been held in my home and that I had in part attended. Subsequently I moved to Milan, where shortly afterward my parents, aided and abetted by the British intelligence service, and knowing that I still had the weapons I had possessed at the time of my discharge from the army, orchestrated a phoney arrest with a view to frightening me and persuading me to leave Italy. In fact, this fitted in with their plans because they, fearing the advent of the Republic, were organizing a general exodus of the family.

I went to Spain and to Portugal, from where, still in the July of '46, I eluded the surveillance of my parents and returned to Italy, taking up residence in Milan.

I then began to work for the party on a regular basis, at first in the press and propaganda department of the Bietolini branch office, and then in the Duomo branch, at first in the youth sector and then in press and propaganda. This was in April 1947.

In the July of '47 I married Bianca Dalle Nogare, who
had come from the PSIUP and who had been a member
of the PCI for a year. I attended the Youth Festival in
Prague in the summer of '47.

In the meantime, I had come of age and so the administration of the inheritance left me by my father came to
weigh on my shoulders.

In the summer of '48, following the attempted assassination of comrade Togliatti, I was arrested together with
some other youths for having posted unauthorized placards.

It was subsequent to this arrest that the Duomo
branch office put me in charge of press and propaganda
activities.

I was also a member of the branch office committee.
In November, I attended a six-month series of evening
classes run by the local Communist Party Federation.
These classes were remarkably important for my theoretical training as a Communist activist. The histories of
Italy and the political economy I studied there gave me a
whole new perspective on the bourgeois notions I had
learned on normal scholastic courses, while the study of
the history of the Russian Communist Party prepared
me particularly well to deal with the practical problems I
had to face in my day-to-day work for the party.

At the same time I was called in to head the Financial
Committee of the Milan Federation. How did these
posts within the party influence my political formation?
How did I perform these tasks?

My work with the rank and file in the Duomo branch
of our party was certainly very useful to me. As a liaison
officer between the various cells, I got to know the comrades, their shortcomings and their strengths. I learned
to recognize the responsibilities connected with the
party's various aspirations and requirements. I learned to
control, at least in part, my impulsiveness and my
impetuosity; I learned method in debate, in the work of

persuasion and clarification that I had to carry out
among the comrades. I learned to spot concealed opportunism, both behind compromises and generic extremist
statements. Of my work as head of press and propaganda, I have to say that too often I erred in taking too
much upon myself, and only toward the end did I make
concrete efforts to obtain some co-workers and to guide
and direct them in their work, which is a more difficult
task. I therefore fell into the trap of empiricism, thus
losing the overall view of the work I had to do in order to
concentrate solely on one sector or another. The fact that
today I can make this criticism of my grass-roots work
for the party is, I believe, the best demonstration that
this work was not negative and served to further my ideological training.

The job with the Financial Committee of the
Federation was from various points of view rather less
fruitful. I brought to the task a certain lack of experience in the field of business. Above all, I lacked the
qualities required of a doer (in the business field), while
in this case there was less demand for managerial qualities (based essentially on common sense) than for the
technical skills possessed by a doer (I also became aware
of this shortcoming of mine in my own work, but
recently I seem to be on the road to improvement). At
the end of '49 the Financial Committee was rightly
incorporated into the Administrative Committee and I
became an activist on this committee. In the autumn of
'49 I was once more arrested by the political section of
the Milan police. A group of young bank robbers
arrested shortly before, some of whom had been members of the PCI (expelled when their provocative
activities had come to light) had stated under questioning at the police station that I had financed their gang,
which had strange connections with the world of espionage. I was released on the day after my arrest, but this
did not deter the gutter press from unleashing a violent

smear campaign. I had in fact met these young men in the period during which they were members of the PCI, and some of them had also taken part in a summer camp that, in my capacity as the youth officer for the Duomo branch office of the party, I had organized in the summer of '48.

I have had no contact with them whatsoever since their expulsion from the party, far less have I financed their enterprises or lent them money even on a personal basis.

After my arrest, I was transferred to the Federation cell and my political activity was limited exclusively to my work with the Administrative Committee.

Now, by attending the party's regional school, my aim is to attain two basic goals:

1. to further my theoretical knowledge by learning a study method and by applying myself to the study of the themes and the writings of those who have led popular movements, who have led the party to power in some countries, and who in other countries are still leading it in the struggle against domestic and foreign imperialists;

2. to learn from three months of collective life to live in a community, therefore modifying my character, and to learn what it means to work alongside other comrades. I feel that this second objective is especially important because of the particular conditions in which I live, and because by so doing I may improve myself and thus work better for the party.

Feltrinelli's 'autobiography' caused a sensation in the offices of the Milan Federation. Lidia Lefebre, who worked there as a secretary in 1950, recalls the great impression it made on everyone: a mixture of admiration for a comrade who had exposed himself so openly, and of pride in the party's powers of attraction.

* * *

I have met some of the comrades that had dealings with my father in the early fifties.

Giovanni Pesce, who had been awarded the gold medal of the Resistance, met Giangiacomo in the offices of the Milan Federation of the PCI or perhaps late one evening in the corridors of *l'Unità*, as they waited for the first edition to appear. He says: 'The first time it was I who approached him. I said hello and he greeted me without smiling. That missing smile made me feel a little uncomfortable and I sensed he was not an easy person. This aroused my curiosity because I have never liked easy people, or hail-fellow-well-met types, as they say.'

The days of the Resistance held great fascination for everyone and within the ranks of the Left its leading figures were venerated. The battles waged by Pesce's combat unit, the Third Brigade of the GAP, against the Germans were legendary; as were the epic deeds of those who had fought the Fascists in Spain.

At this time, Feltrinelli also met Vittorio Vidali. I think the person who introduced them was Giuseppe Zigaina, the painter from Cervignano del Friuli. Vidali's curriculum was an impressive one: prison, woundings, mutilations, a life on the run between Algeria, the USSR, France, Germany and Austria. A spell in the America of mobsters, Sacco and Vanzetti, and Rudolph Valentino. The Spanish Civil War and the command of the 5th Regiment of the International Brigade. Mexico and the 'Giuseppe Garibaldi' anti-Fascist alliance. The marvellous Tina Modotti. After twenty-five years, his return to his native Trieste was dogged by the rumour, vague but never really denied, that he had been among the killers of Leon Trotsky.

The twenty-year-old Giangiacomo must have really got a kick out of talking with characters like Vidali. And if there was something that really interested him in the underground movement, it wasn't necessarily heroic deeds and guns: if anything, he was struck by the spirit of 'getting things done'. Historic events generated expectations that required a sense of initiative and strength of spirit for the future too, just as in the days of the Resistance movement. What they had done was only the first part of a grandiose process still to be completed.

Giovanni Pesce: 'When we met, what Feltrinelli wanted most was for me to explain why the Resistance, despite its victory, had been half cancelled out by the political and economic interests that had handed power to the same ruling classes that had given birth to Fascism and the monarchy.'

I never met Pietro Secchia, the party number two at the time. He has been described as the strong man of the Resistance, the insidious shadowy figure that lived above Togliatti in a condominium in Montesacro, whence he manipulated both the leader and the entire party network. 'One branch office for every bell tower' was his motto. They say that he was often in disagreement with the official party line and that he acted in close connection with the 'supreme' party on the other side of the iron curtain. It seems that he was a difficult man, with a subtler intelligence than current historiography would lead us to believe.

While Secchia had a friendly relationship with Feltrinelli, he would often tell his factotum, Giulio Seniga, that he thought Giangiacomo was an able manager of his own business affairs, but less open-handed with the party.

Between September of 1950 and the following summer, Feltrinelli made various trips to East Germany, Czechoslovakia, and Hungary. He went there openly, to see to some fairly unimportant commercial matters. Meissen porcelain from Germany, vacuum flasks, refrigerators, and gas cookers from Czechoslovakia, stuff like that. But the party was his partner in these ventures, at least fifty-fifty. Secchia introduced him to the Czechs as a comrade who 'enjoys our full confidence'. In reality these were dealings of little account, but they boosted his status as a businessman who worked with Eastern Europe. A fat wad of confidential reports was added to his file in the political archives kept by the Ministry of the Interior and by the military intelligence service.

* * *

The house in piazza San Babila where Bianca and Giangiacomo went to live was a normal apartment, furnished in a sober but functional style. Bianca was the one who tried to create a pleasing ambience. A couple of dogs had the run of the house and on one wall, among the old masters, it seems there hung a portrait of Stalin.

Political activity took up almost all their free time. This meant very little social life and few friends. During the day, Feltrinelli the businessman struggled to elude the traps laid for him by his rapacious mother. He knew he had learned in a hurry, in the field, and therefore he took care not to expose himself too much. He had good sense, and a sixth sense, too, especially in his choice of colleagues (he promoted as his assistant a young accountant of proven Christian faith, Gaetano Lazzati) upon whom he apparently lavished encouragement and trust.

His holdings were concentrated in construction (with the 'Edilizia centro Milano' and the Compagnia imprese e costruzioni, which both owned important real estate in Milan and Rome) and in lumber and lumber by-products. Within the parent company, Feltrinelli industria e commercio legnami, there was a difficult co-existence with the Accademia dei Lincei, Antonio Feltrinelli's 'heir'. There were also other important holdings in the construction sector (Ferrobeton) and in that of building materials (Loro & Parisini). Then there was a majority stockholding in the Banca Unione (the Banca Feltrinelli until 1918). The stockholders in this small but distinguished private bank, which stood near the Milan Stock Exchange, were anything but united. As well as his mother and his sister, Giangiacomo's fellow shareholders were the Bastogi corporation and the Vatican Bank. So, a young businessman, ostentatiously Communist and in a period of high Stalinism at that, was the principal stockholder in a merchant bank, side by side with a representative of the Vatican's IOR,* the minority partner.

* L'istituto per opere religiose, or IOR, is the Vatican bank.

Giannalisa prepared for a tough fight; at least, this is the way Lazzati remembers it. She wanted to oust her son from the board at all costs. She succeeded, but even this wasn't enough for her.

During a street demonstration, perhaps in the days of the 'legge truffa',* the police arrested Giangiacomo right next to the Banca Unione. He was carrying a copy of l'Unità. The telephone lines of the bank management were red hot: 'It's a scandal, a scandal!' The scandal in question was the newspaper he was carrying. Giangiacomo's mother again moved to force her son to sell his stockholding. And that's what he did, I believe in '53. About twenty years later, the Vatican found itself in partnership with the notorious Michele Sindona,† this time as the majority shareholder.

Politics came into everything, contaminating life and business. Feltrinelli was doing deals with politics and he was a good deal as far as politics was concerned. A straight question: how much importance was attached to the party card number 0735668 in the name of Giangiacomo Feltrinelli? 'A lot, a lot,' comes the reply in chorus, with closed eyes and much nodding of heads, from three men who were party leaders or officials at the time: Armando Cossutta, Gianni Cervetti, and Elio Quercioli.

But as to just how much 'a lot' really amounted to I have never really understood. All I have is anecdotes: 'he would make up the losses on the federation's balance sheet'; 'a million a month for the Milan office of the newspaper'; or the story about the local party secretary Alberganti, who, when he couldn't pay the wages, would make himself look good by saying 'I'll see to it' and going off to phone you know who.

These things were well known at the Ministry of the Interior. Since 1948, Feltrinelli, a 'major financer' of the PCI, had been under the systematic surveillance of the Milan police.

---

* According to this law, decried as a fraud by the Left, the coalition that won 50 per cent of the votes would obtain 65 per cent of the seats in parliament.
† A shady financier, who was involved in the Vatican bank–Banco Ambrosiano scandal and in the P2 affair, Sindona met his death in mysterious circumstances while awaiting trial in prison.

They kept a record of his business activities, his arrests, his travels, the people he invited to dinner, and the money given to Togliatti for the administrative elections – everything. In the August of 1951, the Office of Confidential Affairs received a report from the Milan police in which it was alleged that Feltrinelli had salvaged the publishing house 'run by the Communist son of the president of the Republic' (namely Einaudi).

The three men I interviewed, Cossutta, Cervetti and Quercioli, offered similar descriptions of the relationship between Alberganti and Feltrinelli. Although there was an age difference of twenty-five years between the two men, they were linked by strong ties: 'Alberganti always protected and defended him!'

Giuseppe Alberganti, whose roots lay in a blend of anarchism and labour unionism, had been a partisan in Emilia and possessed the physical courage of the intrepid man of action. He was one of those who had never given up on the X hour, the hour of the barricades. They say that after the strike called following the Togliatti assassination attempt, he did not return to his post at the Federation: he just couldn't stand the idea of facing all those workers who were tearing up their party cards because they were not allowed to go into action.

I am sure that my father was fond of Alberganti, who treated him with a quasi-paternal regard. But shortly before he died, the nonagenarian 'Fuma', the painter and former secretary of the Duomo branch office, told me of his innermost conviction: 'On the day of the revolution, Alberganti wouldn't have struck him off the list of those to be taken out.'

Obviously there's no telling, perhaps it was an insinuation and no more, but let's imagine that there was in fact someone, and someone there must have been, who saw things that way. Perhaps Giangiacomo himself was aware of this. He may have been very young, and terribly enthusiastic, but he was intelligent and probably he was learning to deal with people, to keep everybody sweet, *to take their measure* and – why not? – to be suspicious. The fact remains that he did not see the Communist

cause as a bandwagon to be abandoned whenever it was con-
venient; he was not just 'close' to the great party; he was much
more than a supporter. Communism was very much his ideal.

Feltrinelli's network of contacts extended further than
Milan, naturally. In Rome, the man in charge of the PCI's
publishing activities was Amerigo Terenzi: a man with a blunt
manner and red hair. One source, I don't know how reliable,
says that Feltrinelli made a large financial contribution toward
the purchase of printing presses needed by *l'Unità* in Rome
and by *l'Ora* in Palermo (a Sicilian newspaper sympathetic to
the Communist line). Apparently this machinery was delivered, ready for use, direct to the party. Cossutta says he seems
to recall that the presses were financed in another, let's say in a
more traditional way, but his recollections concerning this
matter are somewhat vague.

The man who really counted was Secchia. That there was a
strong bond of trust between Feltrinelli and Secchia has
already been pointed out. How far that trust extended is proven
by a brief note in Secchia's hand, written on the day that
marked the end of his political career. It was 26 July 1954 when
he learned that Giulio Seniga, his trusted right-hand man, had
flown the coop a few hours earlier with the party's secret cash
fund: 421,000 dollars plus some confidential documents (the
exact sum was revealed to me by Seniga in 1996). Secchia wrote
down a chronology of those terrible moments:

> At eight in the morning I came across the first theft, he
> [Seniga] had taken everything from Bundazia [the *nom de
> guerre* of Oddino De Laurentis], and then from all the
> others. I took Valli everywhere I went in order to have a
> witness if any sums were found or if everything had dis-
> appeared. In this regard it has to be said that he [Seniga]
> did not manage to go to G.Giacomo's apartm. or to
> Turchi's and in these two places I found all the sums
> deposited.

So, it would seem that a part of the PCI's reserves was

hidden in a Roman house put at the party's disposal by Feltrinelli, but, according to Seniga, there was another Feltrinelli 'safe' in Milan that he did not want or was unable to 'visit'.

In the early fifties, Palmiro Togliatti would occasionally go to dinner in the San Babila apartment. When he came to Milan, his every move was top secret, for security reasons, and the party preferred him to eat in the houses of comrades in order not to attract attention. In passing from the hall to the living-room of Giangiacomo and Bianca's home, he was obliged to steer a zigzag course through the piles of books lying on the floor.

* * *

The idea is simple. It is not possible to study the workers' movement without first undertaking the great task of collecting sources, material and documentation. Thought that looks to the future cannot be detached from memory, and this is a perpetual tension. It is necessary to reconstruct the threads of a tradition that Nazism, Fascism and the war have cut. We must take stock of a world that resembles an open wound and find the right instruments with which to remedy matters. This is the 'thing to do'.

If this is what Feltrinelli and Del Bo talked about, and if this is what they were aiming at, the result of their challenge can still be seen today. All you need do is take a tram to piazza della Scala in Milan.

Here you get off, and after passing a few banks and bars with marble-topped counters where the clerks take their lunch, there is the low doorway that leads to the reading room. A domed ceiling pierced by thick bull's-eye windows: you need light for reading. In the room you have to be quiet; people come a long way to study here. Ladies and gentlemen, what would you like to see? A cultivated librarian can take you to the private chapel for religious services, dating from grandfather Carlo's time; today, below the crimson banner of the Paris

Comune, there are two hundred periodicals from the time of
the comunards and the First International. On returning to the
reading room, you can see a first edition of the *Encyclopédie*,
together with a collection of original editions of the most
important works of the Enlightenment. In the back, among
the ranks of metal shelves, it takes a little time to get your
bearings: the sections on the old economists, Russian populism, English industrialism, the Spanish Civil War, the
French, German and English Utopians . . . there are over three
hundred thousand books. And thirty thousand periodicals. But
a discerning eye will spot a rare edition of Thomas More's
Utopia alongside first editions of Rousseau's *Social Contract*,
Bayle's *Various Thoughts on the Occasion of a Comet*, Mary
Wollstonecraft's *A Vindication of the Rights of Woman* and
Saint-Simon's *Political Discourses*. Verri's *Il Caffè* close to the
satirical journals of the Risorgimento, *Civiltà Cattolica*,
Viesseux's *Anthology* . . . Or Cattaneo's reflections on the 1848
uprising in Milan, Herzen's *Thoughts*, the essays of the phys-
iocrats, the pamphlets on the effects of the industrial
revolution . . . And that's not all. For, if your interests run to
something more sophisticated, you have to go down to the
basement where cartoons and caricatures from the siege of
Paris, May 1871, stand next to Marx's working notes, Engels's
notes, Victor Hugo's letters to Garibaldi, the letters of the
young Bakunin, Proudhon's correspondence from exile in
Belgium and the canvas-backed notebooks in which Angelo
Tasca* kept an account of his years in Paris, as well as his
correspondence with Salvemini†, Rosselli,‡ Togliatti, and
Nenni.

On reaching the exit, just before you get your breath back,

* (1892–1960). A political exile in Paris. A founder member of the PCI, he
was expelled in 1929 for his criticism of Stalin.
† Gaetano Salvemini (1873–1957). A historian and an opponent of Fascism
from the start. He taught at Harvard in the thirties.
‡ The Rosselli brothers, anti-Fascist intellectuals, assassinated by
Mussolini's thugs in Paris: Carlo (1899–1937) was an economist; Nello
(1900–37) a historian of the Risorgimento.

it's up to you if you wish to spend a few minutes looking at the only extant copy of the *Patriotic Journal of Corsica* (1790) or the collection of *Die Neue Zeit* (1883).

Every library embodies the fascination of its construction, of its intrinsic rationality, of its unpredictable nature. That's why its development is a journey that wends its meandering way through a maze of tempting possibilities – perhaps a new collection here, maybe a new section there – in search of an unattainable completeness. It is a pattern that resembles a blot of sepia ink; in some parts the punctiform structure is denser and in others it is more tenuous. But it cannot be denied that there is a 'body', an equilibrium, a great centre of strength.

In April 1951, a confidential report informed the chief of police: 'Within the sphere of the various activities of the PCI, we ought to include the work of the well-known Communist businessman GianGiacomo Feltrinelli, resident in piazza San Babila 4, which is made up of an enterprise, already well under way, aimed at attracting young people of all classes desirous of culture to a library that bears the name of the aforementioned Feltrinelli and is located in a building owned by the same Feltrinelli – or at least so we have been assured – in via Domenico Scarlatti nº 26.' According to this information, received from 'very reliable sources' this 'little university of Marxism' was in reality a meeting place for 'young Communist fanatics' who are given a training in culture as well as in the work of 'action squads'.

In fact, Feltrinelli sometimes took issue with his youngsters when he found them in the bar across the way, absorbed in hard-fought billiards games. This was apparently as near to action as this particular squad ever got.

In the first offices of the library, not far from Milan Central Station, a group of young intellectuals got down to work. While Giuseppe Del Bo, starting from 1948, was the main source of inspiration, between 1950 and 1952 Feltrinelli created its real structure. From Rome, following a request sent to the PCI,

came the high-school teacher Franco Della Peruta* (recommended by Gastone Manacorda), the philosophy student
Gastone Bollino (the secretary of the Rome University cell)
and Franco Ferri, a graduate of the Normale di Pisa University,
who had been chosen by a group of colleagues very close to
Palmiro Togliatti. These were joined by the socialist Gianni
Bosio, the founder of the magazine *Movimento operaio*, and the
first bursars or collaborators, like Stefano Merli and Luigi
Cortesi. Strictly speaking, almost none of these persons
belonged to the generation that had fought in the Resistance,
and this further underlines the awareness that a historical epoch
had come to an end. As scholars, they recognized that the
inherited canon had been delegitimized. Retaking possession of
the history of the workers' movement, which was their declared
aim, implied the systematic and unified collection of all the
material that had survived the war, the book burnings and the
censors. This was to be done by updating both the documentary structure and the bibliographic research methods, without
neglecting an analysis of the social problems that were already
germinating.

Feltrinelli's investment necessarily called for specialist personnel, recruited almost exclusively from the ranks of the
activists in Sesto San Giovanni, the Milan suburb known as
'the Italian Stalingrad': two employees to look after administration, two for secretarial duties, one delivery man, three filing
clerks. It was necessary to forge ahead in the creation of the
inventory of archival sources: books, pamphlets, periodicals,
one-offs, manifestos, flyers and photographs. The material
began to flow in.

The researchers combed the stores specializing in old books,
region by region, and delved into the address lists, family by
family. The result of their efforts was an increased store of
documents on the Risorgimento and Italian socialism. Franco
Della Peruta spent most of his time working on the Italian

* (1924–). Professor of the History of the Risorgimento at the University of
Milan.

section, while Del Bo supervised the acquisition of collections of old foreign publications, especially French material. This was because Feltrinelli wanted to give the primary line of research an international slant right from the outset, for which he had already made several trips to various European countries. Many years later, he spoke to a German journalist about his first hunts for material:

> It was in '48. Germany was still in ashes and ruins. Only the cultural and literary spheres showed some signs of life. On one of my frequent trips to Hamburg, in a bookshop, I learned that someone in Osnabrück was selling a first edition of *The Communist Party Manifesto*. Together with Professor Del Bo, I immediately left for Osnabrück. On the one hand we almost wanted to draw out the thrill of waiting, but on the other we were afraid that someone might get there before us. So, having arrived early at our destination, we waited in the car, eyes peeled. But we were the ones to be spotted: a stranger came up to the car and asked if, by any chance, we were the friends interested in the collector's item. Then he took us to a dusty attic, where we found a couple of enormous bookshelves. The first of these contained the most comprehensive library of socialist literature I had ever seen: articles by Trotsky, court-case documents, party circulars, manifestos and resolutions. I bought the lot for forty thousand marks. I did not let that 'treasure' out of my sight until I had transported the thirty boxes to my apartment in Milan. Naturally I missed out on a really huge bargain: the second shelf was also of extreme interest. It contained the most valuable collection of erotic literature I had ever seen . . .

Between Feltrinelli and Del Bo there was a fraternal relationship. Both men whose lives had not followed a linear course, they were linked by a common ideal of a just, lay society. Sometimes Giangiacomo would listen to his friend's advice,

other times he would play his cards close to his chest. There
was also a playful aspect, and no lack of amusing episodes.
They were like friends who were still kids.

In a legal deposition made when they were kids no longer,
Del Bo was to say this of his friend:

> Given my fraternal contacts with Feltrinelli, I wish to
> describe what I feel was his character. He was undoubt-
> edly a man of considerable intelligence, impulsive, with a
> tendency to take the lead. He seemed wary, but in reality
> he was prepared to embrace other people's opinions with
> enthusiasm and to espouse their cause if he thought fit.
> But he was just as prepared to abandon a cause, without
> standing on ceremony, if he felt it was outdated or did
> not serve his way of thinking. His enthusiasm was easily
> aroused. He believed in the things he did.

'Uncle Sergio' was a born diplomat and an able organizer
with a talent for weaving a network of relations. In addition, he
was a talented librarian and a man of shrewd commercial sense.
His scientific skills were occasionally criticized, perhaps for
good reason or perhaps because of the particular role he played
at the court of the 'prince'.

But Del Bo did not become the first curator of the Feltrinelli
library. When the Associazione Biblioteca Giangiacomo
Feltrinelli was officially established, on 24 December 1951, my
father agreed with the top echelons of the PCI that the post
ought to be given to someone with direct party links. The
choice fell on Franco Ferri, a pupil of Delio Cantimori, the
eldest of the small 'Roman' group.

This was typical of the form of control exercised by the PCI
over the cultural institutions within its sphere of influence. The
principle was that of 'joint management', and that's how things
went at the Biblioteca Feltrinelli, at least until a certain date.

Inevitably, Del Bo was bitter about the post he had been
denied. Apart from the personal disappointment, perhaps he
was afraid that Feltrinelli was excessively taken by his political

enthusiasms and might lose sight of certain scientific and cultural scruples. Giangiacomo decided to send him to Paris.

On the banks of the Seine stood the little store owned by the antiquary and bibliophile Michel Bernstein, a member of a famous family of exiled Lithuanian Mensheviks. His contribution was essential for the establishment of the collections on the French Enlightenment, Utopian Socialism, the Paris Comune, and the Fourierist movement. Bernstein could track down the libraries owned by the scholars or politicians of the turn of the century, he knew the Russian *émigrés* of Paris and he kept a check on the state of health of a few old men who had books in their cellars ready to be bought up outright. He could also provide the addresses of pharmacists, who were considered fairly important authorities, living in small provincial towns, often the only persons who tended to keep a few papers during the war. Del Bo stayed in Paris for over two years, between 1952 and 1954, and Feltrinelli frequently visited him there.

Giangiacomo was not only a Communist, he was also an *aficionado* of Citroën cars. That is to say, he drove his Citroën with the skill that comes with great familiarity, without bothering too much about denting the wings (a sure sign of a 'bourgeois' mentality); and while he was a terrifying driver, he was also a tireless one. His forays with 'Uncle Sergio' as they combed Europe in search of books and papers were to become authentic family legends: 'That time when Sergio nearly had his first heart attack because of the way Giangiacomo was driving the car, with a broken window, at three hundred kilometers an hour . . .' And it was thanks to these missions that the two travellers in the black Citroën were soon able to avail themselves of a network of experts, consultants and dealers, all of the very first quality.

In Holland, they went to Herbert Andreas, a very special character. Born in Hamburg in 1914, as a young man he had developed a passion for history, mainly of the origins of the workers' movement and Marxism. In the early thirties he changed his name to Bert, as a tribute to Brecht, joined the German communist party, contributed articles to his local newspaper and published an anti-militarist novel, *Mata Hari*. About midway through the decade, after a couple of arrests, he opted for exile in Holland and continued his subversive activities with the International Red Help organization. After an adventurous war, Andreas settled in Amsterdam, where he established himself as a collector and bibliophile. His first contacts with Feltrinelli date from 1951 and he was to work closely with him for ten years or so. Thanks to Andreas, and despite the fact that at that time there was scant interest in Germany in the history of the socialist movement, the sections on Marx–Engels and on German social democracy and the Hegelian left began to take shape. Bert Andreas was also perhaps Feltrinelli's first contact with the Marxist–Leninist Institute of Moscow (IMEL).

Another source of literature in the German language was an enthusiastic pioneer of research who lived in Zürich: the anarchist Theo Pinkus; in England, Eric J. Hobsbawm himself went through lists of antiquaries, albeit only very occasionally; for Russian matters, there was a scholar of the calibre of Franco Venturi to oversee populism and Decembrism. For the United States there was Luigi Aurigemma, Giangiacomo's childhood friend from the Museo delle Terme in Rome, whose official reason for his journeys to America was that he was in search of material on the Utopian colonies of the nineteenth century. But if he chanced to come across some documents on the McCarthyist wave, in full flow at the time, so much the better. Aurigemma often went to Paris and when Feltrinelli went there to see Del Bo, they would go off to dine on snails.

Those trips and the frequent visits to Paris were good for Giangiacomo; the change of air and the water gurgling in the gutters gave him the sense of a great city, beautiful and free. In the end he took a shine to a lady dining at the next table in the Deux Magots. I think this was the beginning of a real and intense love story, but affairs of the heart deserve a minimum of discretion.

* * *

The heroic period of the 'Archives of the Revolution' was the first half of the twentieth century: thefts, confiscations, bombs, rescues, adventurous handovers. One of the primary goals of the Revolutionary movements was to halt the dispersion of manuscripts, letters, books and newspapers, notes, reports and minutes, particularly the works of Marx and Engels and their contemporaries. On 2 February 1921, Lenin wrote to David Borisovich Ryanazov, the director and co-founder of the Marx–Engels Institute in Moscow: 'Can we not buy [. . .] the letters of Marx and Engels? Or copies of them? Is it possible to take the collection of extant writings and bring them together in Moscow? Is there a catalogue of what we already have?' The situation was by no means promising. After the First World War, the rich inheritance of books left to German social democracy had been dispersed. In the Soviet Union, most of the works in circulation were photographic reproductions of material that was either inaccessible or impossible to find elsewhere. Even the publication of the works of Marx and Engels was a sketchy affair and editions were often incomplete or rehashed.

Things began to get moving in Berlin, but the real action was in Amsterdam, thanks to the efforts of Nicolaas Wilhelmus Posthumus and Nehemia de Lieme. The former was a real pioneer of economic history in Holland, an enthusiastic captain of industry; the latter was the founder of an insurance company whose profits went partly to finance the cultural development of the working classes. Posthumus came from the social democratic tradition, De Lieme from the liberal socialist school of thought. In 1934, the two men joined forces to found the International Institute of Social History. In the space of a few months, thanks to the help of invaluable associates, Posthumus clinched a string of spectacular deals: the Parteiarchiv of the SPD, the libraries of Max Netlau and Karl Kautsky, the archives of Leon Trotsky, Mikhail Bakunin, Wilhelm Liebknecht and Valerian Smirnov.

But the results achieved after much labour in the twenties and thirties risked destruction with the establishment of Nazism and the coming of the new barbarism. Much material was lost, while research became more and more difficult. It was 1946 before the Institute in Amsterdam managed to recover part of the documentation confiscated by the Germans during the occupation after 1940.

After the Second World War, the plan to create a temple for the 'Archives of the Revolution' became a real obsession for Moscow. The Institute of Marxism–Leninism sent one hundred and twenty-seven 'correspondents' out into the world. The forms of Marxism were multiplying, and the Cold War was on its way.

The Soviets noticed the Italians in 1952. The first information came from their embassy in Rome, while in Moscow the first special 'top secret' document was drawn up on 4 April 1953. It was addressed to comrade Pospelov, one of the secretaries to the Central Committee, a former director of the Institute of Marxism–Leninism, and soon to be elected to the secretariat of the first Central Committee of the post-Stalin era.

> The Information Committee of the Ministry of Foreign Affairs of the USSR reports as follows on the Feltrinelli library in Italy. In Milan there is a large private library on the history of the international workers' movement, composed of over seventy thousand books and documents. The library belongs to Giangiacomo Feltrinelli, a well-known collector of bibliographical rarities, manuscripts and documents regarding the history of the European and especially the Russian revolutionary movements. In particular, the Feltrinelli library holds three complete collections of the newspaper *Iskra*. In December 1952 a certain Bernstein, on behalf of Feltrinelli, negotiated the purchase in Paris of the original of an unpublished letter by V. I. Lenin. The letter (eight pages in French) was allegedly written by Lenin in 1908 to a French journalist who had lived in Russia and had later published some articles hostile to the revolutionary movement there. Some time ago, associates of Feltrinelli discovered in Paris two

archives (a police archive and a private one), containing documents regarding the Paris Comune. Feltrinelli is presently negotiating to buy these archives. In the USA, another of Feltrinelli's associates has collected a large amount of material on the history of the First International. In March this year, Feltrinelli informed a functionary of the Soviet embassy in Italy that he was holding talks with Rüter, the head of the Amsterdam archives, regarding the publication of some material from this archive, including what appear to be the originals of over five thousand letters by Marx and Engels. Feltrinelli said he was prepared to finance this publication. Nevertheless, as Feltrinelli has pointed out, there are numerous difficulties. In particular, the Amsterdam archives have apparently aroused the interest of Columbia University (USA), which is prepared to buy the contents for three million dollars. According to Feltrinelli, the Americans want to falsify the letters by Marx and Engels held by the archives in Amsterdam. In the course of the same meeting, Feltrinelli expressed the desire that a functionary of the Marx–Engels–Lenin Institute go to Italy to see his library. That same functionary could prepare the way for the temporary transfer to IMEL of the most valuable material of which the Feltrinelli library has only one copy. Feltrinelli justified this request by explaining that, should the political situation in Italy worsen, reactionary elements might try to sabotage his library. Many precious documents might therefore be destroyed, given that the library has no armoured rooms. The same opinion was expressed in December 1952 by Paolo Robotti, who is a candidate for membership of the Central Committee of the PCI, in the course of a conversation with the Soviet ambassador to Italy. Feltrinelli is very rich and owns numerous industrial and commercial companies. According to information from top-level functionaries of the PCI, Feltrinelli supplies the Communist Party with financial support.

Six days later, the heads of Agitprop and the department in charge of relations with foreign Communist parties, both offshoots of the central committee of the CPSU, sent out a second document, whose contents were basically similar to those contained in the document of 4 April. It landed on the desk of Nikita Khruschev, the prime candidate to succeed Stalin. The note suggested that it might be worth approaching Pietro Secchia to sound out the idea of using Feltrinelli as an intermediary with the institute in Amsterdam (Moscow could not hold negotiations directly: the institute was headed by persons 'hostile to the USSR'). Secchia, the deputy chairman of the PCI, was said to be the middleman through whom Feltrinelli passed on 'important material support' to the party. Moreover, the note advised the intervention of the Soviet embassy in Holland with a view to obtaining accurate information on the materials kept in Amsterdam and also on the heads of the International Institute of Social History. In conclusion, it was also urged that Giangiacomo Feltrinelli be invited to come to Moscow, perhaps camouflaged among one of the many foreign delegations due to make visits on the occasion of 1 May.

And there matters rested for a while. Feltrinelli let it be known that he would have preferred a personal invitation. However, in the Kremlin they had other fish to fry: the man who could not die had not been dead for as much as a month, and the furious clash between Khruschev and Zhukov against Beria was already under way.

Talks began again in July 1953, when Secchia went to Moscow for a briefing on the new line regarding Beria. It is probable that the Feltrinelli affair was at least mentioned. The required personal invitation materialized after the summer and the trip was made in the very last days of 1953, when Giangiacomo arrived in the Soviet Union via Vienna and Prague. He was accompanied by his wife Bianca.

The great capital city of Moscow was celebrating Old Year's Night. To reconstruct the other purposes of the visit, we have to use our intuition. On his arrival at Pushkinskaja ul. 15, my father must have walked along the red carpet together with the heads of IMEL, reviewing all the busts and the icons on display. Then he would have visited the cellarage, where the doors are in cast iron and archivists wearing aprons show you picaresque little drawings by Lenin aged twelve and things of that kind. Then they would have taken him to the upper floors, where any conversation was always preceded by a glass of steaming hot tea.

The central subject of conversation was the collaboration between IMEL and the Biblioteca Feltrinelli in Milan. The first lists of things to be exchanged were drawn up. Moscow was interested in copies or microfilms of Marx's correspondence, as well as that of the members of his family, Engels, and the writings by Lenin kept in the archive of Camille Huysmans,* including the lists of material on the First International. In their turn the Soviets agreed to satisfy the counter-requests for microfilms, books and registers of contents.

Feltrinelli found himself in a strange position, as the third side of a triangle that could not be closed: Milan, Moscow and Amsterdam. With the Dutch, 'co-operation was restricted to persons with the same view of things', recalls Rein Van Der Leeuw, then a young functionary with the Institute of Social History. Feltrinelli was also the only person who could contact and work with the Soviets; he promised them he would do all he could to find out what was kept in the institute in Amsterdam. In particular, he had to find out about the Marx–Engels archive that Columbia University was also interested in acquiring. He was to try to get the Dutch to give him an inventory, to buy a part of it or, at least, to get hold of a copy. More generally, he declared his willingness to search for valuable documents in the West, in mutual agreement with the Institute of Marxism–Leninism. He made the same promise to the Dutch, with whom he was on excellent terms. His role was to build bridges between two worlds that did not communicate

---

* (1871–1968). A Belgian socialist who was Secretary to the Steering Committee of the 'Socialist International' in the forties.

with each other, as well as to look after the interests of his own library. Up-to-date research on the sources of Marxism could not be made without the help of the Soviets, but relations with the Dutch were just as vital.

The idea of temporarily moving a part of the Milan archives, mentioned in the Pospelov report, did not seem to get off the ground in the course of the talks with the Soviets. But the fact that Feltrinelli had thought about it should not surprise anyone: at that time, a part of the archives of the PCI was still in Prague and there was talk of sending it to Moscow for safe-keeping. In Italy, after the electoral clash that had brought down the *'legge truffa'*, the troops had closed ranks and the international climate encouraged and fed the growth of a cold-war paranoia from which no one was immune.

Despite the good intentions, the lists of proposed exchanges and the ceremonial, it is legitimate to suppose that the meetings held in Moscow in early 1954 only partly matched the expectations of those involved. Perhaps the nomenklatura showed its more monolithic side. And perhaps the Soviets found it difficult to understand this strange type of Italian.

3

In the late afternoon of Saturday, 18 June 1955, four young men and a girl met in a bar in via Manzoni, just a stone's throw from La Scala opera house. One of the four was the fledgeling publisher Giangiacomo Feltrinelli, whose twenty-ninth birthday it was that very evening. The other three men were his editors, while the girl was his willing secretary, interpreter, cashier and telephonist, who always went around with a stenotype machine fresh from America under her arm, as expensive as it was superfluous. The little group decided to make a toast: to the new publishing house and its first books!

The two books still hot from the presses were *The Scourge of the Swastika*, by Lord Russell of Liverpool (translated by one of the editors, Luciano Bianciardi) and the *Autobiography* of Jawaharlal Nehru.

They had left the advance copies on the desks in the office, because they wanted to forget the bitterness of a few misprints, a few 'typos' of the kind that elude the watchful eyes of copy editors and proofreaders and then, when the book is nicely printed and bound and jacketed, stand out with brazen insolence as if for sheer spite.

In a television interview given ten years later, in 1965, the publisher recalled that these two books were no casual choice.

> They corresponded to three of the principal threads that
> made up the leitmotiv that the house had developed
> with particular care: the first was a consistent and
> coherent anti-Fascism; the second involved the quest for
> a form of coexistence between countries with differing
> economic and political structures that – and this was the
> third thread – did not accept the crystallization of the
> politico-economic geography of the day, but worked on
> the assumption that it was possible for the new forces of
> the Third World, the countries that were emerging from
> colonial domination, to find their own equilibrium and
> to take their place forcefully in the global political
> system.

Back in 1955, in the bar in via Manzoni, those present were well aware that it was only a beginning, that the real difficulties were still to come, and that anyone could print two books, but that you need ideas and means if you are to last.

All of them, Feltrinelli included, shared a common experience. In the immediate post-war period, in 1949 to be precise, the editorial department of an evening paper, *Milano Sera*, housed in the former headquarters of the hundred per cent Fascist *Popolo d'Italia*, had launched a series of low-cost, conveniently priced (100 lire) paperbacks: the Universale Economica del Canguro. Corrado De Vita, the editor of the newspaper, backed the launch with a high-profile promotional campaign.

The idea was to revive a glorious Italian tradition of the late nineteenth century, when a few publishers, Perrino, Barbera, and Edgardo Sonzogno (to mention only the most important names), with an eye to the educational–humanistic aims of the nascent socialist movement, had gone after the mass market, printing the classic literature of the whole world and offering the books at the absurdly low price of 25 cents.

Against this background, during a period of reconstruction that also included culture, the colourful dust jackets of the new Universale series began to emerge at the rate of one a week. 'A book a week against obscurantism' was the slogan that announced the first four: *The Confessions of an Italian* by Ippolito Nievo, *The Indiscreet Jewels* by Denis Diderot, the *Life of Jesus* by Ernest Renan, and the scholarly essays of the English scientist J. B. S. Haldane. In the provinces, the occasional priest would put retailers on their guard against the books published by Canguro: better not to have them on display.

One month before (in May 1949), Rizzoli had launched *Bur*, another renowned 'universal' library destined to enjoy enduring and well-deserved fame. Both ventures, albeit for different reasons, were linked by the idea of exploring the new possibilities of the popular paperback book. When 'popular' did not mean a low quality product – quite the opposite.

Canguro got off to a remarkable start: the readers liked what they saw and print runs reached a peak of thirty-five thousand. The rate at which new titles appeared made it necessary to create a regular working structure right away, complete with a business name: Cooperativa del libro popolare. But everybody shortened this to 'Colip'. More editors were hired and they were set to work under Luigi Diemoz, a man of great refinement who was painstaking to a fault. He looked like a Hapsburg aristocrat, right down to the monocle he wore in his left eye.

The readers' committee included Ambrogio Donini, Lucio Lombardo Radice, Gastone Manacorda, Concetto Marchesi, Carlo Muscetta,* Giancarlo Pajetta,† and Carlo Salinari. Togliatti's contribution to the series was to write an introduction to Voltaire's *Treatise on Tolerance*.

It ought to be added that the decisive impetus for the constitution of the cooperative came from the PCI, on the advice of

---

* (1912–). A historian of Italian literature, literary critic and professor of Italian literature.

† (1911–90). A leader of the PCI, he was to play a key role in relations between Feltrinelli and the party. A Stalinist and a die-hard supporter of the workers' movement, he was known for his wit.

the party leader in person. 'I remember one thing very clearly,' recalls the art historian Mario De Micheli: 'It was Togliatti who pressed for and later took the decision. Both De Vita and Feltrinelli assured me of this.' And this was why, in the early days at least, the editorial office in Milan was under the strict control of the central cultural committee in Rome. Ambrogio Donini, the historian of religion in charge of the party's publishing activities and a member of the Colip board, was the middleman between Milan and Rome.

Among those who co-operated with the new publishing house was Giangiacomo Feltrinelli, still very young and already passionately enthusiastic about the publishing business. His presence within the co-operative, at first as a simple financial partner, was soon transformed into a far broader commitment, especially when things began to take a less favourable turn. After the initial enthusiasm, in fact, it soon became apparent that something was wrong. Booksellers did not earn much out of Universale's publications: the list price was too low. As a consequence, within a few months sales had plummeted. Things seemed to have gone into a dangerous spin until, at the last moment, the call went out for someone to help the company avoid the worst: and so my father found himself directly involved in the way things were managed. This was toward the end of 1950.

The publication of a new book every week was resumed, print runs were more prudent, prices slightly increased, and the distributor changed: 'The new management, thanks to the impetus provided by Feltr., has succeeded in re-establishing a little order and a good part of the accumulated debt has been paid off.' Thus Ambrogio Donini, in a letter to Giancarlo Pajetta dated February 1951.

But it wasn't just a matter of accountancy: the need to broaden the range of publications had become a pressing one. As the months went by, the Universale Economica label became more and more restrictive and less suited to a robust body that had outgrown it, and promised to grow even more in the future.

In the course of a meeting of the readers' committee held in September 1951, Feltrinelli made a speech on 'New publishing ventures to be undertaken by Colip in support of the Universale Economica series':

> Booksellers are not very much interested in selling U.E. books because the profit margin is minimal. On the other hand, the only venture hitherto undertaken by Colip is the publication of the U.E. catalogue. The situation in other publishing houses is different as their popular editions are part of a far broader output, which makes up for the small income deriving from the low-priced series. Colip has to go the other way, backing up the Universale Economica series with more profitable publishing ventures that make for greater profit margins, for Colip and retailers alike. That way, booksellers would treat our low-priced production with more respect.

It seemed that Feltrinelli had made a good point and the house launched two bigger series, one devoted to literature and the other to history. This led to the publication of *The Social History of the French Revolution* by Jean Jaurès and *Italia qual è* (Italy as it is) by Francesco Saverio Merlino. Giorgio Candeloro* was commissioned to write a great history of Italy.

But realizing this project inevitably required immediate financial resources and this was not always simple for co-operatives of this kind. Once more, Feltrinelli stepped into the breach with systematic injections of fresh capital. In the most difficult period, his contribution amounted to over five million lire a month, which fell to a million around mid-1952 before falling again to seven–eight thousand lire in March 1953.

His was the support of a committed militant, which made it possible to consolidate the enterprise, and, with hindsight, it proved a good investment too. For the Colip project did not need to be merely supported or broadened, but completely

* (1908–1988). Professor of the History of Political Doctrine.

reinvented. And the day came when Feltrinelli was obliged to wind up the accounts of the co-operative and shoulder the deficit. The venture ended, the idea remained.

In the meantime, the features of the Italian political landscape were changing, because huge changes were under way in world politics. Even in the cultural field, it seemed as if there were a greater willingness to accept other points of view. The PCI began to take less interest in Colip's activities because the need for an 'anti-obscurantist' offensive was no longer a priority. Other urgent matters and new issues were beginning to emerge.

Having laboriously attained the goal of two hundred titles, in early 1954 Canguro took the plunge: publication was suspended to make way for the establishment of the newborn Giangiacomo Feltrinelli Editore.

* * *

Nineteen fifty-five must have been a tough year.

In Italy, three days after the launch of Feltrinelli Editore, Italy was rocked by the usual government crisis: Mario Scelba's first government was ousted to make way for a new administration led by Antonio Segni. Within the Christian Democratic Party, a struggle began over the inheritance left by De Gasperi. As far as the Communists were concerned, Scelba was the inventor of the '*celere*', the motorized riot police who broke up 'seditious' demonstrations with a liberal use of batons and rifle butts. In this case, 'seditious' meant everything from the protest against the use of chemical weapons in Korea, the tilling of uncultivated land on the part of unemployed farmworkers, or any form of protest by laid-off workers.

In Rome, there was a new ambassador with an energetic approach to the prevention of Communism, Claire Boothe Luce, while America was still going through the aftermath of the anti-Communist campaign unleashed by Joseph McCarthy and his numerous acolytes on the Senate subcommittee on investigations: the electric chair for Julius and Ethel Rosenberg had recently underlined the effects of their crusading zeal.

Claire Luce immediately won over the Italian national press. (Indro Montanelli* of the *Corriere della Sera* wrote to her, saying he wanted to devote himself to clandestine terrorism against Communism before it was too late.) The support of Scelba and the Vatican was a foregone conclusion. In the spring of 1955, the Italian premier had made a trip to the United States, complete with a visit to the Empire State building and a triumphal motorcade through a Brooklyn decked out with Italian flags, some with the arms of the House of Savoy, others with the symbols of Fascism.

America's new ambassador soon enjoyed the unconditional support of Italian industry and high finance, whose leaders had little fear of an imminent Italian Communist revolution but could not tolerate their influence in the labour unions and factories.

Italy's biggest company, car builders Fiat, set about reorganizing their personnel department. Every worker had a dossier and uniformed supervisors and informers were at work inside and outside the factories. Fiat also encouraged the establishment of a 'yellow' labour union, a pro-management organization detached from the political left.

The Fiat company buzzed with rumours of plant restructuring, modernization and automation; in other words, the adoption of modern American methods. All this was in the interests of cost-cutting. To speed things up, labour militants were detailed to special departments from which it was easier to dismiss them on the flimsiest of grounds: insufficient productivity, prolonged spells of sick leave, or on the basis of other treachery cooked up by the personnel office.

The newspapers commented on the defeat of the farm labourers and on the flight from agriculture. And in the south,

---

* (1909–). One of Italy's most famous journalists and writers and founder of *Il Giornale* and *La Voce*.

in the other Italy, people were still dying of starvation in the
outlying districts of the cities and on the great landed estates of
Puglia, Calabria and Sicily.

In Milan, you saw the same southern faces: alarm clocks set
for four thirty a.m., cold rooms, cold water, hot curses. And
every morning the same train for the workshops, the steel mills,
and the chemical, textile and food processing plants. Immigrant
workers from the south found labour unions with their backs to
the wall and bosses who were inventing coaxial cables, plastics,
iron and tubes, and domestic appliances. They never smiled.
Outdoors, as in London, they breathed that compound of
smoke and water that later became known as smog.

The journalist Giorgio Bocca* left Turin for Milan in the
mid-fifties:

> The Milan of those days had a capitalist heart, social
> democratic rhetoric and a radical culture. The heart lay
> in piazza degli Affari,† in the head-office buildings of the
> big banks and insurance companies, in the stock
> exchange, in the offices of the stockbrokers. Social dem-
> ocratic rhetoric hung in the air in City Hall, at La Scala,
> in the offices of charitable organizations like the
> Martinitt orphanage or the Pio Albergo Trivulzio old
> folks' home, in the meetings of the cultural section (run
> by the socialist Ferrieri) of the AEM, the city's power
> company; the radical-aristocratic culture was for a few
> but important none the less, it was to be found in the
> houses of the bourgeoisie or in those of the enlightened
> aristocracy, the heirs to Verri and Beccaria.

And the girls, how were the girls?

Like lots of others, when evening came Giangiacomo would

---

* An influential features and leader writer with *Espresso* and later with *La
Repubblica*.
† The home of the Milan stock exchange.

drink a glass of punch down in Brera,* meet up with friends and, if the evening was free, he could choose from the cinema (at the Durini they were showing *The Roman Holiday of Mrs Stone*) or – why not? – a cabaret starring Walter Chiari.†
Backstage with Maria Callas, Giangiacomo was charming, but he slept in his box while she was singing. He played his role as the enlightened rich man for Paolo Grassi's‡ Teatro Piccolo ('My dearest Giangiacomo, thank you. No further comment. For your promptness and simplicity. Very sweet of you.'); took part in the activities of the House of Culture organized by Rossana Rossanda;** and went to hear Banfi and Vittorini speak (television had barely begun in Italy). He had a shaky marriage and a girl who wrote him honeyed letters from Paris.

* * *

The new publishing house was underpinned by a shrewd entrepreneurial insight.

1955 was a turning point, and not only for Italy. The cultural climate of those days, fervent, restless, full of promise and menace, was seeking a form of expression that was different from journalism, but one that would be just as aggressive and striking; there was a desire to move beyond a certain academic culture, whether Liberal or Catholic or Marxist, then dominant in the biggest publishing houses, and to try out original and heretical forms of thought.

All this fitted in perfectly with a specific plan. In September 1952, Feltrinelli had set up a distribution company called Eda (Editori distribuiti associati) to promote Colip and other Italian publishers but also to import prestigious foreign names like

* Milan's colourful 'artists' quarter'.
† Popular Italian comedy actor who starred with Anna Magnani in Visconti's film *Bellissima*.
‡ (1919–81). The founder and director of the Teatro Piccolo in Milan.
** A zealous PCI official, and a friend of Jean-Paul Sartre, she rebelled against the party and helped found *Il Manifesto*, whose position was to the left of the PCI.

Puf, Plon, Oxford, Juillard, Pergamon Press and Reclam. (Eda was headed by Franco Osenga and Adolfo Occhetto, the father of Franco, later to become a Feltrinelli manager, and of Achille Occhetto, the last leader of the PCI before its dissolution.) A few years later, in 1956, Feltrinelli Libri Spa was established to see to the running of small bookshops: Giangiacomo Feltrinelli intended to create a single circuit (publisher plus distributor plus bookshops).

In the meantime, the task of consolidating the Feltrinelli Library was well under way and a research team was working on the difficult process of reorientating the study of the workers' movement. Occasionally, in the new headquarters in via Scarlatti, the President of the Republic, Luigi Einaudi, would drop in to consult the archives.

The only thing that seemed to be missing from this well-articulated plan was a newspaper, an enterprise that acts like a drug on all publishers. With the failure of *Milano Sera*, an evening paper founded in 1945 and promptly labeled 'crypto-Communist' by the Ministry of the Interior, the idea of Feltrinelli's possible entry into the world of daily newspapers was strongly advocated by the PCI. The space left vacant by *Milano Sera* could be occupied by a new venture in competition with the other evening papers. Feltrinelli was extremely enthusiastic about this idea and he set to working on it day and night, without letting any of his team know about his plans. It was a real case of that peculiarly Italian kind of stopgap tactic known as a 'fuga in avanti'; the administrative staff were kept in the dark right to the last. But with the journalists all hired, only a few days before the launch, Feltrinelli put everything on hold. Something did not add up. His people explained this to him without mincing their words. In reality, it was the basic publishing project that had lost its appeal. The PCI had not kept faith with the initial agreement, with the 'agreed conditions'. Feltrinelli reminded both Amerigo Terenzi and the party leadership of this in a letter dated 28 October 1954. The new paper was to have 'inherited nothing from previous ventures' and to have 'no connection with the tradition of pro-Communist

newspapers'. It was to have contributed to 'a new political orientation in the country, by surrounding itself with all those
national forces that, although they could not be considered supporters of the party, nevertheless shared some common views
on fundamental foreign and domestic policy issues'. The initial
agreement also called for a broadly based share package in order
to avoid only one person (Feltrinelli) having to face all the haz-
ards of isolated exposure.

The reasons for the sudden decision to drop the project were
explained without any polemical intent, the aim being to foster
'a calm analysis of the situation'.

According to Cossutta, the project was opposed by President
Einaudi himself, whose threat to reveal dossiers on the past
activities of the Feltrinelli family was sufficient to prevent the
creation of a politically aligned newspaper.

At first, the new publishing house, whose head offices were in
via Fatebenefratelli no 3, aroused a certain curiosity, largely
because of the founder's name. Italy at that time already
boasted plenty of publishers and, like many of those houses,
the newcomer might have lasted a year or two, or at least this
was how the matter was seen by some condescending observers.
Italo Calvino was the only one to express his good wishes, in the
pages of a news-sheet from the Einaudi publishing house. But
Feltrinelli's position was effectively different from that of his
competitors, as he pointed out himself in the course of an
interview granted to Sandro Viola in the early sixties:

> Compared to other publishers, I had two advantages.
> One was represented by my previous experience; since
> '45, in fact, I had spent years working on the reorganiza-
> tion of the companies within the Feltrinelli group,
> learning about balance sheets, how to assess an executive,
> how to foresee market trends. The other advantage, per-
> haps the more important one, was that the great
> transformation of the country began precisely around
> 1955, just as we were getting started. This arguably

allowed us to grasp the reality of those changes faster than others and to graft them on to the house's commercial and cultural programme.

The offices in via Fatebenefratelli were staffed by a group without much experience in publishing: the first editors, contributors and consultants did not come from universities or other large consolidated structures. In almost all cases, Colip had been their only training ground. They learned quickly.

The first thing the publisher did was to ask his staff to sound out the Italian market. Their reports on every single competitor were complete, detailed and meticulous. The commitment of the people that wrote them is clear, as is the fact that they were on the ball. But who were they?

The most immaculate description comes from Luciano Bianciardi. He had been offered a life and a job in a city that he never really cared for. Plucked from his native Maremma, in Tuscany, Bianciardi, today presented in a rather euphemistic light as 'sarcastic' or 'angry' (I see him as an evil genius with a big heart), described Milan and the Feltrinelli company in a letter to a friend. The letter was published in a recent biography by Pino Corrias.

What are you talking about? Do you think three months of Milan is enough to wipe out thirty-two years in the Maremma? Do you really think I would let this handful of pricks pull a straitjacket over my ass? Because, believe me, it would be hard to find a bigger bunch of pricks than the Milanese anywhere. Folk here are aligned, covered and whipped into line by northern capital; obedient and inflexible, they march along in their rut. And, get this, they don't even complain; on the contrary, they think they are happy. If you ask someone from Grosseto, let's say a wealthy man like Pioppino Bianciardi, how he's getting along, he'll say things like: 'Ah, this is no way to make a living, goddammit. I'm getting nowhere fast', and so on. But ask the same question to a fifty-quid-a-month accounts clerk from Milan and he says: 'I'm getting on just fine.' [. . .]

That's exactly how it is. Living in Milan, believe me, is a really sad business. You're not in Italy here, you're in Europe, and Europe is daft. And all the more so because folk here don't have heart, they're not expansive, even though this is not their fault but can always be put down, as I said before, to the pressure of Milanese capital. [. . .] But if I'm managing to hang on (although I haven't settled in at all, my wife is wrong) it's because I think this: the people in Milan who see things the way we do, that is to say the Communists (even those without a party card, party cards don't count a damn; quite the contrary, I have met some party members here who would do better to go to work for Montecatini, and some of them already have done) have a real battle on their hands. After all, the revolution will be made right here in Milan, there's no doubt, because Milan is the home of our enemies, Pirelli and all those of his ilk. And people of that sort must be fought in Ribolla,* true, but above all here. That's the way it is, believe me.

At work in the publishing house, I have been lucky enough to find some really smart kids and I have become a close friend of one of them, that is to say Onofri, the manager. Onofri is a sort of older and worse version of myself. I mean to say that he is a 'Vitellone',† enthusiastic, generous, rough-and-ready, frivolous, a good sort. Naturally he is also a bigamist. I eat with Onofri every day, and we buck each other up when things go badly. Which happens from time to time. But one thing that is never lacking is *denaro*. In Milan, money runs after you, then it runs away from you. You earn it, you spend it, and you can't do without the stuff. But there's no gravy. The others at the publisher's are good kids too. I'll run

---

* A mine owned by the Montecatini corporation.
† A young provincial unemployed person, from Fellini's film *I Vitelloni*.

through them for you: Giampiero Brega. He works across the desk from me. Twenty-eight, a touch on the tubby side, a degree in philosophy, he tends to play the moralist and is, in his own way, a very good person. Valerio Riva, twenty-five, socialist, tall, bespectacled, with a mouth like a sucker-cup. He looks after fiction, is the most practical one among us, and is potentially the most authoritative. He will go far. Luigi Diemoz, the chief editor. Age hard to guess and never stated. Forty-five? He is small, thin, and worn out by five years of Milan, restaurants and a gastric ulcer. Always bitter, sceptical, he has an enormous moustache.

Libera Venturini, forty, a widow for ten years, completely off her rocker after years at Montecatini. I don't know how she ended up here. Then there are the two girls, Renata and Giuliana, tall and blonde the former, petite and brunette the latter.

Then comes Feltrinelli, nicknamed 'The Jaguar': twenty-eight, glasses, moustache, tall and robust, thick as pigshit, and filthy rich. He has interests in lumber, the construction business, refrigerators and Coca-Cola. Outwardly he is very cordial and free-and-easy: when we meet it's all slaps on the back and phoney punches in the gut. He likes me. Upstairs there are the managers, two of them, and the graphics office, two people there as well. Then, still upstairs, there is *Cinema nuovo*, which is Feltrinelli's thing too. Aristarco, Terzi, a girl and a young kid work there. Aristarco is a king-size ball-breaker who thinks he's the cat's pajamas.

Our office is very pretty, they say: it looks like a perfumery; all modern tables, glass and coloured plastic. The décor is the work of the boss's wife, known as 'Mrs Jaguar', an ex down-and-out who has risen to the heights of wealth and power: she is odious and pretty.

Bianciardi, who was in charge of paperback editions of Italian fiction, did not last long because his unrepentant determination to remain out of step got on everyone's nerves. Most nights he was the last to leave Milan's legendary Bar Giamaica, known in Italian literature as the 'Bar delle Antille' or the 'Portorico'. Even maiden aunts knew that this was the bar frequented by artists whose shaggy manes heralded the long-haired hippy look. Bianciardi was never punctual in the mornings and he was eventually invited to continue working for the house as an out-of-house editor, author and translator. I know that Giangiacomo really cared for him.

The other 'angel with the dirty face' – if I can borrow the sobriquet applied to a trio of Argentinean soccer players on the crest of the wave at the time – was Valerio Riva. He, too, complained about the low salaries, and he too was obliged to do the work of two or even three people: 'There was no book we didn't go after; no translation we didn't redo, sometimes from start to finish; no text we didn't rewrite; and no book ever came out without our coming up with ideas (often surprisingly good ones) for every launch. It seemed as though we could never do enough.' Riva also wrote: 'Absolutely no one wanted to come to Feltrinelli; if anything, people tended to leave. And those who stayed were hated, outside the business.' So where was the fun? 'We were all young, we were all equals. And sure, the level was high. And non-conformist. In short, it was an independent publishing house.'

The third editor, whose interests lay more in non-fiction, was Giampiero Brega. He was to have a long association with Feltrinelli. When this trio was joined by Mario Spagnol, Enrico Filippini,* Giampaolo Dossena, Vittorio Di Giuro, Alba Morino and Attilio Veraldi, with Gerolamo Marasà on the control panel, you could say that they made up the best publishing band of the day. Fair enough, but how to keep the band from breaking up?

Also worthy of mention was the management department run by Silvio Pozzi, a former dispatch rider with the resistance

---

* (1934–88). A journalist and German scholar who introduced some of the most important German-language writers to the Italian public.

movement. After the Liberation, Pozzi worked for a brief
period with the Coca-Cola company; then, thanks to a letter of
introduction from his commandant, he found a position as an
accountant with Eda, the distribution company. Here, he met
Feltrinelli for the first time. Pozzi recalls:

> I met him one day in the head office in via Cavour. He
> came into the waiting room, I was tying up a parcel, and
> he asked me: 'Is the accountant around?' 'Who are you?'
> I asked him. 'Feltrinelli,' he said. Embarrassed, I carried
> on trying to tie up the parcel and first he watched me and
> then he said: 'That's not the way to tie up a parcel. Look,
> first you have to make a kind of slip knot and then you
> can pull it tight.' I wasn't able to do this, it wasn't my job
> after all. So he showed me how it was done. That's how I
> met Feltrinelli.

Pozzi went on to become a lifetime director of the publishing
house and for people like him the term 'feltrinelliano'
(Feltrinelli boy) was coined. According to Pozzi, the editors
saw Feltrinelli as a friend, a peer, they would all go to dinner
together and there was a good deal of familiarity. At the same
time he was the boss, with a rigorous view of management that
scared the younger members of the editorial staff.

But the atmosphere was good. Michele Ranchetti, formerly
an assistant to Adriano Olivetti,* and the first manager of the
Feltrinelli Bookshops, recalls an anecdote that reveals the
shrewdness of the group:

> One time Brega told me the story of one of the many
> rows between Feltrinelli and Bianciardi. Apropos of a
> book that was to be translated, Bianciardi told
> Feltrinelli he had already discussed the matter in suffi-
> cient depth with the 'Deputy-Asshole'. The

* (1901–60). An entrepreneur, engineer, industrialist, publisher and member
of parliament.

Deputy-Asshole? And who might he be? Feltrinelli wanted to know. 'Everyone knows who he is, it's Brega,' shot back Bianciardi. And Feltrinelli laughed, really guffawed, even when he repeated the wisecrack to Brega himself, who, a touch resentful, but as coolly as possible, asked him: 'So who do you think this Deputy-Asshole is?' And Feltrinelli, gleeful: '*You* are the Deputy-Asshole. You ought to feel flattered, because who do you think the Asshole is?'

Founding a publishing house means a lot of adrenaline, especially in this case. Because Feltrinelli aimed at being a really modern firm, where books came out on time, with an accounts department that was buzzing, and where, in the mornings, punctuality was the rule. Riva again: 'Feltrinelli taught us to talk with Italian authors on an arithmetical basis: print runs, industrial, general and advertising costs, list prices, multiplication, subtraction, and addition: if the figures added up, the book could be done, if not, forget it.'

The balance sheet? Losses. Often, almost always. But there was no philanthropic logic behind Feltrinelli's practice of making good on losses: there were no funds to lose for the sake of mere prestige. The following anecdote told me by Silvio Pozzi refers to a later period, but it throws light on the attitude:

One time, it must have been in the mid sixties, Feltrinelli took me to Cuccia,* at Mediobanca, to ask about long-term financing. We made the standard pitch, put forward our request, then Cuccia called one of his people and made the introductions: 'This is the famous Mr Feltrinelli, his hobby is publishing . . .' The remark went down like a lead balloon. Feltrinelli turned on his heel and walked out without even saying goodbye. I just stared at the ceiling, Cuccia was speechless.

* Enrico Cuccia, the legendary boss of Mediobanca, for many years Italy's most powerful banking concern.

From one meeting to the next, in a rather undisciplined and informal climate, with no respect for academic rigidity, books and series took shape. 'Our style corresponds, as is obvious, to a certain aspect of my personality, and people are getting used to it. At Einaudi, for example, they are more systematic in their planning. But we are all ups and downs,' the publisher was to say in public.

Those first titles to be published soon won shelf space for themselves in the bookshops, both because they captured something about culture in those places where culture was really to be found (in Germany, in Russia, in Latin America, in the United States, even in Persia, Egypt and China), and because Feltrinelli had put his money on paperback editions (unfashionable in those years) that, for the first time, were not only of novels but also of non-fiction books and manuals. These were no longer low-priced versions of previously published hardbacks, but entirely new products. It would take too long to go into the matter of how far the situation was affected by the competence of the various consultants like Carlo Muscetta (one among many), or the covers designed by a pioneer of graphic design like Albe Steiner. Moreover, in order to guarantee a visible presence on the shelves of the bookshops, Feltrinelli introduced a special system offering booksellers across-the-board financing for all the titles in a publisher's catalogue, an innovative commercial procedure that is still in use today.

It was not long before Feltrinelli did away with the traditional working method by which all human knowledge was divided up into so many fields, with one person in charge of each section, who in his turn could count on his own collaborators, in descending order. This was the same hierarchical model as the Communist Party's division of the city into federation, zone, cell, and section. One casualty of the decision to sacrifice this system was Fabrizio Onofri, ousted by Feltrinelli following a direct clash between the two that left onlookers dumbstruck.

'At bottom,' recalled Anna Del Bo Boffino, the press officer
at the time,

> we realized we were very lucky, we were living in the eye
> of the cyclone. On the one hand, the office was ruled by
> a sort of party discipline, and we had a comrade who was
> also the boss. But every time Giangiacomo went over the
> intellectual score, so to speak, then everything had to be
> discussed, and at that point the fact that he was the boss
> became a problem: because our boss was also a comrade.

But what does Tina have to say? The boss's secretary, Tina
was simply Tina for friends, enemies, supplicants and celebri-
ties alike: a 'filter' for everyone. While still very young, Tina
Ricaldone had given up her job with the Communist federation
(where she had been Alberganti's secretary) in favour of a position with Feltrinelli in the via Fatebenefratelli offices. There,
she swore an oath of fidelity to her publisher that was to prove
more lasting than any wedding vow.

Tina was and still is a very reserved person; even though she
was on first-name terms with my father, and is to all intents and
purposes a member of my family, when we talk of him she
never says 'Giangiacomo' or 'your father' but invariably only
'Feltrinelli'. Feltrinelli and that's it. 'Feltrinelli', in fact,

> created the publishing house to give a sense to his life
> and to provide the political Left with a tool. He could
> not bear the idea that some people thought of the pub-
> lishing house as being on a par with a factory for the
> production of stock cubes. With many of the people who
> came to work with us, maybe on the strength of a recom-
> mendation, relations were broken off as soon as they
> revealed any sign of bureaucratic attitudes.

But for those who stayed, they were remarkable years, were
they not? 'The feeling was that we were leaders across the
board, and not just the first to acquire the right books. I'll give

you an example: ours was the first house to establish the forty-hour week . . .' To this day, Tina will not stay any more.

Feltrinelli was on the verge of becoming a real publisher, 'with his head in the clouds and his feet on the ground', as someone was to say. But he was more than that. He had a liking for newspapersellers. Tough folks already at work in the city fog long before daybreak. He liked the tradition of the '*pontremolesi*' or '*bancarellai*', the men and women who carried books around in panniers and sold them on the street. He toyed with the idea of setting up a mobile bookshop that might do the rounds of the markets and fairs. Some older booksellers still remember a very young Feltrinelli rummaging through the shelves and the tables with the latest publications, and not only to inquire about the sales of his own editions but also because he was interested in the day-to-day problems faced by booksellers: discounts on orders, problems with suppliers, the pressure applied by the big publishers, the progressive impoverishment of their stocks . . . Problems he was to tackle personally when he took over the first stationer's and bookseller's shop on the outskirts of Milan and other established bookshops in Pisa, Rome, Milan and Genoa. For that project, too, this was a time of meetings, discussions and frenetic business trips.

Some have talked of him as an off-putting man, divided in two by his dual role as 'boss' and 'comrade', and prone to sudden likes and dislikes. Says Carlo Ripa di Meana,* then the manager of a small Feltrinelli bookshop in Forte dei Marmi: 'His real problem, apart from the sad story of his family, was his immense wealth. He was tormented by the suspicion that he was surrounded by people who wanted to exploit him, who were his friends only because his name was Feltrinelli.' This is a typical example of the kind of glib cliché that is regularly served up as what Alberto Arbasino[†]

* A socialist, former member of the European parliament, and founder of the Italian green party, Lista Verde.
† (1930–). Journalist and novelist.

would call rough-and-ready-private-legendary-window dress-
ing.

As a matter of fact, at first sight most people seemed to find
Feltrinelli quite disagreeable. He was a good listener, but rather
slow to offer his confidence, and his aristocratic traits – com-
portment, elocution, manners – were blended with sincere and
humble impulses. He was a difficult man devoted to a certain
type of risk, together with a surprising form of irreverence that
speakers of Yiddish would describe as 'chutzpah'. This was
what made his every gesture inexplicably charismatic, even
when it wasn't.

And those who threw in their lot with Giangiacomo in those
years, and who resisted temptations like idleness, glibness or
opportunism, and adulation, were treated as equals. This was the
real point of his personality: guided by his own highly particular
radar, he could be stand-offish or charming, brusque or exquis-
itely polite. With everybody, and without bias. This freedom in
interpersonal relations allowed him to call himself 'rich' in the
truest sense of the word, unfettered by considerations of class.

In the early years of the publishing house, apart from questions of friendship or compatibility, everyone knew they were
working toward the realization of a great undertaking: to make
up for lost time and to link Italy to world culture.

* * *

'At that time, at first, new ideas were emerging, albeit in a vague
form. Old conceptions were called into question and it was a
period of study and research. We tried to exercise our influence
on all aspects of a rather fluid society and politico-cultural
system. It wasn't a question of lack of commitment, our commitment was decidedly wide-ranging in scope.' This was how
Feltrinelli recalled his early days in publishing in an interview
with the US trade journal *Publishers Weekly* in the mid-sixties.

At its inception, the new publishing house was the interpreter of requirements that were still confused, uncertain and
often contradictory. But despite this, it was explicitly a part of

Italian 'anti-Fascist' culture and its editorial approach was organized along Marxist lines.

In the publisher's introduction to the first historic catalogue, published in 1965, to mark the house's tenth anniversary, Feltrinelli wrote:

> To our way of thinking, anti-Fascism was not and still is not merely a criticism of the outward aspects of the Nazi-Fascist phenomenon, of its errors and horrors, but the search for the images and causes, in the recent and distant past, of the crisis affecting a system that was not resolved with the fall of Fascism itself. This is why we did not restrict ourselves to taking our analysis of the past well beyond the limits set by conventional historiography, we also tried to stimulate and develop an understanding of the present, of politico-economic structures and of the ideas that were developing in this new context, as we sought a solution to those problems that the fall of Fascism had left unresolved.

Much has been said about the 'cultural hegemony' of the Left, practised throughout the post-war period in Italy. The fifties, for example, really was a time when people were searching for a synthesis intended to solve all problems. But (or am I wrong?) what counted were precisely those cultural ferments that, in their desire to be complementary to a political line, ended up diverging from it: against the deference of the Left, and against the intemperance of the Right.

Feltrinelli immediately acquired 'dissonant' books, in other words the liveliest work then coming out of eastern Europe: the acts of the Eighth Polish Plenum, for example, or Lukàcs's *Discourse to the Petöfi Circle*, the *Political Writings* of Imre Nagy, an anthology on labour problems in the USSR, and the Programme of the Yugoslavian League.

Within the Left, Feltrinelli proceeded at a syncopated pace toward the goal of an open society. His decisions were also dictated by his instincts: 'If in 1955 I had not been a Communist

I still would have proposed exactly the same range of material I proposed at the time, because I am sure that it was exactly what contemporary Italian culture was interested in.' He was to say this much later, in the course of an interview.

Forty years after the uprising in Hungary, the Italian press dedicated a lot of space to the final months of that 'terrible' 1956. This resulted in a spate of recollections, historical analyses and anecdotes, like Pietro Ingrao's* account of how Togliatti made a sardonic toast during the first hours of the Soviet intervention. But for the purposes of any summary reconstruction of that *annus horribilis* for Italian Communism it suffices to reiterate what is already known: the PCI's defence of 'socialist gains' (in opposition to the arguments of the Hungarian workers, the intelligentsia, and the students) was to put the party's 'democratic evolution' on ice.

The steady trickle of news about the unheard-of things said by Khruschev in his Report to the 20th Party Congress (February 1956), the fifty-four workers killed by the militia during the strikes in Poznán (June), and the feeling that a tragedy was looming in the interim between the Red Army's first and second intervention in Budapest (23 October to 3 November), triggered a malaise that involved both questions of policy and issues proper to the intellectual sphere. A qualitative leap forward was required in the critical capacities of the entire Left.

The picture was perhaps clearer concerning relations between the PCI and the CPSU and the general agreement within the international Communist movement regarding the various experiences of so-called 'popular democracy'. But even the analysis of the Italian situation seemed to point to imminent strife. There was still no talk of the 'economic miracle', but it was clear that certain concepts expounded by the Third

* A major personality within the left wing of the PCI, he was the editor of *l'Unità* from 1947 to 1957, and President of the National Assembly from 1976 to 1979.

International and by Marxist theory in general – particularly
the naïve expectation that capitalism would be stricken by a
general crisis – were belied by reality, thus making it necessary
to bring certain theories up to date. The sheer capacity for
development of the forces of production and the technical
advances in industrial organization were underestimated. This
was the subject of debate in the Istituto Gramsci* throughout
1956. These were the first and most important signs of dissent.

In the sectors close to the Feltrinelli Library, the debate
hinged on the orientation of historical research following the
closure of the magazine *Movimento operaio* and the polemics that
marked the International Congress of Historical Studies held in
Rome in 1955. The Soviets, making their first ever appearance at
an international congress, cut a pitifully poor figure.

A variety of papers, letters and documents enable us to check
Giangiacomo Feltrinelli's career as a militant. Contacts with
the Communist leadership, at least until 1955, were cordial and
helpful.

In January 1956, Feltrinelli sent a highly confidential letter
to Giancarlo Pajetta, a kind of 'correspondence from Milan',
strictly for internal use, containing comments gleaned from
local circles frequented by 'our opponents'. These 'opponents'
were the most traditional members of the city's economic and
financial élite.

On receiving this missive, Pajetta passed it on to Togliatti,
complete with a comment in which it is hard to say whether the
intention is ironic or patronizing: 'You might be interested in
this letter from the "eye of Moscow" among the millionaires.'
Pajetta would make a name for himself as a wit.

Yet relations with Togliatti remained good. Shortly before
the letter to Pajetta, in December 1955, Feltrinelli had
addressed the party leader in elaborately deferential terms:
'Hon. Professor,' he wrote, 'I am very glad that, after talks with
Prof. Carlo Muscetta, you have agreed to grace our series of

* Research centre run by the PCI.

monographs on Italian and European periodicals with a volume including selected material from *Stato Operaio*,* a task to be undertaken in collaboration with a reliable person of your choice.' The fee agreed upon was, for those days, astronomically large: four hundred thousand lire.

Early in the summer of 1956, Feltrinelli and Del Bo, who had recently been promoted, met with Togliatti at a seaside resort. Important changes had taken place in the top echelons of the library. On 24 May, Feltrinelli had called a meeting with all the employees and a good number of freelance collaborators. The day before, Franco Ferri had resigned after a series of close encounters of a decidedly non-convivial kind with Feltrinelli. In the course of the meeting, the running of the library was officially handed over to Del Bo and a radical change of course was announced. All present were asked to endorse this move explicitly: those who could not relate to the new programme were more or less invited to resign.

What was to be the future of the 'institute' (as Feltrinelli then called it for the first time)? To become a 'duplicate of a cultural committee or of a body like the Istituto Gramsci Foundation' in order to satisfy needs of an immediately popular nature? Or to be a scientific 'institute' with its own instruments, and with policies and programmes that were truly extensive in scope? Or again: was it necessary to deal with modern and contemporary history in general, including all the issues dear to Gramsci? Or was it preferable to adopt a standpoint clearly oriented toward the history of socialism and the study of its origins, toward the social, economic or political sciences? Was some form of geographical limitation necessary or would it be better to put Italian historiographical interests within a broader context?

In Feltrinelli's view, the working hypothesis was very clear and he backed it with vigour: the institute had to have a purely scientific character, it had to make a name for itself in the

---

* The PCI's monthly magazine. It was published in France from 1927 to 1939, then in New York from 1940 to 1943.

history of the workers' movement without a doctrinaire
approach to thematics and methodology, and it had to have an
international outlook. Where 'without a doctrinaire approach'
meant, for example, not overlooking certain areas such as the
Hegelian Left or certain philosophers like Labriola (who were
marginalised by mainstream Italian Marxism), and where
'international' meant attacking the Italian cultural structure at
those points where it was weakest; in other words, those forms
of provincialism that limited even the most authoritative contributions. It was one of Feltrinelli's typical changes of
direction: back to the founding principles of the early days and
then off out of the swamp in which his fellow travelers had
become enmired. Some referred to this as his 'tormented coherence'.

Togliatti, Feltrinelli and Del Bo discussed all this during
their meeting in the early summer of 1956. The party leader
shrewdly encouraged them to press on. It was an important
conversation, the last really fruitful one between them.

The events that followed immediately afterwards were to
throw this fellowship into disarray.

On 23 October 1956, the people of Budapest rose in rebellion
and Soviet tanks moved in to restore order. The brief insurrection was suppressed at the cost of many human lives. But in the
short term, it was hard to establish the extent of the repression;
some talked of dozens of dead, others of hundreds, and some
of several thousands. The lead editorial in *l'Unità* of 25
October was headlined 'From one side of the barricades, in
defence of socialism'. But the party was on the ropes, and shak-
ing like a leaf.

In Rome, the students immediately took a stand: 'The executive of Communist students, having met on 25 October, has
resolutely affirmed its support of the process of democratiza-
tion.' That same evening, the news came in that the CGIL
labour union had also reacted critically. And three days later,
again in Rome, it was the intellectuals' turn to take the field:
they promoted a document that was to go down in history as

the 'Manifesto of the 101'. Signatures were collected at the Rome offices of Einaudi and of the magazine *Società*. The text, censored by the Communist newspapers, was leaked and picked up by a 'bourgeois' press agency. The signatories who did not dissociate themselves were attacked bitterly by *l'Unità* and by the party alike.

On the other hand, there were no public consequences for the eight Communist personalities, from Milan this time, who a few days later signed a similar protest addressed to the Central Committee. No newspaper talked about it. Yet, one dramatic evening, the document was delivered to *l'Unità*. Outside the editorial offices, a group of Fascists was demonstrating against the PCI and the Red Army, while inside, the editor, Davide Lajolo,* known as 'Ulysses', was thundering that he could not publish the document in question. While the verbal exchange was raging, Feltrinelli, who was present, must have thought of sending the whole crew to the devil: PCI, *l'Unità* and its editor alike. The fact that he did not do this was because of the Fascists down in the street. Their shouts reinforced his sense of belonging. He managed to keep calm and to put forward his point of view without doing much more than raise his voice a little.

Here follows the text of the letter to the Central Committee (dated 29 October) that the Milan-based group would have liked to publish:

> The undersigned Communist intellectuals deplore the fact that in the communiqué sent out by the Party Central Office on 25 October ult. the tragic events in Hungary were defined as 'an armed counter-revolutionary struggle, openly aimed at the overthrow of the people's democratic government, at interrupting the march toward socialism, and at the restoration of a reac- · tionary capitalist regime' and that, until this moment, a

---

* (1912–82). Journalist, writer, and editor of *l'Unità*. Elected to parliament in 1963, he was a member of the Central Committee of the PCI until 1975.

clear position has not been taken that recognizes in the origins and fundamental nature of the Hungarian movement a strong plea for socialist democracy.

They also deplore the fact that the arrival of Soviet troops at the behest of government officials and politicians has not been deemed the latest and most serious error of a policy line that the 20th Congress of the CPSU has condemned and abandoned.

They insist that these positions – confirmed by the development of events – are the only ones in line with the Party's socialist and internationalist ideals and with the rational implementation of its political line for an Italian road to socialism.

They therefore pledge their support for this same position in the congressional debate, with a view to arriving at a correct approach to the theoretical and political problems that these events have reintroduced in such a compelling fashion to their conscience as militant Communists.

Luigi Cortesi, of the Biblioteca Feltrinelli
Giuseppe Del Bo, of the Istituto Feltrinelli
Giangiacomo Feltrinelli
Enzo Modica, of the Milan editorial office of 'Contemporaneo'
Giuliano Procacci,* of the Istituto Feltrinelli
Rossana Rossanda, of the House of Culture
Vando Aldrovandi, of the Libreria Internazionale Einaudi
Marcello Venturi, of the editorial office of *l'Unità* in Milan

The signatories, almost all of them within Feltrinelli's orbit, were summoned in the space of a few hours and shut up in a room inside the Federation offices for a brusque rebuke and a

* (1926–). Professor of history.

reminder of the need for discipline. Armando Cossutta and the party official Italo Busetto were both called in to restore order. Cossutta, on the point of liquidating even 'hardliners' like Alberganti in the name of the 'Italian road to socialism', proposed mediation and promised transparency during the imminent pre Congress debate; everything is postponed, for the time being be good!

But by that time the lid was off and the real item on the agenda regarded 'directing the requirements and aspirations of the various currents within the party'. Feltrinelli's speech before the National Cultural Committee in mid-November was conceptually strong.

A few days later, Feltrinelli threw himself into the Congress of his new party section, in via Milazzo. Hours and hours of discussion and thousands of cigarettes, hundreds of preambles, a single conclusion. Locked up for five endless days in an area meeting held to discuss everything, 'from manhole covers to Peking'. The words were heavy as living beings, and the winners were those who showed the most tenacity.

The concluding motion deplored the fact that the national dignity of the Hungarian people had been impaired and, at the same time, criticized the 'generic nature of the criticisms' made by the leadership of the PCI on the subject of de-Stalinization. The provincial Congress, held shortly after, and the national one, held in Rome that December, were not so satisfactory.

The Galileo company owned Italy's most advanced factory in the optical field. One of the hands, Valerio Bertini, a true-born Tuscan with a French accent, was a delegate to the 8th Congress of the PCI. He met Feltrinelli in the corridors of the conference centre in Rome's EUR district. A friend stopped to give a warm greeting to the tall, thin, bespectacled young man, dressed entirely in grey, and a touch staid and stiff. The friend later told Bertini that the young man was a Communist from Milan, a fat-cat who had served with him as a soldier in the Volunteer Corps on the Gothic line during the winter of 1944. A bit of a 'fanatic', according to the Roman volunteers, a character who would willingly go out on patrol even on stormy nights, who never shirked, and who washed himself, stripped to the waist, every morning. Shortly after that, Bertini was introduced to Feltrinelli by Giuliano Procacci.

Bertini had just wound up the speech with which he hoped to persuade the Congress to repudiate the aggressive, barely socialist and totally undemocratic policies of the Soviet Union. His wish was that the party would without prevarication take the 'Italian road to socialism'. But his speech, pointlessly aggressive and sarcastic, overly colourful and presumptuous, met with more grumbling than applause. It was then that Feltrinelli went up to him and said: 'You're right. But don't kid yourself: they'll cut your balls off.' And since it was clear that this Bertini had talent, Feltrinelli hired him a short time after, thinking to use him in one of the bookshops. Bertini could also write and Feltrinelli published the novel that the young man had in his drawer.

The historian Giuliano Procacci provides us with another illuminating episode from that same period (a couple of weeks after the second intervention in Hungary): 'One morning I went to the Feltrinelli library, with which I had been collaborating for a bit. When I got there (before opening time), I found the door open. In the reading room was Giangiacomo Feltrinelli, absorbed in the pages of *Das Kapital*. You could see from his face that he had been up all night, "Nothing makes sense here," he said to me, "we're in the shit right up to our necks."'

It was not long before people began to notice Feltrinelli's agitation. 'They tell me that you apparently harbour some doubts about the outcome of the Congress,' wrote Mario Alicata* on 29 December 1956.

> I can understand that, given the complexity of the
> problems that the party has had and still has to tackle;

---

* (1918–66). In charge of the PCI's cultural policy from the end of the war until his death. One of Togliatti's most trusted men.

but it strikes me as superfluous to insist that these reservations can only be overcome by discussing them in depth with other comrades. It seems to me that it is much more important to hold this discussion with you, because of the particular responsibilities that have fallen to you, and given the diversity and importance of the projects that depend on you.

Alicata was in charge of the National Cultural Committee of the PCI. After the events in Hungary, on meeting a comrade, he said: 'I took all my Bartók discs and I broke them, I broke them all.' Making the 'o' sound even more open than his Calabrian accent required. He proposed to Feltrinelli that they meet as soon as possible and emphasized the fact that their meeting would be 'anything but personal', a marvellous periphrasis for 'Comrade Togliatti would also like to meet you' on that occasion. But when they met, on the last day of the year, only Alicata turned up. Togliatti did not show.

The conversation was not very productive. They talked a little about everything, and, in particular, on a project for a new politico-economic magazine to be launched in Milan. The idea was that it should be devoted to analyses of economic structures, on the consequences of their transformation, and on the types of development under way in the various sectors of Italian society. Feltrinelli set out his conditions: a guarantee that there would be no political interference as far as research was concerned, and the presence on the editorial staff of a man who had been under a 'shadow of suspicion' for some time, Antonio Giolitti.* For too long, evidently. And in fact, the project came to nothing.

But in the meantime, in January 1957, Feltrinelli had another row with Lajolo, the editor of *l'Unità*, because the latter had published a polemical reply issued by *Pravda* in response to an article in the Polish periodical *Nowa Kultura*. But Lajolo had neglected to give the Polish point of view.

---

* (1915–). Law graduate, politician, member of parliament with the PCI, editorial consultant and Minister of the Republic.

As a publisher, Feltrinelli had excellent contacts with intellectuals in Yugoslavia, Hungary and Poland. In Poland, the house had profited from the good offices of Eugenio Reale, a former Italian ambassador to Poland, a personal friend of Gomulka's, and a supporter of a 'third way' between a capitalist and a Stalinist regime. Reale had recently been expelled from the PCI for this reason.

But the library was the epicentre of a different way of thinking, even with regard to the political prospects of the day. Del Bo, Cortesi and Della Peruta were joined by Procacci, Enzo Collotti* (for the German section) and Luciano Cafagna.† Cafagna, an expert on economic history, joined the team in January 1957. The six men were thinking in terms of a new classification for the existing collections of material, and promised new research programmes.

The closure of *Movimento operaio* was interpreted as a gesture of intolerance on the part of orthodox Communist historians. Basically, the real problem was that of going beyond the classic boundaries established by the history of the working and agrarian classes. This was why, as Gianni Bosio's magazine was closing, the library, later to become the institute, launched the *Annali*, its most important publication. The idea behind the *Annali* was to set up a dialogue with the *International Review of Social Science*, published in Amsterdam.

Until that time, Italian historiographical research had been limited to studies of the workers' movement in Italy and of the pre-Fascist period. The history of the Third International and the history of the PCI itself was under a taboo, terrain into which it was hazardous to venture. But, as was clear right from the first numbers, this was precisely the ground that the *Annali* series was most interested in exploring.

The series *Il pensiero socialista* (Socialist Thought), produced

* (1929–). Professor of contemporary history at the University of Florence, a member of the Historical Institute of the Resistance.
† (1926–). A historian, formerly professor of contemporary history at the University of Pisa.

by Feltrinelli in collaboration with the library, was on the same wavelength. Among the first publications, Hilferding's *Finance Capital* and Kautsky's *The Agrarian Question*, with an introduction by Procacci, were of particular note.

Between 1956 and 1957, within the Feltrinelli Library they were debating about how Italian big business was changing, about technological development and industrial relations. This 'training ground' had a name: 'The Centre for Study and Research into the Italian Economic Structure'. The round table was made up of Nino Andreatta,* Antonio Giolitti, Silvio Leonardi, Siro Lombardini, Franco Momigliano, Claudio Napoleoni, Paolo Sylos Labini, and Massimo Pinchera. Most of these men were not Communists.

And in fact the party protested, suspected, and hurled anathemas, especially because of the unforeseen presence of certain party members like Bruno Trentin (Research Centre of the CGIL Labour Union).

> Dear Comrade, it has come to our attention that you took part in a meeting called by the Feltrinelli Library in Milan to launch a study centre devoted to the Italian economic structure. [. . .] We were surprised by the fact that you did not deem it correct to discuss with us the line to be followed, and in any event by the fact that you did not feel it your duty to inform us about the meeting itself and of any results that may have emerged from it.

The letter was signed on behalf of the party leadership by Luigi Longo. It was 12 March 1957.

Feltrinelli's reply, dated 4 April, was rather brusque:

> I should be grateful to you if you would clear up the matter because it strikes me as really inconceivable that obstacles be put in the way of a programme of scientific research into such an important sector [. . .]. Moreover,

* Right-wing Christian Democrat and future minister.

to this day comrades have never been required to obtain
official authorization prior to attending the meetings and
encounters organized by the library, as if the library were
a political organization whose work and development did
not fall within the general ambit of our cultural and
political struggle.

'It is clear', declared Luigi Longo* in a letter dated 8 April,
'that you have been ill informed regarding the tone of the
letter.' No rebuke was intended, but the failure to notify the
party regarding the participation of Communist experts in the
meeting gave the impression that there was a wish to maintain
an atmosphere 'if not of secrecy, at least of a confidential
nature'. There was a risk of providing grounds for rumours put
about by 'the adversary' regarding the 'political' purposes of
those meetings: 'On the other hand,' continued Longo, 'it
would have been natural for the Communists invited to take
part to exchange their ideas in advance [. . .], all the more so
since, perhaps owing to an oversight, not all the comrades well
versed in economic issues were invited to the conference by
the directors of the library.'

According to Bruno Trentin,[†] when asked about this forty
years later, the presence of those Communists in the group was
a sign of just how open the conflict now was, especially between
the party and the labour unions.

Beset by a thousand doubts, Feltrinelli kept up his party
membership in 1957, abstaining from public declarations and
letting off steam in private conversations. Disquiet, disagreements and breaches troubled all parts of the Communist
world: directors of the foundation (Fortichiari), representatives of the days of clandestinity (Reale), exponents of the

*(1900–80). One of the founders of the PCI, Longo was with the
International Brigade in Spain. He was secretary general of the PCI from
Togliatti's death (1964) until 1972.
† Leader of the powerful metalworkers' labour union during the 'hot
autumn' of 1969.

generation of the 1940s (Giolitti, Onofri) and of the partisan movement (Raimondi, Seniga). And now also intellectuals like Muscetta and Calvino were giving up their party cards, and more. Their defection, in the summer of 1957, provoked an exchange of letters between Feltrinelli and Giorgio Amendola, the leader of the pragmatic right wing of the party. The correspondence between the two is a perfect reflection of that troubled period.

A good number of people had pinned their hopes on Amendola following his speech during the National Congress of the PCI in April 1956. In commenting on the 20th Congress of the CPSU he had maintained that Italian Communists ought to feel free of external 'mortgages'. But following the events in Hungary, as happens within the logic of power, he had become more Catholic than the Pope, leading the 'anti-revisionist' offensive.

The occasion that brought Feltrinelli out into the open, in a confidential letter, sprang from a statement made by Amendola to the daily paper *Il Giorno*: 'The loss of small fringe groups of intellectuals is not an important phenomenon'; the PCI's recent bad patch had affected only a few, and 'only that fringe least in touch with the masses'.

This is how Feltrinelli replied to him, on 7 August 1957:

I must tell you that it is not my intention to indulge in any unnecessary self-defence, in so far as, without fear of presumption, I neither feel myself to be [a member of any] 'fringe' nor am I lost to the working class and the Party, nor again do I feel I am part of the 'dead wood' as D'Onofrio has defined some comrade intellectuals, whoever they might be. But I do feel that I must express my opinion with regard to the statements quoted earlier.

First of all, it seems to me that the comrade intellectuals that have abandoned – not without a long and painful crisis – the Party or that have, at least temporarily, ceased being active party militants or have left the politico-cultural front cannot be defined as a 'fringe' (of what, indeed? the party? the socialist movement?), and thus be erased and disposed of in dismissive gesture.

We are not dealing, moreover, with a few isolated cases, but with a group of scholars of national stature: philosophers, historians, men of letters, jurists and artists. The fact remains, however, that these comrades have not only brought lustre to the party, the working class and the socialist movement, but have also represented one of the strong points that have enabled us, since the fall of Fascism, to undertake a wealth of politico-cultural projects; one of the strong points that that have enabled the party to integrate more fully with Italian society, thereby paving the way for a range of initiatives that have contributed to the winning of more than one battle in favour of democracy and socialism. (. . .)

These displeasing defections from the party are also serious, because, contrary to your statements, they do not affect only certain 'fringes' (and I shall dwell no longer on the impropriety of this term), but a far broader stratum of the rank and file: workers, housewives, and the simple militants in our cells and sections. (. . .)

That this situation holds within the party is a serious matter, both because it involves comrade intellectuals and the ordinary comrades in the street cells and in the workshops. And the problem is all the more worrying because not only is it still with us, it is worsening. And this is so despite the 8th Congress, which had done much important preparatory work for the renewal and reinforcement of the party, with a view to linking political action more and more closely to the reality and the exigencies of the Italian situation, by concretely articulating a programme of political activity capable of lending substance to the watchwords of the party's most important assembly.

The congress itself – in proclaiming that the party was more and more oriented toward the Italian road to socialism and in greeting with approval the results of the 20th Congress of the CPSU – assumed, implicitly and explicitly, the necessity, albeit without neglecting all the vitality to be found in the experience of international workers' movement, for an original ideological formulation of the problems of socialism.

This result – all things considered a positive one – could and had to lead the party to becoming a lively centre of attraction and debate in which to draft programmes for political action, not only for all comrades, but for the Italian democratic movement as a whole. Can we honestly say we have succeeded in bringing this situation about? I do not think so.

Amendola's reply, lengthy, preoccupied, and touchy, was not long in coming.

The fact that over the last year a certain number of comrade intellectuals have left the party is certainly not an unimportant phenomenon. (. . .) It also pains us on a human level, when it signifies a breach in the old bonds of a friendship born during the struggle against the Fascists. What responsibility must we bear for having been unable to prevent this breach? What must we do?

In my view, there is no doubt that, during the dramatic events of 1956, some comrades, who had joined the party on the wave of the struggle against the fascists and the war of Liberation or in the course of the battles for peace and democracy of the last decade, began to manifest substantial ideological differences that, after having been bottled up for a long time, subsequently exploded into the open. (. . .) This emerged clearly in '56 when the pre-Congress debate hinged above all on the two central problems 1) of the international proletariat; 2) of democratic centralism, problems whose just solution depended on the working class's leadership of the struggle for democracy, problems that therefore developed into the

struggle for socialism. (. . .) Regarding these two problems – proletarian internationalism and democratic
centralism – an ideological conflict emerged, which
prompted several comrades to leave the party. When this
was accompanied by a loyal and sincere explanation, we
considered it as a painful event, but one that it was better
to accept as the expression of divergences that have to be
reckoned with. But we had to react with the tools of
political struggle and with expulsion when those who left
slammed the door behind them and launched defamatory
attacks, twisting the party's position the better to slander
it. In various cases, therefore, we adopted different atti-
tudes, from expulsion to political criticism with
acceptance of resignation, to simple registration of differences. (. . .)

I really did not underestimate the importance of the
withdrawal from the party of a certain number of comrade intellectuals. This is a political problem that must
interest and concern us. The thing to do is to help the
best ones to return to the party fold (and some have
already returned) and to help those comrades who have
still to make up their minds by discussing matters
frankly with them and by not driving them far from the
party. Nevertheless, let me tell you that since I joined the
party in 1929 I have seen many leave! Shortly after I
joined, Silone left, to be followed later by Spinelli, Rossi
Doria, Bonfantini, Valiani, and then, after the war, by
Vittorini, Balbo and many others. They all left declaring
they wanted to fight 'better' for socialism. Where did
they end up? What did they achieve? But we carried on,
because while these people were leaving, on the basis of
the party's political activity others came to us and offered
us their support. Today, too, the essential thing is to
pursue just policies that, faced with the threat to Italian
democracy represented by the DC, may express the
needs of that part of the Italian people that wishes to
continue along the road to democratic renewal and

socialism. If we manage to develop a broadly based plan
of political action, as in other crucial moments, in the
heat of the struggle other groups will join us and
strengthen our party.

I am proud to have been a Communist since 1929.
And more than ever I feel I have chosen the right road.
And this is why it pains me to see comrades falling by the
wayside and leaving us. My hope, therefore, is that you,
after having emphasized the seriousness of the situation,
will make your contribution to containing it. (. . .)

Giangiacomo must have read and reread this letter, nerv-
ously nibbling at his moustache with his teeth, struck by the
generosity of the reply, flattered perhaps, but by no means
relieved. Amendola could have done little more to ameliorate a
reply that, given the context, could only be disappointing.

Between the first putt-putt of the Fiat 500 and the first beep-
beep of *Sputnik*, the political world was rife with intrigue and
discord. But perhaps politics was not the only theatre of existence, perhaps one could live without the party; the 'apparatus'
was not everything.

Matteo Secchia, Pietro's brother, was certainly an 'appa-
ratchik' when he went to confer with the undersecretary of the
Soviet embassy in Rome. It was 12 August 1957. The diplomat
was to note down in a diary, five days later, an account of the
visit: 'Feltrinelli has yet to state that he wishes to leave the
party, but he has already stopped contributing funds.'

The return to political life after that summer was marked by
Mauro Scoccimarro's report to the party Central Commission.
His speech immediately revealed a departure from the previous
official line. The non-Communist press noticed the breach, but
it was talked about more than it was understood. However,
insiders who knew the party machinery could not ignore the
terms of the question. Above all when (and this held for many)
Communist militancy was bound up with concrete prospects of
renewal. Hold it! The 8th Congress had created new elective

controlling bodies and the traditional wheeling and dealing of the party bureaucrats was still going on? And what price the new statute, which made party membership independent of ideological adhesion, when adherence to Marxist–Leninist doctrine was considered decisive in the choice of a leader? Did this not presume that a non-Marxist party member must recognize the superiority of Marxism, even when he or she is not Marxist? So, was it to be a party of the masses, or a party of Marxist cells?

No answers to these questions were forthcoming and the pill became very bitter for Feltrinelli when Scoccimaro defined 'the right of individuals or groups to their own autonomy and freedom of initiative in cultural and ideological activities' as a 'deviation', and not as a democratic requirement. Weighty words. Feltrinelli noted in his journal: 'The old concept forms a homogeneous and tight-fitting block, the new concept has until now been unable to express itself except as a series of disconnected ideas'.

More than ten months had passed since the Congress, he had seen people leave, he had been prudent, he had deluded himself, he had attempted to say his piece: nothing doing, no response! He had entered that 'grey area' reserved for those whose loyalties had become suspect. Perhaps it would have been better to get out of the way, possibly without a sensational row.

In the meantime, the first great best-seller in the history of contemporary publishing was about to be born.

The 'blue period' was beginning.

4

The secrets shared by Boris Leonodovich Pasternak and Giangiacomo Feltrinelli have aged in an old office safe in via Andegari. In this safe, my father also hid the photos of a trip to Denmark and some Garibaldi memorabilia. The key had disappeared, we needed a blacksmith and an oxyacetylene torch to open it. Inside was the Feltrinelli–Pasternak correspondence. After forty years, if a secret changes hands it slips away like quicksilver.

I'd like to start with an article by Giangiacomo Feltrinelli published in the *Sunday Times* of 31 May 1970. At the time Feltrinelli had already disappeared (in the sense that he had gone underground) and no one knew what identity he had adopted. The article, commissioned by the editor Sir Denis Hamilton, ended with the phrase 'I am where no one can find me'.

The cascade of events had so affected Feltrinelli that the original text was in the third person, as if not written by him but 'by sources close to the publishing house'. The draft is dated 15 March. This was the only time he ever spoke of things that had happened long before.

In 1955, immediately after the establishment of my company, Giangiacomo Feltrinelli Editore, I was contacted
by Sergio D'Angelo, who at that time was running the
PCI bookshop in Rome and was about to leave for
Moscow as a member of the party editorial staff working
on an Italo-Soviet radio programme. He suggested that
he act as the USSR literary talent scout for my Milan-
based publishing house. A few months later, D'Angelo
told me that an amazing novel written by a Russian poet,
Boris Pasternak, was about to be published in the Soviet
Union. I asked D'Angelo to get in touch with the author
and to request a copy of the manuscript so that a translation might be made immediately. After first publication
in the Soviet Union, Russian authors enjoy no copyright
protection. By starting the translation right away, I
would have had the chance to publish at the same time as
the Soviet publisher and thus to secure the copyright on
the work in the West. By agreement with the author, the
manuscript was delivered to me in Berlin in the summer
of 1956.

Establishing the rights with regard to works coming out of
the Soviet Union was crucial. If a publisher, let's say from
Europe or America, managed to publish *Doctor Zhivago* in the
thirty days subsequent to its appearance in the USSR, then he
would have secured exclusive rights for the Western market.
According to the Berne convention, his would be the first edition. The Soviets had not signed the Berne Convention. But
one day over the statutory thirty and the work would have
become 'public domain' and anyone could print his own edition, without exclusive rights or any obligation to pay royalties.
The attorney Antonio Tesone, the Feltrinelli company's legal
advisor, made a careful study of the case.

But, apart from the question of rights, the reconstruction in
the *Sunday Times* corresponds to the version of the facts provided by Sergio D'Angelo on various occasions and perhaps it
might be useful to recapitulate the various events that

occurred before the summer of 1956. Most of these are already known.

One year after Stalin's death, in spring 1954, Boris Pasternak's name came to the fore following the publication of some poems in the magazine *Znamya*. They were written as an appendix to a novel he was working on, *Doctor Zhivago*. The novel was finished in 1955. Pasternak sent copies to the Goslitizdat publishing house and to a few literary reviews. Then he waited for their decision.

In the winter of '55, Sergio D'Angelo agreed to become a scout for Feltrinelli in the Soviet capital. He had worked with the house occasionally in the past.

D'Angelo left Italy in March 1956. He was working with Radio Moscow, the gospel according to the Soviets broadcast in all the world's languages. A few weeks after his arrival, during a cultural events programme, he came across news of the probable publication of *Doctor Zhivago* by Boris Pasternak: 'A novel written in the form of a diary covering three quarters of a century and ending with the Second World War.'

D'Angelo was quick off the mark. He sent the information on to Milan and Luigi Diemoz asked him to get in touch with the author right away.

In early May, on a beautiful sunny day, D'Angelo arrived in the Writers' Village at Peredelkino, the wooded area just outside Moscow, where Pasternak often spent time with his second wife Zinaida, his younger son Leonid, and sometimes with Evgeny, the son born of his first marriage with Evgenya Lure. More or less fifteen hundred metres away as the crow flies, on the other side of a small hill, stood the holiday residence of Olga Ivinskaya, the woman with whom Pasternak had been in love for almost ten years and who helped him in his work as a translator.

Pasternak received D'Angelo and listened to him with apparent surprise. He was lost in thought for a long time. He was not at all convinced that his book would be published in the Soviet Union: he had spent a year waiting for a reply that never came. In the end he decided to go along with his guest's request. He had already sent the book to be read by a group of Polish writers who had visited him some time previously, and he was also in contact with the Prague publishers Svet Sovetov about a Czech edition.

When D'Angelo came to take his leave, the poet permitted himself a bitter bon mot: 'You, Sir,' he said to D'Angelo, 'are as of now invited to my execution . . .'

On 13 May, Feltrinelli drafted a first letter to the author and, I am sure, he understood right away that this would be a thorny affair. For this reason, he preferred to handle it personally and, when D'Angelo went to Berlin to have a visa renewed, he went to meet him. It was the end of May or the beginning of June. The two men dined in a restaurant. There, they met two blondes who worked for the Siemens company, and they danced with them. But they never took their eyes off the big package left on the table wrapped in a raincoat. It contained a typescript in Cyrillic.

As soon as he returned to Milan, Feltrinelli sent a telegram to the Slavic linguist Pietro Zveteremich ('please come right away') to ask him for an opinion, which he received within a few days. Zveteremich wound up his reader's report with these words: 'Not to publish a novel like this would constitute a crime against culture'.

On 13 June, Feltrinelli sent off his first letter to his future author, in French. In the beginning, at least, they always used French. 'If ever you receive a letter in any language other than French, you absolutely must not do what is requested of you – the only valid letters shall be those written in French.' How Pasternak's message arrived, written on a cigarette paper, I do not know.

The correspondence between publisher and author was made difficult by the length of time it took for letters to arrive. Every exchange required a suitable intermediary to whom the envelope might be entrusted for mailing or personal delivery.

Feltrinelli later introduced the banknote method: the messenger was 'safe' if he could show Pasternak the missing half of the banknote in his possession.

Milan, 13 June 1956

Dear Sir,

We are very grateful to you for letting us have your
novel, entitled *Doctor Zhivago*.

Even a cursory reading confirms the enormous literary
importance of your work, which presents us with a vivid
portrait of Soviet reality.

Once more, we should like to express our gratitude for
your allowing our publishing house to publish the story
of *Doctor Zhivago* in Europe for the first time, and also
for entrusting us with organizing its publication in other
countries, through the assignment of rights to other publishers.

We therefore submit to you our proposals for settling
the question of authorial rights, both for the Italian edition and editions in other languages.

With regard to the Italian edition, we feel we can offer
you the highest royalty rate customary in Italy, namely
15 per cent. Given the high sales price, the rather high
publishing costs in our country, and finally the translation costs, which will have a considerable effect on the
cost of production, we would not be able to increase this
percentage. As for the foreign rights, we propose, as is
customary, to pay you 50 per cent of the rights received
by us. The money due to you shall be paid into an
account to be opened here, which will be of use to you
for travel or other expenses in Europe, or alternatively
into an account with the State Bank of the USSR.

These are the most important points of the contract,
two copies of which are enclosed with this present letter;
please be so kind as to send us one signed copy should
you be in agreement.

Yours sincerely,

Giangiacomo Feltrinelli

A cordial letter, standard and efficient. Everything ought to
have gone smoothly. On 30 June, Pasternak replied, again in

French. Before he sent the letter off, he showed it to his sons
Leonid and Evgeny.

Today, Evgeny has a face like a woodcarving, exactly like his
father. I owe most of this reconstruction to him. He was thirty-
three at the time: 'We fully agreed with that letter even though
we knew it might have led to dangerous consequences. Our
father was prepared to make any sacrifice as long as *Doctor
Zhivago* was published. We fully supported his wish, we were
also ready to do anything. My father thanked us and said that
he had been hoping for our understanding.'

Evgeny recalls that his father recopied his reply, something
he usually never did:

Moscow, 30 June 1956

Dear Sir,
Your proposals are admirable, and I shall sign the contract
with pleasure. Although I am not entirely uninterested in
money, here we live in conditions that are completely different from those in your country. It is no merit of mine if
questions of money are non-existent or entirely secondary
for me. In any event, keep all that is due to me under your
protection, I entrust it to you unreservedly, and don't let's
talk any more of this until I come to you or bring up this
matter myself. I am particularly glad that the novel will
come out and be read in your country. If its publication
here, promised by several of our magazines, were to be
delayed and your version were to come before it, I would
find myself in a tragically embarrassing situation. But this
is not your concern. In the name of God, feel free to go on
with the translation and the printing of the book, and good
luck! Ideas are not born to be hidden or smothered at
birth, but to be communicated to others.

Make sure the work is well translated. In this regard,
Professor Lo Gatto has much praised and recommended
the poet and translator Ripellino, in Rome.
Yours sincerely,

B. Pasternak

P.S. Please be so kind as to send me a telegram acknowledging receipt of this letter.

A fine letter, showing a sincere lack of interest in economic issues. 'In fact,' says his son Evgeny, 'my father got by with the bare essentials. His study was modest in size, he dressed very simply, and he avoided futile amusements, travel, holidays and all that derives from the pleasure of spending money.'

But the alarming thing about this first reply to the Italian publisher is that the Soviets knew about it right from the start: maybe not everything, but definitely something. Recently, in Moscow, an important document came to light. It is stamped 'top secret', the date is 24 August 1956. The sender was general Ivan Serov, chairman of the National Defence Committee of the Soviet of Ministers of the USSR (commonly known as the KGB). The recipient was the Central Committee.*

The National Defence Committee of the Soviet of Ministers of the USSR is in possession of a series of facts from which it emerges that in the May of this year the writer B. Pasternak, through Sergio D'Angelo, a speaker with the radio of the Ministry of Culture of the USSR, an Italian citizen and a member of the Italian Communist Party, delivered to the Italian publisher Feltrinelli a manuscript of his unpublished novel, *Doctor Zhivago*, for publication in Italy.

In the letter of 3 July of this year addressed to Feltrinelli, Pasternak officially agrees to the publication of the novel and asks that the honorarium due to him be left in Italy. On handing over the novel, Pasternak set the following conditions: that the publisher, subsequent to publication of the work in Italy, assign the rights to the novel to French and English publishers.

Pasternak asks Feltrinelli to make sure that the novel does not come out in Italy before it is published in the

* KGB Archives

USSR. Feltrinelli replies that the novel will be published around April 1957.

It is known that in the April of this year Pasternak delivered *Doctor Zhivago* to the editors of the magazine *Novy Mir*. The work was reviewed, but permission for publication has not yet been given. On 9 August of this year, Pasternak sent a letter to a certain Danil Georgevich Reznikov, resident in Paris, in which he expresses his doubts regarding the possibility of *Doctor Zhivago*'s being published in the USSR: 'I realize perfectly well that [the novel] cannot be published now, and that this is how it is going to be for some time, perhaps for ever: so grand and so unusual is the freedom of spirit with which existence is represented in the work, existence in its totality, existence in the world; so free and new is its conception of the world.'

In referring to the delivery of the book to a foreign publisher, Pasternak wrote to Reznikov: 'Now they will tear me limb from limb: I have this foreboding, and you shall be a distant and sorrowful witness to this event.' At the same time Pasternak sent Reznikov a manuscript of 'People and Situations', which he had written as an introductory essay to the collection of poems published by Gozlitizdat. He also asked Reznikov to do as he wished with the essay, as if it were his property.

The essay is constituted of a detailed autobiography of Pasternak, accompanied by an assessment of the work by some Soviet poets, in particular by Mayakovsky, Cvetaeva and Yashvili. In the essay Pasternak also expresses his opinion on the possible causes of their suicide and of that of the writer Fadeev.

Boris Leonidovich Pasternak, born in 1890, is a Jew, has no party card, and is a member of the Union of Soviet Writers.

During the revolution and in the years that followed, he joined the petty bourgeois literary school known as the acmeists. A typical feature of his work is

estrangement from Soviet life and a celebration of indi-
vidualism. For a long time Pasternak did not publish
almost any of his works, with the exception of a brief
cycle of poems.

Between 1946 and 1948 he wrote the first part of the
novel *Doctor Zhivago*, which reflects his idealistic view of
the world. The magazine *Novy Mir*, to which he sent the
manuscript, refused to publish the novel because it was
ideologically unacceptable. Subsequently the manuscript
of the novel was passed from hand to hand in literary circles.

In those same years Pasternak established contacts
with a series of collaborators in the British embassy in
Moscow, through whom he kept up a correspondence
with his sister, who lives in London.

In conversations with some of the representatives of
the embassy he made anti-Soviet statements.

It was thanks above all to these contacts that, between
1946 and 1948, Pasternak made a great deal of propaganda in the English and American press, creating for
himself an aura of the 'great poet-martyr' unable to
adapt to the reality of Soviet life.

The KGB report both clarifies and complicates matters. In
the correspondence found in the safe together with the
Garibaldi memorabilia, there is no trace of the letter of 3 July.
There is the letter of 30 June, whose contents are similar to the
one that, according to Serov, was dated three days later.

This leaves two possibilities, or on second thoughts, more
than two: the first hypothesis is that, in some remote archive,
the letter of 3 July really does exist. But why two letters in the
space of three days with the same content? Besides, unlike
Pasternak's message to Danil Resnikov, nothing in Serov's 'top
secret' message regarding the alleged letter of 3 July is in
inverted commas.

The reasonable suspicion arises that there exists no correspondence for that day. Perhaps they were referring to the letter

of 30 June, perhaps they got confused, perhaps 3 July was the date on which the police intercepted the missive of three days before. But why should the Soviets have then allowed the letter to reach Milan? In the envelope, probably, there was also a contract: 'I sign without reservations,' wrote Pasternak on 30 June. And if it is true that the documentation was intercepted, why not use it to frame the poet in public? There was no shortage of either pretexts or trials.

This brings us to hypothesis number three: the Soviet police intercepted nothing at all. Perhaps someone talked about a letter sent on 30 June or 3 July, and disclosed some relatively pertinent information: for example, the publisher's request to assign the rights in England and France, or Pasternak's plea requiring Feltrinelli to ensure that the Italian edition did not come out before the Soviet one (while the letter of 30 June says the exact opposite), or the fact that plans had been made to publish the Italian edition in April 1957. Who was present 'when the novel was handed over'? Who could have known about the correspondence between Pasternak and his Italian publisher?

The poet's family, perhaps prompted by jealousy, have always encouraged the suspicion that Olga Ivinskaya had supplied information to the secret service. Even the contemporary press in Moscow today takes it for granted that Olga was an informer. But this equation is not only vulgar and ungrateful, it also risks sending us off the track. An informer? Everybody was an informer in the most rumour-ridden society imaginable. If Olga passed on information, then she did so in a well-meaning, 'positive' way, in other words by omitting inconvenient details and presenting the most reassuring versions in order to make future mediation possible. In a letter to Khruschev, dated 1 March 1961, Ms Ivinskaya admitted: 'The Central Committee suggested that I keep Pasternak away from possible contacts with foreigners.' And in another part of the same letter: 'It was futile to point out that it was the Central Committee that had previously suggested the name of D'Angelo and that through D'Angelo I managed to keep the publication of the novel in Italy on hold for a year and a half.'

Olga Ivinskaya had already served a three-year spell of internment (she came out in 1953). She was not the only person directly involved in the affair, and the solution of our mystery might bring us to other leads, unverifiable at present. Perhaps some sprightly old domestic had been bustling in and out of the room just as D'Angelo and Pasternak were discussing the deal, or perhaps D'Angelo himself had played the role of 'mediator'. In any case, in August 1956 the news was circulating freely within the machinery of the Soviet apparatus, this can be said with certainty. The day after Serov's note was sent, 25 August, the KGB once more informed the leadership of the CPSU of the effective delivery of the manuscript and, in a separate communication, they also informed our old acquaintance Pyotr Pospelov, who had by then become the secretary to the Central Committee.

On 31 August, the Foreign Minister Dimitri Shepilov defined Pasternak's novel as 'a ferocious libel against the USSR' and gave notice that 'the Department for Relations with Foreign Communist Parties, through some friends, is taking steps to prevent the publication abroad of this anti-Soviet book' (cf. *Le dossier de l'affaire Pasternak*, Gallimard). This means that the matter was probably discussed around some samovar with the Italian Communists, in Russia on vacation or on other business (we are between the publication of the Khruschev report and the Hungarian uprising).

The tone adopted by the Soviets was both concerned and agitated, even though, I suppose, at the time they still thought that everything could be sorted out. Perhaps with the help of their Italian comrades.

Giangiacomo's article for the *Sunday Times* adds this:

While the Italian translation was proceeding, publication in Moscow was postponed and the rumour began to circulate that I had received a copy of *Doctor Zhivago*. The PCI (of which I was a member at the time) received a request to check out that rumour. I confirmed the matter with Togliatti, the secretary general of the party. At that

time I received no request to suspend publication of the
book in Italy, I was only asked to ensure that publication
in the West was concomitant with publication in Moscow.

The autumn was highly eventful.

While the Soviets were making up their minds, Feltrinelli
was invited to return the original of *Doctor Zhivago* temporarily. The request was made by Pietro Secchia and Paolo Robotti,
on their return from a trip to Moscow. The Soviets had asked
the two Italian leaders to take all steps necessary to clear up the
'affair'. Secchia had talked of his good relations with the publisher, reassuring them: they would give it a try.

On 24 October the Department for Relations with Foreign
Communist Parties received, via the embassy, a euphoric message from Robotti: the problem was solved! Within a short time
the manuscript would be back in Moscow. The communication
was endorsed by Leonid Brezhnev (cf. *Le dossier de l'affaire
Pasternak*).

But the truth was quite different: Feltrinelli, alarmed about
the pressure upon him, had decided to keep the manuscript
(until then in the possession of Zveteremich in Rome) in his
own home.

January 1957 brought a series of sensations.

The umpteenth delegation from the PCI, this time led by the
deputy leader Luigi Longo, made a visit to Moscow. Despite a
fairly heavy agenda, Suslov and Ponomariev brought up the
Zhivago affair, showing the Italians letters from local writers
expressing their indignation with Pasternak for his ideologically
incorrect attitude.

The Soviets were disappointed. After months of secret talks,
reassurances, and inter-party negotiations, they found themselves empty-handed. Yet again, they asked the help of the
leaders of the PCI, who looked at one another and spread out
their arms in that eloquent Italian gesture that says 'We're
sorry, but what can we do about it?' Irritated, the men in
Moscow decided to change their tactics and take the bull by the
horns, breaking their menacing silence over Pasternak.

But, as can happen in a chess game, this change of tactics led to a wrong move, one that triggered an inexorable march toward checkmate. Pasternak was summoned by Alexey Surkov, the secretary of the Union of Soviet Writers, who offered him a formal contract drawn up by Goslitizdat, the state publishing house. But he was given to understand that it would be necessary to make a few cuts or maybe even write a completely revised version. Then he was forced to send a telegram to his Italian publisher. The aim was to play for time.

further to the request from the goslitizdat publishing house novaya basmannaya 18 moscow please to hold Italian publication of the novel *Doctor Zhivago* for a half year until first september 1957 and the coming out of the soviet edition of the novel send reply telegram to goslitizdat

pasternak

The telegram reached Milan on 14 February 1957. It was in Italian, more or less. But as soon as Pasternak left Surkov's office, he wrote to my father, in French this time. The date was 6 February.

Dear Sir,
Our state publishers are putting pressure on me to send you a telegram requiring you to suspend the Italian publication of my novel until they bring out their modified version of it. I would propose that you postpone publication for, say, six months at the outside. Grant this deferment, if this does not clash with your plans, and send your reply by telegram not to me but to the address of the State Publishers: Goslitizdat, Novaya Basmannaya 18, Moscow.

But the sorrow that, naturally, is caused me by the imminent alteration of my text would be far greater if I thought that you intended to base the Italian translation upon it, despite my enduring desire that your edition be strictly faithful to the authentic manuscript.

Another question: I was the one who saddled you with the burden of the matters covered by art. 4 of the contract while inviting you to deal with the business of the other foreign translations. I have recently made some great new friends in France, who are prepared to work together with me and who are connected to the best publishers, Gallimard and Fasquelle, for example. I am prepared to offer you any supplementary concessions you may desire with regard to article 2, if you would hand over the matter of the French edition to the group of French translators about whom you will receive a letter from Madame Jacqueline de Proyart, my representative in Paris for literary matters and the leading member of the group. Otherwise, if you do not wish to give up the management of the novel in France, at least give consideration to Mme de Proyart, Mlle Hélène Peltier and Monsieurs Michel Aucoutourier and Martinez as translators, of whose services you must avail yourself in accordance with the meaning and purview of art. 4. Please do come to an agreement with them, really, I pray you, it is my burning wish. And pardon me for importuning you so much. Yours

B. Pasternak

Jacqueline de Proyart, a student living in Paris, of noble origins and a fervent Catholic, arrived in Moscow in early 1957. She knew little or nothing about Pasternak, not even if he was alive or dead. She chanced to meet him. He was a most fascinating man and she offered to help him with the translation of his works into French. She was on friendly terms with Gallimard, and she would do something for the novel, in France at least. And whoever might this unknown Italian publisher be?

On receiving Pasternak's letter, Feltrinelli immediately informed Zveteremich:

I am writing only to tell you that it will be necessary to finish Past. within 3 months. The Russian version is coming out in September and in order for our contract to be valid, and by that I mean that if we are to be able to sell the rights, the book has to be on sale by 2 September. I am prepared to make some sacrifices, a compromise, provided I can go to print by that date. Assure me of this and make me any proposals you may have. I talked to Moravia about a review but he didn't seem enthusiastic. I'll bring the matter up with Bassani.* In the meantime, make haste.

Then he waited until a reliable courier was available before sending a letter to Moscow on 22 March:

Dear Sir,
Some weeks ago I received the news that your novel 'The Story of Doctor Zhivago' will be published in Moscow next September. Allow me to tell you how pleased I am about this. The Italian translation is proceeding and after the news of the forthcoming publication in Moscow I have insisted that my translator finish the translation as fast as possible. Yours sincerely

Giangiacomo Feltrinelli

Despite all the assurances, the days passed too slowly for Pasternak; his health and morale were suffering, while the time gained by the Soviet authorities was very little. Moreover, there was enormous tension in the top echelons of the CPSU. This became very clear during the summer, with the expulsion of the so-called 'anti-party group' (Molotov and company) and the clampdowns ordered by Khruschev.

In this atmosphere, the Soviets received the letter from Feltrinelli informing the state publishers of his intentions. It

---

* Giorgio Bassani (1916–2000), journalist, novelist, lyric poet, publishing manager, vice president of RAI TV.

was dated 10 June, a good three months after Pasternak's
telegram:

Dear Comrades,
With this letter we wish to confirm that we shall not proceed with the publication of Pasternak's novel 'The
Story of Doctor Zhivago' until it comes out in the USSR
in the month of September. Now that we are finally free
to express an opinion on the manuscript, we can confirm
that this is a novel of remarkable literary value, whose
author is comparable with the great Russian writers of
the nineteenth century. In our opinion, Pasternak's prose
recalls that of Pushkin. His is a perfect portrayal of the
nature, soul and history of Russia: characters, things and
events are rendered clearly and concretely in the finest
spirit of realism, a realism that ceases to be merely fashion and becomes art.

The reflections of the protagonist and of the various
characters in the novel on their personal destiny and on
that of their country are on a level so high as to tran-
scend the boundaries of current political contingencies,
whether the reader agrees with their political judgments
or not. This is an aspect of the work that might give rise
to some controversy. However, it seems to me that the
importance attached to these reflections in the work is
irrelevant and moreover, after the 20th Congress, the
divulgation of certain facts no longer surprises or per-
turbs us.

Moreover, Western readers will for the first time come
into contact with the voice of a great artist, a great poet
who has made, in an artistic form, a detailed analysis of
the course of the October Revolution, the harbinger of a
new epoch in which socialism became the only natural
form of social life. For the western public, the fact that
this voice is that of a man foreign to all political activity
is a guarantee of the sincerity of his discourse, thus
making him worthy of trust. Our readers cannot fail to

appreciate this magnificent panorama of events from the history of the Russian people, which transcends all ideological dogmatism, nor will they overlook its importance or the positive outlook deriving from it. The conviction will thus grow that the path taken by your people has been for them a progressive one; that the history of capitalism is coming to an end and that a new era has begun.

We have expressed in complete sincerity our opinion of Pasternak's work and we hold that its debatable aspects are more than compensated for by the arguments in favour of its publication. We have reached this conclusion not only in consideration of our interests as publishers, but also in line with our political convictions, of which you are well aware. Moreover, you are also well aware that, as far as we are concerned, political opinions and the business of publishing are inseparable.

It is important for us to be able to express our point of view, given that there have been some misunderstandings in the past regarding Pasternak's book and above all given that you have suspected that we wished to lend this publication a sensational character, which is absolutely not our intention.

Yours sincerely

Giangiacomo Feltrinelli

Eight days later, Zveteremich sent a telegram to Milan ('Dear Feltrinelli, I have completed the translation of *Doctor Zhivago . . .*') and on the 20th of the same month Pasternak sent a new message:

Dear Sir

I have been ill now for three months, first at home, then in hospital, and now in a sanatorium near Moscow. I thank you again for having granted the postponement requested by the state publishing house (Goslitizdat). But this is really all I have to ask of you. All the rest is superfluous. I would be deeply pained, grievously

disappointed, if the Italian version of the work, in a form
faithful to the Russian manuscript, were not published
by your house on 1 September. Any delay in [the publication of] the Italian edition would hold up the
appearance of the other foreign translations, whose realization I have always subjected to your control (for
example, in France, in England, in Czechoslovakia and
elsewhere). Here in Russia, the novel will never come
out. The troubles and misfortunes that will perhaps
befall me even in the mere event of foreign publication,
that is to say without an analogous publication in the
Soviet Union, are matters that must not concern us,
either me or you. The important thing is that the work
sees the light if nothing else, and do not withhold your
help from me. Yours very sincerely,

B. Pasternak

In July 1957, Molotov and his faction having been ousted
from the Politburo, Khruschev was firmly in the saddle. Lazar
Fleishman, the best biographer of Pasternak, pinpoints the
moment:

That same summer they published a selection of his
[Khruschev's] speeches to assemblies of the intelligentsia. These speeches were to serve as party guidelines.
Since Zhdanov's day, no Soviet leader had expressed his
opinions on literary and artistic matters. It was the first
time that Khruschev had spoken on the subject and the
publication of those speeches left no doubt about the fact
that it was the conservative front rather than the liberal
one that enjoyed his full support in the field of cultural
policy.

Fleishman also recalls that, in the summer, two episodes
occurred that infuriated the Soviet authorities. The first of
these was the publication of some excerpts from *Doctor Zhivago*
in the pages of a Polish quarterly, which was moreover perfectly

in line with official culture. How could this have happened? Evidently there were many copies of *Doctor Zhivago* in circulation and this preview – they thought – might be a pretext for the subsequent appearance of the novel in the West. Especially since a magazine run by Russian *émigrés* in Münich – and this was seen as a second humiliation by the Soviets – had printed some poems attributable to Pasternak without citing him as the author. It was necessary to intervene.

Evgeny Pasternak explains: 'In early August, at the request of Suslov and Pospelov, the Central Committee drew up various statements in an attempt to deal with the problem of the plans to publish the novel in Poland and Italy. At Goslitizdat they wanted to have the text modified, hoping that Feltrinelli would have waited until September for the author's corrections.'

The leadership of the Italian Communist Party was once more informed so that suitable countermeasures might be taken. A substantial delegation from the PCI, including Longo, Alicata and Spano, arrived in Moscow for the World Youth Festival. The young expert in Slavonic studies, Vittorio Strada, was also making a visit, his first, and he managed to meet and get to know Pasternak. Strada still remembers his surprise when, as he was leaving, Pasternak took him to one side to whisper in all serenity: 'Vittorio, pass this on to Feltrinelli: tell him that I want my book to come out at all costs.'

Let's go back to the *Sunday Times* article of May 1970:

In the summer of 1957 I heard rumours of the definitive cancellation of the plans to publish *Doctor Zhivago*. Shortly afterward, the author requested me to proceed with publication in Italy and the West, independently of publication in Moscow, and to ignore other instructions that he might in future be obliged to transmit to me. The agreement between Pasternak and me was that I would shoulder all the responsibility for publication, in order to provide the author with some protection from the Soviet authorities.

August witnessed the beginning of the strategy orchestrated by Dimitri Polikarpov, the head of the cultural section of the CC, and Alexey Surkov, the secretary of the Writers' Union, both as surly and forbidding as their names suggest. Pasternak was summoned peremptorily to humiliating meetings in which harsh words gave way to threats. Instead of Pasternak, who was physically debilitated, the two men often dealt with Olga, who was acting as his representative. A new postponement, this was what was expected of Pasternak; a last attempt to stop everything. Otherwise, without putting too fine a point on it, they would have him arrested.

I have recommenced working on the manuscript of my novel *Doctor Zhivago* and I am now convinced that what I have written can in no way be considered a finished work. I consider the copy of the manuscript in your possession as the first version of a future work that will require radical rewriting.

In my view it is not possible to publish the book in its current form. This would go against my rule by which only the definitive draft of a work may be published.

Please be so kind as to return, to my Moscow address, the manuscript of my novel *Doctor Zhivago*, which is indispensable for my work.

Boris Pasternak

The text of this letter was agreed on with Polikarpov and Surkov on 21 August, transcribed in Russian and sent in the form of a telegram.

Sergio D'Angelo, present yet again, was to describe the events in a long article for a Soviet studies magazine. He recalls how Olga rushed to visit him, tears in her eyes, asking him to help her persuade Pasternak to agree to send the telegram. When the pair went to see the poet, he greeted them with angry words: no motives of friendship or affection could justify their charitable mission; they were disrespectful to him, treating him like a man with no dignity. And furthermore, what would

Feltrinelli have thought, the publisher to whom Pasternak had just written to say that the publication of *Doctor Zhivago* was his principal aim in life? He would have taken Pasternak for a madman, a coward.

Only after an explanatory discussion was Pasternak persuaded that, given what had been arranged, no further message (especially if not written in French) would have been believed. In any case, it was no longer possible to block the publication of the novel. And so, finally, he agreed to send the telegram.

'The fact that he was not arrested', wrote Sergio D'Angelo, 'was thanks to Olga Ivinskaya.'

On his return to Rome, Velio Spano, the 'foreign minister' of the PCI, laid his report before the party leadership. It was 14 September:

> In the course of the meeting of the Central Committee of the CPSU the question of Pasternak and his book was again raised. The Soviet comrades, still concerned over its possible publication by Feltrinelli or some other Western publisher, again asked us to take steps. In this regard they gave me the letter of injunction signed by Pasternak and asked me to ensure that one of us show it to Feltrinelli in order to corroborate the position adopted by Pasternak himself.

Alicata went to Milan with the copy of the text used for the telegram. It had been decided to hold the meeting with Feltrinelli in the rooms of the Milan Federation of the PCI, in piazza XXV Aprile. The art historian Mario De Micheli bumped into the publisher, who was hunkered down on the steps in front of the offices, ten minutes before the meeting: 'I'm not giving in', said Feltrinelli. De Micheli also recalls how violent Alicata became as he furiously brandished the bogus letter of injunction from Pasternak.

When all this was going on, the translator Zveteremich, who had been in contact with Pasternak for some time, was in

Moscow, and he spoke of his time there in a letter to Feltrinelli
dated 5 October:

> In Moscow the atmosphere created around the book is
> very ugly. They are turning it into a big scandal. Its pub-
> lication has been defined as 'a blow against the
> revolution'. Clearly in bad faith. Especially since I have
> had complete confirmation that the book was to come out
> in the USSR. I have seen the contract between P. and the
> Soviet publishers dated 7/1/57, as well as a letter to P.
> from a writer who spoke of a magazine that intended to
> publish excerpts from it. I met the copy editor. It seems
> that in the CC of the CPSU, Pospelov and others
> thought it should be published. Everything changed as a
> result of the pressure applied by the Writers' Union,
> which in this case has been more intransigent than the
> party and forced its hand. [. . .] P. asks you not to pay any
> heed to this and cannot wait for the book to come out
> even though they have threatened to reduce him to star-
> vation and have already deprived him of work previously
> commissioned. P. entreats you not to let it be known that
> you have a contract with him on the basis of which you
> have assigned him a certain sum. An agreement is fine,
> but nothing concrete regarding payment. This would
> aggravate his situation in a way that is hard to foresee.
> His safety depends on people believing that he will
> receive nothing. [. . .] D'Angelo is not afraid of any con-
> sequences of the scandal caused by the publication of P.,
> excepting perhaps that he might be invited to leave the
> USSR, something that does not bother him. So he
> thanks you for worrying and tells me to reassure you.

In the course of a visit, Pasternak gave Zveteremich a brief
message for his publisher.

Dear Sir,
I should like to send you my heartfelt thanks for your

touching concern. Forgive me for the injustices that have befallen you and for those perhaps yet to come caused by my wretched fate. May our distant future, the faith that helps me to live, protect you.

Boris Pasternak

Between the end of September and the beginning of October, Alexey Surkov, the president of the Union of Soviet Writers, descended on Milan. Where the false letters, the indirect messages and the pressure had all failed, now he had come to do the job himself, in a tête-à-tête with Feltrinelli. They were closeted in the publisher's office for three hours, and their angry shouts could be heard throughout the whole floor. Surkov ('a hyena dipped in syrup', according to Feltrinelli) could not have failed to note the faded photo of Pasternak hanging on the wall at his host's back. Seeing how things were turning out, Surkov too played the card of the extorted telegram. The reply: 'I am well aware of how documents of the kind are obtained.' Yet again, it was no deal.

Taking his time, for by then it was only a formality, Feltrinelli replied on 10 October to the telegram Pasternak had sent at the end of August.

Dear Sir,

I have received your letter and your telegram with the following text [. . .]. I should like to express my amazement and make the following points:

1) In the text in our possession we see none of the shortcomings you criticize in the manuscript, namely that it is an 'unfinished work', and 'a preliminary draft requiring thorough revision'.

2) We have an agreement with you according to which you granted us the right to publish your book. This agreement was made after you signed a contract with the Goslitizdat house for publication in the Russian language. This contract does not contain any clause that makes publication of the book

abroad dependent on publication in the Soviet Union.

3) Further to the telegram that you sent at the beginning of this year in which you asked us to wait a little, until such time as the book was published in the Soviet Union, we willingly agreed to postpone foreign publication. But today, seeing that the Soviet publisher has no intention of publishing your work, we no longer see any reason for postponement.

4) In order to avoid any further tension in Western literary circles, created as a result of your wholly regrettable telegram, and following the various talks held in Moscow between foreign delegates and some representatives of Soviet political and literary circles, we advise you to make no further attempts to hold up the appearance of the book, something that, far from preventing publication, would lend the entire affair a tone of political scandal that we have never sought nor wish to create. In any event, in consequence of your initiatives and those of the Writers' Union (in Italy and in England), we shall decline all responsibility with regard to the repercussions that the appearance of the work will certainly have as a result of the lack of tact shown by some of your functionaries.

Yours sincerely,

Giangiacomo Feltrinelli

We do not know when Pasternak received this letter, but it is certain that it reached him very late. The absence of a prompt reply is a positive sign: *les jeux sont faits*, and ideally it was the time to drink a toast. But the atmosphere was ruined by the need to carry on making pseudo-statements in order to intimidate the Italian publisher and his French and English colleagues. The text was more or less the same for everyone. This is what Pasternak was forced to write to Feltrinelli (on 23 October):

Mr Feltrinelli,
I am stunned by the fact that I have still to receive your
reply to my telegram. I asked for the manuscript to be
returned to me as soon as possible because I had come to
the conclusion that the work still needed polishing and
that it was still unfinished. I feel that any publisher with
a respect for literature and his own reputation cannot
refuse the request of an author who considers his manuscript provisional and for this reason asks for it to be
returned.

Your failure to reply leads me to think that you, in
spurning the direct instructions of the author and in
spite of his clear and express wishes, have none the less
decided to publish the novel. I do not know if the laws of
your country give you such a right. And in this case we
are not dealing with a formal right either, because both
my telegram of 13 February 1957 and the subsequent
letter expressed beyond any doubt my wish not to publish the novel in a version that is still provisional.

Decency demands that the author's wishes be
respected.

Neither I nor any other writer from my country could
allow his manuscript to be published against his will.
This would be a clear-cut and crass infringement of the
rights an artist has over his work, a violation of his will
and of the freedom of that which flows from his pen.

The request that the manuscript of the novel be
returned also holds for those French and English publishers to whom you have given a copy.

Boris Pasternak

But the letter sent to Feltrinelli a few days later, on 2
November, was of a quite different tenor. It has never before
been published, and this is what it said:

Dear Sir,
I can find no words with which to express my gratitude.

The future will reward us, you and me, for the vile humiliations we have suffered. Oh, how happy I am that neither you, nor Gallimard, nor Collins have been fooled by those idiotic and brutal appeals accompanied by my signature (!), a signature all but false and counterfeit, in so far as it was extorted from me by a blend of fraud and violence. The unheard-of arrogance to wax indignant over the 'violence' employed by you with regard to my 'literary freedom', when exactly the same violence was being used against me, without this being mentioned. And all this vandalism, disguised as concern for me, for the sacred rights of the artist! But we shall soon have an Italian Zhivago, French, English, and German Zhivagos – and one day perhaps a geographically distant but Russian Zhivago! And this is a great deal, a very great deal, so let's do our best and what will be will be!

Do not worry about the money owed to me. Let us put off the financial issue (for me, there is none) until we have a more sensible and humane system, when, in the twentieth century, one can once more keep up a correspondence, travel. I have unlimited faith in you and I am sure that you will watch over what you have put aside for me. Only in the unhappy event of their cancelling my benefits and cutting off my food supplies (which would be extraordinary and there is no sign of it happening), well, I would try to find a way to let you know in order to take advantage of the offers you have made me through Sergio, who, as his name suggests, is a real angel and lavishes all his time and his soul on this regrettable affair.

Yours very sincerely,

B. Pasternak

It is the kind of letter that every publisher would like to receive at least once in his lifetime.

The message also contains an important reference to the rights payments regarding *Doctor Zhivago*. Judging by the receipts kept in the famous safe in via Andegari, periodic payments in roubles began in December 1957. The receipts, written and signed by Pasternak or Olga Ivinskaya, refer to 12,800 roubles delivered on 21 December 1957, 4,000 on 7 June 1958 and another 1,000 that same month, 10,000 in October, 5,000 on 17 February 1959, 3,000 on 28 March, and 5,000 on 1 August. All this serves merely to give an idea; these were not the real sums.

At first, the middle man who made the deliveries was Sergio D'Angelo; then, as we shall see, other channels were used.

To return to the fall of 1957, on 25 November Pasternak again wrote to Feltrinelli:

Dear Sir,

Yesterday I finally received your esteemed reply, dated 10 October, which had therefore been wandering about goodness knows where for a month and a half. As I am unable to go into the details, I hasten to thank you with all my heart for the fact that all has ended well, thanks to your shrewd foresight, which has informed all the ramifications of this extraordinary affair. I am enormously obliged to you.

I am not wont to indulge in the immodest tomfoolery of identifying myself with the voice of truth in person; but I am bold enough to hope to share the tension and the aspirations of all those who love their native land, life, the truth and beauty with a diligent and grateful love. Now, just as you have done a very, very good thing for me, over and above all measure, so you have striven a great deal for the beautiful, just cause.

I was greatly pained by the fact that I had made a certain name for myself thanks to trifling things like a few verses, disparate like contemporary poetry in general (and my own), fragmentary, incomplete and limited to vague expressions, in such great times, which demand that one live in a resolute and responsible way, expressing one's thoughts without reserve. Thanks to a lengthy prose work, which cost long and arduous toil, it has been possible to put an end to this state of shame and suffering, and to begin a new chapter of my vocation, a new period of my life; it has come, infinitely late, but it has come. You be the judge, therefore, of how grateful I am to you for having helped it into the world!

I have an important question for you. None of this could have come about without the assistance of S. D'A., who has been our indefatigable guardian angel. While such sincere help cannot be measured in money, do me a big favour, when he returns to you, repay him for all the countless occasions in which he has lavished his time and energies [on my behalf], in the following manner. Take a considerable amount from the sum that you are holding for me for the future and give it to S. D'A. You and he must agree upon a suitable sum, and then double it. May we meet again in a distant future, dear friend and artificer of my new kind fate (in spite of its fearful consequences)! Yours,

B. Pasternak

D'Angelo, to whom Pasternak read and handed over this letter, put a large 'no' in the margin of the part concerning him, drawing a pencil line through the text. After Pasternak's death, he was to say that he had never refused that most generous compensation (which was never formally requisitioned): all he had done was to 'reserve [the right] to accept'. Years afterward, he was to claim a good half of the author's royalties.

It is clear that, in the letter, Pasternak uses the expression 'double it' in reference to a remuneration for D'Angelo. But a remuneration redoubled is not at all the same thing as a half-share of all the profits.

In 1965, five years after the death of Pasternak, D'Angelo sued the Italian publisher. The courts threw out the suit.

November 23rd 1957: *Doctor Zhivago* is the book of the hour.

The first figures from the bookshops in the centre of Milan were comforting: the first print run (12,000 copies) was selling like hot cakes. The publisher presented the book with a jacket design by Albe Steiner (much appreciated by the author, simple, elegant: '*très bon goût . . . très noble*'). The text of the novel was introduced by a 'Publisher's note' that summed up the 'official' version of the publication. Pasternak had suggested this to Zveteremich in the course of their meeting: there was no reference to contracts or correspondence between the author and the publisher.

> Regarding the preparation of the Italian edition, there was an exchange of letters between the publisher and the Soviet publishing house regarding the worth of the book and its publication date. On that occasion, an agreement was reached to the effect that the Italian edition would not be published before the month of September 1957. At the end of the summer, when the publication of *Doctor Zhivago* was imminent and there was nothing to suggest that in the USSR any difficulties had arisen over publication, we received a request from the author that we return the manuscript to him as he was anxious to review it. We were unable to grant the author's wish inasmuch as the book was already at an advanced stage of preparation and was also ready for publication in other countries, and on the other hand the modifications that the author apparently intended to make to it did not arrive in time [. . .]

In the winter of 1957, *Doctor Zhivago* was in translation with the most important publishing houses: S. Fischer, Collins, Pantheon and Gallimard. In Italy, it was reprinted every two weeks.

In the only interview given in those weeks, Feltrinelli declared that the publication of the book amounted to an 'explicit protest', it was a phase in that 'battle for tolerance' that Togliatti – years before, in his excellent preface to Voltaire – had described as 'still topical and not an easy one to win'. This irreverent quotation from one of the books produced by Colip brought the first chapter of the 'novel within the novel' to a close.

'Was that publisher prompted by the greed (not necessarily commercial) to bring off a major publishing coup, or was it that, in his heart and in that of his advisers, there lurked the intention of striking a blow at the motherland of socialism?' Perhaps it was neither of the two, comrade Alicata.

* * *

To sum up. *Doctor Zhivago* was to be published in the Soviet Union and, owing to the fact that the USSR was not a signatory to the Berne Convention on authors' rights, Western houses were free to publish it without contracts and economic rewards. The only way to obtain exclusive world rights, which counts economically and provides protection for the work, was to have the translation ready within the critical thirty days following publication in the USSR.

On the Italian side there was no lack of willingness to wait for the original edition, at least until Pasternak's real letters arrived. But, after publication in Italy, it was no longer permitted to talk of contracts and letters, even in the event of highly personal attacks. And, in fact, letters and contracts made no further appearance: they were 'classified'.

Feltrinelli took complete responsibility for printing the book and he did not do this as the paladin of anti-Sovietism (not even Pasternak would have wanted that) but simply because he was convinced that the work was good. Within the closed ranks of the Soviet leadership it was thought to the last that the book would not be published in Italy (at least not until after publication in Moscow): Feltrinelli, at bottom, was 'one of ours'. This made the diplomatic, political, and cultural defeat of the world's first or second power all the clearer and more wounding. Of course, Khruschev could have taken the trouble to read that long novel, something that much later he was to confess he had not done. It really must be said that he underestimated the power of a book.

There is an emblematic photo of the Soviet defeat. A paparazzo immortalized Anastasy Mikoyan, the vice president of the Council of Ministers, as he was gloomily observing the window of the biggest bookshop in New York. The picture was taken on an official visit in the winter of 1958. *Doctor Zhivago* was the only book on display, many copies piled up in the window.

Had the CIA or an agent acting on their behalf orchestrated the publication of the novel, the impact would have been different: half the world would have cried conspiracy and complaints would have been made about this most ignominious of ignominious speculations. But, this way, everyone was caught by surprise: it was too complicated to prepare a counter-propaganda campaign at the last minute.

By the way, it may be that the CIA did have a hand in matters, perhaps in attempts to pirate the book. I read somewhere that Her Majesty's secret service was also involved. They allegedly photographed the typescript at Malta airport when the plane Feltrinelli was travelling in made a bogus emergency landing. But what James Bond was up to in the window seat of the last row, smoking Turkish cigarettes, is a story still to be told.

The strange thing, at least thinking about this affair with hindsight, is that Feltrinelli didn't become the paladin of anti Sovietism even afterwards, once the book had been published. Yet it would have its advantages for him (maybe even a trip to the top of the Empire State building). The tragic thing about the history of Communism is that being anti-Soviet always means being anti-communist and you really could not be a Communist and go against the October Revolution, the echo of which was still too enormous.

Feltrinelli never spoke or wrote a word in the language typical of a former Communist and, to tell the truth, he was never to be an ex-Communist. His personal stance on *Doctor Zhivago* is well explained in a letter to Bert Andreas, dated 23 December 1957. The German scholar had written to him

shortly before, worried about the sensation over the Pasternak
case. Andreas was in agreement with the reasons for publication, but feared that the repercussions might affect the
activities of the Feltrinelli Institute. This is how my father
replied to him:

> Pasternak. The question is not purely literary but also
> has a political significance. I cannot, nor do I wish to
> avoid this. The political significance certainly was not
> hostile to the Soviet Union *tout-court*, but to certain
> powers that still hold very important positions within it.
> In this sense the whole affair was suggested to me by the
> Soviet Union itself. If Tito and Gomulka have taken an
> autonomous stance, then this has political significance as
> far as the Soviet Union is concerned, but it will not lead
> to these gentlemen returning to the good graces of the
> capitalists.
> Several people understand all this, even in the USSR.
> No harm whatsoever will come to the institute out of
> this. The ladies in M. are not so stupid. When they were
> here, they showed that they had understood the situation
> rather well. Orders from on high can hinder good rela-
> tions, but even if this were to happen, they would be
> restored again in the future. It is inevitable and cannot be
> otherwise. On the other hand, all this cannot but improve
> relations with other Institutes.

The phrase 'the whole affair was suggested to me by the
Soviet Union itself' introduces a new mystery: with whom was
Feltrinelli in contact? Was one of the 'ladies in M.' really lend-
ing her support?

I understand only the dynamic of events. An Italian publisher is in opposition to the plenipotentiaries of a political
system with which he identifies, but considers devoid of innovation. Once the sclerotic Moloch had been defeated, the
USSR would have begun to show vigorous signs of emancipation. Feltrinelli was the plenipotentiary of his own highly

particular republic, represented by himself, his books, his writers, his ideas and his money. He wanted to deal on an even footing with the super-power. It was his policy.

The 'novel within the novel' was to continue for many episodes, with the publisher continuing to defend his copyright and the motives that underlay his editorial decision. After the initial enthusiasm, however, personal interests, opportunism and speculations like those made by Alicata were to make their appearance. Was it or was it not the first great bestseller in contemporary [Italian] publishing?

Doctor Zhivago remained in Feltrinelli's bloodstream like the most ecstatic drug, like one of the deepest human experiences. He had had the proof that his profession could have an influence on great events.

This is what he wrote to Pasternak, in his own hand, at the foot of a letter dated September 1958:

> Thank you for *Zhivago*, for all that you have done for us. In these times, in which human values are forgotten, in which human beings are being reduced to robots, and in which most people are trying to flee from themselves and to solve the problems of their own ego by living in stress and mortifying what remains of human sensitivity, *Zhivago* has provided a lesson that cannot be forgotten. And every time I do not know which path to take, I know that I can go back to *Zhivago* and learn from him life's greatest lesson. *Doctor Zhivago* will always help me to rediscover the simple and profound values of life, even when they strike me as being definitively lost.

'Zhivago', it is clear, had become the keyword for everything that was adventurous, that made life worth living.

* * *

After the publication of the novel, Feltrinelli had to withstand the assault of the PCI, punctual as a Swiss watch.

The party leadership had been unable to absorb the sequence of events around *Zhivago*, and even less so the statements made to the *Corriere d'informazione* about the 'explicit protest', and the 'battle for tolerance'. And what should it say about the cocktail party given in the foyer of the luxurious Hotel Continental, a stone's throw from the publisher's office, where *Espresso*'s literary critic Paolo Milano had launched the book? Some party leaders thought this offensive, a real humiliation. They decided to grasp the nettle.

Alicata was appointed by the leadership to investigate Feltrinelli's activities and to sound out his position. The first to express themselves were Alberganti and Scotti, on behalf of the Milan Federation, who met with my father for this specific purpose. Their report was sent to Alicata on 18 November 1957.

In the PCI of those days, the examination of a particularly thorny problem was carried out at all levels of the organization. Now it was up to Alicata to say his piece. On 28 November, he sent a report to the leadership in which he announced that comrade Rossanda had recently summoned Feltrinelli to the Federation offices in Milan for talks but he had yet to receive her report.

On 8 December, Rossana Rossanda sent her report to Alicata.

Dear Mario, as I have already told comrades Longo, Amendola, and Barca, I have had the conversation with Feltrinelli as arranged. I shall now sum up the positions that emerged, and my own point of view.

1) At first, Feltrinelli refuted my accusation of having 'blown up' a scandal for reasons of publicity. He stated that this had not been his intention; that there would have been no scandal if the book had not been prohibited; that he had restricted himself to giving some interviews to 'condition' the opposition press. On this point, which I demolished completely, he ended up by recognizing that he had

been wrong to give the interviews; and that these had objectively damaged the Party. He told me that he was deeply sorry about the outrage expressed by the comrades.

2) For the future, he admitted he would have to keep a careful watch over publicity for the publishing house and promised that there would be no more scandals. He informed me that he was about to publish a series of books, one or two of which might prove to be delicate, like a collection of works dealing with the labour unions in the USSR, edited by Longo's son, and an old book by Nagy. He told me that he was prepared to discuss his publishing programme with us. On this point, I simply told him that, in my opinion and independently of the position the P. might take in his regard, as long as he remained in the P. it was absolutely necessary to hold frank and ongoing discussions – and not on a personal but strictly political level. He stated that he desired such discussions in order to avoid further problems.

3) As far as concerns his position within the P. and on my telling him that we were all angered by the fact that a member of the P. with a party card in his pocket should launch that sort of campaign; that none of us was prepared to admit that these were the terms of any political struggle; and that if he did not intend to defend his own position correctly, like all of us, I and many comrades like me thought that it would be better if he were to leave – he struck me as sincerely contrite and concerned. He maintained energetically that he was firmly convinced by the line adopted by the 8th Congress, and that he wanted to stay in the Party.

4) In conclusion, the conversation lasted two and a half hours. He was very worried, confused and, if my judgment is not completely wrong, at a certain

point even distraught. He begged me to assist and help him, not as a person, but as the Party; even though, at first, he clung to some confused positions of principle regarding freedom of debate, etcetera. He betrayed the same agitation toward those of us who had gone to the cocktail party: a decision taken by me in order to defuse all further talk of scandal. In fact, our presence was noted, many people came to talk with us, and we spoke our minds plainly to them, making light of the whole affair. Feltr. surrounded us, thanked us, and apologized to us. At that point the affair petered out; barely reviewed by the papers, the book has already vanished from the window displays. The general impression was that the P. had behaved in a balanced fashion and, by attaching scant importance to the matter, it had given proof of its strength. So much for the story. My opinion is that Feltrinelli is governed by a blend of vanity and confusion, and not by any real bad faith. While his 'direction', or at least 'conditioning', is a possibility, there is no concealing the fact that this would be difficult, both owing to his weak character and to the atmosphere that surrounds him – even though all of his people have received the clear impression that they have overstepped the mark, and have been gripped by a certain fright and the desire to shift responsibility on to others. On the other hand, while 'conditioning' would be difficult, it would none the less always be preferable to letting the publishing house and the institutes drift, beyond all possible action or control on our part. I hold that a disciplinary measure such as expulsion would not estrange all comrades and sympathies from these bodies: by creating a certain atmosphere of persecution, it might increase the confusion. The problem remains, in any event, of giving F. official notice, as

I have done personally and perhaps others too, that he has overstepped the mark. I am still of the opinion that this could be organized in accordance with the usual practice, in Milan, even within his own cell: but I am alone in thinking this; a tough reprimand from the cell, in my opinion, would be more instructive, for him and for everybody. Comrades Longo, Amendola, and also Alberganti and Scotti feel instead that the matter should be dealt with in Rome.

Rossana Rossanda

At this point we ought to fade to black (we already have all we need to understand): Rossanda was – and still is – an important figure on the Italian left and times were different then. Subsequently, she was to take a different political path, but every time I meet her I cannot help thinking of that party at the Hotel Continental. I see her standing there in silence, with her cane hidden up the sleeve of the overcoat that she did not take off.

The dossier on Feltrinelli having been well and truly opened, it was decided to fix a meeting with him in Rome: 'The party leadership feels that it is necessary for comrades Longo, Ingrao, and Alicata to hold a meeting with you to clear up a few matters.'

On 17 December, at four in the afternoon, Feltrinelli strode into Botteghe Oscure* and, for three hours, he remained on the second floor talking with Longo, Alicata, and Bonazzi. Ingrao was not there or did not come. Longo started the ball rolling, with a series of sweeping criticisms. 'A tough start', Feltrinelli was to note later. Alicata then took over, saying that the first rift in the relationship dated from June 1956. Feltrinelli corrected him, reminding him that it was in fact precisely in that period

---

* From the name of a street in Rome, where the PCI had its party headquarters. It is worth noting that Botteghe Oscure also lent its name to one of the world's most prestigious literary revues, founded by Princess Caetani and directed by Bassani. The magazine was the first to feature *The Leopard*, and a young poet called Pasolini.

that 'the last frank talks' had taken place (the occasion on which Togliatti and Feltrinelli had discussed the library, perhaps?). In any case, 'The sequence of events as related by Alicata is precise and reliable, in so far as he traces the onset of tension with the party from the moment co-direction of the institute ceased following Ferri's departure.' But here are the 'charges', according to Feltrinelli's notes:

Pasternak. The scandal and its repercussions for the Soviets, as well as his personal position vis-à-vis the USSR. It was odd, even typical if you will, but this point appeared only second on the list. The impression almost arose that it was dealt with in a generic way, with embarrassment.

The publishing house: 'there have been no more exchanges of ideas, apart from Pasternak'. Sure, no contacts, replied Feltrinelli, 'but look at your attitude!'.

A lack of relations between the Istituto Feltrinelli and the publishing house. The Institute was no longer 'co-directed' while the publishing house still employed a group of heterodox, non-'organic' intellectuals.

In conclusion, Longo and Alicata asked for a preventive discussion of the tricky cases that might crop up in future. The reply was blunt: 'Unacceptable, this would lead to paralysis and total control.'

The meeting was over, and everyone went his own way. The party leadership produced an internal memo deploring Feltrinelli's behaviour, deemed 'incompatible with the duties of every militant Communist'. Duties that involved 'realizing, in one's own field of activity, the party line' and 'defending the party from all attacks'. This was also established by article five of the statute.

> Feltrinelli's attitudes, which appeared to be aimed at
> fomenting the anti-Soviet and anti-Communist cam-
> paign led by our class enemies and certain political and
> intellectual groups who have taken sides against the
> party, cannot be justified even by the freedom of cultural
> research and the autonomy of the bodies run by comrade

Feltrinelli. Consequently, the party leadership invites comrade Feltrinelli to bear this criticism in mind and to remember his duties as a militant, so that the matters complained of here may not be repeated.

In other words, bye bye comrade Feltrinelli . . .

The sequence of events of June 1956, the last period of marked 'frank relations', is significant. Between May and early August, it was all happening: it was the time of the changing of the guard in the management of the Feltrinelli Library, of the meeting between Feltrinelli, Togliatti and Del Bo, of the arrival of the *Doctor Zhivago* typescript, and of the exchange of letters between Feltrinelli and Amendola. By an ironic quirk of fate, and just to make the whole affair even more bizarre, June was also the month in which Nikita Khruschev decided to write to Palmiro Togliatti, apropos of those letters . . . Yes, the 'Archives of the Revolution', the Marx–Engels correspondence of which there had been talk two years before, of the Institute of Amsterdam, of the Americans who wanted to buy the letters . . .

To comrade Togliatti
The Central Committee of the CPSU has been informed that Columbia University, USA has recently been negotiating with the Institute of Social History of Amsterdam regarding the purchase of the archives held by that Institute containing a series of original documents by Marx and Engels, previously kept in the Archives of the German Social Democratic Party, some documents by Lenin, and also material on the history of the international workers' movement. To the best of our knowledge, comrade Feltrinelli has contacts with the Amsterdam Institute and enjoys the confidence of that institute. We believe that with his help it would be possible to have information about the chances of securing documents and material of interest to us. Actually, we would like to receive an accurate list of the original

documents by Marx, Engels and Lenin as well as comrade Feltrinelli's opinion regarding the price for which
the proprietors of the archive might be prepared to sell.
It is clear that if during negotiations the owners of the
archive should propose the sale, together with the most
interesting documents, of other documents too, then we
would have to accept. In this case it would be desirable to
know the contents of the material on offer, the overall
value and any other conditions of sale. In the extreme
case whereby the original documents were not for sale,
we might ask comrade Feltrinelli to inquire about the
conditions under which photocopies might be obtained.

Please speak with comrade Feltrinelli about our interest in this matter and let us know whether he agrees to
carry out this mission and what his proposals might be.
We wish both the preliminary talks and the possible
acquisition of the material to be effected by comrade
Feltrinelli in his own name, for his own library, without
letting it be known that the Institute of
Marxism–Leninism has an interest in the matter. All
expenses connected with the purchase of this material
shall be totally reimbursed by us.
Regards from the comrade
    Secretary of the Central Committee of the CPSU
                                            Khruschev

Togliatti told Alicata to meet with Feltrinelli and to show
him the letter. The publisher, having gathered the appropriate
information, replied to Alicata by letter, the latter referred its
substance to Togliatti and the leadership of the PCI replied to
the Soviets with another letter that, essentially, was a repetition
of Feltrinelli's letter to Alicata.

                                            23.7.56

Dear Comrades,
Comrade Feltrinelli has supplied us with the following
information about the talks between Columbia

University and the Institute of Social History of
Amsterdam.

1. The talks were held 3–4 years ago in the atmosphere created by the international cold war.
   Formally, an agreement was reached on the following bases: Columbia University earmarked 5
   million dollars for the institute's Marx–Engels
   archives, which were to be transferred to America
   for the time necessary for photocopying and publication of the documents, but these last were to
   remain the property of the Amsterdam Institute. In
   fact, the agreement was not finalized and it lapsed a
   year later. It would seem that the work of cooperation specified in the agreement was never
   undertaken, nor is it under way at present.

2. The Amsterdam Institute never intended and still
   does not intend to sell the archives, which is apparently expressly forbidden by its statute.

3. Last year the Institute completed a summary inventory of the Marx–Engels archive. We have managed
   to obtain a copy of this inventory, which has been
   transmitted to the Marx–Engels Institute of
   Moscow.

4. In the present situation, it is practically impossible
   to have access to the archives of the institute and
   this holds especially for the Marx–Engels archives.
   The management of the institute is planning, in the
   long term and in direct relation to its human and
   economic resources, to publish its archives. None
   the less it ought to be borne in mind that the institute, whose orientation is vaguely social democratic,
   is financed by donations from banks and from the
   Dutch Education Ministry and so as long as the
   present political situation holds there is little reason
   to think that the task of publishing the
   Marx–Engels archives will be undertaken with any
   particular energy.

5. Given this situation, proposing the purchase or
requesting photocopies of the material in the
Amsterdam Institute would produce no result.

Comrade Feltrinelli sees only one possible way of
examining the documents that interest us, and that is to
offer to provide the Amsterdam Institute with the people
and the financial means with which to publish their
archives, including, of course, the Marx–Engels archives.
A similar proposal was made by comrade Feltrinelli at
the time of the talks between the Amsterdam Institute
and Columbia University, but the proposal, although it
was not rejected, was not followed up.

At present, comrade Feltrinelli could make this proposal once more, depending on the availability of the
necessary finance (certainly not 5 million dollars, but
nevertheless a large sum) especially as he is now planning
the construction of an institute in Switzerland, controlled by him, through which it would be easy to act.
The acceptance of this proposal by the Amsterdam
Institute would make it necessary for us to set up an efficient group of scholars and specialists, but comrade
Feltrinelli maintains that with the Marxist forces in Italy
and in other countries it would be possible to carry out
the work with the maximum scientific rigour.

Please let us know your views regarding comrade
Feltrinelli's letters and whether you feel that he should
make this proposal to the Amsterdam Institute.

Fraternal greetings

As we have seen, the events that were to occur immediately
afterwards upset all plans. The protagonists were less willing to
cooperate and talks were broken off. *Zhivago* was to overwhelm
everything and everybody.

* * *

Act two of the persecution of Boris Pasternak began in October

1958, after the announcement that he had won the Nobel Prize for Literature. The Soviet press unleashed an avalanche of accusations, the Writers' Union demanded his expulsion and, had he dared accept the prize, they would have deprived him of his citizenship and had him exiled. Yet again, it was Polikarpov, in agreement with Suslov, who orchestrated the whole operation.

In a recent book of memoirs, Gerd Ruge, a correspondent with German television in Moscow, gave a good description of what was happening around Pasternak:

The press campaign grew from day to day. *Liturnaya Gazeta* introduced a special column called 'Wrath and indignation', featuring the hate letters of the readership, letters written by people who had not read the novel and who roundly condemned the author. During a public meeting of young Communists, attended also by Nikita Khruschev, the leader of the Konsomol, Semitastny, defined Pasternak as 'a pig who fouls his own trough', and called for the writer's expulsion from the motherland.

Groups of young Communists demonstrated in front of the house in Peredelkino, waving banners bearing the word 'Judas', and security guards had to take care that the house was not taken by storm or set on fire. There was a doctor on hand, ready to step in should Pasternak attempt to take his own life, like Mayakovsky or Yesenin: another suicide would have shocked millions of readers and would have exacerbated the scandal. In fact, according to the memoirs of Olga Ivinskaya, on 28 October Pasternak apparently asked her if it would not have been better to commit suicide together.

In the end, Pasternak decided to refuse the prize and sent off a telegram to the Swedish academy on 29 October and he wrote directly to Khruschev, two days after, to explain how the threatened exile to the West would have meant death for him. Perhaps he sensed that the last chapter of his life had opened.

Yet 1958 had begun with his great joy at leafing through the Italian edition of *Doctor Zhivago*.

Here is his reaction, in a letter to the publisher dated 12 January of that year:

Dear Sir,

I do not know when I shall have the opportunity to express my immense gratitude for all your amazing achievements, of which I am the beneficiary and the witness. I appreciate the circumspection with which you have granted interviews, and also your regard for me, which I can sense from the appearance of the book, given to me by a German journalist, and by the excellent translation, which is highly praised everywhere. The good fortune that has smiled upon my book, the editions that sell out rapidly, all is due principally to you, and full of reverence I bow before your kindness, your talent and your lucky star.

If in my turn I have been of use in some way, I have a request to make of you – grant me this wish.

Since your edition has enjoyed such a fabulous success, allow me to express a hope, the hope that I might see the work published exactly as it was written, in the original language. So, give me leave to place this delicate matter (bound up with consequences that will perhaps prove fatal to me, the way all fancies of a 'Zhivagoesque' nature do) in the prudent hands of my good friend from Paris, Madame Jacqueline de Proyart. After clearing up the economic issues with you, the lady, I believe, will choose to have the work published by Mouton of The Hague, the publishers most consonant with it from a political point of view. I cannot see anything in this that might jeopardize or harm your interests, since every book in Russian put on sale will carry below the title a statement declaring your reservation of all rights regarding foreign translations, and a most extensive declaration of your copyright. But should this request of mine run contrary to your interests, I beg you to meet me half-way all the same, and I shall indemnify you for any losses in the manner provided for by the clauses contained in article 2 of the contract. Give me leave to confer material authority regarding all literary questions concerning my Russian texts upon Madame de Proyart, and do not hinder her in this activity. I shall number you among my most wonderful friends, to whom I shall forever be an insolvent debtor. Among those [friends] there is also, even more cherished, Madame de Proyart. I do not want any discord among my friends. Please, sort things out with Madame for the best. Do not write to me, do not bring up the question of money. Behave as you have always behaved with me, maintain the same silence. I embrace D'Angelo with affection, tempestuously. All his acquaintances send him their fondest greetings. Please pass on my enthusiastic compliments and my infinite gratitude to dear Zveteremich, whose work reveals him to be a master of his art, a wizard.

Yours

Boris Pasternak

Over and above the declarations of friendship, this letter is extremely important because it explains some questions that would become relevant in the future. The first concerns the position of D'Angelo, who had returned to Italy and was employed for a time by the publishing house. The second, more important, concerns the role of Mme de Proyart. She had met and befriended the poet in January 1957 and, on the strength of this familiarity, she now felt she had a role to play in the management of his interests.

The odd thing is that the letter sent on 12 January 1958 never reached Feltrinelli. Given by Pasternak to Hélène Peltier, one of the French translators who was on a visit to Moscow that January, the letter was in an envelope containing other correspondence for Madame de Proyart. But she kept everything and forwarded nothing to Milan. Perhaps this was because her legal rights as an agent had not been defined with sufficient precision or, who knows, perhaps she thought she was much more than a mere proxy, or perhaps she was unaware that, according to international law, *Doctor Zhivago* was to all intents and purposes an 'Italian' book and that a Russian edition was subject to the same contractual obligations as a translated version in English, German or French.

Jacqueline de Proyart only recently gave the letter to Evgeny Pasternak, and her failure to forward it at the time generated some serious misunderstandings and even friction between the publisher and the poet's solicitous lady friend.

But it is easier to follow the evolution of the entire affair through Feltrinelli's own words. From the *Sunday Times*:

> While the literary world was acclaiming *Doctor Zhivago* and its author, I became aware of the first signs of a long battle between me and a variety of persons and institutions (all connected with the same circle of anti-Soviet activities that, in one way or another, was connected to the CIA). I had commissioned from a Dutch printer a limited number of copies of *Doctor Zhivago* in Russian and, to my surprise, a different, pirate Russian edition appeared in Holland. It would appear that someone had printed an edition on the request of some Russian *émigrés* in Paris, who had certain relations with the Americans. At the same time, at the International Expo in Brussels, some Russian émigrés were distributing copies of another pirate edition, on the Vatican stand! These events put me on my guard.
>
> As a result, I strongly opposed the political use that anti-Soviet circles might make of the book and of the consequences that this might have for the author. I was also seriously worried that my copyright might be jeopardized. I therefore took legal action against the pirate editions circulating in Holland, Greece and Argentina and in all cases I managed to come to an amicable agreement.

As to how far these suspicions (perhaps they were certainties) were plausible, I really do not know. But I do know, thanks to direct evidence, about the vicissitudes of the attorney Tesone, who was then taking his first steps in the legal profession, and who found himself catapulted into the most complex of international intrigues in the field of copyright. It was in everyone's interest to defend the contract and to prevent the work from falling into the public domain. In order to block a pirate edition, Tesone flew all the way to Buenos Aires: on that occasion it was to prove child's play for him. 'As soon as I arrived, I went to the Plaza but I could not sleep because of jet lag and I went down to take a stroll along calle Florida. After a hundred metres I was assailed by a newsvendor with a copy of *Doctor Zhivago*. I unearthed the printer within two days.'

Throughout 1958, the correspondence between Feltrinelli and Pasternak slowed down. Both were employing maximum caution. On 5 September, almost a year after the publication of the Italian edition, Feltrinelli sent his author an affectionate statement.

Dear Friend,
First of all, let me clasp your hand with feelings of wholehearted friendship and gratitude.
    From time to time, I have had indirect news of you, sometimes good, sometimes of a kind that had me worried about your state of health. I hope, and the most recent news I have received confirms this, that you have now recovered from your indisposition of last spring, and I entreat you, also in the name of the innumerable friends you have everywhere, to look after yourself and not to risk your health for any reason.
    Now I should like to say a few words about the success of *Doctor Zhivago*. In figures: in Italy we have sold about 30,000 copies. An enormous number for the Italian market and hard to beat even for the most famous

authors. But these figures have a significance that goes
well beyond this. We have had cases of youngsters who,
during their lessons at school, read *Doctor Zhivago*, page
after page, passing it on from hand to hand. We have the
testimony provided by the dozens of people who have
written to thank me for having published this work.
Wherever I go, people talk to me of *Doctor Zhivago*, the
best-loved book in Italy at the moment. Now I shall cite
only a few lines of a message the Italian writer Carlo
Cassola sent to me.

'Today I finished reading *Doctor Zhivago*. No contemporary book has aroused in me so much enthusiasm, so
much emotion, so much intellectual pleasure, or so much
comfort and serenity as this one has.'

Doctor Zhivago has already come out in French and is
about to come out in England, America, Germany,
Holland, Denmark, Sweden, Finland, Norway, Israel
and Mexico. In Sweden it has already aroused enormous
interest in the Swedish Academy.

And there is more. In Italy, *Doctor Zhivago* has won
the prize awarded by the booksellers, a fact that reflects
an appreciation of its literary qualities as well as its success in terms of sales. I am also sending you the most
important reviews to have appeared in the Italian press
as well as a few that have arrived from abroad.

Now we are preparing your autobiographical essay for
next November, and I should like to ask you, dear friend,
to require one of your friends in Moscow to find the
photos mentioned in the list I am enclosing along with
this letter. We should like to illustrate the book with
photos of the characters, of the works, and with reproductions from magazines, etc. that are mentioned here. I
am also enclosing a copy of Chekhov's *Cahiers*, which we
published last year, to show you how your essay will be
presented. Could you have someone find the material we
need? Perhaps you already have it in your own records? I
hope I am not importuning you with these requests of

mine, but time is very short: we must have everything as soon as possible!

I end this letter, dear friend, with the hope I may finally meet you one day. Thank you for *Doctor Zhivago.* Yours,

Giangiacomo Feltrinelli

Pasternak ticked off a few items on the list of material requested, and crossed out others. At that time he was thinking of sending Feltrinelli a painting by his father, who was an artist, which shows Prince Trubetskoy intent on making a sculpture of his young grandchildren. In his autobiographical text Pasternak talks of the prince, who taught along with his father in the school of painting. Trubetskoy had been assigned a new studio whose skylight gave on to the kitchen of the Pasternak household. That picture was a great present for Feltrinelli, and Pasternak wrote on the back of the canvas: 'I send you this picture as a gift, my dear friend. It was in this very atelier, built adjacent to the window of our kitchen, as is described in my autobiography, that the prince modelled his grandchildren.'

It was 19 October 1958. The poet was not to have the time to arrange the complicated delivery of the materials Feltrinelli wanted. Four days later, his life was turned upside-down: he had won the Nobel!

'Infinitely grateful, moved, proud, amazed, confused' was his first reply by telegram to the Academy in Stockholm. Even Giannalisa thought it well to congratulate the winner: just for once, was she or was she not the publisher's mother?

5

The Aurelian way was a strange summertime manger-scene with its oleanders, electric lights, wickerwork screens, spaghetti *al burro*, wall posters, magic pine car air fresheners, little shrines with television sets and the reflected glitter of the sand all around. On San Lorenzo's night (in August 1957), the usual Citroën was heading for the Argentario. With Giangiacomo there was a Roman girl who was perhaps not a beauty, but who was said to be a character. The couple arrived at Giannalisa's house overlooking the sea where she had left the children to spend the winter after the long sojourn in New York. With them there was only governess number 17. Giangiacomo woke up Benedetta, the youngest: 'Come on, there's someone I want you to meet.' The introductions were made in the enclosed space between the roofs, lying down on the still warm stones beneath the shooting stars. That is how Benedetta recalls the encounter.

The Roman girl was Nanni De Stefanis, the daughter of a Roman playwright. In those days, Feltrinelli was spending more and more time in Rome: he had had enough of the fog, the late-night meetings at the branch office, the ghastly office curtains; in Rome, for a good night on the town, all you needed was a white shirt and a couple of gypsies *à la* Django Reinhardt. Nanni was on the poetry circuit and the typical small restaurants, the *trattorie*, were still typical.

With Bianca, it seemed that things had been going badly for some time; in fact, the couple were practically separated. Before Rome, Giangiacomo had run off too frequently to the Deux Magots and Françoise; Bianca, in 1955, had been seduced by Renato Mieli, an ex-editor of *l'Unità*. Formerly secretary to Togliatti, Mieli was suspected of being an English spy and was rumoured to be on the point of leaving the PCI. I think that Giangiacomo loved Bianca, despite her rather uncompromising character. In Italy, divorce was still in the future, and there was only one way to get rid of a spouse, apart from murder: you needed a decree of annulment issued in a foreign country and this then had to be endorsed by an Italian court. Something only the rich could afford, obviously, it was a tortuous and costly process. The loophole, usually, was that of *impotentia coeundi* on the husband's part.

Nanni could have made the right companion for Giangiacomo, she would have brought a touch of Rome to Milan. With her, life would have taken a more stimulating turn, perhaps a more amusing one. At first, the couple went to live in the family home, in via Andegari, refurbished for the occasion.

One day, they took the car and after an ice-cream in the square in Vigevano, after driving through Lomellina, the rice fields of Mortara and the mosquitoes of Casale, they discovered the skeleton of an ancient castle on the top of the hills around Monferrato. At the foot of the hills there stands a village. In the mid-eighteenth century, a young disciple of the school of Juvara,* certainly an amateur, had indulged his whims in a unique enterprise. He designed a two-fronted belvedere that was to link up with the village by means of a strange system of steps, underground passages, walkways and

---

* Filippo Juvara (1678–1736). Italian architect whose baroque style was tempered with classicism. He worked in Turin for the royal house of Savoy.

paths. The construction he imagined was devoid of depth but really spectacular. Around the axis of the central tower, exploiting the sloping terrain, terraces, towers, arches, hallways, exedras and balustrades were designed to blend in with exotic plants, gardens, palm trees and orange and lemon groves. Everything complied with a rigorous symmetry in which even the trees had their own specific place. The spectacle is neoclassical, the syntax strictly Baroque, and the quiet is Arcadian.

But this was not the scene that met Giangiacomo on his first excursion with Nanni. The only archaeological survey from the time provides us with another image. The '*Bollettino storico-bibliografico subalpino*' of 1942 reported that the construction had been 'left at the mercy of the elements and neglect' and was in 'a desperate condition. [. . .] The castle lies lifeless, crumbling, roofless, and at certain points, like the ceilings of the covered stairways in the gardens, there have been some serious cave-ins.' In place of the hanging gardens and the flowerbeds, there grew 'brushwood, ivy and nettles'.

The village below is called Villadeati. In 1944 it was the scene of a Nazi reprisal, which culminated in the slaughter of eleven people. A squad of partisans had sought refuge in the ruins of the castle.

It was going to take one, two, or maybe three years, and truckloads of gravel; there were bricks to be piled up, seeds to be sown, but in the end the place was restored and, in a certain sense, it resembles him. According to the historian André Corboz, the castle of Villadeati is 'an atypical complex, impossible to classify under a single label'. It is a folly, 'in which formal quality none the less prevails over bourgeois vanity. At Villadeati the space already belongs [to the age of] the hot-air balloon, and no longer to that of the horse-drawn carriage.' There are photos of Feltrinelli with a wheelbarrow full of mortar working on a cryptoporticus. He was trying to build himself a piece of future.

But things did not work out, and there was no helping that. It wasn't clear whether or not Nanni was putting it on, but she was unstable. She did want to marry him, but she wasn't prepared to give up her Roman connections. She was unhappy in the new city. The wedding was celebrated on 19 June 1957, but the marriage didn't last as much as a year. These things will happen, and when they do, they hurt. Two marriages, two failures. Perhaps the time had come to go away, to get a change of air, to be alone.

And in fact, in July 1958, Feltrinelli set off with his backpack and his tent and headed north, towards Scandinavia, with a stopover in Hamburg to meet some German publishers. During this trip, he wrote from the lagoon of Grado to his friend, the painter Giuseppe Zigaina, who was about to get married. The letter was a long one in which Feltrinelli bared his soul, also to himself.

Dear Pino,
I am still on my travels and I hope that you will continue to behave sensibly and that you will not get cold feet at the last minute. I really think, dear Pino, that you must not have doubts. And this is not because I want to see others go through the troubles that have come my way. But for what little, very little alas, I can understand, and above all because I am not emotionally involved in the matter, I think you couldn't have made a better choice. On the other hand, even though I feel galled, scorned and humiliated, I still agree with what Zompitta said about marriage a couple of years ago. To my way of thinking, nothing could be better for a man like you, with your wealth of experience, than choosing the right wife and to have from her what only a wife can give, if she loves you, if she is a balanced person, morally, intellectually and physically. And when the crises come along, the doubts and the problems, you will always find in her love the comfort that a man needs. And then there are children. You see, Pino, I envy you. I think you will have all the things I have always desired and do not have. Once, because of inexperience on my part, or on the part of

both, and maybe even out of my malice or imprudence, I
spoiled and destroyed something beautiful and sound.
The second time around, I got a taste of my own medicine and I reaped the hurt I had caused another. I envy
you, Pino. Because you have all the experience a man
needs to be able to choose, to know what to do and what
not to do, and I seem to see Bianca's qualities in Maria.
Only with far more sweetness and humanity than she had
then. As long as you don't do anything silly, you will be
very happy. So say hello to Maria from me, and my fondest good wishes to both of you. And while we're on the
subject, it is sad Pino, to get to thirty-two years of age, to
find the road ahead barred, and to realize, when you have
had the sincere love of a woman, full of faults, but none
the less a sincere and honest person, that you have played
with life and love to the point of throwing it all away.
And on reaching the point in which you are mature
enough to give and appreciate what you could and had to
receive, nothing, there was nothing to receive beneath a
thin layer of appearances. But enough – otherwise there
is a risk of my falling into self-pity. Anything but that. I
have gained in strength and calm these last few weeks.
Being alone, the contact with nature, and travelling has
given me serenity, and so I can talk of these things with
calm and awareness. At this moment I am travelling from
Naurk to Honnersgung (Nordkapp) on board a small
motor ship. We are travelling through the Norwegian
fjords, among mountains still laden with snow, on a sea
that is, I would say, dark periwinkle-blue under a sun
that never sets on the horizon. It is a magnificent spectacle, at times almost terrifying. I left the car at Kiruna in
Sweden and when I get back there on Sunday morning I
want to take the road for the north once more, and see
these same places from the land. The solitude here is
immense. Last week, after a visit of 7–8 days to
Stockholm, I took an inland road right across Sweden
(1800 km) and in about ten days time I expect to be in

Helsinki. I think this is one of the best trips I have ever made. On the one hand, I am sorry to be alone, because many things are too beautiful to be seen alone. On the other, I don't regret being alone and I am almost enjoying myself. The Swedish girls are a delightful spectacle and they are really bewitchingly beautiful. But no adventures. A bit because I was in contemplative mood and a bit because as the sexual problem doesn't exist, the idea of sex is not sufficient reason for two people to get together. That's my theory at any rate. I am racking my brains in the search for a handsome and useful present for you and Maria. Well, Pino, I shall go up on deck to make an inspection and check to see that everything is shipshape. Fondest wishes to you and Maria, from your Giangiacomo

Perhaps it was to ward off bad luck, but here there is no mention of the press photographer Feltrinelli had met in Hamburg on the outward journey, in the office of Heinrich Maria Ledig Rowohlt. 'I introduced them, I invited her to a party in Giangiacomo's honour. They got to know each other better, they got on, I would say that they understood each other immediately and, when they left the party, I don't think they needed anyone else . . .' It may be that after that meeting, born under the auspices of the publisher who was a friend of Faulkner and Hemingway, there was a brief encounter on the way back home. Perhaps in Copenhagen, at the court of another publisher, Otto Lindhart, with whom it is still a pleasure to talk of books to this day.

The girl, says Rowohlt, made a name for herself for having photographed Pablo Picasso, Ernest Hemingway, Gary Cooper, Gérard Philippe, Greta Garbo and Anna Magnani, and she learned about photography by interviewing Erwin Blumenfeld in New York. The girl looked like a blend of Audrey Hepburn and Leslie Caron.

* * *

Have you read *The Leopard*? Did you like *The Leopard*? So begins a society piece published in the winter of 1958–9:

> When the book came out, the question came from friends who frequented literary circles; then it came from colleagues, then from acquaintances. By now you hear it in the theatre or coming from the row behind in the cinema. In fact, any cheap cardboard yellow cover, lying on a table, sticking out of a pocket or a handbag, now makes you think of a copy of *The Leopard*. Anyone buying or receiving the book that has just come out is advised to hang on to it: it is, in fact, almost a bibliographical rarity.

'Yet,' Eugenio Montale was to take it upon himself to explain elsewhere, 'Lampedusa, who was this person? Until the other day no one could say that this was the name of a writer . . .'

The Leopard arrived in the bookshops in December 1958. As a result of a blunder. The plan had been to publish the book early in the New Year. The Christmas schedule was already very crowded and Osenga, the sales manager, insisted that 'safer' books should have precedence. But, owing to a misunderstanding, a few advance copies were sent to the critics and Carlo Bo unexpectedly wrote a review for *La Stampa*. There was nothing else for it but to rush the book out as fast as possible.

Feltrinelli was to admit, during an interview, the serendipitous nature of 'Operation Leopard': '*Zhivago* called for a difficult decision to be taken in isolation. Who could have advised me in that situation? In short it was not, as is almost always the case with best-sellers, and as it was with *The Leopard*, a stroke of luck.'

In reality, the publishing histories of the two books are to some extent analogous. As with Pasternak, Feltrinelli was never to meet the author of his second, huge publishing hit. Giuseppe Tomasi di Lampedusa, duke of Palma, died of lung cancer in July 1957. His was to be an overwhelming posthumous success.

'In the bookshops, delicate ladies of a certain age, "angry young men", and petit bourgeois who usually read the glossy magazines all asked for *The Leopard*, almost with the same unwitting passion they had asked for *Doctor Zhivago* some time before.' This was what they managed to write in *Rinascita*, the theoretical magazine of the PCI, thereby inviting the ironic darts of the critic Geno Pampaloni: 'In a country that divides into a mass of apathetic people and a discordant clique of sophisticates, the fact that a book not only sells tens of thousands of copies but moreover has pretensions to being considered "good" is in itself more than amazing, it is scandalous. And such people view the book with the same mistrust that they reserved for *Doctor Zhivago*.'

As with *Zhivago*, the publishing history of the new bestseller contained a sensational rejection. In fact, at first, there was the oversight at Mondadori, perhaps the fault of some superficial readers, then there was the critic Vittorini, who at first may not even have read the manuscript. All could be explained, like the ideological anomalies in the novel that prompted a refusal from Einaudi, and justified on the basis of 'coherence'. Vittorini argued his case in a long letter to the author, views he was to repeat publicly: even though 'serious and honest', this was a static, conventional book that denied history. Cassola's *Il soldato* was better, or Testori's *Il ponte della Ghisolfa*. These works, which had also just been published by Feltrinelli, had more life and were 'steeped in our history'.

The events that led to the publication of *The Leopard* form a new, albeit minor 'novel within the novel'. The protagonists were a friend of Bassani's, Elena Croce,* the daughter of the great Italian philosopher, who had remembered the manuscript that had lain for a long time in a drawer before she finally sent it to Giorgio Bassani; and Bassani himself, the 'sparrowhawk' recently recruited by Feltrinelli during his Roman period to direct a series of works by contemporary authors. Elena had

---

* (1915–94). A remarkable essayist and German scholar, she was an indefatigable defender of literary culture.

written to Bassani, telling him that the novel came from an
'aristocratic young lady from Palermo'. Bassani swooped on
the text and managed to recover, after a great deal of diplomacy
and detective work, the text of the denouement with the
famous ball as well as the original manuscript. Then, after publication, it was the critics' turn to have a ball: was the novel
'right-wing' or not, and what should be considered 'left-wing'?

By this time, Feltrinelli thought that these were pointless
polemics: so what if Mario Alicata had labelled one of his
books as 'decadent' for the second time? Probably he was as
bored by this as he was by the twittering of the ancient aristocratic crones in their hats (at the zenith of their splendour) that
packed the amphitheatre where Lampedusa's book was
awarded the 1959 Strega prize.

The Prince of Salina and Doctor Yuri, the unexpected protagonists of novels that were historical as well as ahistorical or
superhistorical, coexist somewhere like two characters in a
mirror. They look at and recognize each other from far off. But
while *The Leopard* was 'the restless ghost of Italian literature
after the second World War' (the definition is that of Alfonso
Berardinelli), *Doctor Zhivago*, in its own country, was an even
more awkward ghost.

* * *

In 1958 Feltrinelli was formally an 'ex': after fourteen years as
a party member, he was no longer carrying a party card in his
pocket. In fact, he was rumoured to be 'on the point of joining
the PSI Italian Socialist Party, for whom he is to present himself as a candidate at the next political elections'. This is what
was said in a confidential report to the chief of police on 11
January. The purported leak was subsequently rebutted by two
'first-rate' informers, each unaware of the other's work: 'the
news is unfounded' (7.2.1958).

After years as a militant activist, breaking with the party is
often the prelude to weird existential crises whose effects are
not always cathartic. There is a real case study to be made of

this: how many 'exes' have we had and how many do we still have? Moreover, precisely because the party is an austere thing, it is unforgiving. The context is always 'strained to the breaking point' and as for the political conjuncture, well, the conjuncture is always a 'decisive' one. And it is this unforgiving nature that engenders the contempt that suddenly smothers you, leaving you with no place to turn. To the right, there are all those faces you have always detested, to the left, there is that strange family that doesn't want you any more.

Both Feltrinelli and the PCI played down his breach with the party and there was no sensation-mongering on either side. Feltrinelli said he was 'disappointed'. And no more.

That the breach was a real one, however, emerges from the ineffable author of the police report (4.2. 1959): 'It seems that today, especially after the publication of *Doctor Zhivago* and the works of some American authors, the breach between Feltrinelli and the Communists is complete.'

The officials of the American State Department who were examining his request for a visa prior to a visit to the USA came to the same conclusion.

The Consul General in Milan, Charles Rogers, sent Washington the memorandum of his meeting with the Italian publisher.*

Feltrinelli is a young man, well dressed, and gives the appearance of a wealthy background. Above all, he gives the impression of a person who takes himself very seriously. His expression is grave and he attaches importance to the thoughts which he expresses. He has a mission, that of achieving a better world for the 'downtrodden'. Judging by his views as expressed during our conversation, his state of mind seemed more analogous to that of a nineteenth-century social reformer rather than that of a 12-year member of the Italian Communist Party. At the outset of our conversation he seemed ill at ease, but as

---

* FBI Archives, Washington.

the conversation led into a discussion of his political
ideas, he relaxed somewhat.

He said he had joined the Communist Party in 1944
because at the time, due to 'historical coincidence', it
seemed to him the most effective instrument to combat
Fascism and to bring about the rapid development of
true democracy in Italy. By this he intended to imply not
simply a parliamentary democracy but a utilitarian state
in which the conditions of life of the lower classes would
be greatly and speedily improved. He left the party in
1957 when he became convinced that this historical coincidence no longer held true and that the Communist
Party, due to its relationship with the Soviet Communist
Party, both mechanically and philosophically, no longer
was a suitable instrument for the achievement of the
objectives which he wished to support. When he left the
party, he did so in a quiet fashion and without creating a
dramatic issue which, through its attendant publicity,
would create an image of him as an 'anti-Communist'. It
is his aim to be a leader of left wing intellectualism and,
in order to retain his influence in left-wing circles, he
wishes to avoid the label of anti-Communism. He has
stated publicly only once that he is no longer a member
of the party. This was at a press conference in London in
the fall of 1958. His present focus of activity as a left-
wing intellectual leader is the Giangiacomo Feltrinelli
Institute of Milan, a centre of socialist studies, of which
he spoke with a note of pride. [. . .]

Feltrinelli has no present intention of associating himself with any other political party in Italy. He is not
prepared to accept political slogans which he is unable to
test in advance for the purpose of establishing their
validity. When I asked him how he would describe himself as a political thinker, he shied away from the term
'Marxist' or 'revisionist'. Under the present circumstance, he said, it is impossible to define a 'Marxist'. As a
father of political thought, Marx had unquestionably

made a great contribution to human development but in
the light of 100 years' experience, many of his assump-
tions and theses were evidently erroneous. In response to
my question as to his estimate of Lenin, Feltrinelli said
the he was not entirely of one mind. While Lenin was
unquestionably a brilliant and important political
thinker, one could not overlook the results of his work. It
is difficult to separate Lenin's ideas and intentions from
their consequences. Apropos of 'The State and
Revolution', Feltrinelli also expressed his conviction that
the powers of the central government under ideal circumstances should be diminished and that many
functions of the government be delegated to the local
community. He did not argue that the central government be 'withered away' altogether since there were
obviously many functions which needed to be performed
by it which could not be performed locally. He mentioned in this context that he had just returned from
Sicily, but there was no opportunity to question him further on his activity there.

Feltrinelli is especially interested in the problem of the
individual's relationship to society in a technological civ-
ilization. He appeared to believe there was a parallel
between the pressures to which the individual was subjected as a result of the imposition of doctrine by a
tyrannical government under Communism and those
self-induced pressures of standardization and social convention under capitalism. For these reasons, he said, he
was particularly anxious to observe at first hand the
effects of the evolution of modern society in the
American democracy. He has a number of introductions
to intellectual circles in the United States.

Feltrinelli had not been in the USA since the days of Doctor
Gottlieb, or whatever the hell Giannalisa's dentist was called.
He was the best. And when he moved his practice from Vienna
to New York, grandmother thought it only logical to remain

faithful to him and not to do without his precious skills, especially for the children's sake.

But owing to his Communist party card, Feltrinelli had been
unable to show his face in the USA since 1945. Even as an 'ex',
he still did not have that right. But now Washington took only
three weeks to grant the request, probably as a result of the
'Pasternak effect'. In fact, the publisher had asked to go to the
United States in order to deal personally with various business
matters regarding the management of the rights of his most
important author. The *Herald Tribune* and the *Washington Post*
attached particular importance to the *nulla osta* signed by
Justice Minister William Rogers.

This time, Feltrinelli left for America with his new love, Inge
Schoenthal. It was to be a long trip. First stop Mexico City and
a quickie marriage bureau, then the United States and a whole
galaxy of publishing contacts, followed by Cuba in search of
Hemingway, and then back to the States again. All in four
months: from Christmas to April 1959, with a brief return to
Italy in between. This interlude overseas was the line of demar-
cation between one life and preparations for a completely new
one, sanctioned by a honeymoon spent between Zihuatanejo
and Baja California.

> We began to publish in 1955 and, apart from some rare
> exceptions, those first books were rather poor. Now I
> have come to America because we are publishing books
> that are better, much better, and we'd like to publish
> books that are even better still. I felt that personal con-
> tact with American publishers could be an important
> step for the development of our business and one that
> would give me some first-hand knowledge of literary
> production.

These were Feltrinelli's opening remarks in his first American
radio interview. He spoke excellent English and the man who
was firing the questions at him – Barney Rosset, the publisher of *Evergreen review*, the best magazine of the cultural

avant-garde – presented him as an 'intense' man, who made a strong impression.

New York gave them a really special welcome. The Americans noticed a felicitous resemblance between Mr Feltrinelli and *Doctor Zhivago*. But the aura of *The Leopard* also helped to arouse intense curiosity. A curiosity that was reciprocated.

There were important encounters and new friends were on the horizon. One of these was the same Barney Rosset, who was an editor at Grove Press, 'a quick-witted, dynamic forty-year-old', noted his Italian guest. They spoke at length about Beckett. Feltrinelli took out an option but, unfortunately, did not clinch a deal. By way of compensation, they got on right from the start. The same thing happened with Jason Epstein (one of the future founders of the *New York Review of Books*), who by twenty-eight had made it to the top job at Random House, 'a real *enfant prodige*, a sort of Brega'. And also with Mike Bessie, then with Harpers, 'intelligent and witty, with a profound knowledge of Europe', and even a friend of Luigi Barzini. It was the same story with Bill Jovanovich, the Montenegrin who ran Harcourt Brace, and with Roger Straus, to this day in charge of one of America's most admired publishing houses, and above all with Kurt Wolff, Pasternak's American publisher and Feltrinelli's real host.

There men were to become his friends in the world of publishing, together with Heinrich Maria Ledig Rowohlt and Gottfried Bermann Fischer, a close friend of the Mann family who played the cello with Albert Einstein. These are the names of the older generation, one that had created the cultural framework of an epoch in which books had yet to become stock cubes.

One black day, Rosset was to have words of real praise for Feltrinelli: 'We had the convictions, he had the courage'. For his part, Wolff said: 'He was the first and only *homo novus* we had met.' Perhaps they were both thinking of those first frenetic encounters in New York in the winter of 1959.

And after the publishers there came the inevitable contacts with authors: in his radio interview, Feltrinelli said he was on the trail of Jack Kerouac. And we know that he approached Nabokov, then an old man, about *Lolita*, an approach that failed basically owing to incompatibility of character. Feltrinelli proposed to Nabokov that he bring out a Russian edition, thereby incurring the (fairly benevolent) strictures of Alberto Mondadori, who had Nabokov under contract. Things went better with Karen Blixen: oysters, champagne and a deal for *Out of Africa*. Then he dropped in on Arthur Miller at the playwright's home. The famous wife was in the next room, unable to decide on which outfit to wear. Giangiacomo and Inge played for time, talking and talking, but the famous wife did not make an appearance.

Some like it hot, and, given that heat was the name of the game, my parents moved on to Havana, in search of Hemingway. Inge had interviewed the writer three years before and now wanted to introduce him to her husband. In the great casinos the roulette wheels were still spinning, but only out of inertia, and instead of Hemingway, who had taken himself off because he was in bad shape, the couple found a revolution only a few weeks old. 'A magnificent city', Feltrinelli wrote to the faithful Tina, 'very chaotic, with Hispanics, Blacks and Chinese, humming with life and colour. Every so often, scattered here and there, you come across bearded guerrillas, complete with pistols and sub-machine-guns, lounging on big chairs in front of public buildings, guarding against the enemy.'

Having taken one of the last flights out to Miami, the journey continued by car toward Washington, Baltimore and New York once more. A Ford Mustang lurked in the rear-view mirror for a good part of the trip: the FBI?

* * *

On his return to Italy, the publisher threw himself back into the Zhivago affair. He had to come to an agreement with the University of Michigan Press in Ann Arbor about a new Russian-language edition of the novel. By way of a precautionary measure, he decided to begin preparation of his own version in Cyrillic.

In the meantime, Pasternak's *Autobiography* had been published in Italy in December 1959, together with a collection of poems translated by Sergio D'Angelo. But let's pick up the thread of the article Feltrinelli wrote for the *Sunday Times*:

> I received various letters from Madame Jacqueline de Proyart of Paris, with instructions for the publication of the autobiography. Madame de Proyart said that Pasternak had granted her the widest powers of attorney. I knew nothing of Madame de Proyart's position and relations between us grew more tense. I was worried because, in such a delicate matter, it might have been dangerous to involve a third person who was not acquainted with all the details. Frankly, I also resented the fact that she enjoyed the privilege of being able to travel and have direct contact with the author, something I could not do as I did not have a Soviet visa.

So it was back to the sequence of questions and answers to be enclosed in a sealed envelope and entrusted to the hold of a plane and to hands that sorted the mail in a hangar. On 2 February 1959, Pasternak sent a reply – from Peredelkino, via Paris – to Feltrinelli's letter of 5 September 1958. The publisher had sent Pasternak a first statement regarding sales of *Doctor Zhivago* one year after publication, with a grateful postscript in English ('Thank you for *Zhivago*, and for all you have taught us').

> My very dear friend,
> I begin this letter by begging you to convey to your good lady mother, Giannalisa Feltrinelli, my humblest apologies, and my bitterest remorse, as well as my warmest thanks for the beautiful and inspiring telegram that she honoured me with on the day, so fateful for me, of my joy. Tell the dear, dear Madame Giannalisa that on

reading her missive, among the others received that day, I could not hold back my tears and now, as I dash off these impetuous lines, I can barely resist a new bout, at the mere recollection. Tell her too – since such solicitous and penetrating words always express the entire being of those who utter them, better than a hundred portraits – tell her that for the rest of her life she will always remain so young, adorable and passionate, something that will come to pass, moreover, even without my wishes. I bow respectfully before her. I also thank you for all the flattering exaggerations that you kindly wrote in your letter of 5 September 1958 – 5 September, now fancy that, how long ago it is now! But we must not be surprised by the fact that only now have I found the time to reply to you.

As for my feelings for you, of which you are well aware, words can never suffice, even were I to express my gratitude night and day. I have often assured you, and I repeat this, that it is to you I owe not only the success of the book, but far more: this entire phase of my life, distressing, deadly dangerous, but full of significance and responsibility, dizzyingly enthralling, and worthy of being accepted and lived in glad and grateful obedience to God. I shall confirm everything to whoever may make criticisms or show interest and curiosity: I mean to say your rights regarding the publication of *Doctor Zhivago*, translated in all languages, your honesty, your generosity to me, your fairness in all disputes concerning the translated versions of *Zhivago*. One example: when the Indian publishers approached me, I forwarded all their proposals directly to you.

In the same way, on the request from the Galeria Libertad of Montevideo, who challenged your rights over the Spanish version of the Dr, I told them that the rights were yours and that such disputes were futile.

But let's change the subject altogether. Recently there has sprung up a numerous group of critics, translators and publishers, who are sensitive, devoted and benevolent towards me, who write about me, translate me and publish me. And instead of finding in me gratitude and joy, as they would have every reason to expect, given that they have covered me with gifts and gladness, they find in me, as I was saying, ingratitude and an enigmatic sense of bewilderment. They are saddened, the poor souls, and they waste time speculating about what mistake they can have made to deserve my hostility, wondering whatever it is they can have done to me, apart from pure unadulterated good. They are wrong. They are not the cause of my suffering, I am unhappy and irritated with myself. With me, with my face in some of their photos, so realistic they capture the traits of an ugliness that is characteristic but not something that I would boast about having reproduced. With some passages in my prose works, with some old and unfinished poetry, which I would have preferred to forget and whose imperfections I am reminded of thanks to the perfection of their translations.

If only I knew what to do about all this, how to conduct myself, if only I had some fixed point of view, if only I were able to give clear and precise instructions. Is it possible to suppress everything I did before the Dr, the *Autobiography*, the recent poems, and the translation of *Faust*? Perhaps I am wrong to criticize, to refuse everything *en bloc*? Against my will I have devoted fifteen years of my work to the countless bulky translations that take up a whole shelf in my bookcase. My work in the original language is not vast, it is limited in choice. Can I neglect this part entirely? When I am the one who has my writings to hand, I can make a selection. I have put together a selection of my poems from all the periods for the state publishing house. I hoped that, once this book came out, it might have served as a model for all the foreign translations. But it was rejected. None of my work is going to be published here any more, either the translations or my works in the original language. And conducting business, making decisions and coming to agreement by means of a mail service that is so uncertain, slow and ill disposed, over such distances, with such tight deadlines – it is a torment, an unsolvable problem, a wretched misfortune. Hence, therefore, the need, the reason why I find myself obliged, while still having full confidence in you, to create, to recognize in a foreign country another myself, an adviser, who meets my requirements in taste, in rigorous selectivity, in critical competence, and who has like ideas regarding what is to be done, to be accepted, avoided, refused, desired and striven for, amid all the excessive occasions that present themselves a bit too frequently and practically everywhere in my favour.

I cannot contemplate either rivalry or conflict between you and Madame de Proyart, my *alter ego*, who, like me, understands and makes allowances for the ambiguous position that I was obliged to impose upon you out of necessity, forcing you to put up with my statements in silence and without objecting, and even though infrequent and reserved, my words were nevertheless hypocritically slanderous of your honour as they suggested you had acted without my knowledge or against my will, statements made by me with your permission – statements whose falsity the world was able to understand and forgive – statements made solely under conditions of extreme and unspeakable coercion. Well. But there always has been a good number of imbeciles who, incapable of imagining the deadly weight of this yoke, of this mawkish and gilded cruelty, took my false accusations as the gospel truth, with a view, perhaps, to ruining your reputation with unjust criticism. I have cost you dearly, and this pains me, and my second soul, Madame de Proyart, will never forget your merits and your sufferings in all this ambiguous and delicate situation.

To conclude this interminable letter, I shall talk of money and I shall ask you a few questions. I hope that the entire sum (of money) is kept somewhere under your protection. I am infinitely grateful to you for this and I beg you to see that everything continues in this way. The fact that I am completely lacking in curiosity regarding the various details and how much it all amounts to must not amaze or hurt you, almost as if my attitude were a form of indifference. Truly I have no desire to know all these things, as I do not dare and have no right or chance to think about them effectively. I think that only in a hypothetical case, and that is if they wanted to starve me out, would I decide to avail myself of an official remittance of cash from abroad. The financial authorities would have agreed to this deposit in foreign currency, but for the rest of my life I would have been poisoned by the perpetual accusation of treacherously keeping myself on foreign capital.

But I want to begin using this money in another way. With your help and permission I want to make some small pecuniary gifts, by bank order, to some persons. Here is the list (of names and sums); I pray you transfer:

1. Ten thousand dollars to my younger sister Mrs Lydia Slater, 20 Park Town, Oxford, England.
2. Ten thousand dollars to my elder sister Josephine Pasternak (to the address of my younger sister, in the event of your not being able to find that of Josephine).
3. Ten thousand dollars to Mme Jacqueline de Proyart, 21 rue Fresnel, Paris XVI.
4. Ten thousand dollars to Mlle Hélène Peltier-Zamoyska, Maison St-Jean by St-Clar-de-Rivière, Haute Garonne, France.
5. Five thousand dollars to Mr Michel Aucoutourie.
6. Five thousand dollars to Mr Martinez (ask Mme de Proyart for both addresses).
7. Five thousand dollars to the Italian translator Pietro Zveteremich. Mr Feltrinelli knows his address.

8. Ten thousand dollars to Mr Sergio D'Angelo, via Pietro d'Assisi 11, Rome.
9. Two thousand dollars to Mr Garritano, to be paid in Italy or at his temporary domicile in Moscow.
10. Five thousand dollars to Max Hayward.
11. Five thousand dollars to Mrs Harari (the two English translators, whose English address can be had from Collins).
12. Five thousand dollars to the Danish translator Ivan Malinovski in Copenhagen, at the address of Gyldendal publishers.
13. Five thousand dollars to Reinhold V. Walter, care of S. Fischer Verlag.
14. Five thousand dollars to Mr Karl Theens, museum director, Stuttgart-Degerloch, Albstrasse 17, Germany
15. Five thousand dollars to Mme Renate Schweitzer, Berlin West 30, Marburgerstrasse 16.
16. Five thousand dollars to John Harris, 3 Park Road, Dertington, Totnes, Devon, England.
17. Ten thousand dollars to Gerd Ruge in Germany.

I end this letter in great haste. A thousand thanks to you

Yours B. Pasternak

As had happened before, this letter never reached its destination and remained in Mme de Proyart's personal archive. For what reason? Perhaps, yet again, Jacqueline de Proyart was not entirely satisfied or was not prepared to settle for second best. Pasternak had hinted at the prospect of her playing a specific role in the management of his literary estate. But, now, her role was described in a rather confusing and embarrassing way, without the necessary clarity. Her position might still be misinterpreted as that of a mere confidante regarding matters of taste or critical selection.

This time, Mme de Proyart expressed her point of view to Pasternak. He agreed to let the letter drop, and said he would write another. Feltrinelli was to learn about de Proyart from de Proyart herself, without any prior intimation from Pasternak.

D'Angelo, by then back in Italy, on bad terms with the PCI and briefly employed at Feltrinelli, was in touch on his own account with de Proyart and with Pasternak himself, thanks to the Moscow correspondent of *l'Unità*, Giuseppe Garritano, who was also one of the beneficiaries on Pasternak's list. Incidentally, one of the reasons for the non-arrival of the letter of 2 February might have been a last-minute intervention on the part of Olga Ivinskaya, a move requested by Garritano himself, who was perhaps afraid of something and wanted nothing to do with the list.

The feeling was that a lot of things were happening without Feltrinelli's knowledge.

Unaware of these goings on, Feltrinelli received a letter from Jacqueline de Proyart. She presented herself formally, complete with power of attorney, claiming to supervise 'all the rights' to Pasternak's works in the West. Amazed, Feltrinelli could do little else but write once more to his author. He did this on 16 February 1959, having made a brief return to Italy from the USA.

From then on, the courier most frequently used to pass correspondence on to the poet was Heinz Schewe, the Moscow correspondent of the German daily *Die Welt*. Ruge, who is mentioned in the following letter, is Gerd Ruge, a correspondent with German television and a colleague of Schewe's, who was also involved in this kind of mission.

Dear Pasternak, dear Friend,
Last month I tried to reach you in all kinds of ways, but in vain, all efforts failed; now I have found a new way, and I hope this letter may reach you.
Months have gone by since my last letter, months full of anxiety and life, sorrow and admiration, humiliation and joy.
Following the political free-for-all that has livened up these last few months, *Doctor Zhivago* is still being read

by thousands and hundreds of thousands of people all over the world, and continues to be appreciated for its worth, and for all that it is capable of giving and teaching humanity. Recently, Ruge brought me news of you, he told me that you are in good health, and that made us feel easier. Dear friend, look after yourself. We have just published the *Autobiography*, of which I am sending you a copy. Only after its publication did I come to know of a certain Madame de Proyart, who informed me that you apparently wish to have only the second version published, with a different ending.

Alas, the version you delivered to me was the first one, and before now I never received any instructions regarding your preference for the second, which has been published by Gallimard.

And with regard to Madame de Proyart, I must confess to you that it came as a sore blow to me when I learned of your having nominated her your representative for Europe, without a word to me, when for a long time I was the one who in practice had the honour and responsibility of representing you. For reasons I quite fail to comprehend, Madame de Proyart has thought to declare herself only now, all but reproving me for not knowing what she herself has concealed from me for a long time.

I have borne all sorts of humiliation without batting an eyelid, but this last blow is the hardest of all to take. I have conducted, I think, all the various publishing operations, with their considerable burden of responsibility, in conformity with your instructions, or, when these were not available, in the spirit of your wishes. Now, to find myself bereft of your trust, of the support of your authority, is an unexpected surprise, and an extremely painful one.

Madame de Proyart is causing me many problems with regard to the *Autobiography*, which you entrusted to me and for which, even though we have been unable to draw

up a contract, I felt responsible, handling its publication
in several countries, as I did with *Doctor Zhivago*. As a
matter of fact, Mme de Proyart is calling into question
everything I have done, hindering me and threatening
me with legal action regarding ventures undertaken
before she declared her position. She is demanding that I
hand over all contracts to her. Agreed, I will do so, if this
is your wish. I wonder, dear friend, why I must be
threatened and treated like a fraud by Madame de
Proyart. This too is a humiliation I do not think I
deserve.

But, dear friend, I ask you to explain once more the
following points, on which your thinking, even in the letters to Madame de Proyart, is not clear:

1. Can the Russian-language editions of *Doctor
   Zhivago*, one in Europe and one in America, be considered as included in the contract we stipulated for
   this work?

2. With regard to the profits deriving from the editions of *Doctor Zhivago*, what are your wishes? That
   I entrust them to Madame de Proyart, that I hold
   them for you here or in Switzerland, that I have
   them sent to you by diverse means and in what
   annual quantity, or that they be held and managed
   in common by me and Madame de Proyart?

3. Our contract for *Doctor Zhivago* does not contemplate the rights for a film version. What is your
   wish? Do you want a film to be based on it? (In this
   case, please, sign the letter herein enclosed and send
   it back to me [document no. 1]). I am of the opinion
   that a film version could be made in one or two
   years' time, but this is up to you, I cannot know
   what your wishes may be. What percentage would
   you want? The same as for the translations of
   Doctor Zhivago? Do you have sufficient faith in me
   to leave me sole control over production? (I shall
   not conceal the fact that any collaboration with

Madame de Proyart would lead only to disaster:
there is nothing like incompetence for spoiling all
ventures.)
Dear Pasternak, I am saddened at having to subject
you to commercial questions, and at boring you with my
worries and my anxieties, but it is indispensable for me to
know your opinion.
Dear friend, let me know all you need and desire.
I am, as ever, your friend.

Giangiacomo Feltrinelli

P.S. In any event, it is necessary for you to sign the letter
of attorney herein enclosed (document no. 2), which is
indispensable if I am to be able to take more effective
action against all arbitrary initiatives.

So sign both documents, if you would be so kind, and
send them to me, along with your wishes and your opinions.

Giangiacomo Feltrinelli

P.S. Please send your reply to Olga. Mr Schewe will
come to collect it in a week's time.

The two enclosures for signature were a letter of clarification
regarding the rights to *Doctor Zhivago* and a letter of attorney
for the cinema. There was talk of two projects for a film version
of the novel, but neither Feltrinelli nor de Proyart had power of
attorney. In this case, too, Feltrinelli had to call on his lawyers
to nip the film plans in the bud. Without clear instructions,
the copyright could not be defended for long. But Pasternak,
for the time being, did not sign.

For the first time, Feltrinelli had to face the issue of relations
with Paris. He must have pondered for a long time over the reasons for Pasternak's recent decisions regarding de Proyart: what
were they up to? Why nominate a new agent? Probably, thought
Feltrinelli, Pasternak has faith in de Proyart, and in her attorney husband. He could communicate with them at no risk, and

then she spoke to the poet as an expert in Slavonic studies, asking his advice on the philological aspects of the various translations, and so, of course, she was good for the 'need for taste, for rigorous selection, and critical competence'. But was this enough to subvert a perfect relationship between publisher and author?

As the correspondence reveals, it is hard to think that Pasternak was dissatisfied with the management of his contracts. Not even from an economic point of view. He knew that his earnings were in the West and that it would be difficult to dispose of them at that time. Publishers from all over the world were paying his royalties into a Swiss bank. *Doctor Zhivago* was by right an 'Italian' book, but one whose contract could neither be shown nor officially registered in Italy: it would have been the proof that Pasternak had made a deal directly with a foreign publisher. For this reason, Feltrinelli required foreign publishers to pay royalties into the Swiss account, while he did the same for the author's share of Italian sales.

In the meantime, Schewe had become the most reliable middleman for the cash consignments to Moscow, the ones whose receipts were initialled by Pasternak or Olga. Their principal source of income derived from the roubles furtively purchased in some north European port.

But let's get back to Madame de Proyart. While she had a sincere concern for anything that might encourage or help Pasternak, her behaviour betrayed signs of an overweening ambition. For example, she thought she could do a job about which she knew nothing better than anyone else. By superimposing herself over Feltrinelli in the management of the rights to the *Autobiography* she caused bewilderment among Pasternak's publishers. Her activism also concealed some obscure points, like the role she had played in the business of the pirate Russian-language edition distributed at the Vatican stand at the Brussels Expo. This edition was subsequently adopted by the University of Michigan Press, complete with numerous typos that Pasternak was to complain about to the Italians.

It is worth remembering that de Proyart had not forwarded

to Feltrinelli the letter that Pasternak had sent a year before, the one containing the reference to the edition published by Mouton. Both parties were unaware of de Proyart's failure to deliver the letter. Feltrinelli had to bend over backwards to establish, at the last minute, his copyright on an illegal and certainly imperfect edition; in his turn, Pasternak thought that Feltrinelli had not followed his instructions for the Russian-language edition of the book. On the strength of the author's trust, de Proyart had played things her way and, as the Italians strongly suspected, perhaps on behalf of others.

In mid-February of 1959, the problem of relations with de Proyart suddenly worsened: alarmed publishers called in from all over the world. Five days after his last letter, Feltrinelli again wrote to Pasternak.

Milan, 21 February 1959

Dear Friend,
The more I think of the situation that has been created following Mme de Proyart's position, the more I am filled with consternation. Today's telephone call from Kurt Wolff in New York – amazed and indignant about what has happened as a consequence of the power of attorney you have conferred upon Madame de Proyart – has persuaded me of the necessity to appeal directly to you requesting you to revoke automatically all powers vested in Madame de Proyart by signing enclosure no. 1 and adding the title of the *Autobiography* in your own hand. All must be signed in the presence of Ruge or Schewe, who must be asked to countersign the above-mentioned documents (without forgetting the date).

Dear friend, I imagine that, by conferring the mandate upon Madame de Proyart, you meant to do only good, but in all honesty allow me to tell you that the thing has had some highly negative effects.

I would advise you not to take similar initiatives in the future. If you wish me to pay the lady money, tell me the amount, and I shall do so.

You have attained a position of universal esteem and now much caution is required both in business and in making statements to the press.

In my opinion, you can have faith in two people, Ruge and Schewe, and if one day they should no longer be in Moscow I shall always manage to establish a contact with you. In case of emergency, have someone you trust take a letter addressed to me to the Italian Embassy: it will reach me in a few days.

Dear friend, forgive my frankness. Let me know what you need. Make no statements to the press regarding your next books. If you are writing, write. Then, we shall see.

If I could come to Moscow I should like so much to embrace you, and chat with you and explain so many things to you. Yet I feel that one day this will be possible.

Giangiacomo Feltrinelli

The correspondence between author and publisher was getting in a tangle, above all because of the unpredictable amount of time required for transmission and delivery. The letters for Pasternak were sent to Schewe's office in Germany and thence, through a kind of diplomatic bag, to his home in Moscow. Finally, Schewe would take them to Olga.

In early April, when Pasternak rewrote the letter of 2 February (the one that had remained in Paris), it seemed as if he had not yet received the letters sent by Feltrinelli on 16 and 21 February.

Dear, great, and noble friend,
The despondency that has accompanied me of late has now been compounded by the great sorrow caused me by the suspicion that my letter of January, addressed by me to your good lady mother, the admirable and marvellous Giannalisa Feltrinelli, has gone astray somewhere and cannot now be found. At this time I could not restore the contents to you and this is not even necessary. I shall

merely repeat my warmest thanks, expressed in the vanished letter to your good lady mother for the honour she
generously desired to make me with her felicitations of
last autumn; also, I shall express my gratitude to you,
Sir, for your long and sweet letter in two languages (half
in French, half in English), for your generosity, for the
sentiments you have nurtured for me, and for all you
have suffered on my account (ignoble accusations of
imaginary non-performance that worked to my detriment or of sham negligence, which you have had the
goodness to simulate), for everything, for everything.
You are well aware that I am hindered in my affairs to
the point of paralysis, that I can neither take any decision
concerning them, nor keep up a correspondence, that my
hands are tied in my attending to them from a distance
and even in my taking an interest in them. In such conditions of complete separation from me – you have acted
with supernatural infallibility, like some divinity of fate,
I have no reproaches to make you if not for the fact of
your having spoiled me and dazzled me with your splendid, inexhaustible successes. If I may be granted the
right to dream or hope of surviving, I would like to
imagine a completely different period, two or three years
hence, calmer, more joyful and tolerant, in which I
should be able to forget *Doctor Zhivago*, supplanted and
put to flight by three new works, regarding which I
should deal first with you through a completely free and
licit exchange of letters, or better still, by meeting you in
the flesh during my trips to Europe.

I have determined to write 1) a theatrical piece in
prose on the serfs on the eve of their liberation; 2) a
poem on the theme of love and freedom, personified by
some Serbian female figure (instinctive appetites, a lover
of independence, the mountains, the sea, the world of
the Adriatic, with a hint of the style of Mérimée); 3) a
novel on the way the ancient and the contemporary world
are interwoven, set in the early days of our era

somewhere in the Iberian peninsula and in some imaginary excavations in the Caucasus. (You could encourage and give your blessing to the venture by sending me material, books on points 2 and 3, so that I may know more about the Yugoslavian situation and on the topic of archaeological digs – life, events, documents, interesting and dramatic ideas, and by passing on to Fischer and Collins this same request for published sources.)

In the meantime, the singularity of the current situation has created, together with my relations with you, other relations, which are in no way deleterious either to your rights or your interests, or to my esteem for you, but which are none the less just as important and respectable.

Your fine Russian-language edition of the novel abounds with errata, of which a considerable part probably could have been avoided if the text had been edited by Madame de Proyart, who knows the work well, not only because as a Slavonic scholar she had a hand in the French translation of the work, but also because she still has in her possession manuscripts revised and corrected personally by me.

It is an entirely natural consequence of our meetings if Madame, who is now familiar with the projects I have discussed with her and the written texts I have entrusted to her, has taken on this burdensome responsibility and has gradually become my ever more exclusive and plenipotentiary agent. In all this there is no trace of offensive preference to the detriment of any other friend of mine, or of discontent or disapproval in anyone's regard. I wish that during this lengthy period in which it has been impossible for me to act, exercise an influence over things, choose, keep up a correspondence, enjoy the fruits of your business activity and my ideas; during this period in which not only am I unable to know the results of all these things but am even unable to want to know about them, I want your two functions, yours and that of Madame, to be clearly and efficaciously separated. I want you to continue to profit from your contract regarding the novel in translation (which is doubly advantageous for me, both in a moral and a material sense) and that you may profit from all new agreements you intend to make with the consent and approval of Madame de Proyart.

I want you to see Madame as my stand-in, I want her to act in my stead as far as regards your accounting needs, for decisions regarding the allocation of funds or consultations about new ventures. Because for the time being (which is destined to last for a long time to come) I do not exist, either for her, or for you, you must forget that there was a man with this name, you must delete it from your memory.

These were my intentions when I wrote you the letter enclosed herein. I enclose it, recopied word for word in my own hand, along with the letter I am about to write and send to Mme de Proyart. Believe in my devoted gratitude. I owe you so much! All might have gone differently, were I not deprived of the most elementary liberties.

B. Pasternak

P.S. (very important) In the letter addressed to you that went astray, there was a list of sums and of persons to whom I wanted to send said sums as a gift (including ten thousand dollars to Sergio D'Angelo, ten thousand that I now correct to fifteen thousand, to Gerd Ruge, etc., etc.). Fortunately a copy of this list reached Madame de Proyart and is now in her hands. Do not hinder and do not delay these dispositions, dear sir. I wish the donations to the various persons mentioned to be made as soon as possible. Mr S. D'Angelo has offered me material assistance in the extreme event of my finding myself at my wits' end. Perhaps I shall be obliged to take advantage of his offer, but he shall have to consult Mme de Proyart about this, in accordance with the certification

herein enclosed, without troubling you with this problem. B.P.

Enclosed along with the letter was the following statement,
dated 4 April 1959:

I have the honour of confirming, dear sir, that I have
assigned to Madame Jacqueline de Proyart de
Baillescourt full control over the management of all my
royalties and likewise control over the cash transfers I
shall request of you. In my absence, please be so good as
to account to Madame de Proyart for all my royalties,
including those of the novel. I confer upon Madame de
Proyart – or upon whosoever she may wish to designate
in the event of her decease – freedom of disposition.

B. Pasternak

Feltrinelli must have feared the worst on reading these
instructions. He did not understand Pasternak's behaviour. If
only they could meet! In these cases, distance distorts things so
much it muddles up one's ideas.

But the real point, perhaps, was that Pasternak no longer
wanted to know about contracts; and the idea of creating an
alter ego to whom everything might be delegated, while it could
not stand up in practice, was an expedient through which he
thought to simplify his life. Mme de Proyart's hyperprotective
ambition completes the picture: while she saw things differently from Feltrinelli, and she certainly did not understand
him, she was none the less the poet's confidante.

In the summer of 1959, it became necessary to come to terms
with her. Feltrinelli harboured profound doubts, although he
made a virtue of necessity.

The parties met in Milan on 21 July and Feltrinelli sent off
an update to Schewe, who was in constant contact with
Pasternak. Under pressure from de Proyart, a 'theoretical'
agreement was reached on the Russian edition of *Doctor
Zhivago*. It was also agreed that the international contracts for

the *Autobiography* would end up in her hands. The de Proyarts produced the list of the gifts of money enclosed with the famous letter that was never delivered. Feltrinelli ordered the bank to pay out the 120,000 dollars in favour of the persons nominated by Pasternak, but temporized over the delivery of the contracts. The publishing houses of half the world, led by Kurt Wolff, were worried about an eventual changing of the guard in the management of Pasternak. Feltrinelli played for time: 'I am still awaiting a signal from our mutual friend,' he wrote to Schewe. 'Mr Pasternak begs you to have a little patience. He will reply to you soon. Do not lose patience and do not doubt him,' replied Schewe at the end of July.

Almost without anyone's noticing, it was already high summer.

* * *

I met Schewe in July 1994. He is a seventy-two-year-old who has aged well. We met in Vienna, where he lives. Judging by his appearance, you would take him for a clerk. But he spent a lifetime as a correspondent in some of the world's greatest capitals: London, Moscow and Jerusalem. He could be defined summarily as a down-to-earth journalist of the old school, a Cold War veteran. He must have practised his profession with a profound dedication to his newspaper. Now, in retirement, with five years of economic survival left, or at least so he said, he led an apparently solitary, secluded life. When I went to visit him, I didn't have the courage to ask him if he had a family, a wife, friends; but if he had, I would be surprised.

Schewe did not hide his nostalgia for the period in his life that began in April 1958, when the publisher Axel Springer sent him to the Soviet Union as a correspondent with *Die Welt*. 'If I played a part in the Pasternak affair, it was thanks only to Feltrinelli, who needed a safe contact in Moscow, and Springer gave my name to Inge, Feltrinelli's wife.'

Olga Ivinskaya describes him with affection in her autobiography, speaking of him as a 'trusted and devoted' friend, able to mitigate tensions even when the temperature was rising fast, and Schewe, for all those years, remained very attached to Olga and her daughter, Irina. Of Feltrinelli he says: 'He was all I wanted to be and was not.' Of Pasternak, he recalls the encounters in Olga's house, over the hill, where the poet would arrive emerging from the wood: 'It's as if I could see him now. He would come toward us almost at a run, until he was breathless, and he would embrace us and he would be the only one to talk (with me, he spoke splendid German with a Marburg accent), and he would tell us all he had seen, heard, or received.'

I got straight to the point and asked him about that 1959: what was going through Pasternak's mind? And the Feltrinelli–de Proyart dispute? 'The atmosphere surrounding Pasternak and his family became explosive after the Nobel. Living conditions became incredibly harsh when they deprived him of any chance of earning. What's more, there were the press campaigns, the police surveillance, and the permanent fear of making a mistake.' This picture was made worse by the poet's *naïveté*: 'He was a real child, incapable of disappointing or saying no to all those who, perhaps even in good faith, attempted to climb aboard the *Zhivago* bandwagon . . . Olga had to protect him all the time.'

The journalist has a clear recollection of the rumblings of the coming turbulence between Feltrinelli, de Proyart and Sergio D'Angelo. Pasternak suffered on this account: 'He was a generous man, not greedy at all. In his serene moments, when he was not afflicted by depression, he used to joke about the money he had outside the Soviet Union and, like a real Russian aristocrat, he liked to make presents, always with the impulsiveness of a young boy.'

And the roubles smuggled into Soviet territory, what did Schewe remember about that?

I took in sums on Feltrinelli's behalf, seven or eight times, for a total of about a hundred thousand roubles. Obviously this involved the risk of arrest and heaven knows what else, even though I sometimes had the impression that my guardian angels let me get on with it, considering that, out of caution, I never took in sums that were too large at any one time . . . I think that Ruge also made cash deliveries in Feltrinelli's name.

At a certain point, Pasternak and Ivinskaya thought of getting Olga's daughter Irina out of harm's way by having her marry a Westerner, thus guaranteeing her the right to leave the country. Irina could have married Schewe himself; but, although she was fond of him, she would not hear of it.

* * *

'It is a great sorrow for me that F. and J.P. have not found any common ground,' wrote Pasternak to his French friend Hélène Peltier on 21 July 1959. The total power of attorney conferred upon de Proyart failed to remove the burden of the management of his works from the poet's shoulders. For his part, Feltrinelli was champing at the bit as he felt he had been penalized without reason. 'I am for all of his projects, I would never refuse him anything,' Pasternak confided to Peltier. But now signing the documents sent from Milan in early spring (he had finally received them) meant annulling the prerogatives granted to de Proyart.

Olga gave the clear impression that she was on Feltrinelli's side. Schewe quotes one of her comments: 'Giangiacomo's arguments express what I have been thinking and saying for goodness knows how long.'

The situation was distracting the poet from what really mattered to him, his writing. Finally, he screwed up his courage and wrote to my father and also to de Proyart. From then on, Feltrinelli and Pasternak carried on their correspondence in German.

Early August 1959

Dear friend,
Contrary to my habit of writing to you in French, this

time I am writing in German, because this missive will
be read by our mutual German friend, who in this way
will be better able to judge the clarity of my text,
together with the sense and the usefulness of my decisions. My friend, I owe you and Madame de Proyart
exactly the same apology. The confusion I have created
around you and between you is an insult to Madame as it
is to you. Of all this I am guilty, both with regard to
Madame and to you. I have no need to give you new
proof of my unlimited faith, of my esteem and admiration. Today more than ever, I am prepared to repeat:
granted that I am in some way the one who wrote the
novel, you are and remain the sole creator and artifice of
its pilgrimage around the world, of its destiny and of its
success. Must I perhaps again add how great and spontaneous my enthusiasm and gratitude for all this must be
and is? I have no wish to deny the fact that I received
your letter and the contract almost a month past. Forgive
me for the delay, with which I have probably caused you
profound vexation. Forgive, too, the sincerity with which
I now make my confession to you with open heart. I have
put off terribly reading your mail because I expected that
it would procure me worries far greater than those I
effectively encountered on leafing through it today – but
things went in such a way that at the same time, roughly
a month ago, I finally got started on a work that seemed
about to see the light at that very time – and I dared not
run the risk of putting to flight with gloomy thoughts the
work that had barely begun, before it had firmly rooted
itself in my existence. I want to sketch in the scope of
this letter right away. It will not be possible to exhaust all
the arguments here. I have an hour left in which to finish
this and in which to dash off a few lines to Madame de
Pr. My efforts of today must therefore be aimed solely at
ensuring that we may both rest easy in spirit once more.

   That you are not just a business genius but have also
shown yourself to be a gentleman whose feelings for me

are cordial and disinterested is also known to Mme de
Proyart, who will never deny this. When, two years ago,
I began to confer full powers upon Madame, I did not
mean by that to limit my trust in you. You certainly
cannot have thought such a thing! But which of us could
have imagined then that the world would have shown
such great interest in us? Would it not have been ridiculous presumption on my part if I, already at that time,
had burdened you not only with the contract for the
novel but also with an infinity of other commitments? It
was not possible to foresee so much success (from a commercial standpoint, not from that of my secret *amour
propre*). This is why I delegated Mme de Proyart to take
care of the *Autobiography*, of the novel in Russian, and
the poems, etc. – in the sense of an additional task to be
seen as complementary to my relations with you, and not
as my imposing a limit or a barrier upon you.

The part that follows is addressed partly to you, and
partly to Mme de Pr. You will understand the reason for
this at the end.

I have reread Feltrinelli's letter. I was wrong. He is not
threatening anyone with anything. It is my duty to
defend him. He had no recourse to such low methods.
But he is right. I have confused the issue beyond measure and I stand guilty before him and above all before
you. Forgive me, therefore, both of you.

What are my wishes? (The same ones as ever, but for
brevity's sake I shall not talk of the past and shall limit
myself to the present and the future.) I want the marketing of my present and future works to enjoy success
abroad without let or hindrance, in all forms of editions,
original and translated texts, adaptations for cinema and
radio, etc., etc., and I want this marketing operation to be
set up, managed, directed and supervised by Mr
Giangiacomo Feltrinelli of Milan, my principal

publisher. For this reason, therefore, I agree to all the
ideas and proposals made by him and drawn up in contractual form, despite the fact that I am legally unable to
sign contracts, this being one of the many states of
necessity in view of which I delegated Madame de
Proyart to be so kind as to act in my stead with her
authority, her advice, her reputation and her signature.
In standing in for me, in my eyes she has become a
person who has the same unconditional faith in Mr
Feltrinelli as I do, a sort of moral support for his ventures, always so remarkable and fortunate.

How did I see Mme de Proyart's role as my substitute?
I thought that if Mr Feltrinelli had had need of my opinion (of a consenting opinion, not a veto) he could have
asked Mme de P. If he (not I) found it useful for himself
to make me an annual statement of accounts, he could
have turned to Mme de Proyart, without even telling me
about it, given that at present all these issues are for me
impossible, inaccessible and indifferent. Finally, if Mr
Feltrinelli (he not I) wished to make deductions or payments in my favour (I have need of them), he ought to
consider Mme de Proyart as the proprietress, without
even informing me. May Madame forgive me the exigu-
ousness of the functions that I have reduced her
responsibilities to and the informal way I required her to
act in my stead, but it is a question of being Pasternak
for Feltrinelli, in the rare cases in which he may have
need of me, the way one needs another person when
one's own person is no longer enough.

My wish is that Madame de Proyart, with her goodness and her friendship for me, and Mr Feltrinelli, with
the strength of his experience, savoir-faire, talent for
inspired and fortunate ventures, and generosity, will constitute the two poles of this bifurcated plenipotentiary
mandate, or, should this be impossible, to kindly invent
some other system of power of attorney and regulation,
geared to the state of powerlessness in which I find

myself, which both must understand and which must
inevitably be respected.

[. . .]
Be so good as to copy all this part written in French for
Madame de Proyart, and send it to her at rue Fresnel,
Paris XVI. I wanted to do this myself, but the need for
haste is such that I cannot and I do not want the letter to
arrive late. One more thing. Nothing is needed here. Mr
D'Angelo's suggestion that he might help me was made
during an acute crisis, which now seems to have passed. I
can promise you nothing regular, nothing statutory. I
trust you more than I trust my conscience and my
memory. Nothing is recorded, and you will see no
receipts. If money arrives, it is used up and only the
gratitude that derives from it is not forgotten and grows.
All the rest slips my memory. But do not even think of
transferring everything here, it would be folly. Madame
de Proyart is there to help you with this. Accept, I pray
you, my feelings of deepest admiration, gratitude, devo-
tion, and friendship.

Yours B.P.

I am sending this without even rereading it.

This letter represents a final attempt to settle a dispute that
so far had resisted resolution. Feltrinelli, relieved by this recon-
firmation of Pasternak's faith in him, was convinced he had the
problem solved. He took a plane for Paris but, full of opti-
mism, he ended up by rebounding off the door of the de
Proyarts' home in rue Fresnel.

Milan, 25 October 1959
Dear, most esteemed Friend and Master,
I certainly take no pleasure in thinking back on these
recent days and on the, unfortunately fruitless, talks in
Paris! Mainly because I have the feeling that all these

complications deeply disturb and irritate you, and also because it seems to me that for the first time I have not managed to carry out a task entrusted to me by you. In any case, please forgive me if today – something I shall do again next week – I write to you on matters that I am the first to admit are rather distressing.

I have shown Mr Pr. the letter you addressed to me (of which I have sent you another photocopy), and I have done all I could to make possible the union you hoped for. I even committed myself, in accordance with the wishes of Pr., to ensure that: a) Madame de Proyart will have the right of veto over all ventures and negotiations regarding the performing rights (cinema, television, etc.) to *Doctor Zhivago*; b) and that I shall, naturally, provide Madame de Proyart with regular statements of the financial situation.

In exchange for this, I requested: a) a contract for the Russian-language edition of *Doctor Zhivago* (in accordance with our epistolary agreements); b) a contract regarding the subsidiary rights to *Doctor Zhivago* (with the above-mentioned limitations); c) a contract (in conformity with the contract already drawn up for *Doctor Zhivago*) for the *Autobiography*; d) a formal option for the marketing of your future works.

All this was opposed: lack of time in which to check out the documents, the absence (for the first week) of Madame de Proyart, and continual objections to the limitations of the powers of attorney mentioned in your letter, to the point that I began to feel certain that the de Proyarts did not want any agreement, until such time as they might try to trick you into contradicting what you have told me in your letters. At that point I broke off the talks.

This, unfortunately, is how things stand: there are two ways of viewing your power of attorney – your interpretation, expressed very clearly in the letter you sent to me, and that of de Proyart.

De Proyart's interpretation differs from yours not only in terms of the role and responsibilities held by the de Proyarts or by me concerning all publishing matters, but also in terms of the fact that the de Proyarts believe themselves to be, in my regard, not only your representatives, but also the 'proprietors' of all the rights. And in their capacity as 'proprietors', they deal with me with an eye to their own interests, respecting your will solely when your will coincides with their interests. *Please read the note at the end of the letter right away.** This state of affairs proves that the *pouvoir bifurqué* you bargained for does not and cannot work! The task you entrusted me with, to see to the marketing of your works in the West and to defend them from the attacks of speculators and pirates has been made impossible, or at least arduous, now and in future, by the power of attorney you vested in the de Proyarts. Impossible, because the Proyarts refuse to make available the contractual documents you prepared – arduous, because they understand nothing about publishing and the related legal problems (to become an attorney in the publishing field requires years of highly specialized training, of which Mr de Proyart has none).

If I am to continue acting as principal publisher, we need to find a completely different solution. I have talked at length about this with my attorney, Mr Tesone, dwelling in particular on your problems of security, on your wish to publish and market your works without let or hindrance all over the world, and on how we can respect our commitments to you in this regard. We have come up with certain ways and means that demand determined decisions on your part – but I shall go into all this in more detail in my next letter, on the basis of documents (which are in the course of preparation).

And now let's talk of other things!

Did you receive the books? Do the overcoat and pullover fit? What do you think of *The Leopard* and

Durrell's book? Your ideas and opinions interest me very much indeed. Can you read Italian?

I would so much like to introduce you to the work of one of our young Italian writers. At present there are no translations of Testori, and I also fear that the best parts would be lost in translation.

What is new and important today in Russian literature? Could you let me know something about this? There is a possibility that I may come to Moscow with an Italian state delegation, within the ambit of cultural exchange agreements due to be endorsed by Italy and the USSR in the near future. I have already taken the first steps in this direction. Do you think that, once I get to Moscow, I may come to visit you, or will you be obliged at that very moment to accept an invitation to the Caucasus? Forgive me for the lengthy epistle, but it was really necessary to say everything! Do not deny me your friendship. Your sincerely

Giangiacomo Feltrinelli

* The de Proyarts' attitude toward me is not the work of Madame de Proyart, but only of her husband who, being an attorney, is well aware where his interests lie. Madame de Proyart does not have so much as a smattering of legal matters and has to submit all negotiations and legal interpretations to her husband. That she is not wholly in agreement with her husband emerges from the following example: recently she showed me one of your letters that her husband had forbidden her to show me!

That year, Schewe had taken his vacation when the summer was already almost over and he did not go back to his job in Moscow until mid-October. He delivered a few presents to Olga and, as he talked with her, he realized it was a tricky moment. The matter concerned Schewe directly, given that a letter that Irina had sent to him, when he was on holiday, had been intercepted by the Soviet authorities. A couple of tough-looking men had visited Olga, leaving her in no doubt that Irina would do well to stay away from him.

That Schewe was under surveillance was beyond doubt. All foreign correspondents were; and he, in his improbable guise as a secret agent, was obliged to keep a low profile, without exposing himself to excessive risks or making any overly bold moves.

Schewe made haste to get in touch with Pasternak and on Sunday, 24 October, thanks to Olga's good offices, he obtained a meeting at the house in Peredelkino. Boris arrived in a rush, puffing from his exertions, but stayed to chat for a good three hours. 'I don't understand why my friends cannot reach an agreement, surely there must be a way . . .' he said, going straight to the point. He felt responsible for all those misunderstandings: 'I am too poorly versed in contractual matters'. He really did not know what to do, and was frightened by the idea of damaging one of the parties.

'The whole story', wrote Schewe to Feltrinelli, 'is causing him enormous bitterness, and is undermining his ability to concentrate on his work.'

Work consisted of a few translations from which he would have earned a little income. When Pasternak mentioned the theatrical drama he was thinking of writing, he struck Schewe once more as 'a man full of strength and expectations'. 'Even though here in Russia it will go the way of *Doctor Zhivago*,' he heard Pasternak say, 'they will hang on to the manuscript for an eternity, checking it over and over again, and in the end nothing will come of it.'

As far as possible trips abroad were concerned (there were rumours of a visa for Belgrade or Warsaw), Pasternak would hear none of it and Schewe advised Feltrinelli to forget any thoughts of adventurous encounters.

As far as Schewe was concerned, that Sunday in Peredelkino, with the sound of fresh snow being compacted underfoot, the important thing was Olga's determined stance in favour of Feltrinelli: 'She is one hundred per cent on our side, and is exerting all her influence over P.' Olga confided to Schewe that they were receiving a continuous flow of correspondence from France, drafts of documents, letters of intent for signature and also a copy of the Gallimard edition of *Doctor Zhivago*, complete with a dedication written by Madame de Proyart. All this *'Papierkrieg'* once more caused Pasternak to lose heart, and on Olga's advice, he imposed a four-week period of silence: thereafter, he did not reply to any further correspondence from Paris.

The time had come to make the right move and to take a chance: Feltrinelli wanted to clear things up, even at the cost of pushing Pasternak, and he sent off a new and definitive contract for signature. 'It is a last-ditch attempt on my part to come to an agreement and to spare Pasternak the alternative of having to choose between Madame Pr. and me,' he wrote to Schewe. He added: 'Since 1956 I have borne all the responsibilities and all the consequences, positive or negative alike, he cannot turn his back on me now.'

The text of the document drawn up by Tesone followed that of 1956 and, with a view to preserving the continuity of the original contract, the new one was back-dated. The new addition, as compared to the initial contract, concerned the film rights and a commitment regarding the author's future works. The remainder is made very clear in the accompanying letter.

Milan, 13 November 1959
Dear and most esteemed Boris Pasternak,
Doubtless you have no desire to deal at length with the Proyart–Feltrinelli dispute. And this is why I shall deal very briefly with that issue in this letter. I am enclosing a draft contract, which I pray you to sign, for the following reasons:

1. This is a contract to all intents and purposes complementary to the one signed by us in 1956. We have added some riders as per the instructions contained in your last letter dated August 1959.
2. The contract is to be seen within the purview of the power of attorney you conferred upon Madame de Proyart. Do not gainsay that power of attorney!

3. This contract will certainly be recognized by
   Madame Pr. (Unfortunately, your August letter was
   not deemed an authoritative statement of will, a fact
   that has caused the distressing present situation,
   which makes it necessary for you to intervene on all
   counts once again.)
4. This contract will prevent all further future misunderstandings with Madame Pr.
5. This contract does not mean choosing between
   Madame de Proyart and me (a choice that has
   struck me at times as ineluctable!) It involves no
   injustice or indelicacy in anyone's regard.
6. This contract integrates Madame de Proyart's
   power of attorney as far as the film rights are concerned. These rights are not included in her powers
   of attorney. In order to make a film, today or in
   twenty years' time, a contract must be signed by
   you, in the case in point, this contract.
7. I pledge NEVER to make this contract public, even
   in the event of legal disputes. The advantageous
   aspect of this contract lies in the fact that it enables
   out-of-court settlements for legal disputes that
   would normally require a lawsuit. Without this contract, in my capacity as representative of your
   interests, or with a view to defending your interests,
   I would inevitably have to appear before a court, or
   drag others into court. A public suit aimed at chal-
   lenging the power of attorney (which is less
   common in private bargaining) would put you in
   great difficulty. You might withdraw the power of
   attorney. If you do not do this, you will always be,
   as far as your government is concerned, fully
   responsible for every move made by the holder of
   that same power of attorney!!!
8. I would be very glad if I have managed to give you
   a clear picture of the situation and if I have persuaded you of the advantageous aspects of this

contract and of the need to sign it. Were things otherwise, I would be greatly saddened. I will not bore
you now with thousands of explanations. Warmest
good wishes,

Yours Giangiacomo Feltrinelli

This enervating and staccato correspondence was made more
complex by the arrival of a new letter from Pasternak, who had
not received the last two from Italy. This letter has been lost (it
was not in the safe), but it must have brought good news:
Feltrinelli was extremely happy about it. He took pen and
paper to write a reply, perhaps a little on the sentimental side.

Milan, 19. 11. 59

My dear Boris Pasternak,
You cannot imagine how much joy your latest letter has
given me! (It crossed mine in the mail.)

I am glad about what you say about yourself and your
work, even though unfortunately the underlying tone of
your letter was extremely sad and depressed. It gave me
enormous pleasure to learn that you are once more concentrating on a great work and that in future you will no
longer have to do translations. Naturally I shall send you
regular 'deliveries' through our friend H. But may I be
permitted to advise you, for reasons of diplomacy, not to
neglect translations altogether?

I am waiting most anxiously for *Blind Beauty*; the title
is splendid. But it would be better if not too many people
knew about it at present, otherwise it might cause an
enormous song and dance and disagreeable publicity for
all of us, don't you think?

The things you say about the 'humiliating concessions'
you are obliged to make distressed me greatly. I am
proud of you and full of admiration, for the faith you
have in yourself, without lowering yourself to any compromise.

If only things here in the West could be organized in

such a way that you would have no further reason for sadness, or any need to worry about all these matters!

Unfortunately, my Christmas presents will not arrive until after the festivities, since our friend H. will return to M. only in early January. Please give him a list of ALL the books you are interested in. Wishing you all the very best, your most devoted

Giangiacomo Feltrinelli

* * *

On 5 November 1959, Schewe sent to Milan a close-up of Pasternak, taken at Peredelkino on Sunday 25 October. He thus fulfilled a promise. In exchange, Feltrinelli sent off a photo of himself and Inge for the poet. On that same Sunday at Peredelkino, photos were also taken of Olga and her daughter, but the two women thought they had not come out all that well. They decided to take other photos on the next occasion.

In the meantime, Olga had let slip important secrets that Schewe reported, within quotation marks, in his correspondence with Feltrinelli. Pasternak feared that the clash between Feltrinelli and the de Proyarts might lead to a trial and a public scandal. In the Soviet Union, his position was still hanging by a thread, the atmosphere surrounding him was only slightly easier and his finding himself once more publicly exposed for any reason might spark a new crackdown, perhaps a definitive one. Feltrinelli's reassuring letter of 23 November was not long in arriving, via Schewe: 'Under no circumstances shall I allow it to come to a trial between Mme de Pr. and me.'

Another secret was even more serious: '*Der Klassiker fühlt dass er älter wird*', or 'The Grand Old Man [which was Schewe's and Ivinskaya's nickname for Pasternak] feels that he is getting old'. 'He is often tired. He would like not to feel forever under the knout, always working on new translations to earn a few roubles. He would prefer to concentrate entirely on his idea for a theatrical drama. But he could only do this if he were completely self-sufficient.'

Schewe noted:

The Grand Old Man has recently received various proposals from people who have offered him large sums in
dollars, deriving from the income from *Zhivago*. They
have promised him they will convert these sums into
roubles and get them to him in Peredelkino one way or
another. Madame Olga had her say in the matter: 'I think
it would be better if everything were to remain exclusively in Giangiacomo's hands. We can trust him. We are
afraid of involving other people in this business. In any
case, they all want a share of the money!'

These words were transcribed for Feltrinelli and sent off,
together with the photograph of the 'Grand Old Man', on 5
November 1959.

In early 1959, Sergio D'Angelo had begun writing to
Pasternak, offering to help him gain immediate access to his
money. D'Angelo maintained that he could bring the money
into the Soviet Union without any risk. In September he had
written to Olga telling her of a meeting he had had in Paris with
Jacqueline de Proyart. She had suggested that he take the
money directly to Pasternak. D'Angelo advised Olga Ivinskaya
to ask for 100,000 thousand dollars, for any eventuality.

Now, on looking back, we need to judge as best we can what
happened. Fundamentally, it was a matter of helping an important friend, who had been reduced to living on a subsistence
level. Nevertheless, and such is the way of the world, some
people in Italy blamed Feltrinelli and Feltrinelli alone for the
extremely serious consequences of these circuitous goings-on.

That November, despite the fact that Feltrinelli had sent off
a few more 'sandwiches' (the word he and Schewe used to refer
to the consignments in roubles), and despite other 'sandwiches'
that were sent off immediately afterward, Pasternak decided to
accept D'Angelo's proposal. 'Thanks to his inner strength,'
comments Schewe today,

Pasternak had always thought he could live for three
hundred years, tolerating with ill grace birthdays,
bunches of flowers, and anything else that might remind
him of the passing of time. Perhaps, that very winter, as
he neared seventy years of age, after all the emotions, he
had realized he was coming to the end of his life. Such a
sensitive man could hardly have failed to notice that his
strength was ebbing. And so, living as he was in conditions of terrible hardship, and knowing that he could
draw on a great deal of money held abroad, he must have
thought 'let's have it here, as much of it as possible, now,
right away . . .' This would have already been tricky
under normal conditions, let alone in such a particular
moment.

> Peredelkino, by Moscow
> 6 December 1959
> I hereby delegate the undersigned, Mr Sergio D'Angelo
> to withdraw one hundred thousand dollars (100,000) of
> my royalties for the uses and purposes he shall communi-
> cate and explain to two other persons in whom I trust,
> Madame Jacqueline de Proyart and Mr Giangiacomo
> Feltrinelli.
>
> B. Pasternak

At the same time, the poet sent a request for ten thousand
dollars to be paid to D'Angelo. It is difficult to establish
whether or not this was a kind of commission for the hundred-
thousand-dollar operation. In the space of three months,
Feltrinelli transferred both sums to D'Angelo.

It may be useful, at this point, to attempt a purely economic
balance with regard to *Doctor Zhivago*, up to the point of
Pasternak's death. If we add the cash gifts requested by the
author in his letter of 2 February 1959 to the more recent payment made through D'Angelo, we get 235,000 dollars. To this
we need to add an unspecified sum for the purchase of roubles
to be transferred to Moscow. Considering that the initial sales

of the rights for Germany, Great Britain, and the United States ought to have brought in 150,000 dollars for publisher and author alike, it can be presumed that a good part of the rights acquired for the years 1957 and 1958 had been paid while Pasternak was still alive. Is this a lot? Is it a little? How much was a dollar worth in a market in which Stephen King and John Grisham did not exist?

Unfortunately, the author of the most adventurous and unexpected of best-sellers, at a time when best-sellers really were best-sellers, was able to enjoy only a derisory part of those profits.

* * *

Christmas 1959, as is only right, seemed to have brought a truce, at least in the correspondence between Pasternak and his publisher. In fact, the poet received an average of over thirty letters a day from all over the world and this distracted him from his theatrical work, also because he felt it was his duty to reply. Moreover, worried letters were arriving from Paris: the de Proyarts had probably sensed the danger of a new agreement between the author and Feltrinelli.

To sign or not to sign now became the real problem for Pasternak; on the one hand, his signature would have definitively cleared up a question that had been troubling him for too long, a problem he wanted to rid himself of; on the other hand, two further problems might have arisen. The first of these again concerned Madame de Proyart. There was a risk of disputes arising over the management of the mandate in the period in which she had acted as his agent. The second fear, in reality, was a source of great anxiety: if the new contract was binding for the author in future too, then there might have been a repetition of what had happened with *Doctor Zhivago*. For example, if the theatrical drama *Blind Beauty* were published, the Soviet authorities might have considered the fact a deliberate repetition of Pasternak's desire to deal directly with a foreign publisher. And this was certainly the harbinger of a new scandal. For the Soviets had come to know that a contract was lying on Pasternak's desk. How they knew, yet again, remains a mystery.

On his return to Moscow (with his 'sandwiches') after the end-of-year holiday, Schewe informed Feltrinelli, begging him to use all precautions in the exchange of letters and advising him, for the future, to set up 'safe' meetings, in some European city. 'In the corridors of power, and this is certain, they know that I am the middleman,' he said to him.

Pasternak and Olga were nervous too: 'They think that they are under surveillance and they are even afraid that there are microphones in the walls.'

Between the end of January and the beginning of February, there were many meetings at Peredelkino with Schewe and, despite everything, there were moments of great serenity. The poet's reassurances, which Schewe later sent on by letter to Feltrinelli, were clear. Feltrinelli was not to worry, Pasternak's faith in his publisher was undimmed; now it was his turn to propose a way of clearing matters up and, without a doubt, Feltrinelli could count on *Blind Beauty*.

But was he doing the right thing in signing the contract? Wasn't it too great a risk?

In the meantime, Pasternak signed it, then he preferred to wait and think it over.

On 20 January 1960, he wrote a new letter: he was tired of this situation that he was unable to resolve. I deduce from the correspondence with Schewe that, ten days later, Feltrinelli must have written to Pasternak. But, unfortunately, there is no copy of this letter either.

20 January 1960

Dear friend,

I have come to know of your new plans regarding the extension of my rights, the placing of the management of my literary affairs more firmly in your hands, and of the complete assignment of all that I have written and will write in the future. I agree. I was ready to sign the contract. I had even signed it when I suddenly noticed a problem. I approve of your idea of backdating the contract and of drawing it up in the form of a supplement. I am fully in agreement with this. I have no need of your reassurances, I know perfectly well that you would never abuse this simulation for the sake of form. But may it not be that one day, without your knowledge and against your will, that this backdating may lead to embarrassing consequences for a series of persons – Madame de Proyart first and foremost – because of a series of documents from the period between the backdating and the present time? Allow me to quote some passages from your letter.

2. The contract is to be seen within the purview of the power of attorney you conferred upon Madame de Proyart. Do not gainsay that power of attorney!

3. This contract will certainly be recognized by Madame Pr. (Unfortunately your August letter was not deemed an authoritative statement of will, a fact that has caused the distressing present situation, which makes it necessary for you to intervene across the board once again.)

4. This contract will prevent all further future misunderstandings with Madame Pr.

6. This contract integrates Madame de Proyart's power of attorney as far as the film rights are concerned.

etc., etc.

You are right on many counts. But organize things so that I come to know all this from Madame; in other words, sort out all these old problems in the light of this brand-new concept together with her; guarantee her a safeguard against all possible abuses of your supplementary clauses, indemnify her if there is any compensation to be made, royalties to be paid, or cases of non-performance regarding any obligation you or I may have toward her. In short, arrange things so that in the part concerning Madame your proposals will be acceptable to and desirable for the person who is my friend and agent and who (as you yourself will see immediately, at the end of this letter) is a nobly altruistic and valued ally in all circumstances. I shall write to Madame, so that she may know that my wishes correspond to yours, namely that I am wholly in favour of the clear-cut division of functions between the two of you and of the concentration of all ventures and of all effective powers in your hands. But do not forget that, once your new rights and your new ventures are under way, I shall not be setting up an office in my home in which to receive your letters containing even the slightest details of your activities, to take decisions or to reply to you. I will not be involved in anything. I must not be disturbed or prevented from working. But there will always be serious cases in which you will have need of my representative, my *alter ego*, who will need to be informed of something or other or whose opinion will be required. As far as I am concerned this *alter ego* can be none other than Madame, my agent, my deputy or substitute.

I hope with all my heart that all will now proceed in accordance with the spirit and the terms of your contract. Help me to ensure that it may be concluded. And (pray do not be offended) free me of the need to neglect my work and to write long letters. Yours,

B. Pasternak

In April 1960 Pasternak relieved Jacqueline de Proyart of her mandate as proxy, with attestations of extreme gratitude. Up to that month, *Doctor Zhivago* had sold 156,000 copies in Italy.

Schewe returned to Moscow in late spring and only then was Feltrinelli able to write the poet a different kind of letter, one that no longer touched on those issues that had risked ruining their relationship. Unfortunately, it was late in the day.

Milan, 15 May 1960
Dear, most esteemed Boris Pasternak,
Unfortunately, the absence of our mutual friend H. S.
these last few months has interrupted our correspondence. Naturally I now take the first opportunity to send
you with this letter, and also directly, through H. S., my
warmest greetings. I have many things to tell you. The
new Russian edition of *Doctor Zhivago* will be ready for
the end of the summer. The text has been revised by
Madame P. and it corresponds to the original manuscript,
which is in Paris. I hope you are in agreement. In conformity with the wishes expressed in your letter (in the
letter I received through D'Angelo), I have transferred to
our friend the same D'Angelo 100,000 dollars of your
royalties, and I hope that by now you have received this
sum, or at least a part of it. In any event, let me have,
through H. S., a few words of confirmation. This would
please me and put my mind at rest. *Doctor Zhivago* is
now selling slowly, but still steadily. In the fall it will
come out in a paperback edition, at the price of 700 lire
(instead of 3,000 lire for the hardback edition). We shall
be printing another 30–50,000 copies. For some time
now, a paperback edition has been circulating in
America. In Rome, a lawsuit is dragging on between two
film companies and us (it is a trial concerning the *Doctor
Zhivago* copyright).

As for other things, here it is spring, or better, already
summer. It is hot, people are thinking of the coming
holidays, at the seaside, in the mountains, or abroad.
There is fervent activity only here in the publishing
house. We are already working on the forthcoming
Christmas holiday, and in part on the spring 1961 schedule. Great literature is thin on the ground. At present in
England and in the USA everyone is talking about *The
Leopard* (the book I sent you at Christmas in the German
edition). In France, *Le dernier des Justes* (a book on the
persecution of the Jews) has been a great success. Camus,

the only representative of the in-between generation of whom one might have expected something, has unfortunately died in an automobile accident, as you will certainly have heard. The other great protagonists of the literary scene haven't produced anything particularly new. The young French writers of the *nouvelle vague* are trying to develop their school further – but they have run aground on a quasi-sterile experimental formalism, despite the fact that their early work represented a search for new themes. Something really new – the result of a combination of the evolved classical form with a content that goes further than the stereotyped 'I love you, you love another man, and the other man loves another woman who in her turn loves me unrequited' – is not to be found. In this, a highly negative role has been played by the French political scene, the endless colonial war in Africa, waged for years with unheard-of brutality, the internal divisions in France over the sense or the absurdity of this war, De Gaulle's taking of power and the rejection of the democratic system (De Gaulle himself has been unable to find an 'issue' in Algeria – *neither peace nor war*), the blackmail to which the whole of France is subjected by the army, which wants victory over the Africans and to impose its power over the metropolitan territory, all this has sundered the '*élan*', the backbone of youth. The Fourth Empire is the age of compromise, of money and intellectual poverty.

In Spain, where writers have been living for twenty years under the dictatorship of Franco and the Catholic Church, perhaps the novel is undergoing a phase of growth. After the great disappointment of 1945 (we all hoped that the end of the war would also be the end of Franco), the Spanish are rebelling once more and have found their 'outlet' (even though this is forbidden in their country) in literature. In Italy, there are two literary movements: the fundamental feature of the first is formalism, which leads to literary acrobatics, the other uses literature as the instrument of a sociological representation. Any attempt to write a novel with a hero, with ideas, with a treatment of the problems facing the individual, with a profound humanity, is rejected almost out of principle.

But all this talk has made me stray from the focal point of my letter. How are you and your family getting on? How is your health and your work? All of us are expecting so very much from you, and from your next work!!! With my warmest and sincerest best wishes,

Giangiacomo Feltrinelli

Not even a week was to go by and Feltrinelli found himself reading a news item that rocked him. Here is his reaction:

22 May 1960

My dear, most esteemed Boris Pasternak,
I had barely sent off my letter of the fifteenth, when I received, alas, a reply to my queries!!

I was deeply distressed to learn from the newspaper of your illness but my worry over your state of health was allayed somewhat by learning a few days later, again from the newspaper, that you had got over the crisis. I hope you are in good hands. Should you need a doctor from here, let me know right away, and I shall do everything to come to your aid. There is no need to add that, should you need medicines or goodness knows what else, you must not hesitate for so much as a second, and let me know immediately.

Do not deny me, I beseech you, the chance to be able to help you even in this most difficult moment.

A thousand good wishes and warmest greetings
Yours,
Giangiacomo Feltrinelli

Schewe did not manage to deliver this last letter; Pasternak was in hospital and died on 30 May.

In a letter to Jacqueline de Proyart, six months previously, Pasternak had expressed the wish that Feltrinelli might pay any price to keep his body out of the hands of the Soviet authorities. He wanted to be buried in Milan, where Olga would have watched over his grave. But the funeral was held in Peredelkino; the Italian publisher was *persona non grata* and there was no chance of a visa. Schewe went to the service. The reports of his standing silent and composed alongside the coffin strike me as plausible. To a colleague who had elbowed his way through the crowd, Schewe apparently said: 'Yes, I know, I am neither taking notes nor taking photographs . . . but I am burying a friend.'

Bombarded on all sides, Feltrinelli dictated a brief press communiqué: 'The death of Pasternak is a blow as hard as that of the passing away of a best friend. He represented the personification of my non-conformist ideals combined with wisdom and profound culture.'

Olga Ivinskaya gave the signed contract for *Doctor Zhivago* to Heinz Schewe and asked him to take it to Milan.

* * *

In 1959 Feltrinelli published translated versions of *The Rain King* by Saul Bellow, *Out of Africa* by Karen Blixen, *The King's Mother* by Kazimierz Brandys, *Aleph* by Jorge Luis Borges, *The Setting Sun* by Osamu Dazai, *The Ginger Man* by J. P. Donleavy, *The Promise* by Friedrich Dürrenmatt, *Howard's End* by E. M. Forster, *Homo faber* by Max Frisch, *The Habit of Loving* by Doris Lessing, and *Portrait of a Man Unknown* by Nathalie Sarraute . . . 'There was a moment in which Feltrinelli was an Italian publishing house only because its head office was in Milan. I don't think any other Italian publisher received perhaps more manuscripts from abroad than from Italy,' wrote Valerio Riva. And, more recently, Michele Ranchetti: 'We were a benchmark for all the publishers in the world, who looked to us to point the way forward.'

Toward the end of the fifties, Feltrinelli travelled the world and, with the exception of the Soviet Union, all doors were open to him. During a visit to London, the press talked of him as a 'miracle man'. A British journalist followed him from one appointment to another for an interview: 'I managed to talk to him only when he was dashing off to the Reform Club, where he made Sir Stanley Unwin wait for over twenty minutes. This is something that an English publisher would not easily allow to happen.'

But Doris Lessing received an invitation to breakfast at the Ritz: 'In those days, they had yet to invent the "working breakfast", but during the meeting we discovered that neither of us usually took breakfast. All we took was coffee and orange juice.' Feltrinelli told her of his problems with Pasternak's novel and said that he appreciated her books. Doris Lessing recalls: 'I was struck by his vitality. In fact vitality is often associated with celebrity.'

By the end of the fifties, Mr Feltrinelli was barely thirty-three and sported a big black moustache.

6

Now I am going to have a word with Ingelein. We understand each other straight off. I invite her to have a drink with me and I assume the tone my mother and I reserve for great occasions. She is ready to tell me many things. Her part is of decisive importance; a party to this story and one of its leading figures, she has never given in.

She has no trouble remembering the crucial moments, the encounters, the clashes, the journeys, who was there and who was not, the newspapers always full of news. In theory, I could start with the questions and take notes. In theory. But we can do without the charade. It's her thing, and when she wants, if she wants, she can do it by herself. Perhaps we have already talked about it during all those oblique moments spent together and now there is not much to add. Yes, I know, you need to struggle and to believe that nothing is impossible: with good luck and courage, there is no such thing as the impossible.

When did the sixties, so different, when people thought anything was possible, begin?

If the sixties were really the story of the magic carpet

(everybody talks about it, but only a few witnessed it landing on the doorstep), then I ought to say that I saw it. Someone briefly opened the door and a for a second I saw it. It was red, bright red, but maybe I had got hold of the wrong end of the stick, taken chalk for cheese. It would be nice to be able to understand times past but in reality there are only different times for people who are always the same. And, to tell the whole story: 'No period of past time is so unknown to us as the three, four, or five decades that separate our twenties from those of our father.' This, at least, was how an important Austrian author put it.

Clearly, the sixties began when the fifties were finally brought to a close (this may seem obvious, but it isn't). As far as Giangiacomo Feltrinelli was concerned, the sixties began in via Andegari, where he brought together family, business, the publishing house and also his important library: 'Here, in this old house, in the centre of Milan, where my father lived, to whom at this time my thoughts turn with infinite gratitude, for all the things he allowed me to do and to have done.' These were fitting words with which to inaugurate the premises of the Istituto Giangiacomo Feltrinelli. It was 25 March 1961. Alongside the Education Minister there was the empty seat reserved for Palmiro Togliatti, who was invited but was busy elsewhere.

On the birth of Carlo Fitzgerald Feltrinelli, the fourth floor was completely inundated with flowers. Even the bathrooms. It was a real party, and the cheering went on and on. From the Agnelli family to Pietro Secchia, half of Italy sent telegrams. Secchia also took the trouble to come in person. His friendship with my father dated back to the old days in politics.

The odd thing was that when Feltrinelli left the PCI he was considered to be a 'right-winger', but the man he stayed in touch with was Secchia, the 'hardliner' of the party, by now merely a senator. One might have suspected a strong political bond between the two, but as far as Feltrinelli was concerned, the internal life of the party was no longer of burning interest.

Contact with Togliatti was frequent but indirect (and concerned only the activities of the Institute), while Secchia was a friend and they saw each other from time to time.

Upon the conclusion of the customary round of congratulations, the 'strong man' of the Resistance movement confided in his secretary–chauffeur, who was waiting for him in the car: 'Goodness knows why they chose "Fitzgerald" as a middle name for their son. It can't have anything to do with the American president, can it?' After running through the few other Fitzgeralds he had any notion of, Secchia probably forgot all about it.

Enrico Filippini, a young German scholar destined for future success, felt that a wind of change was blowing through via Andegari, that something was changing. He was to speak of this in a scintillating society piece written a little later:

> One day the walls of the publisher's changed colour: they all became *fauves*, cadmium yellow, traffic-light red, dark green; perhaps Inge had a hand in this: the young man had understood that now one went about subversion in a different way and that gestures had to become more radical and less conventional [. . .]
>
> Economically speaking, being a publisher means having a lot of money at your command and being prepared to gamble with it, or not having any at all and wanting to make lots of it. In the second case, the results are often harmful to the public; the first case requires you to have at least some good reason, for example, a belief that culture is a very important thing, which is worth the effort of getting up every morning at murderous hours, working twelve hours a day, committing yourself to lunches discussions dinners discussions travel discussions and lunches, living with misfits and neuropaths, stirring up a bit of a social whirl, hitting the headlines . . . Culture: the classics, history, literature, psychoanalysis, psychiatry, economics, politics, history,

the classics . . . The beat generation, planning, the avant-
garde, the rearguard, the problem of race, neutron
physics . . . everything that happens in the deep
universe . . . Yet culture is not merely a massacre of
problems, a cemetery of concepts: culture is either the
stuff they taught us at or university or it is the new kind,
the kind that you make, the kind that attempts to dispel
the stagnant miasmas of the first variety. There is always
the risk that culture contains something subversive . . .
And so, watch out: the young man could be, is, a subversive [. . .]. He spends his days and sometimes even his
nights in a cadmium-yellow office full of books, ashtrays,
Mies van der Rohe armchairs for meetings, and photographs, drives his car at alarming speeds, spends weeks
aboard his yacht on the North Sea, Friday evenings he
leaves with his wife and son for a castle perched above
the village of Villadeati, and there he dreams up and dis-
cards book series, projects, contracts among hunting
trophies, a real Finnish sauna and a swimming-pool,
amid books on Italian history and books on sexology,
quality paperbacks and avant-garde novels, and magazines in four languages [. . .]
      The young man started his business in the gloomy
fifties, cold war, neo-realism, immobility, and at that time
he dressed as a neo-realist, a woollen vest and any old
shirt: *commitment* . . . His latest image is frankly better:
light-coloured clothes, striped shirts, stupendous ties . . .
And it is not a matter of fashion, it is a matter of
culture . . .

Feltrinelli was usually at work by seven thirty. It was a good
time to begin some letters or perhaps to hold briefing sessions
with his colleagues. The family apartment was on the same
floor as the office. 'At that hour the publishing house was
deserted and strangely silent,' recalls the philosopher Paolo
Rossi, 'whereas normally one was caught up in a highly charged
atmosphere.' The door of Feltrinelli's office was open and

visitors would find him not at his desk but in the armchair
beside the window (on the right as you went in). On the floor
there would be books, newspapers, mail, notes and an open
packet of Senior Service cigarettes.

In this room, when the offices were bustling with activity,
Tina would fix the rhythm of appointments. In early 1962,
more or less, Feltrinelli met with the critic Cesare Garboli to
work out the details of a contract for a new edition of Dante's
minor works that Garboli was to edit for the Universale
Economica series.

Garboli recalls the scene in his book *Falbalas*:

Feltrinelli was sitting on the other side of the desk, and
he was asking me about my work on Dante. 'And these
minor works, are they interesting?' I do not have a ready
wit, unfortunately. My instinct is to lend assistance, not
to strike. I think that the intention behind Feltrinelli's
question was to discuss or to examine the advisability of
reprinting works that were already so well known.
Moreover, the physical presence of a person, the event
that unfolds when we are in the presence of a person in
flesh and blood, in short the theatrical power of reality,
prevails, in me, over all other faculties and throws everything into crisis, I cannot defend myself; it is more
powerful, so to speak, than my mental strength; and I let
myself be invaded because it strikes me as fair to honour
reality and its sudden right to exist. For a moment, I
doubted that *Vita nuova*, the *Convivio* and the *De vulgari
eloquentia*, the works that are, in my view, the proof of
the existence of reality, nay, the proof of my very existence, were 'worth republishing', works worthy of
reappearing in public and of being readmitted to a cultural circuit. Never have Dante's minor works emerged
in such bad shape as they did from that meeting.

Something of the kind must have happened on other occasions. While many heard Feltrinelli talk competently about

books and culture, others like Garboli recall him as being 'thick as pigshit'. Colourful expressions aside, perhaps both versions hold some truth.

'Do you read a lot of books?' I once asked him toward the end of the sixties. He replied that he read plenty of them but not an excessive amount.

In an article for *King* magazine, Feltrinelli provided a few witty definitions of his business. He said that publishers can be defined in thousands of ways: that they are unlikely to change the world (A publisher cannot even change his publisher), that they must not take themselves too seriously, and that they have absolutely nothing to teach anyone. 'Publishers', he maintained, 'are handcarts, people who go around with the sign "printed pages for sale", they are conveyors of messages [. . .]. Knowing nothing, they must know everything, everything of use.'

The basic idea was that publishers must shoulder the responsibility of selecting what it is desirable for people to read, thereby providing 'necessary' books with an outlet. He felt that people who read are in any case richer than those who do not. They are more autonomous, can orientate themselves better, and there are many things that people ought to know about. The old décor inherited from the provincial academic tradition is not of much use, its wainscoting, its pompous and backward-looking erudition. New instruments and new languages are needed: 'because everything must and will change'.

But Feltrinelli was not some kind of publishing Barnum who chose books by leaping through a ring of fire. The famous morning sessions in the deserted office served to direct and plan series like the 'Philosophy of Science' library created by Ludovico Geymonat* in 1960; the 'Library of Clinical Psychology and Psychiatry' series directed by Gaetano Benedetti and Pier Francesco Galli; the 'Fisb' ('*I fatti e le idee. Saggi e biografie*') library; the 'Mathematics Series' inaugu-

---

* (1908–90). Professor of the History of Philosophy at the University of Milan.

rated in 1963 by Lucio Lombardo Radice and Edoardo
Vesentini; and the 'History of Science' library edited by Paolo
Rossi* and Libero Sosio. There were many innovative things
(consult the playlist!), Jacobin books guaranteed to shake
Italian readers out of their parochialism.

From the 'Philosophy of Science' to the 'History of
Science', on leafing through the catalogue between the two
series that were born at each end of the decade, one sees a
clear attempt to think of contemporary culture as an intrinsi-
cally scientific culture. But what fields of knowledge were
covered? Logic and mathematics, naturally, but also psychology, anthropology ('cold history' as opposed to 'hot history'),
'human sciences' and literature; that is, philology, linguistics
and semiotics.

In a preface to the famous book by Charles Snow, Geymonat
wrote:

> Today, no one can be so blind as to fail to realize that the
> existence of two cultures, as different and as far apart
> from each other as the literary–humanistic culture is
> from the scientific–technical culture, constitutes serious
> grounds for a crisis in our civilization; it marks a rift that
> grows deeper from day to day, and threatens to transform
> itself into a real barrier to comprehension, deeper and
> more pernicious than any other subdivision.

To narrow the gap between the 'two cultures' was, in brief,
the theoretical basis of the publishing plan.

'It was an adventurous "home-grown" operation,' says a witness who wishes to remain anonymous, 'piloted by enthusiasm,
without deference for tradition. Compared to other publishing
houses, Feltrinelli did not pursue a "cultural policy".'

It burned with its own fire.

* * *

* (1923–). Philosopher and professor of the History of Science.

In order to demonstrate my powers of memory, I have to talk about the four trees.

On the first, we would stay hunkered down and silent. There were deer all around and it was usually Christmas. I have spoken of this one already.

The second is a cedar of Lebanon over sixty foot high that has been happily flourishing since Napoleon's day. A lightning strike mangled its top, but this is merely an aesthetic problem; the bark is incredibly resistant. There are many things to be discovered beneath the cedar: animals' lairs, ravines, car racing tracks, hidden lives, roots that disappear into the ground. Where its shade ends, the lawn begins. The lawn is the English-style lawn of Villadeati, and in the summer the Bermuda grass runs wild. My father's nicotine-stained fingers would try to weed it out and I would help him with this absorbing task. I also used to tag along when he went into the vineyard for the grape harvest, or if there was a plant to be pruned, a greenhouse to be heated, an engine to be repaired, or a swimming-pool to be cleaned. Saul Bellow maintains that algae used to grow in the pool (as they do in the Adriatic). He talks about this in a short story. They are not algae, Saul, but needles from the cedar of Lebanon, and I would float along with them through a life without shadows. One foggy morning, I saw my father leave, not down the main drive but along the path that runs through the shade of the big cedar. My days were no longer to be so peaceful.

The third tree boasts the biggest cluster of magnolias I have ever seen. I won't say anything about the white flowers, everything is sweet on the shores of Lake Garda, even the tomatoes in the pasta sauce. That house (the 'Bavarian mausoleum') is in reality a labyrinth in which it is easy to get lost among the corridors and the anterooms. There are mirrors, stairways, billiard tables, baldachins, and even a bunker dug out by the Germans. The emergency telephone handsets hang down in the darkness. In the village there is talk of ghosts, but there is the warmth of our lunches in the kitchen and the veranda steps are the perfect place to chat. From here, we can look at the lake and

Monte Baldo with its topping of snow is like a Japanese post-card. Once a day, the tourist excursion boat passes. The local guide explains that this was Mussolini's last residence and that the famous Doctor Zhivago also lived here. The tourists take snaps: you don't often see magnolias like these.

The fourth tree isn't really a tree at all. It is perfectly straight, with stays instead of branches. The *Eskimosa* is a hull about sixteen metres long and is based in Porto Ercole. The boat is named after Ingelein, who has high cheekbones like a Laplander or an Eskimo. The white cap with the black visor and the garnet red band looks like a Danish student's cap, but on the captain it looked like a captain's cap. If the captain had been merely a blend of impetuosity and impatience, he would never have tolerated all the things you need to do to keep the prow straight. The engine was never used; if there was no wind, you could always play chess in the cockpit. On coming into harbour, the sails were kept hoisted until the last moment and the final manoeuvres were silent.

Biagio Sabatini, the mariner from Porto Ercole, has left us his memoirs. I shall choose a very Nordic page dealing with the summer of 1961. Biagio had only recently joined the *Eskimosa*:

On 22 July we were in Bergen. For the next two days, we explored the surrounding area. Rain and wind obliged us to put in at Teisthl. As soon as we could, we set sail again. Mr Feltrinelli had decided to push as far north as possible. We got as far as Trondheim. We explored the Sogne Fjord, Alesund, Kristiansund and many other smaller fjords. We stopped only to take on fuel. The weather never really set fair: always showers and a gusty wind. But we were expecting that, it was about mid-August, a bit late in the season for those latitudes. Some journalists came on board at Trondheim. They asked us loads of questions, in English. Only Mr Feltrinelli replied. All I understood was what was translated for me. I began to suspect they had never seen a sailing yacht flying the Italian flag before. Trondheim is a really charming town, standing on the various ramifications of Trondheims Fjord, but we didn't have the time to visit it at our leisure. We left almost immediately, after having seen Mrs Feltrinelli and a guest off on a plane for Bergen, where they were to wait for us.

Outside Trondheims Fjord we hit a heavy squall. We were heading into a south wind, which obliged us to reef the gaff-sail and to press on aided only by the foresail and the mizzen-sail. We kept on hoping things would calm down as we forged ahead, but the situation got markedly worse. Mr Feltrinelli realized that it would be dangerous for us to carry on, and so he decided that we would anchor in the next sheltered place we came across. About ten miles ahead of us there was a fjord, in the lee of a promontory. We decided to take shelter there. But the unfavourable winds and currents we encountered as we came up to the point behind which lay the fjord literally stopped the boat, and despite all our efforts we couldn't move forward so much as one metre. And as if these problems were not more than enough to worry about, a gust of wind ripped the foresail from the boom. I ran to get it before the wind dragged it into the sea. Mr Feltrinelli tried to start the engine, but this was not possible as the batteries were flat. All we could do was to hoist the storm jib, a small and very resistant sail, and try to carry on with that. But hoisting it proved a hard job. I had to open a key-bolt but it was stuck, I needed a screwdriver. It was necessary to go fetch the tools from inside the yacht, but I couldn't leave the bows or the wind would have dragged the jib into the sea. Mr Feltrinelli could not leave the helm, from where he was steering the endangered boat, and there was no question of his moving from there. There was a guest on board, a gentleman from Milan, but he was so seasick that only when it was impossible to do otherwise did we decide to ask his help. Crawling along the deck, suffering God knows what torments, and stopping frequently to vomit, he finally

managed to hand me the screwdriver. I managed to hoist
the storm jib. But the unfavourable winds and currents
continued, despite the hoisted sail, to prevent us from
entering the fjord; the situation was still precarious. Mr
Feltrinelli handed me the helm and went to check the sea
charts. All we could do was to seek shelter astern. He
found a place a few miles astern, Hovofjord, a tiny bay
with a particularly tricky entrance, no more than five
metres across, while the *Eskimosa* was about 3.80 metres
wide. We were encouraged to attempt the passage by the
fact that we sailing before the wind. But it was risky and
Mr Feltrinelli and I feared for the boat. With every
minute that passed, he would ask me: 'Say, Biagio, are we
going to make it?' I replied by joking that if by any
chance we didn't make it, the land was so close that all
we had to do was jump to reach it. Luckily, everything
went well. Inside the bay we found a flat calm, it seemed
like a dockyard basin: as if the pandemonium out on the
open sea had nothing to do with that corner of the world.

* * *

Cuba, Cuba, Cuba. Everybody has had something to say about
Cuba. In the early sixties, no matter how far away you were,
you had to reckon with Fidel Castro. For many, he was syn-
onymous with a dangerous extravagance that soon became an
obsession for them. In his *Age of Extremes*, Eric J. Hobsbawm
wrote:

> Probably no head of state during the brief century [. . .]
> had a more enthusiastic and impassioned audience than
> this bearded man in the crumpled camouflage uniform,
> who always arrived late for political rallies and then
> spoke for hours, uninterruptedly, communicating his
> rather confused thoughts to the attentive and consenting
> multitudes, of which I too was a part. For once revolu-
> tion was experienced as a sort of collective honeymoon.

Where would it have led? Somewhere there had to be a better future.

It's well known that one day Feltrinelli, too, stopped over at José Marti airport, but his decision to go there was carefully considered, not a revelation on the road to Damascus. According to Nadine Gordimer, whose *A World of Strangers* was published by Feltrinelli in 1961, Giangiacomo was aware, for example, even then, of the wretched fate of the Kurdish people.

The early sixties witnessed the last act of the old colonial powers. The outcome of the Suez crisis (contemporaneous with the Hungarian uprising) accelerated a process that was already well under way in Asia. Now it was the African countries' turn to fight for freedom.

These were issues that interested Feltrinelli, both as a publisher and for their political importance (the two things coincided). The first signs or symptoms are to be found in a letter he sent to Ben Barka, the leader of the Moroccan Union Nationale des Forces Populaires, and another sent to Sékou Touré, the president of the Republic of Guinea. Guinea had been independent since 1958. In the summer of 1962, Feltrinelli went first to Nigeria and then to Ghana (the former British Gold Coast, independent since 1957) to attend the Accra conference, the only publisher to do so, I believe. Promoted by the Ghanaian president Kwame Nkrumah, the conference was one of the first international meetings of 'non-aligned' politicians. The theme was nuclear disarmament. Representing Italy, there was also Lelio Basso, an authoritative figure of the socialist left. The British Labour Party peer, Lord Kennet, who was also present, today observes with some amusement that, in all likelihood, the whole thing had been organized by the Ghanaian president for reasons of personal prestige. But whatever was really going on, at least one person thought it was worth going all the way to Accra.

Feltrinelli had been doing his bit as a publisher since 1956, when

he presented a translated version of *Outlaw Africa* by the
Jeansons, a French married couple. The book was considered to
be the theoretical bible of the nascent anticolonialist movement
in Europe. 1960 witnessed the publication of *The Algerians at
War*, a reportage by Dominique Darbois and Philippe Vigneu. A
copy of this book was dispatched to Havana: it was Feltrinelli's
first contact with Castro, who sent his thanks. In 1962 Feltrinelli
brought out another book by Francis Jeanson, *Problems and
Perspectives in the Algerian Revolution*. Jeanson had been unable
to find a French publisher, but Feltrinelli had a French version
printed and distributed in France under his own imprint.

Juan Goytisolo's novel, *The Surf*, was banned in Franco's
Spain and hailed in Italy as the finest work produced so far by
the new generation of Spanish writers, very close in spirit – we
read in the blurb – to Pasolini's *Ragazzi di Vita*. The book was
launched in February 1961 in a theatre in Milan, accompanied
by a projection of a documentary on the conditions facing
domestic migrant workers in Spain. The film had barely begun
when a group of ex-paratroopers, subsequently stopped by the
police, interrupted the event by throwing smoke bombs. The
Madrid press picked up the story, denouncing the provocative
significance of the event and speculating on the meaning of
the incidents. Feltrinelli's response was simply to send two
functionaries of the publishing house to Barcelona, ostensibly
to protest and deny but with the secret intention of distributing
his books in Spain. But nothing happened, apart from a certain
outcry in the local press. The Italian publisher's name, however, became taboo in those parts and also, more importantly, a
passport affording him entrée into the circles of the intellectual
opposition.

In the public sphere in Europe, the problem of the freedom of
the press was now seen in a new light. As far as Feltrinelli was
concerned, the picture was anything but idyllic. In Italy, every
other month his books were banned by public prosecutors who
appealed to the courts to lay down the law in aesthetics. In
France, the publishers and writers who had denounced the

crimes perpetrated by the military were put on trial, as in the case of *Deserter*, a book that told the dramatic story of a young man who had refused to fight in Algeria. In West Germany, in the fall of 1962, the *Der Spiegel* case exploded like a bombshell when the Defence Minister Franz Josef Strauss accused the weekly of having violated state secrets and engineered the arrest of its publisher Rudolf Augstein.

After having sent off dozens of telegrams to half of Europe, Feltrinelli drew up a letter of condemnation to be sent to the German ambassador in Rome. It was signed, among others, by Giorgio Bassani, Paolo Grassi, Alberto Mondadori,* Elio Vittorini, and Eugenio Scalfari.† The confidential affairs office of the Italian Ministry of the Interior also took an interest in the matter: who had allegedly supplied *Der Spiegel* with the sensitive documentation? Feltrinelli, of course! Feltrinelli versus Strauss, NATO's principal ally in Europe. Fascinating but unlikely: my German source does not corroborate the story.

But to get back to the growing threat to the freedom of the press, we have to talk of the pre-emptive censorship employed in socialist countries, where the few publishing houses were state-owned, a fact that prevented the publication of certain works *a priori*. In Spain, however, publishers were obliged to submit their manuscripts to the offices of the Ministry of Information, which sent everything back with cuts, marks in red and blue pencil, and an accompanying note on paper with no letter heading, for a yes or a no.

These issues aroused animated debate everywhere.

At the end of 1961, at a meeting organized by one of the most authoritative magazines published in West Berlin, Feltrinelli replied to questions on Pasternak, on *Arialda* and on Miller. He was to do the same in Paris a few months later, nor was there any lack of opportunity in Italy.

*

* (1914–76). Journalist and publisher.
† (1924–). Law graduate, important journalist and writer, Scalfari founded *Espresso* and *La Repubblica*.

With the Algerian crisis at its peak, the Istituto Feltrinelli offered asylum to two or three political refugees or 'deserters', just as the conviction that determined action on the issue was required was coalescing in political and intellectual circles in Milan.

On 1 November 1961 various newspapers ran a paid appeal, which provided a good indication of the political climate and of just how much was at stake:

> For 7 years the forces of French conservatism have been waging a ruthless war on the Algerian people. A people is being oppressed and exterminated because it is demanding freedom, independence and social justice.
>
> 800,000 dead is the bloody toll of this war: men, women, and children have been killed in the fighting, butchered and tortured in the course of roundups and police operations.
>
> 1,500,000 Algerians languish in the concentration camps of North Africa.
>
> Tens of thousands have been imprisoned in France for years.
>
> In order to defend their economic interests against all the interests of the French people, the colonialist forces are tending to open the door to fascism and military dictatorship.
>
> By riding roughshod over the traditions of the enlightenment and democracy, French conservative forces and some military circles are a threat to democracy, and a hotbed of intrigues against democratic and progressive forces in Europe.
>
> The freedom of the press is seriously threatened in France. Algerians and French citizens are being persecuted and hunted down with methods that will remind world public opinion of those employed by the Nazi-Fascists. Citizens of Italy, it is necessary – on this, the centenary of the Unification of Italy, mindful of the traditions of freedom of our Risorgimento, and of the

traditions of democracy and progress expressed by
Garibaldi and Mazzini – to support the Algerian people
in their struggle for independence as well as the democratic and progressive forces within France today.
Their struggle is our struggle. Italians, we ask you to
make a strong expression of indignation against the fascist forces at work in France and against the war in
Algeria.

The first signatories were Basso, Feltrinelli, Grassi, Piovene
and Vittorini. Academics and intellectuals were swift to follow
their lead.

In the meantime, in France, the forces orbiting around the
Parti Socialiste Unifié (the United Socialist Party led by Pierre
Mendès-France) and the left-wing Catholics of 'Témoignage
Chrétien', were facing a decidedly delicate situation. Apart
from still unallayed fears of a putsch led by the generals and the
forces of the OAS, the end of the war in Algeria made it imper-
ative for France to return to its democratic traditions. It was
necessary to reverse a process that was exploiting the emergency to make steady inroads on parliamentary democracy.
From France there came requests for political, intellectual and
even economic solidarity.

The network of those who supported these appeals provides
a good definition of the Milan of that time. Gilles Martinet
(one of the founders of the PSU) wrote to Feltrinelli, who
agreed to ask for the support of his writers, but also for that of
publishers like Alberto Mondadori, of business people like
Roberto Olivetti and of journalists like Italo Pietra. A similar
task fell to Paolo Grassi, who, apart from the world of the theatre, drew in the socialists and the backers of his Piccolo
Teatro. Aldo Bassetti also had a list, as did the bookseller
Vando Aldrovandi, who involved the publishers Einaudi and
Lerici and the representatives of the great industrial families
like Giulia Devoto Falck and Giulia Maria Crespi.

This was the Milan accustomed to popping into the well-
known Bar Biffi for a plate of risotto *al salto* and a glass of

good wine. The journalist Eugenio Scalfari says that at least
once a week he would find himself at the same table as the
banker Renato Cantoni and Giangiacomo Feltrinelli.

But it is not true that Feltrinelli was always prepared to back
demonstrations, appeals or requests for help. He had learned
how to make himself respected and how to dissociate himself
from knee-jerk activism. When Giovanni Pirelli and Rossana
Rossanda, excessively sure of his willingness, took it for
granted that he would help with the preparations for an exhibition in the name of the 'Committee for the birth of the
Algerian nation', he replied in brusque tones: 'I am sorry, but I
have no intention of complying with your order to pay a share
of the expenses involved in setting up the exhibition. I certainly would not have refused to contribute to this fine initiative
had the request been made in a politer fashion. Seventeen years
in politics ought to have taught you that you cannot act by
"decree".'

* * *

After the death of Boris Pasternak, the bleakest chapter of the
'novel within the novel' began with the arrest of Olga Ivinskaya
and her daughter Irina. They were sentenced to the labour
camps: eight years for Olga, three for Irina. Olga was arrested
in mid-August 1960, Irina in September.

During the month of June, about half of the hundred thousand dollars requested by Pasternak had been taken to Moscow
by fiduciaries of Sergio D'Angelo. A married couple, the
Benedettis, arrived by car, travelling on tourist visas, with no
problems at the frontier. In the boot of their car there was a
suitcase full of roubles, almost half a million in all, but the
banknotes had recently gone out of circulation and were hard to
change. The couple had not taken even the most elementary
precautions. There were witnesses to the delivery of the money
and Olga went straight out and bought a brand new motor-
scooter for her youngest son . . . too much for even the most
compliant of police forces.

A few weeks before, while Pasternak was still alive, the Garritano family (he was a correspondent with *l'Unità*) had also brought a large sum in roubles. The sender was again D'Angelo. In that same period, the couple was asked to send Feltrinelli an envelope with the receipts and a will drawn up by Boris in Olga's favour. Although the Garritanos had tried to present Feltrinelli in a poor light on more than one occasion, Olga had appealed to them to send those papers to Italy. (Heinz Schewe was not in the Soviet Union at that time.) The Garritanos told Olga they planned to leave for Rome the following day, but they went off on a trip to the Caucasus instead and lost (or allowed someone to take) the documents in the middle of a terrific rainstorm. An 'imprudence', says Giuseppe Garritano today, but he says it as if it were still an open wound for him.

After the Garritano 'incident', Olga broke off relations with everyone except Schewe and Feltrinelli. To them she sent desperate letters, worried about what might happen to her, fears that were soon to prove all too well founded. When the secret police arrested her, they searched the house and found a letter in Italian in which she was advised to communicate only with Schewe. Feltrinelli had already tried to put her on her guard as far as D'Angelo was concerned: 'Unfortunately,' says Ivinskaya in her autobiography, 'owing to the circumstances (and often owing to imprudence on our part) we disobeyed Feltrinelli's warnings and we continued to write to "dear Sergio". We were to pay dearly for this.' And this was how the 'our ingenuous conspiracy' came to light. Many years later, shortly before she died, Olga talked to me about it. She spoke about Pasternak, herself, Feltrinelli, D'Angelo's emissaries, the suitcases full of banknotes, the letters, the haste, and all the moves prompted by fear.

The events in Moscow in the summer of 1960 again reverberated around the world. Feltrinelli sent off a communiqué to the press agencies: 'It is my opinion that Olga Ivinskaya is not responsible either for the transfer of the sums, or for the destination of those same sums. For, on the one hand, the order to

make the transfer was made by Pasternak alone and, on the
other, Pasternak himself had said that it was immaterial
whether the roubles were handed over to him or to Mrs
Ivinskaya.' The communiqué also clarified the matter of the
roubles that came from funds at Pasternak's disposal in
Western bank accounts and the role played by D'Angelo
(whose name was not quoted) in the transmission of a part of
these funds to Moscow.

Not long after, a third-rate weekly whose political affiliations
lay in the murky area around the right wing of the Christian
Democratic party, unleashed a barrage of accusations against
Feltrinelli. He was accused of having deliberately betrayed
Ivinskaya, leaving her at the mercy of the Soviet police.
Feltrinelli commented to Schewe: 'It is a provocation so base it
leaves you breathless with anger.' The articles were apparently
orchestrated by the former Communist Reale and by D'Angelo
himself, who was soon to become the US correspondent for
Fiorino, a magazine belonging to the same publishing group.
The suspicion that D'Angelo and Garritano, for reasons of
their own, were connected with someone in America or (more
probably) in Russia crept into the correspondence between
Feltrinelli and Schewe.

Feltrinelli and Schewe kept in touch in order to record all information coming from Labour Camp 385/14. There, five
hundred kilometres from Moscow, the wind was so strong that
you had to walk backwards. Olga had to be helped. But how?
By provoking a new head-on clash with the Soviet authorities?
By soliciting a protest on the part of the international community? Or, instead, by tackling the problem from another angle:
by seeking what little chance there was of talking, making a
deal?

In 1961, some important information was revealed. This
emerged from a report dated 9 May that was drawn up by
Pospelov, the former secretary to the Central Committee of the
CPSU, who had recently been reappointed head of the
Institute of Marxism–Leninism.

From 25 to 29 March 1961 comrade E.A. Boltin, the deputy director of the Institute of Marxism–Leninism of the Central Committee of the CPSU, on finding himself on a mission to Italy, visited on our behalf the Giangiacomo Feltrinelli Institute for Social Studies in Milan with a view to finding out more about its work, and was present at meetings on the activity of the said institute attended by comrade Luigi Longo, the deputy secretary general of the CC of the PCI, comrade Secchia, a member of the CC of the PCI, and by other party leaders.

There follows a description of the activities of the Istituto Feltrinelli and the presence is mentioned, in the library, of many Soviet publications and of the letters of Marx and Engels. Only passing mention is made of the publishing house, 'the same one that published Boris Pasternak's novel *Doctor Zhivago*'. Finally came the proposal that the Central Committee invite the top echelons of the Istituto Feltrinelli 'to establish scientific contact and to discuss the form that possible cooperation might take'.

Since early 1959, Del Bo had been trying to bring about a rapprochement with Moscow. He felt that this was necessary in order to complete certain projects of paramount importance, like the bibliographical study of the works of Marx and Engels that the Istituto Feltrinelli had been working on for several years. The study was destined for one of the forthcoming 'Annali' series. Del Bo had written to Togliatti on 26 February 1959, to explain the situation. Relations with the Institute of Marxism–Leninism of Berlin were good, as they were with similar research centers in Prague, Warsaw, and Budapest: 'As well as swelling our store of documents, these relations have procured us contacts and links with individual scholars that promise new and interesting developments.' With the Moscow Institute, at least apparently, things were not going badly: the exchange of documents had been 'extremely considerable'. Del Bo does not say how fatiguing it was to hold a dialogue

with the Russians. He mentions only that direct meetings had
ceased. The last one had taken place in 1957, when comrade
Evgenya Stepanova had visited Milan shortly before the publication of *Doctor Zhivago*. On that occasion, Stepanova, an
historian with the Institute of Marxism–Leninism, had proposed that Del Bo visit Moscow.

Del Bo, almost two years later, had asked Togliatti if the
time had not come to accept that invitation: 'What is the path I
must follow? [. . .] Do you think I ought to speak to them
directly, or must I refer to you with regard to this issue?' He
made it clear that a renewal of contacts might prove 'really
useful and important'.

After the breach between Feltrinelli and the PCI (December
1957), Del Bo had always been the one to maintain contacts
with the central office of the PCI. He was scrupulous about
this. He wrote a letter to Alicata, the party's 'Minister for
Culture', in which he referred to the activities of the Institute.
But the letters were too vague and Alicata complained about
this. With Togliatti, on the other hand, the approach was highly
deferential. At bottom, the party leader was also one of 'the
best contributors to the "Annali".' Del Bo had written to
Togliatti, congratulating him on his essay on the formation of
the Communist leadership between 1923 and 1924. Togliatti's
contribution, which was to be published in the third volume of
the series, contains an important new battle cry: to reconstruct
the history of the PCI as an integral part of Italian national history. That Togliatti's piece was published in the 'Annali' of the
Istituto Feltrinelli was a signal not to be underestimated.

Regarding Del Bo's plans to visit Moscow, Togliatti had
sought the advice of Alicata, who gave his opinion on this at the
end of 1959:

> I believe that we ought to point out to our Soviet com-
> rades the advisability of re-establishing contacts between
> the Institute of Marxism–Leninism and the Feltrinelli
> Library. However, Del Bo must be made to understand,
> in an appropriate manner, that without our intervention

such contacts would be impossible to organize, at least
for the time being, given the reservations that those in
charge of Institute of Marxism–Leninism have concerning Feltrinelli's activities overall.

In 1960, with the deepening scandal over *Doctor Zhivago*, it
became impossible to take matters any further. On 15
September 1960, the economist Piero Sraffa noted this remark
made by Del Bo: 'On account of Pasternak, the Soviets want
nothing to do with Feltrinelli either as a publisher, or as an
institute.' But in 1961, after the Soviet visit to Milan, Del Bo's
trip to Moscow finally received the green light. He was accompanied by the historian Enzo Collotti. Late that summer, for
almost two weeks, the Italian delegation was the guest of the
Institute of Marxism–Leninism and the meetings proved cordial and highly fruitful, especially about the opportunities for
exchanging documents. Collotti recalls that General Boltin (a
famous military historian), his chest laden with medals and
accompanied by an honour guard, was waiting to greet the
Italian delegation at the foot of the aeroplane steps. It cannot be
that far from the truth to suppose that Del Bo used the situation, and his skill in diplomacy, to sound out the possibility of
a conciliatory solution to the Ivinskaya case. According to
Collotti, who was not supposed to know anything about it, the
Pasternak question was in fact one of the principal reasons for
the visit.

The fact remains that some weeks after Del Bo's return to
Italy, the second important episode of the year occurred.
Feltrinelli decided to hand over to the Soviets, that is to the
administration of the Marx–Engels–Lenin Institute, some of
the original letters received from Pasternak during the turbu-
lent months following the publication of the novel. What was
the sense of this gesture? He explained this himself to
Pospelov: 'There is no need for me to tell you how important
these papers are to me from a human standpoint. But I deprive
myself of them willingly if this decision may be considered a
step toward bringing this affair to an end.'

Feltrinelli and Del Bo attached great importance to this initiative. The envelope containing the letters was handed over to
Secchia with precise instructions. On 11 October, Del Bo
urged:

Make sure that T. takes the envelope with him and deliv-
ers it personally to Pospelov. This is extremely
important, according to me. Should T. feel that it is
unsuitable for him to take it, give the envelope back to
Leonardi and we shall think over our next move here in
Milan. Agreed? Do not try other ways. Thank you and
interpret Giangiacomo's words as a concrete step in
everybody's best interests.

'T.' obviously stands for Togliatti, who from the 14th was in
Moscow for the 22nd Congress of the CPSU. On 12 October, it
was Feltrinelli's turn to write to Secchia:

I hope that this gesture of 'unilateral disarmament' on
my part may lead, when a suitable occasion arises, to a
consideration of the possibility of alleviating the lot of
Mrs Ivinskaya and her daughter: as well as easing my
mind, a pardon or a reduced sentence that might lead to
their release would also offer the Soviets an advantageous
way of ending the polemic with intellectual and political
circles in London and Paris, a polemic that might otherwise drag on for a long time. Perhaps it may be possible
to draw the Soviets' attention to the fact that, should
international politics enter a phase of *détente* in the near
future, they might do something for the two Ivinskaya
women as part of the variety of acts and gestures to be
made. I should be really grateful to you if you would
intercede, directly or indirectly, in this regard. I enclose
for your attention an English article containing some
statements made by Surkov, whose style is unsuited to a
polemic between a Soviet personality and the Western
world.

Secchia wasted no time in replying:

I have received the envelope, which I immediately had delivered to the person we agreed upon; in fact I was lucky because I was able to speak to him of the matter right away. Your gesture and your initiative were appreciated both by me and by him and we hope that the friends to whom your gesture is addressed will also take things in the desired spirit.

To what extent these 'friends' actually did appreciate Feltrinelli's move we do not know, but from spring 1962 onward vague hints began to circulate about the possibility that something might be done for Olga and Irina. And in fact, Irina was freed just before the summer, after serving half her sentence. Was this the effect of the 'diplomatic' mission entrusted to the good offices of Secchia and Togliatti? Perhaps. This is what Feltrinelli wrote to Schewe on 2 July 1962:

My feeling is that what little I have managed to do for the liberation of O. and I. ought not to be made public, especially with regard to Irina. There have been contacts between the Party here and the Party in M. Perhaps I have done the Russians a favour by handing over the documents you know about. But Irina must not know this. All the Russians have done in relation to the liberation of Irina and perhaps, before much longer, of Olga, they have done of their own free will, without pressure or negotiation. We have to save their face and it would be better if the girl knew as little as possible of the background.

As part of his attempt to secure Olga's liberation, which occurred in 1964, Feltrinelli had also put pressure on Fidel Castro, whom he met in the beginning of that year. At least, this was what Olga told me. She was never to meet my father.

As soon as Olga was freed, she took steps to keep herself and her daughter by having cash sent from the West. I have been unable to establish whether this aid, by that time tolerated by the authorities, depended on that 'what little' Feltrinelli had been able to do previously.

In early 1964 Giangiacomo Feltrinelli and Metro-Goldwyn-Mayer came to an agreement for the film version of *Doctor Zhivago*, on the basis of a flat fee of 450,000 dollars. The first drafts of the contract mention ten potential directors: Federico Fellini, Luchino Visconti, Vittorio De Sica, David Lean, Carol Reed, Elia Kazan, Stanley Kubrick, Billy Wilder, Peter Ustinov and Joseph L. Mankiewicz. The choice fell immediately on Lean. The Italians insisted that the treatment, screenplay and dialogues be based strictly on Zveteremich's Italian translation. The idea behind this was to prevent any errors contained in other translations from 'misrepresenting or distorting the author's ideas in a way that might lead to their being attributed with a meaning and a political orientation that was not in conformity with his will'. This was how Feltrinelli put it in a letter to Carlo Ponti.

Many years later, I called Ponti in Los Angeles to learn more. He did not have fond memories of the long and difficult negotiations. In that rasping voice of his he said: 'Right from the start, the plan was to have David Lean as the director and, as for Feltrinelli, he didn't give a damn, all he wanted was the money.'

Whichever way things went, the Americans did their best to create a product that would satisfy even the most sophisticated viewer. The winner of five Oscars, *Doctor Zhivago* broke all records in Italian cinemas, showing for six hundred days. It is still the seventh most popular film of all time. 'It was the tops as a commercial and an artistic film alike,' says Ponti. 'Yet,' he continues, 'Feltrinelli didn't even come to the première, to the great chagrin of the executives at Metro who wanted his opinion, but he didn't give a damn, he didn't give a damn for anything or anybody . . .'

At first, they thought of going on location to a certain part of

Yugoslavia, the only country conveniently close to Italy's eastern frontier where the book had been published. There, moreover, it would have cost less to hire extras. Feltrinelli delegated the attorney Filippo Carpi de' Resmini, who was a trusted friend as well as his cousin, to handle film-related business from Rome.

Filippo, who was a kind of uncle to me, would always tell the story of when he, Carlo Ponti and his wife, Sophia Loren, visited Marshall Tito's summer residence to champion the cause of the film. Tito received them all on the pier, he was cordial, and a real gentleman with Sophia, but he hedged over the proposals made by the tiny Italian delegation. Better to let the matter drop.

Ponti denies the episode. He had known Tito well for a long time, the Yugoslav supremo would have immediately given the film the green light: but he did not want David Lean, considered to be too much of an anti-Communist. But Ponti came up with a splendid anecdote: through the embassy in London, the Soviets sent a letter to Lean, inviting him to travel all over the Soviet Union. Once he got to know the way our people live, they said, he would no longer have wished to direct a film based on *Doctor Zhivago*.

So Omar Sharif with his moustache and Julie Christie with her limpid gaze went off to Spain with David Lean, where they had a whole neighbourhood of Moscow reconstructed. The film was shot on location in other countries too. There is a photo of the set in Finland, with Feltrinelli meeting Yuri Zhivago in the snow. But Ponti does not remember this: 'He didn't give a damn, he just didn't give a damn.'

More or less at the same time, shortly after Olga's liberation, Feltrinelli made official contact with the Soviet authorities and in particular with Professor Volchov, the President of the College of International Jurists of Moscow, the official representative of the Pasternak family. This was an important innovation: for the first time it was possible to sit around a table and deal in a conventional fashion. After going to

considerable lengths to sound out the real intentions of the
parties, the Soviets made a first visit to Milan and nominated
their own Italian representatives. For his part, Feltrinelli produced a statement of the proceeds from *Doctor Zhivago*. At
first, especially after the film, the Soviets' aim was to secure a
tacit agreement that would solve, solely for the past, an exclusively economic problem. Feltrinelli's position was different.
Here is the text of his letter to Professor Volchov during the
summer of 1966:

It seems to me that the time has come for frankness and
loyalty, all the more fitting by way of a tribute to the
memory of the late Poet. I cannot forget that, solely
because Pasternak gave me a mandate to publish and
market his work, he was obliged to endure the harshest
condemnation and persecution, which profoundly embit-
tered the last years of his life. Nor can I forget that it was
only for this that he was expelled from the Writers'
Union, banished from the literary community, publicly
accused of treachery and disloyalty toward his native
land, and even induced to disavow the fact that he had
ever assigned me the task of publishing his great novel.
In short, wounded in his most inviolable sentiments and
morally lynched for having entrusted me with the task of
introducing his famous work to the world of readers.
    All this belongs to the recent past, a past that lives on
in everyone's memory, a past that, unfortunately, we have
yet to recover from. But I believe that times will change
and I am certain that you, too, as a man of honour, will
agree with the need to avoid proceeding any further
along this line, which would be the case were any attempt
made to bury this sad business under a discreet silence:
with the mere presentation and the settlement of an economic dispute related to the publication of the book
which was officially branded infamous, almost as if it
really had been an act of treachery and vileness.
Fortunately, however, some things are beginning to

change, as is proved by the fact that these economic
demands can now be championed by the most authoritative representative of the official body of the Soviet legal
profession, in other words, by the president of the
International College of Jurists in Moscow. Introduced
and accompanied, in the talks held with me, by a functionary of the Soviet embassy in Rome.

The time is therefore ripe, in my opinion, for all of us
to take a more open and sincere step forward, including
those who at the time showed no mercy to the noble
figure of the late Poet. Moreover, I feel that I would be
betraying the faith that the late lamented author had in
me were I not to take the trouble to make – unfortunately, by now, only to his memory – at least those
(minimal) amends due to his qualities as a man, a citizen
and a writer.

To this end, I maintain that it is indispensable to
dispel the pall of clandestinity that has until now hung
over my relations with Pasternak and finally to emerge –
as we say here – into the light of day. I am therefore
authorized to propose to you, in the name of the publishing house represented by me, the stipulation of a
standard publishing contract with the Poet's heirs, which
may define the past and at the same time obtain all the
appropriate blessings, approvals and authorizations on
the part of the various competent Organizations,
Associations and Bodies in your country. With the
express support, in any event, of the Union of Soviet
Writers and through those reasonable forms of publicity
that can be reasonably discussed and agreed upon.

It took a good three of four years to reach an agreement
regarding the past, the future, and Olga who, formally, had no
right to anything. The Soviets made several visits to Milan,
where they learned to wind spaghetti around their forks,
amused themselves and discussed business. The talks were very
long and very tough. Professor Volchov never went anywhere

without his fountain pen, with which he claimed to have signed death sentences at the Nuremberg trials. But, in the course of one endless afternoon, he hurled it against a wall in a fit of rage. That pen was his pride and joy and he broke it beyond repair.

The year 1969 finally led to a handshake: the Soviet State Legal Advisory Office would receive a six-figure sum in dollars (but their clients, the heirs, were to receive much less, I fear). A final calculation was reached by deducting what had been transferred to Pasternak during his lifetime (the Legal Advisory Office accepted the principle) as well as the considerable expenses incurred in the management of the copyright. A standard contract was to bind the parties (Olga Ivinskaya included) for the next twenty years.

After so many battles, this was for all parties the logical, if not the ideal conclusion to negotiations that had been vitiated by the passage of time.

In 1989, in Moscow, attorney Tesone renewed the rights to *Doctor Zhivago* and struck a deal for the first publication of the novel in Soviet territory. It was the time of perestrojka. In accordance with the terms of the 1970 contract, the rights were freely available. The magazine *Novy Mir*, which was supposed to have published the book thirty-five years before, was ready to do so now. Only four words were requested in the copyright line: '© Giangiacomo Feltrinelli Editore Milano'. And that is how it was. It made a symbolic and solemn end to the 'novel within the novel'.

After the Soviet Union had collapsed, I met Olga Ivinskaya shortly before she died. She was bedridden, but had ensured there was no lack of vodka and cigarettes for our warm embrace. Then she wrote me a letter about Feltrinelli and Pasternak and about two stars that meet in space like the stars in Lermontov's poem. The day after our only meeting, I made a visit to Peredelkino, which my father would have loved to have seen.

* * *

Andrey Voznesensky sent off a collection of his poems to Boris Pasternak when he was only fourteen. It was in 1946. As in a dream, the maestro replied, granting the boy his lifelong friendship. One day he pronounced the word 'Feltrinelli' in his young pupil's presence and, as fate would have it, Andrey was also to become aware of that name. This happened only a few months after Pasternak's death, when the world was picking up speed so fast that in Moscow people were suddenly talking of 'Jack' (Kerouac), while in London Andrey himself was all the rage. 'He has taken off like a rocket in the starry firmament of poetry,' wrote the *Observer*.

The following pages deal with Voznesensky's encounter with my father in Paris (late 1961, early 1962?), while the meeting in the Kremlin, the one in which Khruschev polemically interrupted Voznesensky's speech, occurred in March 1963. Voznesensky recalled these events in January 1997:

One fine day they called me at my hotel in Paris and a honeyed voice told me that signor Feltrinelli had come to meet me. The voice inquired if I would like to accept.

Now it must be made clear that this was my first trip abroad. I was in ecstasies over the way the most important French newspapers (*Le Figaro*, *France Soir* and *Le Monde*) had greeted my poetry recitals; I had literally lost my head.

A black limousine with shades drawn was waiting for me at the corner of the hotel. A snake-like smile hovered on the face of the silent man who was to accompany me. It seemed like a scene from a thriller. I don't remember where they took me, perhaps it was a villa in the suburbs or a secret apartment. We sat down in the lounge to wait.

And then, impetuously, he strode into the room. Tall, with a tennis player's build, slightly curved shoulders, dressed in a grey suit. In his eyes there shone a sad and frenetic light. But the most important thing was his moustache, curving downward, in the style favoured by Ukrainian terrorists. There is a kind of grub that lives in

the woods and moves by arching its back that is said to
bring good luck. Would Feltrinelli's moustache bring me
good luck or not?

I sensed in Feltrinelli a certain adventurous passion
that is really dear to me. Perhaps, precisely for this
reason, a current of reciprocal liking began to flow
between us. He played the part of the one who likes to
set universal principles ablaze, and I was a legendary
figure in the stadia of Moscow. He wore trousers with
cuffs, like mine, while the silent escort's had no cuffs,
like all Parisians at the time. Amused, I pointed this out
to him. We spoke briefly of *Zhivago* and he toyed with
his moustache, curling it, as he told me, in tones of
wonder admixed with disgust, of the episode in which
that syrupy hyena Surkov had gone to visit him, presenting himself in Pasternak's name, to ask him to stop the
publication of the novel. Feltrinelli offered me a lifetime
contract for the world rights to my work. Until then, I
had never signed a contract: Soviet law prohibited direct
contact with publishers. And now the chance had presented itself! Almost a signing fee! I accepted, but only
for the Italian rights. I was behaving like a consummate
actor, knocking back the whisky in one gulp. They
offered me an incredible advance. I don't recall now, but
for someone like me, who had never received a cent from
publishers, it was a mind-boggling amount. I was left
dumbstruck with surprise. I refused. The silent escort
grew even more silent at this brazenness on my part. 'So
how much do you want?' Plucking up my courage, I went
for a figure that was ten times higher. This, I thought,
was how one deals with publishers. Feltrinelli paled, and
dashed out of the room. The escort shot me a glance
from over the rims of his glasses, doubtless thinking
something like 'Will you listen to this crazy Russian!' I
said to myself: 'Andryusha, now you've blown it!'

Three minutes later, the door was thrown open;
Feltrinelli came in wearing a calm but determined

expression. He said: 'OK. How would you like to be
paid? By cheque, or would you prefer a draft to be sent to
your bank?' 'No. I want it all right now. In cash!' In
those days I didn't even know what a cheque was, while
in practical terms, as far as the Soviet authorities were
concerned, having a bank account meant you were a CIA
agent. 'OK, OK,' said the moustache, looking at the ceiling, 'but in that case you'll have to come to Italy.'

And so I perpetrated the second crime. Soviet citizens
could not ask foreign consulates for a visa directly. This
was possible only through Moscow, after a special commission had vetted the request. But I went to the Italian
consulate in Paris and, three days later, there I was in
Rome. Imitating an American accent, I told the cab
driver: 'Take me to the best hotel.' The luxurious hotel
in piazza di Spagna was swarming with Americans and
wealthy cardinals. I knew that I was going to have to
spend all the money in only one week. I was positive
that, on my return to Moscow, the road to Europe would
be closed to me for ever. And so I bought fur coats and
jewellery for all my friends. I set to drinking myself to
death and, when I left the hotel, I forgot a drawing by
Picasso that someone had given me as a present.

[. . .]

It was not long before the punishment arrived, in the
form of Khruschev brandishing a raised fist in fury: 'Mr
Voznesensky!' he yelled. 'Get out of this country! You
have done nothing but slander our system; you are trying
to provoke a Hungarian uprising here! Go off to your
friends abroad . . .' The hall of the great assembly room
in the Kremlin resounded with a babble of voices:
'Shame! Shame! Get out of the country!' And all this
because I had said that Lermontov, the genius Pasternak
and Akhmadulina belonged to one direct line of descent.
Which made the secretary general hit the roof. For
Khruschev, not long before, had defined Pasternak as a
pig that shits in his own plate, and now this one here

starts saying he was a genius! That windbag Khruschev just couldn't appreciate straight talk. Feltrinelli was a straight talker.

I don't know whether the great leader had come to know, from my dossier, of my criminal association with Feltrinelli. The vitriolic articles about me made no mention of this, but as far as I am concerned it was the real cause of the accusations. 'Now Shelepin will prepare your passport!' yelled the atomic power.

Shelepin, the Minister of the KGB, blurted out: 'You didn't come to the Kremlin in a jacket and tie but in a pullover. You are a beatnik!' No one in the room knew what a 'beatnik' was, but everyone shouted in chorus: 'Beatnik! get out of this country! . . .'

Ingenuously, under the illusion that they would not find me, I took refuge in one of the Baltic countries. I would spend hours lying down in the woods, observing the sky overhead. At a certain point, on a dead branch outlined against the sky, I saw a tiny slow-moving figure. I recognized it: it reminded me of a moustache. It was going toward the sky, arching its back. Slowly. Then it disappeared over the horizon.

I am certain that Feltrinelli was glad to publish Jack Kerouac's *The Subterraneans*, even more so when the book was confiscated owing to its presumed obscene content. Barney Rosset arrived from America in his capacity as the first publisher of the work, and Kerouac sent a letter to the judge (who was from Varese, I think), admitting that he had not so much as a smattering of law, but adding that he did know the sole foundation of jurisprudence: 'The judge is always right!'.

And Testori's play *Arialda*? It was the same year and the same fate: 'Highly offensive to the common sense of decency, for the turpitude and triviality of the events considered.' Visconti was working on *Rocco and His Brothers*, all too freely based on Testori's novel *Il ponte della Ghisolfa*. Visconti came across a copy of *Arialda* and, enthusiastic, he had it staged by

Paolo Stoppa. At the première in Milan, the company was obliged to interrupt the performance. The theatre resounded with whistling, shouting and bigoted insults. Feltrinelli jumped to his feet, facing the infuriated crowd: 'You provocateurs, cut it out, you provocateurs!' The Surveillance Committee for theatre scripts got down to work beneath the ozone-free sunshine of 1960.

Many other Feltrinelli books were being vetted for obsenity. In particular, Selby's book, *Last Exit to Brooklyn*, with his stories of 'perverts', and Henry Miller's two *Tropics*. Since 1960, my parents had met Miller in Italy on various occasions. It was impossible to publish the *Tropics* in Italy. But in the publishing house there was great enthusiasm for them. With a trial inevitable, Feltrinelli asked some eminent psychiatrists to demolish the paradigm of 'obscenity', in other words that elusive whiff of corruption that according to the lawmakers causes irreparable psychological damage.

This time, Feltrinelli did not manage to convince Tesone, the lawyer in the Pasternak case, to whom he gave a copy of an invaluable little publication, *The Trial of Lady Chatterley*, so that he might prepare himself for a trial of 'unprecedented dimensions in Italy'. The two men argued bitterly: Tesone felt that Miller's *Tropics* represented too much of a risk and he tendered his resignation for a while. Feltrinelli carried on doing things his way. But with a difference . . . *Tropic of Cancer* began to circulate in 1962, in a Feltrinelli edition printed in Bellinzona and kept in stock in the Gondrand warehouses in Basle. A notice on the cover said 'Paperback edition for foreign sale only, the publisher prohibits its export and sale in Italy'. This served to prevent confiscation, but – as the accountant Pozzi recalls – 'we had the books transported from Basle to the Maison di Livre Italien in Nice. We would go by car to pick them and return to Italy via the customs post at Ventimiglia carrying two or three hundred copies, never any more. We brought the books into Italy and sold them under the counter, but not in Feltrinelli bookshops.' The bookseller Bertini sold them: 'I picked up some *Tropics* at the 1962 Frankfurt Book Fair.

Feltrinelli made me pay for them. He wanted a cheque. If you
end up in jail that's your fucking problem, he said to me.' On
his way back, Bertini avoided Switzerland and crossed the frontier at the Brenner pass. But the customs men stopped his
Lancia Appia series III, perhaps because the load made it look
a bit down on the springs. 'The trunk was full of *Tropics*, mixed
with foreign publishers' catalogues. I told them I had come
from the Frankfurt Book Fair. I thought I'd had it. "What a lot
of books on cancer", said the customs man. "Yeah", I said,
"it's a nasty business".'

'Thanks for all you are doing, I take my hat off to you
Italians for having been so professional, thanks for being so
understanding . . .' Henry Miller wrote to his publisher and
also to Veraldi, Riva, Bianciardi and Praz, who had worked
with painstaking determination on the editing and translation.

Knowing Miller's habits, when the author visited Gargnano,
Feltrinelli had a ping-pong table set up under the big magnolia
where some hard-fought matches were played out. The *Tropics*,
in a single volume, were not officially published in Italy until
1967. A magistrate (from Lodi, I think) ordered a new trial.
But the times had already begun to change.

On the evening of 13 February 1965, Nanni Balestrini,* the
editor and poet, set off down via del Corso, in Rome, on his
way to a show. A small local theatre was presenting the first
night of an adaptation of Rolf Hochhuth's *The Deputy*, with
Gian Maria Volonté. When Balestrini got there, he found five
jeeps, an armoured car, and two police vans: no one was allowed
in, the show was prohibited. Scuffles followed and the young
poet was frog-marched off by the cops, the soles of his shoes
dragging along the ground. It was at that point that he spotted
his employer arriving, dressed to kill, in the company of Mary
McCarthy. Moustache to moustache, he heard Feltrinelli yell at
the cop: 'Let him go, he is one of my associates.' The scene was
so paradoxical that the captive was freed. The prohibition of
the show caused a scandal because the police action was so

* One of the founders of Group 63. A leftist, he was close to Toni Negri.

brutal. The public was made up of Italian critics, but also of foreign observers. The Minister of the Interior of the Moro* administration had to issue a note. Two days later, the show was staged in the warehouse of the Feltrinelli bookshop in via del Babbuino.

The Deputy was an indictment of Pope Pius XII's failure to speak out against the Nazi atrocities, and a savage critique of the moral and political responsibilities of the Catholic Church. Feltrinelli believed strongly in the book: '*Doctor Zhivago*, Hochhuth's *The Deputy* and the experimental work of the Italian avant-garde', he wrote in the catalogue published to mark the house's tenth anniversary, 'were episodes in the same battle for freedom of expression against any power that held the analysis, criticism, or creative work of a poet or a scientist to be offensive to legitimate ideals, illustrious men, or glorious traditions; for nothing is ever absolute and untouchable, nothing is ever beyond historic or literary criticism.'

To celebrate the anniversary of the publishing house, they threw a big party at Gargnano in the summer of 1965. Grisha Von Rezzori turned up with Anita Pallenberg, the girlfriend of Keith or Mick of the Stones.

* * *

Group 63: something was happening. This calls for a short account.

It all began in Palermo in October, in the form of a spin-off from an experimental music event. It was an era in which conferences were becoming 'interdisciplinary', the idea being that various languages might in some way coincide. Why not extend

* Aldo Moro (1916–78). A member of parliament since 1946, Moro held ministerial posts with several governments. The leader of the DC since 1959, he served as prime minister on various occasions. He was to replace Leone as President of the Republic but on the day of the investiture of the new government he was kidnapped by the Red Brigades. 55 days later, his body was found in the boot of a car.

the scope of the weeklong event in Palermo to include a discussion of the new literature? The idea arose from an
off-the-cuff suggestion made by Filippini and the young poet-
editor Nanni Balestrini had gone to work on organizing it. The
cry 'everybody to Palermo' shook up Italian intellectual circles.
The overnight sleeper 'avant-garde' was born.

The concept of 'the open work' was no longer a question of
mere poetics, it became a concept for operating at all levels of a
complex society. And this called for writers capable of using
diverse disciplinary languages. This was Group 63: enormous
eclecticism and the maximum of innovation, where what
counted, even more than results, was *attitude*. The discourses
of the establishment (wasn't that how they put it?), those of
left-wing conservatism and conservatism *tout court*, began to
betray a sense of uneasiness for the first time. The general climate was changing, perhaps it had already changed some time
before, but it did not become obvious until literature was
affected, and literature bacame the place where all of these
changes converged.

Group 63 was foreshadowed in 1956, with the foundation of
the magazine *Verri* run by Luciano Anceschi (Giangiacomo
Feltrinelli's first tutor). The group of poets known as the
'Novissimi' gravitated to the magazine: it was no longer possible to write a certain type of poetry. And Anceschi's teachings
were attuned to the moment: phenomenology plus structural-
ism seemed to catch the very point of the century. Then, three
years later, Umberto Eco wrote an essay titled '*L'opera in movimento e la coscienza dell'epoca*', which was later included in his
book *The Open Work*, published by Bompiani in 1962: it
became the watchword of the 'culture' of the sixties.

The name Group 63 was borrowed from a German prece-
dent, Group 47, with which the Feltrinelli publishing house
already had dealings. The similarity with the German group lay
in the question of method. The authors held public readings of
their works, they refuted 'tradition', prized innovation,
accepted the consequences of aggressive, destructive, even self-
destructive debate: a novelty as far as Italian Arcadia was

concerned. But there were also parties, dances, gatherings round the pool, brawls, exhibitions, and concerts.

The idea of forming the group came from via Andegari, but the headquarters were in the bookshop in Rome's via del Babbuino. It cannot be said that Feltrinelli had exclusive rights to Group 63, but (along with Bompiani) it was its principal outlet in the world of publishing.

However, as the novelist Alberto Arbasino put it, as a publishing house, 'Feltrinelli had the luxury of possessing two souls'. His was not only the house that had published the misunderstood *Leopard*, and the series directed by Giorgio Bassani, but also the young writers who defined Bassani and Cassola as the Lialas* of 1963.

Was the literary world of the fifties really 'boorish, smothering, and triumphally smug' (as the young writers believed)? And as for the 'provincial fuddy duddies' in Feltrinelli's Roman offices, in via Arenula, unable to repeat the miracle of *The Leopard* every year, were they really so many 'spongers'? On the other hand: did the 'theoretical glaciation'(as the older generation would have it) of Group 63 really exact tolls! Did their writing represent the funeral offerings of our literature? And when Feltrinelli sacked Giorgio Bassani, did he think that by so doing he was celebrating 'one of the blackest days in Italian literature'? Oh, of course, he did this by breaking into Bassani's desk drawers by night and having his office sealed off. And he even raised his voice when Bassani showed up late the following morning. But, for all that, this did not mark the advent of some kind of literary terrorism, some bookish St Bartholomew's Night. Feltrinelli's was merely a justifiable demand that his own staff, his own offices, his own archives, his own writing paper and his own salaries were not used to divert his own authors toward other publishers. Bassani had become so disenchanted with the new wave in literature that he had begun to move his authors away from such contamination. Bassani was

---

* Liala. Pseudonym of Amelia Negretti (1897–1997), successful author of romantic novels (an Italian Barbara Cartland).

never to admit this, all he did was to take issue with the 'so-called' Group 63.

In Feltrinelli's view, the books produced by the avant-garde were 'necessary', and they represented one of the house's twin souls. And this was why a special series was created for them: '*I materiali*', launched in 1964. Edoardo Sanguineti, a writer who was ahead of his time, recalls that the publisher kept a low profile and left his writers to get on with things. And while the smart boys in the Milan offices waved goodbye as they set off for Palermo airport, there are those prepared to swear that they saw an ironic glint in Feltrinelli's eye.

Fratelli d'Italia (1963) was the emblematic work of this moment in Italian literary history. Its publication was opposed by the very man in charge of the series (Bassani), who disliked its chaotic blend of genres, found that it lacked what he called the 'filter of memory', and could not bear either its virtuoso passages or its fragmentary nature. In a press communiqué, Feltrinelli cut internal and external disputes short: 'I have no wish to get involved in the row over the novel. In my opinion, what Alberto Arbasino has produced is, first and foremost, a book, which some will read as a novel, others as non-fiction, and perhaps others again as a pamphlet or a collection of newspaper articles.'

In his next book (*Paese senza*), Arbasino reflected at length upon his time with Feltrinelli:

> Giangiacomo was typically shy and aggressive, highly puritanical, and capable of bursts of exaggerated good humour, but virtually incapable of relaxing. Needs, none. Desires, out of the question. He had some typically upper-middle-class traits: the habit of assessing – directly and without any polite beating about the bush – the economic side of operations, right down to the managerial affectation of taking pencil and paper and making spot calculations of costs and proceeds; changing the subject to ask polite questions about things that

interested the other party, whenever the conversation languished; and the unconfessed but tangible fear that people frequented him only because of his money, which resulted in a certain reserve that made it hard to forge simple and relaxed relationships. But the managerial tone would disappear instantly on leaving the office for a lunch or for the weekend: as if he had determined to draw a sharp distinction between Business and Private Life.

I have no wish to be falsely ingenuous, but I do not understand why every so often he was thought of as an eccentric Milanese: of course, in a milieu where ninety-nine out a hundred go to Portofino, or at most on safari in Kenya, someone who goes to Cuba seems more extravagant than he would in London, where for every one who goes to Brighton there are ninety-nine who go to Samarkand or Kashmir. But through the continuous restlessness and the many enthusiasms that followed, one sensed above all an enormous vivacity, an inexhaustible capacity for exuberance. I remember, for example, the long-cultivated plans for a *History of Taste in Twentieth-Century Italy* (which was never written because I went off the idea), and a euphoric enthusiasm for coloured paper napkins and games, which the various Feltrinelli bookshops were full of for some time . (If Italian cinema were not idiotic and non-committal, with material like this a new minor Orson Welles could make a new minor *Citizen Kane*.)

As far as working together was concerned, my recollection of the planning and preparation of a wide variety of extremely different books, the professional meetings and the face-to-face talks is one of extreme efficiency and competence. There were even moments of irony: Rizzoli would never manage to steal an author from him, he would say, smiling, because otherwise he would have evicted the AC Milan soccer team – of which a member of the Rizzoli family was then the owner – from their

offices on the ground floor of via Andegari, an address
that Rizzoli very much wanted to keep. And even though
Feltrinelli surrounded himself with associates who were
more experimentally oriented than professional, so much
the better for the future: for the dust jackets of my most
adventurous books they would choose a Fra Galgario or a
Cy Twombly. [. . .] Around 1962, when the manuscript of
Fratelli d'Italia was ready, Giorgio Bassani (who was in
charge of the fiction series) was against it because the
novel struck him as a disordered and scandalous jumble of
fact and fiction, and moreover he feared that it would be
interpreted only on the basis of gossip and polemic. All
Giangiacomo said was: any blame to be taken is taken by
the director of the series when he discovers and endorses
nonsense. But if the nonsense is the work of an author
who is already well known, all the blame falls on him.

The brawling excursions of the *Fratelli d'Italia* were per-
ceived in many quarters as a social slander on a national level.
Feltrinelli said:

This book is a product of this society, and is no better
and no worse than that society: perhaps for the first time,
a certain [section of] society has seen itself in the mirror.
I understand the surprise, but I am surprised by an
indignation that smacks of bad faith. We are all what we
want to be, and why be ashamed of what we are and of
what we want to be? [. . .] In the novel Arbasino
describes places, habits, expressions, and events common
to a certain section of Italian society. I mean to say that
blend of café, literary and theatrical society, in short the
snobbish world of the Milanese and Roman intelligentsia. Intelligent, unconventional, sometimes cynical.
And sometimes presumptuous and arrogant.

The shade of the big cedar of Lebanon welcomed Arbasino
for the launch of *Fratelli d'Italia*:

Villadeati, with the local wine and salame and grappa, was an extremely pleasant 'high place' of conversation and relaxation in springtime and in the autumn. [. . .]

There, we still have an ever more distant recollection – for almost all of us are dead – of a crowded September party, and a great rustic Sunday lunch, in an Italy that was still carefree, with a youthful and highly urbane Milan that today may seem a mixed grill cooked up between the Urbino of Baldassare Castiglione* and the salon of the Countess Maffei. [. . .]

But at Villadeati on that Sunday now as distant as *Gone With The Wind*, the village band was in the loggia playing traditional Piedmontese dance music, and 'all of Milan was there', Giangiacomo was handing out the sausages and the chicken to Wally Toscanini,[†] who was sitting on the lawn saying 'How delightful, how delightful'; Giannalisa and Inge, dressed in red, were chatting in German from a tower to a balcony; and Pietrino Bianchi was gazing ecstatically upward and exclaiming 'All right, this is how the Italian cinema should have been, this is how *La notte* should have been made' . . . And then Pietro Ferraro (dead) flew low overhead in his plane, dropping leaflets bearing good wishes for Giangiacomo and Inge, messages that wound up even in the plate of sweets I was sharing with Ernesto Rogers (dead) . . .

* * *

Milan was proud to be the technocratic capital of the new Italian capitalism. In the city two hundred art galleries were opened and conceptual artists stayed in the Torre Velasca[‡] with wall-to-wall carpets and trilingual secretaries. The mothers of

---

* The author of *The Courtier* (1478–1529).
† The daughter of the orchestra conductor and a well-known socialite in Milan.
‡ Milan's first skyscraper.

my pals in kindergarten talked of Christmas safaris in their red
Morris cars; the driest among them commented on the death of
that decrepit old Communist, Pope John XXIII. Camilla
Cederna* watched over us all with the care of a subversive
entomologist.

On the second floor of via Andegari, above the head office of
AC Milan Football Club, there were the guest apartments for
friends of the publishing house.

Here I have to mention the role played by Inge Feltrinelli,
because here she is the leading lady. She says she was inspired
by Gottfried and Brigitte Fischer's accounts of their home in
Berlin, before the Nazi period, where people like Thomas
Mann or Albert Einstein would drop in for a coffee.

Almost fifty years later, the guest apartments were intended
to be something similar and the guest book is a fascinating list
of a variety of internationally known names. This wasn't
merely a social ritual: the idea was that everyone who passed
though should leave an idea behind them. Examples? The
spring–summer tour of 1965: Ernesto Sábato, Robert Maxwell,
James Baldwin, George Sadoul, John Polanyi (Nobel Prize for
Chemistry), Gregory Corso, Max Frisch and Ingeborg
Bachmann.

The friends. I should like to mention one who was very dear
to me, Roberto Olivetti. He was very much a part of those
years. Roberto was the son of Olivetti founder Adriano Olivetti
(who died in 1960). My father had been on friendly terms with
Olivetti senior. At this point a document from the archives of
the Interior Ministry comes in handy. The document is dated
1958.

On the occasion of a book fair in the Canavese area,
Giangiacomo Feltrinelli went to Ivrea, where he had a

---

* (1911–97). One of the most caustic pens in Italian journalism. An editor
with *Espresso*, she was the author of *Pinelli, una finestra sulla strage*
(Feltrinelli, 1971) and of an inquiry that was to lead to the resignation of
Giovanni Leone, the President of the Republic.

long and fruitful talk with Adriano Olivetti. The two
left-wing industrialists hit it off; judging by what they
said later, they understood each other very well and laid
the groundwork for a joint venture. The meeting was
largely the work of Olivetti, who, at his own expense,
had organized a book fair specifically to showcase
Feltrinelli's publications and had ordered the city to be
festooned with banners bearing the name Feltrinelli in
large letters. The Milanese millionaire was touched by
this and hopes with all his heart that he may have the
strength to leave the PCI [. . .].

In the early sixties Roberto had thrown himself into the
family business, armed with a sincere enthusiasm for electron-
ics and the new technologies. At that time, the 'old' Olivetti of
the engineer Tchou had almost had its day.

Perhaps implicitly, Feltrinelli's friendship with Roberto led
to his becoming less of an outsider in the social world of the
Italian upper class. Giangiacomo had been a guest in the
Agnelli home, but there was nothing for him there; much better
to sit barefoot on the pier at Porto Ercole, or to take a winter
sauna and a cold plunge at Villadeati; even better still was the
impetuosity of two rich, handsome young globetrotters of the
same age consumed by curiosity about a world in which distances were becoming irrelevant. What's more, Anna and Inge
were friends, they became mothers, there was me, there was
Anna's daughter Desire, we had a life in common.

Roberto had no luck at Olivetti. The family stockholders
gave him no respite, he was too far ahead of his time, stubbornly obsessed as he was with microprocessors (the term had
yet to be invented). After resigning from his most important
posts, and after a spell running the Edizioni di Comunità, he
financed the Adelphi publishing house and *Espresso* magazine.

He had realized, I think, that the timing of ideas can be out
of phase with the timing of individual lives. That's why I have
always thought of him as a wise and ironic man. He took my
upbringing very much to heart, helping me over the most

difficult moments (the seventies and eighties), and was always close to me, even when he learned he had the lung cancer that was to carry him off at fifty-seven.

* * *

The ingredients of the Italian 'economic miracle' were, first, integration with the European market, the first government of the centre-left, the labour unions moving toward unity, the new Christian Democratic power structure, and the PCI ever more assimilated. And, above all, a development plan based on the motor car and the consumer society. Then around the mid-sixties, there was the first talk of 'recession' and of the end of the 'miracle'.

The businessman Feltrinelli observed this transformation of Italian society with ideas that were not entirely clear. The publishing house had been in existence for a decade and, given the nature of the enterprise, it absorbed enormous energy and resources. Success and prestige were not lacking, but its size was by no means comparable to those of the great publishing companies. At a certain point, Feltrinelli embarked on talks in a bid to buy into the weekly *Espresso*, perhaps with a view to giving his own group a new importance. But in the end they could not agree either on a price or on who the majority share-holder ought to be.

What has been said about the publishing house also holds for the Feltrinelli Institute. By that time it was acclaimed all over the world, but it was the kind of venture that it is hard to sustain privately. And in Italy there is no point counting on the solicitude of public institutions.

In 1964, Feltrinelli gave serious consideration to the idea of selling the library. In the meantime, he put it 'on ice', as he put it in a letter to the historian Edward (E. P.) Thompson, closed the service to the public and cut both staff and research pro-grammes. There were a few contacts with the Milan town council, but it soon became evident that the only potential pur-chasers able to guarantee costs and continuity were outside

Italy. From the United States both the Harvard University Library and the Hoover Library of Stanford University made inquiries; the historian Ernst Nolte wrote from the German Federal Republic; and Michael Bernstein sent out feelers from Paris. In Great Britain, Thompson, who also informed his government, tried to find a 'European', or, better still, a British, home for the Milanese archives. The name of the omnivorous and already very powerful publisher Robert Maxwell also cropped up.

Apart from these signals, numerous offers were made to purchase individual collections held by the library. But Feltrinelli had no intention of selling things off piecemeal and, in any case, the idea was to keep the fruit of so much hard work in Italy.

Mysterious rumours began to circulate about the goings-on in via Andegari. Rossana Rossanda opened a dossier and found out as much as she could. Her report to Togliatti, dated August 1963, was brief and worried. She spoke of the sacking, in her view on 'political' grounds, of many associates of the publishing house and the institute on the grounds of temporary closure. She suggested the possibility of calling for industrial action. (In contrast with this, the last part of her report is wholly concerned with the situation within the Einaudi publishing house: she saw no problems there.)

Feltrinelli had Del Bo reply to Togliatti, who was following the affairs of the institute closely. The Communist leader talked of the matter in alarmed tones during his last meeting with Piero Sraffa, in July 1964. Sraffa had been in touch with Del Bo for some time. Nenni, then the deputy prime minister, sent a worried letter, in the name of 'socialist culture'. When the rumours of the closure and sale of the library became more insistent, Togliatti decided to step in personally. He wrote to Raffaele Mattioli,* one of the most powerful figures in Milanese financial circles, who had always been on very friendly

---

* (1895–1973). Banker and man of culture, Mattioli was President of the Banca Commerciale Italiana until 1972. He also directed the Italian classics series for the Ricciardi publishing house.

terms with my father. The letter is dated 23 July 1964 and it
begins with a sanctimonious lie.

Dear Mattioli,
I have never had occasion to write a letter to a banker. I
do not know, therefore, if I shall manage to express
myself in a pertinent manner. The matter concerns the
Feltrinelli Institute and its fate, both of which should be
close to the hearts of all Italian scholars. My opinion,
formed through fairly direct contacts, is that intervention
of a certain urgency is required. But I do not think it
advisable to take any steps to exclude Feltrinelli from his
position as head of the institute. This last ought to be
transformed, in my view, into a 'foundation', without
changing either the name or the founder. Having done
this, however, it would be necessary to guarantee annual
running costs. I believe that you too are familiar with the
figures. Now, don't you think that this sum may be put
together through a commitment, at least for a certain
number of years, on the part of a group of banks or the
like? This is the problem I would pose you, considering
that the solution I have suggested might be well received.
But perhaps you know more about it than I do! If possible, bear my opinion in mind. And accept my best and
most cordial wishes.

Togliatti

The leader of the PCI, who died a few weeks later, was never
to receive what must have been a difficult reply to write.
During 1964, Feltrinelli had come to the point where certain
decisions had to be made. What to do? Raise the stakes, seek
new alliances, or give up certain business activities? Havana
provided a good argument in favour of carrying on as before.

* * *

Selling and marketing books in Italy has never been easy. The

fault lies with the schools and the lack of libraries and the sta-
tistics have always been enough to make you blanch. Then
there has always been that story about books being good for us,
that they make us better people, and are even good for our
health, a notion that publishers tend to imply even before they
call in the marketing teams. In reality, reading takes time and
effort, and when we overdo things it leaves us 'blind, con-
sumptive, scoliotic and dyspeptic', as Valerio Riva would put it.

Around the mid-sixties, however, there was talk of a small
'Italian bookselling boom'. Or rather, it was one of those
moments in which it seemed that everything in the book trade
was changing. The technological revolution, paperbacks on sale
at newsstands, distribution networks, the advertising departments: was 'family' publishing really finished? Were we really
moving from 'the consumption of literature to the consumption of books'? Were books to become a consumer item like so
many others? These were the issues that concerned the more
traditional publishers.

How to encourage the spread of literature in Italy? In the
course of a television debate with Valentino Bompiani and
Livio Garzanti,* Feltrinelli insisted on the role of paperbacks
and complained about the lack of time for reading: his idea
was that the working week had to be reduced. With these same
issues in mind, he replied to his colleagues Einaudi and
Mondadori from the pages of the *Corriere della Sera*. Einaudi
was betting on the development of municipal libraries, while
Mondadori saw new possibilities in instalment plans, postal
sales, and in the creation of book clubs and in other commercial
initiatives outside the traditional channels of distribution.
Feltrinelli's view was expressed in a letter published [in the
Corriere] on 2 August 1964:

Sir,
For some time now, I have been trying to drop any pre-
conceived notions as I wanted to see whether it is really

* Two of the biggest publishers in Italy.

true that the worst way to sell books is to sell them through bookshops.

You know that I am still young and a little impetuous: I like to gain the experience I need for my work at first hand. In short, in order to find out the truth, I turned myself into a bookseller; I went into bookshops to see how they sold books, who bought them, who paid for them and who (alas) bought them on credit or (worse still) merely leafed through them. I tried to put myself in the bookseller's shoes, but never forgetting that I am a publisher. And I must tell you that I made some pretty interesting discoveries: the foremost among these is that the criticisms often levelled at this particular instrument that is the bookshop are often based on hearsay, unjust, groundless, and perhaps even (involuntarily) defamatory.

In Italy over these last few years, many new things have been introduced (and I, if you will forgive me for saying so, was the one who introduced some of these novelties). I thought that what was needed above all was a revolution in the way books are displayed, and in the choice of stock. In my bookshop in via Manzoni, in Milan, I am not afraid to display the same book in two or three different places, to show books face-on rather than spine-on, to put the price tag in clear view above each book, or even to present them inside those wire baskets greengrocers use to display fruit and vegetables.

But of course there are more than just Feltrinelli bookshops [. . .] In Milan alone, there are 250 bookshops: it certainly cannot be said that the network is inadequate.

Staffing has also improved remarkably in the last few years. There are still no schools for booksellers, which exist, for example, in Germany and Holland, but there are already young booksellers who are not content merely with learning publishers' catalogues off by heart. Of course, if we had a modern school for booksellers, many of our problems would be solved: and I wonder what costs more, a gigantic advertising apparatus, complex customer administration and heavyweight public relations organizations; or a good school that might produce fifty new booksellers a year, all armed with new ideas and a modern approach.

In June 1966, thirty years before the buzzing cyberworld of amazon.com, a journalist from *La Nazione* asked Feltrinelli what he thought the bookshop of the future might be like. The reporter jotted down a confused jumble of things he had never heard of before: bookshops like jukeboxes, without books, only keys and buttons. You go in, choose a title and press a button. A teletype machine hooked up to the nearest printing works transmits the order. The order is forwarded to the warehouse, and comes to the punched tape containing the text of the book selected. In a twinkling, an enormous offset printer prints out and sends the chosen book to the bookshop in the typeface, language and binding required. 'Or perhaps in the cheap edition, with the pages bound along the top rather than at the side, designed to be thrown away after reading.'

The journalist, incredulous, felt that a round-table discussion was required.

The Feltrinelli bookshops went through their most important phase of development during the early sixties, by which time they had a clearer grasp of the formula that permits a chain of bookshops to develop on a large scale. The first experiments, which had been promoted since 1957, had served as a general rehearsal for gathering information on sales and market trends. Compared to traditional family-run bookshops, the ones in which a counter separated the customer and the bookseller in his dark-grey dustcoat, the Feltrinelli stores were already revolutionary: no schoolbooks, stacks of paperbacks, and the catalogues of the best publishers displayed face-on.

Around 1960, Feltrinelli came up with an idea for self-service kiosks; he had them constructed in Germany. Several were set up in Milan and in various seaside resorts but, as they were not licensed to sell newspapers, it wasn't long before they failed. But the experience did bequeath many ideas regarding the optimum exploitation of shelf space when, between 1963 and 1965, the second generation of bookshops came along.

Once he had changed the top management of the bookselling company, Feltrinelli began the search for larger premises, in busy city-centre streets. The future mayor of Bologna, the historian Renato Zangheri* (who collaborated with the Feltrinelli Institute), accompanied Giangiacomo through the streets of his city in order to calculate the flow of potential passing trade. The historic nucleus of the most important Feltrinelli bookshops began to take shape: in the shadow of the two towers in Bologna, in via Manzoni in Milan, in via del Babbuino in Rome, in via Cavour in Florence (with the blessing of Mayor La Pira). Each store had a history of its own bound up with the personality of the bookseller chosen to run it.

The aim was to persuade people to buy books, come hell or high water. Romano Montroni, who ran the Bologna store, recalls his first brush with this philosophy:

I recall an episode that happened about twenty days after I took over the running of the store. Feltrinelli was pissed off because sales were not going up, quite the opposite. In fact, we had had some totally black days, no one came in and nothing got sold. We had to keep the doors wide open even in winter, and we kept stalls laden with paperbacks on the pavement. Feltrinelli had bought us all red pullovers especially for this. But I had been in charge for twenty days and I still didn't have much of a clue as to what I could do to turn the situation around. OK, our shop was new, and very handsome too, but people still had no reason to abandon the old bookshops in favour of Feltrinelli's shops. People would just walk

---

* (1925–). A historian, a member of the PCI and a former mayor of Bologna, he has also been a member of parliament.

on by. So he came to Bologna and he said: 'Let's have a sale.' I was amazed. A sale? Of what? And he said, still angry: 'Of everything!' 'But these are all new books', I said. At that point, Feltrinelli grabbed a pile of books and began to mangle their edges. 'Not any more they're not,' he replied. 'But there's no need to ruin them all. Sell them all off. Have some placards made up right now, saying 30 per cent off.' He placed an ad in the local paper. We had never offered discounts; on the contrary, we were against the generalized discount policy practiced by almost all bookshops. The whole thing caused a real ruckus, and that sale was the first shock wave. The city woke up to the fact that there was a new bookshop in town . . .

But the sale was only one episode. There were other, less conventional methods of drawing the public. In Florence, they offered roasted chestnuts; in Milan, a barefoot Joan Baez dropped in; in Bologna, they set up the first big meet-the-author events; and in Rome . . . 'In Rome it seemed as if all of the city's cultural life had gravitated to the triangle formed by Cesaretto's *trattoria*, the Plinio gallery and the bookshop in via del Babbuino,' recalls the bookseller Carlo Conticelli.

But hip Martians had yet to land in piazza San Pietro. Again with regard to Rome, the bookseller Franca Fortini has this to say:

A bookshop with a pinball machine: naturally it was Feltrinelli who had had it installed and when he came here, the first thing he would do was to start playing with this thing, either for fun or to let off steam, I don't know which. They took the pinball into the back room, but even the distributor couldn't believe his eyes. In 1965, pinball was at best something you found in a few bars patronized by really young people. You would see the machines at the seaside in summertime, or in some country places . . . And alongside the pinball he put the

Coca-Cola stand, a dartboard, lots of posters on the walls
and he even had them put in a really beautiful juke-box,
like something out of some wild-west saloon, all chrome-
plated and full of records, rock, the Beatles – who were
just getting big – and the songs from the Sanremo song
contest. What kind of stuff? Johnny Dorelli. He was just
a kid but he had won the contest. And Modugno. *Nel blu
dipinto di blu* . . . '*penso che un sogno così non torni mai più*'
. . . And Mina, Celentano, Buscaglione. The high-school
kids would come in and start dancing, the Feltrinelli
bookshop was the first discothèque in Rome. It was a
scandal, these fourteen- or fifteen-year-old kids dancing
in the store to the music from the jukebox. It didn't
happen every day, but it happened now and again, and a
whole lot of serious people got a lot of kicks out of it.

Feltrinelli also 'raided' London; he came back with loads of
stuff, badges, and all the latest gimmicks: Marilyn made up to
resemble Mao, silver belts in the form of snakes, ties, grass-
green miniskirts, mock-leopardskin hats. All this merchandise
was dumped in large wickerwork baskets, like in the street-
markets, by the bookshop cash points. He had a parking disc
made with the message 'make love, not war' on it, complete
with the relevant symbol. And what about the famous spray can
'Paint your cop yellow'? When the Rome police came to confiscate the cans, they took it out on Concitelli, the manager.
'So you want to paint us yellow, huh?', they said to him. And
he: 'For heaven's sake, no! It's only a joke. My cop could be my
boss, or my wife.' But a prosecution followed, and a report on
the matter was sent to the Ministry of the Interior.
　But Feltrinelli did not go hunting for memorabilia only in
Carnaby Street. He also went to Milan's arty Brera district.
There was a boutique there run by a very young blonde girl
who sold pop clothes and art-nouveau bric-a-brac. He was
smitten by her straight away and he invited her to dinner.

*　*　*

Four brief stories are contained by the date 1966. They are not important, nor do they commemorate anything particularly significant: if I close my eyes, nothing comes to mind about '66 (perhaps I ought to know that things were not going so well between my parents, but I don't remember). They are four episodes thrown up by chance, with no common thread, apart from the number 1966. Let the anecdotes speak for themselves.

In January 1966, my father was in New York. I don't know what he was doing there, but I know that Luigi Barzini was also there at the time. The two met on the street, one crossed over on to the other pavement, the other pretended he hadn't seen anything. Benedetta, Barzini's younger daughter, was in town on her own account.

Very beautiful, and very anorexic, Benedetta had stopped feeding herself in the conventional fashion when she was fifteen, thus attempting the only escape route she had to hand. In 1958, she had been taken to a clinic in Zurich, and then to Geneva and Paris. When she was able to do without a drip, Feltrinelli took her with him to via Andegari. 'I'm going to look after you now,' he said, but despite his sincere desire to protect her he didn't seriously manage to look after her. 'It would have been too painful: my illness was the visible sign of a suffering he too had known,' says Benedetta today. Moral: the girl found her way by herself. In 1963, a chance photo for *Vogue Italia* opened the door to the United States and to the court of Irving Penn, for whom she worked for a couple of years. Benedetta was the only one able to compete with the coloured models, being from the Mediterranean and therefore 'exotic'. The rest was Twiggy, wishy-washy little blondes.

In January of 1966 Benedetta was twenty-three. On the night she met her half-brother in New York, they decided to party. Benedetta suggested she introduce Giangiacomo to Andy Warhol. 'I was incredibly proud: for the first time, I was going to take him to a place that was my place.' Andy was there, in his studio, they chatted and Feltrinelli was planted in front of a cine camera for a ten-minute filmed sequence. I found some

frames from the session in a book by Warhol and Gerard
Malanga. The publisher of *Doctor Zhivago* alongside Lou
Reed, Nico and Sally Kirkland.

Apropos of Lou Reed. I don't have any clear memories of my
father in Milan, either in the office or at home. Of course, I
cannot forget when he rushed to the dentist's when I had a
problem with the anaesthetic, or when he dressed up as Santa
Claus for me and my schoolfriends, or the look on his face when
I made a foray into his office. Once he took me to the consulate of an African country, but I don't have many domestic
memories. Only extra-domestic ones. And, with regard to via
Andegari, I have to fall back on the soundscape and attempt an
acoustic digression, if not a psychedelic one.

My parents had little real ear for music. But while my
mother's favourite social occasion was a ball, my father was
fond of folk music, the songs of the Resistance, the Kurds, the
Guatemalans, the Mexicans . . . So, close to the fireplace, on the
fourth floor in via Andegari, a high-quality German record
player, angular and elegant, was well in evidence. And there
were the slim spines of the rows of records: a little classical
music, a lot of modern material. I mean to say, records on the
Italian 'Sole' label, Kurdish, Guatemalan and Mexican music
and, of course, the anthologies produced by Folkway Records,
the Columbia Library, Cisco Houston, Leadbelly, Big Bill
Broonzy . . . But also *Aftermath*, Françoise Hardy, *Sgt. Pepper*,
Coltrane, Jannacci, The Rockets, *Lotte Lenya Sings Brecht*,
Bringing It All Back Home and Mina. Popular music, in short,
for all tastes and in all genres. I have established with precision
that, together with the songs of the Spartacists, *Sgt. Pepper*
was my father's favourite record.

What aroused my curiosity, though, was the sleeve of
Bringing It All Back Home. I discovered it when I was no
longer a kid. And I'm not referring to the songs, 'electric' for
the first time, but the sleeve. The copy I discovered on the
shelf bore a mysterious dedication written in blue ink on the
top right-hand corner: '*Für Giangiacomo von Manuela*'. And

there is also a date: '16.3.66'. As for the photo in the centre of the album, better to describe it in the words of Robert Shelton:

Daniel Kramer's cover photograph, shot through an edge-softened lens, is an essay in symbols. Dylan fondles his cat – named Rolling Stone. Behind him, albums by Von Schmidt, Lenya, Robert Johnson . . . Elsewhere, a fallout shelter sign, a copy of *Time*, a nineteenth-century portrait. Just left of centre on the mantelpiece is Dylan's *The Clown*, a glass collage he made for Bernard Paturel from some bits of colored glass Bernard was about to discard.

In all probability, the 'essay in symbols' was an entirely involuntary creation, just as it is the fruit of pure suggestion to think what I thought, and still think, of the photograph on *Bringing It All Back Home*: that photo looked as if it had been taken in our house, in the very room where we sit down to chat, next to the record player, I recognize everything. When Manuela gave the album to my father, on 16 March 1966, perhaps he listened to it (a present from Manuela gets listened to at least once) and nothing was missing: the fireplace, *Time*, sofa, atomic shelter, album, portrait (nineteenth-century, and fifteenth too), collage, pieces of glass, 'electricity' . . . You can still make the comparison to this day: thirty years have gone by and the fireplace is still where it was, pretty much the same, a few more books and a few less symbols.

In that room, as a child, I found a community that I didn't have the time to judge strange because I was already used to it. Later, and very slowly, I associated many faces and voices with the elements of real biographies. Like the guy who called from the airport saying he was Henry Kissinger. It was Henry Kissinger indeed, then a brilliant professor at Harvard.

But, to get back to the soundtrack, there was a song that fitted the film perfectly. In fact, it was the soundtrack of a film, from that very 1966. I have only seen excerpts of *Un homme et une femme* on television: the director was Lelouch, the stars

Jean-Louis Trintignant and Anouk Aimée. And I don't even
know the title of the song, it is a kind of French-style samba,
smooth, feminine, sexy. Every now and then, they still give it an
airing on the radio and it's like rediscovering my old orange
beanbag: the one I used to stretch out on to stare at the herd of
adults at the trough.

In 1966, the atmosphere in Milan's exclusive G. Parini high
school was electric. It was because of *La Zanzara*, the school
magazine that had run a survey which had escaped the head-
master's attention. The girls and boys at the school had been
asking questions about the use of the birth-control pill, nothing
unhealthy about that. But it was enough to have three students
put on trial. The case became a national scandal: speeches from
public prosecutors, rivers of ink, a full-blown row . . . One
Milanese bookshop acted as a sounding-board for the event
and one publishing house published a detailed account of it.
'Mr Feltrinelli, could we ask you the question that everyone is
talking about these days?, why are you taking part in the Italian
youth movement?' 'Ask me something more specific, I've been
talking since eight this morning and I need to warm myself
up.'

In Florence, high-school girls had to wear black smocks to
school. During a public meeting on the *Zanzara* case, following
speeches by lawyers and teachers, two likeable youngsters took
the floor. They introduced themselves: 'We are students at the
Parini.' Their presence embarrassed the few or the many who
were not yet aware of the news. Yet, not far from there, Don
Milani's* kids were already locked in a public struggle to
defend their right to do something other than military service;
in Rome the death of Paolo Rossi (a socialist university student
and a victim of neo-Fascist violence) became a problem at government level; the Social Sciences faculty at the University of

---

* Don Milani, a dissident Catholic priest, was an ardent champion of the
underprivileged and their right to education. His book *Letter to a
Schoolteacher* become a cult book within the student protest movement.

Trent was in an uproar . . . It was getting more and more difficult not to take notice.

Just before the summer, the town council of Florence
launched an event called 'British Week'. This, too, happened in
1966. To mark the occasion, at the bookshop in via Cavour
they decided to organize an exhibition of Penguin books; the
baskets were full of London-made knick-knacks imported by
Feltrinelli, and the manager Bertini hired Mal and the
Primitives, an English band with a regular gig at the Piper Club
in Rome. The idea was to have them do a show in the shop
every afternoon, from six to six-thirty, just to pull in a few
people. But on the first night, the act went down so well that
Mal was obliged to give a few encores. The following day, they
turned up the amps and things got a bit more complicated.
The din made by the band could be heard as far as away as the
Duomo, and the traffic was blocked by the hundreds of kids on
the sidewalk outside the bookshop.

For the last day of 'British Week', it was decided to hold an
out-and-out happening, still among the books and the shelves.
Surprise visitors included the unconventional singer Patti
Pravo as well as Inge and Giangiacomo. The party went on
until four in the morning. 'It was a triumph'; Valerio Bertini
recalls that in one week they sold almost everything, books and
other things. What was left in the storeroom was engulfed by
muddy waters: on 4 November Florence was swamped by what
turned out to be a historic flood.

The day on which the Arno broke its banks and Ponte
Vecchio risked collapsing, the bookshop was damaged too: the
floor was covered by two and half metres of a stinking blackish
mass that ruined everything. The few books that survived
swelled up on the shelves. They needed a pickaxe to knock
down the shelves. Pozzi, the accountant, rang from Milan:
'How are sales going?' Bertini swore.

On 6 November the only vehicles on the streets were ambu-
lances, army jeeps, and an armoured car with the President of
the Republic on board. The bookshop staff tried to free themselves from the mud. Feltrinelli made a surprise dash to via

Cavour. He was on foot, dressed in mountaineering kit and bearing a bulging backpack, as if he were arriving from a mission across the enemy lines. How had he got through? Had he come by train? Of course not! He didn't say how, but he had managed to slip through the net and the barriers, arriving aboard his Citroen Ds as far as via San Gallo, less than a hundred metres from the store. The car and the backpack were full of all sorts of goodies: ham sandwiches, milk, antibiotics, gas lamps, wax polish for the shelves, various disinfectants, pasta, rice and rags. He appeared at the head of the stairs leading down to the basement full of sludge to ask for a first inventory of the damage. Before leaving again, he thanked the staff one by one. 'I serve the Soviet Union!' yelled Bertini in farewell. They all smiled, even the ones who had not been Pioneers.

In December 1966 there was an international rally in Milan, with the participation of various libertarian groups. Feltrinelli went along for a few evenings and played host to a couple of Dutch anarchists. That same month, the pilot issue of the magazine *Mondo Beat* appeared in the city, duplicated copies run off on makeshift equipment in the offices of an anarchist group.

A small band of youths, far closer to the American beatniks than any product of the local musical beat movement, set up a small tent in the town. They wanted to live in a 'commune' on the banks of the Vettabbia, at the end of via Ripamonti. Six months later the 'squalid camp' of 'New Hoboland' was broken up by police flame-throwers, in the midst of a paranoid press campaign with more than a touch of Grand Guignol about it. They had just enough time to print a number of *Mondo Beat*. From the front page: 'The consumer strike on the part of the Beatniks is a total strike against the capitalist system!'. The author of the article, one Gigi Effe,* lent the magazine a hand after the police 'clean-up'. He was the only one to possess mint copies of *Oracle* and the *Berkeley Barb*. On the strength of the

* Or 'GgF', i.e., Giangiacomo Feltrinelli.

sales of the last number, some of the *Mondo Beat* kids left
Vettabbia for Essaouira in Morocco.

* * *

Giuseppe Zigaina is an excellent and well-known painter. On
looking at his pictures, you can understand why he never left
Friuli. Karstic, lunar, lagoonal landscapes, sometimes with tree
stumps, other times with sunflowers, they are still his obsession. The house, on the road that leads from Cervignano to
Aquileia, is still the same: interiors with lots of woodwork, the
smell of paints in the rooms, the curved lawn in the yard.
According to Giorgio Bocca, Feltrinelli used to practise throwing hand grenades on that lawn. It's not the kind of thing you
do here; if anything, this is a place where people come to relax,
to look for mosaics, to go to Zompitta for barbecues or to
Sistiana to eat fish.

Zigaina has opted for a kind of exile rather than lose touch
with his roots. He draws his inspiration from the evocative
quality of an epic land, rugged frontier country that has often
been fought over. Sometimes I went with him well beyond the
chimneys of Umago, on board the *Oedipus Rex*, a former fishing smack he bought in 1969. Before that, Zigaina had the
Istanbul, a sloop in which he nearly drowned along with Maria
Callas when she was playing Medea on the lagoon.

Zigaina was a great friend of Pasolini, from the days in
Casarsa, just after the war. He was also a great friend of
Giangiacomo, more or less at the same time. With him he had
shared the excitement and the heated debates over the first
exhibitions in Milan, the conversations with Vidali, the construction of the House of the People in Cervignano, the
abortive attempt to open a Feltrinelli store in Trieste, and many
other things again.

One day, Peppino talked to Feltrinelli of Pasolini: he might
have been the right man to direct the new poetry series. But
there were some who were backing another candidate, while
Feltrinelli could not make up his mind, or changed it, and the

series did not get off the ground. Pasolini, who had perhaps already been contacted, learned of the play-off. This was the background, which boded no good at all, to his sole encounter with Feltrinelli. The meeting took place in the early sixties, in summer, at Cervignano; in Zigaina's house. The host was very tense, and the atmosphere between the two guests was frigid. A little white wine was required. Zigaina: 'Pasolini was in grouchy mode, his shyness did the rest. As far as Giangiacomo was concerned, I was sure, mathematically sure, that he had no great liking for Pierpaolo, I can't call it diffidence, but a certain coldness, yes . . .'

But the wine did the trick, the atmosphere became more relaxed, and the talk began to flow more freely. At a certain point Feltrinelli started in on the story of a dream he had had the night before, which he recalled clearly. He told of how he had found himself in the jaws of an enormous tiger, a story of that kind. Pasolini immediately commented on the anecdote with a quip: 'This is a castration complex!'. According to Zigaina, that was the end of the evening. Giangiacomo was mortally offended and the two were never to speak again.

Incomprehensibly, history repeated itself the time I took Pasolini to Gorizia to meet Basaglia,* in a community for the care of the mentally disturbed. On that occasion too Pasolini immediately came out with the line about the castration complex, on account of a tic Basaglia had in one eye. The conversation ceased instantly and Basaglia found a pretext to have us leave. It was because he [Pasolini] was shy, do you see?

I no longer recall on which boat we went out into the lagoon with my father and Peppino; it may have been *Oedipus Rex* or the *Istanbul*. It must have been a year, or at least some months, before the winter of 1969. It was my first visit to the island of

* (1924–80). A psychiatrist. One of the fathers of antipsychiatry, he led the movement for the reform of Italy's mental institutions.

Anfora. It was enormous fun brushing the waves while hanging from the deck by a belt; a great day. My father introduced me to the girl from the boutique in Brera, saying she was his fiancée, but no other comments were forthcoming. We returned at sunset, to the calls of nocturnal animals. On the lagoon, Peppino said, people don't talk much.

* * *

From a certain point onward, at the publishing house the climate was one of 'permanent revolution': 'What youth is against, we are against', and young people were more and more agitated. In the editorial office, there was talk of 'passive resistance', the abolition of the internal combustion engine, world famine, the structure of the Italian family, libidinal neuroses, White Papers and Latin America.

Feltrinelli's reasoning was taking a steadily apocalyptic turn. The capitalist world was on 'the brink of the volcano', and revolution was smouldering beneath the ashes.

Authors were aware of the new climate. Arbasino again, from *Paese senza*:

> In 1968, I was working on two books that were rather too literary (*Super-Eliogabalo* and *Sessanta posizioni*) for the house's image, by then heavily politicized and ideologized, and I told him that I thought the books were perhaps unsuitable, and that perhaps he might be embarrassed by the clash between the image conveyed by my books and his pamphlets. But he wanted them, despite everything: in fact there was a great and moving embrace, followed indeed (in any case, both of us were embarrassed) by a kiss.

Mario Spagnol left the team for Mondadori; Valerio Riva got a separation by mutual consent in the summer of 1968; and when Filippini announced his departure, Feltrinelli pointed a hand gun at him. It all finished in a farewell drink in the bar of the Hotel Continental. The reins of the editorial department were now in the hands of Giampiero Brega, who had returned to the fold after a spell elsewhere. He was a versatile man, in the French manner (a rare bird here in Italy), and highly cultivated. His roots were in the PCI but he was attracted by the most advanced theories of contemporary Marxism. But he curbed and refined Feltrinelli's political impetuosity, kept the product lines broadly based, and watched over the publishing house's various souls. Between 1967 and 1969, Feltrinelli published Castro (*Funeral Oration For Ernesto Che Guevara*), Chairman Mao's *Little Red Book*, the strategies of General Giap, the speeches of Ho Chi Minh, Dutschke's students, and Althusser's readings of *Das Kapital*. They were joined by Lévi-Strauss, Jakobson's linguistics, the poetic texts of Schönberg, Peter Brook's notes on theatre, Panofsky's *Dürer*, Harry Stack Sullivan and Eugen Bleuler. Other popular publications included the Genoan cook Nino Bergese's recipe book and a manual on LSD written by a variety of authors. The purely literary offerings ranged from the new Tom Wolfe to Don Backy (a singer who ran with the Celentano* 'clan'), from James Baldwin to the Feltrinelli K350 series of thrillers. But the real phenomenon came from South America: Asturias (the Nobel Prize-winner), Sábato, Vargas Llosa, Fuentes, *A Hundred Years of Solitude*. The Italian Enrico Cicogna was the first person in the world to translate Gabriel Garcia Marquez, in 1968. The novel in question was not even obviously 'left wing', but it oozed 'magic realism', the ethic of miracles. While our culture was impoverished by its own negations, here was a world of perfect secular happiness. One edition was printed after another; the response was overwhelming and the newspapers for the first time used the term 'cult book'. One of the many reprints came out with a band bearing a quote from the publisher: 'One of the best books I have ever read'.

In 1967–8 the situation was still under control. Feltrinelli

---

* Adriano Celentano, one of Italy's first and enduringly popular rock stars, whose career was launched when he appeared in Fellini's *la Dolce Vita*.

spent more time travelling than he did in Milan, but he always came back knowing his own mind. He still liked making books. He tried to explain all this in an article for *King*:

So I have to define myself: I have to define myself as a publisher; or at least I have to introduce myself, expose myself and explain myself in relationship to the profession that has taken up ninety per cent of my time for these past fifteen years. I could begin with the profession itself and, to make things simpler, I could remove myself from the equation; alternatively I could begin with myself, but in this case, unfortunately, I wouldn't be able to keep the profession out of it . . . So, let's begin with the profession. But I don't want to define the publisher, or better, the Publisher: to my way of seeing things, this is a function that resists definition, or rather one that may be defined in thousands of ways. All you would have to do, in this regard, is to list all those who have made a fortune by publishing books and to make another list of all those who have squandered a fortune by doing the same thing. In contemporary publishing, the former are as numerous as the latter: I am thinking, for example, of Ernst Rowohlt or Gaston Gallimard on the one side, and of Kurt Wolff on the other. Ernst Rowohlt and Gaston Gallimard have made fortunes, in the form of publishing houses, which are both economic and cultural fortunes: Kurt Wolff, the man who 'discovered' almost all of contemporary German literature before the Great War of 1914–18, has scuppered a good number of publishing houses, but culturally speaking he was always right, manifestly right.

And that's how the term 'fortune' has already acquired a meaning that is no longer merely economic, but something subtler; subtler and more ambiguous, a meaning that is, not very metaphorically, 'political'. So let's forget the idea of publishing fortunes on a business level: the behemoths with half a million titles, fifty copy editors, a

dozen low-quality magazines for intellectual 'servants',
or for servile intellectuals, a printing works with super
machinery provided by American 'aid', an intimidatory
apparatus and a 'literary prize purchasing department'.
It is pointless trying to explain how such organizations
work, because today it would be really difficult to create
this kind of super-robot of the book trade, especially
because the creation of such a monster is very far from
my intentions. It may be a flaw, it may be a vice: but even
though I hope my publishing house will flourish economically, I cannot help remembering that it sprang
above all from a mirage; no: from an intention, even from
a need and a desire that I hesitate to define as cultural
only because the word culture, Culture, strikes me as
gigantic, enormous, and worthy of not being continually
brought into play.

So let's say this: even though I do hope that my publishing house will flourish economically, what I am
thinking of, and what I am pursuing is a 'Fortune' in the
second sense. And this is a very tricky thing to explain;
to cut a long story short: I am trying to provide a publishing service that is perhaps wrong in the here and now,
in the contemporary historical context, but will none the
less, I am almost prepared to bet, be proved right in the
historical long term.

Guevara's writings are necessary. I shall try to explain
myself better: in the mixed-up universe of books, of
communications, of values that are often pseudo-values,
of information (true and false), of nonsense, of flashes of
genius, of folly and of opaque placidity, I refuse to join
the ranks of the upholsterers of the world, the packagers,
the painters, the producers of the 'merely superfluous'.
Since the deadly proliferation of printed paper looks like
depriving the function of publishing of all sense and
purpose, I hold that the only way this function can be
restored is by something that, despite fashion, I do not
hesitate to call 'morality': necessary books exist,

necessary publications exist. No matter how paradoxical this may seem, I, as a publisher, fully subscribe to what Fidel Castro has called 'the abolition of intellectual property', and that is the abolition of copyright: this measure serves to ensure that Cuba may have the necessary books, the books that Cubans need. But even in a situation of 'private intellectual property', there are necessary books. Unfortunately, here I am inhibited by a scruple: I should not like to advertise my own books; on the other hand, I am obliged to cite them. And so cite them I will: in the universe of Western letters there is a genre, a literary thing, which is called the novel. Many say it is dead, many say it is alive: people write them, read them, buy them . . . My suggestion is that it is neither entirely alive nor entirely dead, but that certain novels are dead and others alive: the living ones are the necessary ones. Living novels are the ones that capture changes in the world's intellectual, aesthetic or moral awareness, a new sensitivity, new problems, or that propose a model for these new levels of awareness, or that explode the superstition about the unchanging identity of human nature, or that propose new paradoxes – in the here and now, in this sort of purgatory of history. This is why I published (and I cite at random) Pasternak and Velso Mucci, Parise and Gombrowicz, Lombardi and Fuentes, Vargas Llosa and Sanguineti, Balestrini and Selby, Porta and Henry Miller . . . even the heterogeneity of these pairs of names strikes me as vital and amusing. This is why I am publishing the young writers of the Avant-garde.

I shall cite another example: there are political books, or rather books about politics. Many are 'justificatory', in other words, they are books that testify to a failure to take political action. Others, not many, are wholly political books, writings that accompany a concrete political act and that the public wants and has to know about: recently, in three or four days, the bookshops have sold

an entire and considerably large print run of a little book
containing some essays by Ernesto 'Che' Guevara: I
would have agreed to publish this book even if it had not
sold, because Guevara's writings are necessary writings.
In fact I am publishing a little series ('Documents of the
South American Revolution'), made up of books written
by authors (especially 'authors of history') that are not as
well known as Guevara and consequently sell less: I am
publishing them all the same because young people want
them and because it is right that they have them.

Breaking the breast barrier. I shall make one more
example and then I shall stop making examples: once, a
German journalist wrote that I had gone from political
commitment to pornographic commitment; apart from
the fact that I am a supporter of so-called disengagement
and apart from the fact that I call pornographic only
what strikes me as repugnant but not what may violate an
ordinary – or at any rate petit bourgeois – rhetorical
code, I see no connection: it is right, or, as I said before,
necessary, that the bombardment of recent magazines
has achieved this amazing result: the breast barrier has
been broken, and you can show a naked breast on a book
cover. Of course, this is a micro-revolution, but in fact
we must make only those revolutions that it is possible to
make; even though, to my mind, having made one revolution, it is possible to make another bigger one . . .

I don't want to give the impression that I am a man
who sees publishing from a pedagogical standpoint, a
man who feels he has something to teach. So, I would
add: how does a publisher live? A publisher lives under
bombardment, namely the bombardment of printed
paper in a world that has become smaller and devoid of
frontiers, and a publisher is glad of that bombardment:
from the bombs that fall on his desk he must choose the
ones to throw back so that they may explode in the minds
of readers. So a publisher lives surrounded by collaborators, who, because they are intelligent and sensitive, are

often temperamental: during office hours, a publisher must use all of himself and especially his eyes and nose. Manuscripts and books already printed often materialize in the form of a person: of the author, who is often intelligent, temperamental and brilliant: the publisher must use all of himself.

A publisher is a person who spends money to buy titles, to pay royalties, to pay the production costs and the general costs needed to publicize books. Therefore a publisher has to do with people who handle money, with banks, with accountants, with data-processing centres: a publisher must use all of himself and I don't know which part of all of himself.

The publisher is a vehicle for ideas. A publisher must publish books that then must be sold. Therefore a publisher has to do with a sales apparatus, and the technical problems are many, but perhaps, here too, apart from that part of himself that I cannot define, a publisher needs a nose for necessity . . .

Can a publisher change the world? Only with difficulty: a publisher cannot even change his publisher. Can he change the world of books? He can publish certain books that come to be a part of the world of books and change it with their presence. This statement may seem formal and does not fully correspond with my thinking: my mirage, the thing that I hold to be the major factor behind that 'Fortune' I mentioned earlier, is the book that lays hold of you, that book that throws things out of kilter, the book that 'does' something to the people who read it, the book that is a 'good listener' and picks up and transmits messages that may well be mysterious but are sacrosanct, the book that amid the hotchpotch of everyday history listens to the final note, the one that will still ring out when the non-essential sounds have died away . . .

Is it a good thing for women to wear long skirts, or would it be better if they wore short ones? Did the

German social democrats do well to join the Great
Coalition? Why did Senator Merzagora resign as president of the Senate? Is the birth pill a good thing or a bad
thing? What is the ultimate meaning of science for man?
What are the prospects for the labour unions in Italy?
Would it be better to do this book typographically or
lithographically? Can we pay this advance? What is
Italy's position within the European Common Market?
Is it possible to make a psychoanalytic analysis of the fad
for buttons, slogans and badges? Is the new publishing
by chance the one favoured by the Red Guards? Can the
culture industry be justified? Is this the culture industry?
What are students reading and what do they think about?
What is the minimum wage? What is the social function
of obscenity? It appears that the Bolivian General
Ovando wants to sell the *Diary of Che Guevara* for
250,000 dollars: is the publisher still a publisher or a financier of the war of oppression? Is the wave of Black
Power rising in the United States? Will it stamp out bel-
licose imperialism? Is the unrest affecting Italian youth a
purely physical malaise or is it virtually political and
rational? Is there any hope? . . .

What is a publisher? I don't know what a Publisher is,
a publisher *in se*, that is, but I try to understand the reasons why I am a publisher. And I admit: a publisher has
nothing to teach, he does not want to catechize anyone,
and in a certain sense he knows nothing. And I admit: a
publisher, if he is not to be ridiculous, must not take
himself too seriously, a publisher is a handcart, he is a
man with a sign saying 'printed paper for sale', he is a
vehicle for messages, he is at most, to paraphrase this
McLuhan that everyone is talking about, a promoter of
messages that are also massages. And I admit: that the
publisher is nothing, a mere meeting place, where messages are received, rerouted and transmitted . . . Yet: the
right messages must be received and rerouted, and writing that rises to the level of reality must be received and

transmitted. And so: the publisher must throw himself headlong into reality, even at the risk of drowning. Knowing nothing, he must make everything known, everything that is of use, and that helps to make people more conscious at different levels. To dive into reality: to try his 'Fortune'. In this sense, 'Fortune' acquires a real meaning, it becomes a horizon, a triumphant and unfettered life . . . And so: a publisher is nothing, he may think of himself as a mere handcart, but a publisher must also approach his work on the basis of a very risky working hypothesis: that everything, really everything, must and will change.

* * *

The '*Edizioni della libreria*' series made its début with a circular personally endorsed by Feltrinelli in May 1967. It was intended for his nine bookshops, in nine different cities. 'Our Milan bookshop has prepared a series of remarkably interesting political pamphlets. In many ways, this is a necessary adjunct to the party's publicity material on some particularly urgent topics. These are documents and texts necessary for the political training of militants.' The pamphlets were usually short, and sold at an average price of 250 lire; in other words, next to nothing. The first concerned Italy: Secchia's speech before the Senate against the reform of the public security law, and Terraccini on the same subject. But hard on the heels of these came the series 'Documents of the South American Revolution': Che Guevara (*We need to create two, three, many Vietnams*), Régis Debray (*Revolution within Revolution*), the resolutions of the Central Committee of the Cuban Communist Party (*We Accept Our Revolutionary Responsibilities*), Camillo Castano (*Ten Days in Guatemala*), Douglas Bravo (*Guerrilla Warfare in Venezuela*), and others again on Brazil, Puerto Rico, Argentina, Chile, Peru, and Bolivia.

The series rapidly acquired new sections: Africa, Asia, the

Italian debate, the problem of Southern Italy and the student
struggle. A hundred or so titles in all. The standard print run
was four thousand copies. Big sellers were *The Blood of Lions*
by Edoard Marcel Simbu (on the guerrilla war in the Congo)
and *School for the Students*. Feltrinelli differentiated 'militant'
production from the publishing house's programmes, perhaps
in order to maintain a certain equilibrium, perhaps in order to
make the message more incisive. As far as he was concerned,
those little books had become the most urgent thing.

In August 1967 he also published the first number of
Tricontinental, a bimonthly produced by the Organization of
Solidarity with the Peoples of Asia, Africa and Latin America.

It all began during the Havana Conference in early 1966. In
Europe, this had been largely ignored, but it was an important
event. For the first time, there was a meeting that included six
hundred delegates from the neutral governments of Africa and
Asia, from the Communist countries (USSR, China, Outer
Mongolia, North Vietnam, North Korea, and Cuba) and from
international Communist organizations (the World Federation
of Labour Unions and the Federation of Democratic Youth).
The assembly proclaimed the need for 'a global revolutionary
strategy to counter the global imperialist strategy'.
Tricontinental was the new organ of information, made in
Cuba, with English, French and Italian co-editions (published
by Feltrinelli).

'The duty of every revolutionary is to make revolution'; the
magazine was aimed at those who were in agreement with this:
articles on the death of Lumumba, the oil wars in the Middle
East, Ho Chi Minh writing to Johnson, struggle and victory in
Laos, the speeches of Che, news from the Black Power movement in the States. Of particular interest was the third number
(December 1967). The cover featured a fresco by Sebastiano
Matta for *Tricontinental*, a piece by Jean-Paul Sartre (reflections on the Russell Tribunal), the Debray trial in Camiri, then
half-way though, *'Palestina: comandos "Tormenta"'*. For the
first time, a journalist (unnamed) had managed to meet the
leaders of Al Fatah, the group that had given a revolutionary

character to the Palestinian cause. From Damascus, they had taken him by jeep to the secret encampment.

Following the Six Days' War (June 1967) and the occupation of the Gaza Strip, there were 350,000 new arrivals in the refugee camps. The Arab world (not always united) opened its eyes. No more hand-outs from the United Nations; 'the aggressor is a tool of American imperialism!' The men of Al Fatah repeated the slogan to the correspondent from *Tricontinental*. They were seated on bunks, in a little room, among maps, rifles and uniforms. Outside, the yelling of the instructors could be heard. One of them, Abou Ammar, expressed himself with 'serenity and maturity': a hard face, a generous expression. When he took off his military beret, he revealed a pronounced bald patch. He stubbed out his cigarette on the muddy toe of his boot. Suddenly he said: 'There are no wars without deaths, but it is preferable to die killing the enemy and knowing that final victory will be ours rather than to wait for a slow, inexorable death, sitting beneath a tent in the desert.'

Since February 1969, Abou Ammar has been the leader of the Palestine Liberation Organization, Yasser Arafat. I don't know exactly when, but it was in the autumn of 1967 that he granted Feltrinelli his first public interview.

7

It seems that in the early sixties men and women emerged from the stone age, ready to give a meaning to words like 'independence', 'sovereignty', and 'self-determination', even though they had yet to give those same terms an ideological connotation. It was a new vision of the world: all peoples could decide for themselves, no more oppressive systems, full rights for all the new names in the great address book of the world.

All the lonely people, where do they all come from? In order to reply to this question, books had to be made, translated and sent to the stores as fast as possible: investigations written by journalists with guts, photos by the adventurous paparazzi of war. Understanding 'the other' in order to understand ourselves. Politics as the highest form of human endeavour. Through politics, people thought, we can understand everything. It followed that no goal was unrealizable. A bit of courage, a handshake, and we can fight! The vision of the future concerned tomorrow's generation but also that of the day after tomorrow.

Many of these people have now become more realistic; politics has not after all achieved everything. And how naïve the watchwords of that time now seem . . . it was like a bipolar Empire, with its internal conflicts and external inhibitions. The disorderly armies of the Peoples had no room for manœuvre. Perhaps we are all more realistic now, as the scenes of the tragedies become less and less exotic and a dramatically shrinking future looms over a terribly tense present.

Feltrinelli's Cuban adventure can be divided into two phases. The first, between 1964 and 1965, was spent in the hunt for a great book, the memoirs of Fidel Castro. The second, from 1967 to 1970 at the least, was another matter altogether.

The Castro book was to be the big new 'scoop'. A major international best-seller. Or, at least, this was the plan, as had been the case with *Doctor Zhivago*.

A few days before Feltrinelli's editor Valerio Riva left for Cuba, John Fitzgerald Kennedy was assassinated. The first news, sent out by a Dallas radio station, was that the Cuban secret service was responsible. At that moment, Fidel Castro was never at greater risk of being eliminated. Amid the total chaos of that late November 1963, the world rocked on its foundations.

What to do about the plans for the memoirs of the *Lider Maximo*? Carry on, give up, or perhaps it would be better to postpone? Shall we go to the centre of things, or shall we sit in hiding to watch what happens? Riva argued with the travel agency, but he left for Cuba all the same, via New York and Mexico City. Hot on his heels, via Prague, came the Cuban journalist Carlos Franqui.

Over a year before, Juan Goytisolo had introduced Franqui to Riva during a conference of the European Writers' Community held in Florence. The former editor of the daily *Revolución*, for which he was now a correspondent, Franqui wanted to propose a European edition of the speeches of Fidel Castro. He was taken to Milan, where they told him they wanted an authentic book of memoirs, beginning before the Sierra Maestra and perhaps ending with the Cuba of the missile crisis. After I don't know how long, Franqui let it be known that something could be done. This was followed by much

coming and going between Italy and Cuba in order to gather
documentation and draft a first outline to be put before the
author. Riva and Herberto Padilla acted as ghostwriters.

The results of that preparatory work were taken back to
Havana by Carlos Franqui. He was also carrying a roll of
twenty-five thousand dollars hidden in the lining of his suitcase. It was the advance for Fidel Castro Ruiz.

Riva's journey lasted longer than predicted. After stopping over
in New York, he spent a week in Mexico City. It was not easy to
obtain a visa from the Cuban embassy in Mexico City. This had
been tried some time before by Lee Harvey Oswald, who had
become famous in the meantime.

When Riva finally landed in Havana, on 9 December, the
nightmare began. There was no one waiting for him at the airport. Franqui, who should have preceded him, did not show up.
When questioned, Riva declared that he was the guest of Fidel
Castro and that he had come to persuade him to write his memoirs. It was the most inopportune moment for cobbled-together
explanations, without so much as a scrap of official paper and
after a suspicious stopover in New York. The faces around him
darkened.

Riva described his first night in Cuba in a letter to Feltrinelli
dated 20 January 1964:

I couldn't understand what had happened. I was without
a passport and confined to a hotel room on the twenty-
second floor of a skyscraper from which you could see
the poorly lit city. The paint was peeling slightly and the
room was dirty. There was no soap in the bathroom: the
air conditioning did not work very well, and a draught
played directly on my neck. I spent most of the night
pacing up and down the room, wringing my hands and
wondering what was going to happen the next day.

The next day, luckily, Franqui arrived. His return to
Havana had been delayed by a technical fault in his plane.

Seven days stuck in Prague, where he had almost lost the roll of dollars.

Franqui was in a tricky position in Cuba. After the revolution, he had been the most outstanding figure in the cultural information sector. A Trotskyist, with a passion for the avant-garde, he had often argued with the Communists in the columns of *Revolución*. His star began to wane after the birth of *Lunes*, a cultural supplement printed by his paper and edited by a first-rate writer, Guillermo Cabrera Infante. In their attempt to avoid catching 'castroenteritis', the editorial staff was stricken by a painful case of 'castroencephalitis'. The supplement had to close. The official excuse was that there was a paper shortage.

Recently, Franqui had spent a lot of time outside Cuba. He had left his family in Italy. This had not passed unobserved. Again from Riva's long letter:

The business of Franqui's wife and children remaining in Italy could have meant that Franqui had returned to Cuba, but with reservations: that in reality he had already decided to go into exile and that he had become more attached to the publishing house than to the revolution. It would have been really serious if those people had received an impression of this kind. Serious for Franqui, who would certainly have been forbidden to leave the island; serious for the book, because in the situation we found ourselves in, with twenty-five thousand dollars already paid out, without a signed contract, with a manuscript made up of things that were not very well known but not entirely unpublished either (and the only unpublished material concerned the guerrilla war), the suspicion that we were at the centre of a manœuvre that was in some way a counter-revolutionary move could have spelled complete catastrophe.

Despite these worries, for Riva the days passed tranquilly enough. It seemed like the typical holiday in which nothing ever happens. Of Fidel, there was not a trace. Celia Sanchez, his right-hand man, let Franqui know that the Commandante was perhaps on a trip, and that he would hear something within a few days. In Cuba, keeping people waiting is a customary ritual, especially when it is a matter of a meeting with the leader. Riva describes it all very well:

> There is a curious custom in Havana. When Celia Sanchez tells someone that Fidel is going to call him for a meeting, the fortunate mortal must lock himself in his hotel room, with the telephone near to hand, and wait for it to ring. The call may come at any hour of the day or night, but I think this is a legend. My call, for example, came at seven in the evening. The designee must be at his post when Fidel calls. If he calls and does not find you, you might as well pack your bags and go. You are on the blacklist. The role, rank and fame of the person singled out for the 'great honour' is of no importance.

After three weeks, Riva was more and more prostrated as X hour did not come. On New Year's Eve, just to raise his sagging morale, he decided to organize a little private party. But at the crucial moment they called the hotel to tell him to rush straight over to Franqui's house. Castro was expected any minute. Here is the scene, again from Riva's letter:

> Three long American cars arrived at high speed. The first entered the courtyard of Franqui's house, I saw that it was full of soldiers armed to the teeth [. . .]. The left-hand front door of the second car opened and out got a big man wearing an old beret at a crooked angle. He had a short beard, a broad face and a nice smile. 'Franqui!' he yelled, and he moved forward to embrace him. I stepped forward with my hand outstretched and I said to him: 'At last, how are you? I'm happy to see you.' He took my hand, turned toward Franqui and said 'This is the Italian, I suppose?' Franqui said: 'Yes, this is Valerio.'

'Well, Valerio. Welcome to Cuba. And forgive me: I
should have come before but I couldn't. These are terrible times.' He shook his head and dragged me into the
house. He sprawled out on the divan and immediately
said to Franqui: 'You know, Franqui, I've read the book,
it's really wonderful. I never thought it would come out
so well. You've done very well: I really like it.
Stupendous. I gave it to some other people to read: they
all say it's marvellous. I'm really happy. You've done a
good job. What d'you say, can we add anything? I've got
stacks of stuff that perhaps you're not familiar with, I
want to send you it so you can take a look. [. . .] There's
only one part, the one about the battle of Santa Clara: I
didn't write that bit at all: it was Che. The people ought
to be told. You know, I don't want them to tell me that I
filch other people's stuff. Hey, why don't we get someone
to do a thorough job on that story?' Franqui put in a
word: 'It's true, it's not your part, but you will have
noticed that it's all within quotation marks. What do you
say, shall we have Nunez tell that part?' I felt as if I were
sitting on hot coals: all I needed now was for them to
start talking about the good old days. [. . .] Either Fidel
tells the story or that episode is out: there's no arguing
about that. I was worried most of all about Franqui
launching into a discussion of the guerrilla war: he says
he has no memory, but he can even remember the
number of matches he consumed in the Sierra Maestra.
In the meantime, I was studying Fidel: he has a really
strange half-falsetto voice. Sometimes his tone is high
and shrill; other times it is soft and suave. Using his right
hand, he continually played with his paratrooper's beret,
adjusting it over his forehead, over his ear. He was forever crossing and uncrossing his legs. He chose to sit
down on the divan and his posture was not exactly
indecorous, nor – properly speaking – was it relaxed. He
is fat, with a belly and a big backside, but seen from close
up he gives an impression of youth and strength. The

beard looks as if it has been stuck on: the skin of his face
is soft, smooth, childlike. His features are kind, pleasant,
not military at all. He is forever excusing himself, listens
with attention and composure, and never interrupts the
others. He seems shy, but is a great coquet. At first, however, I thought his attentiveness was merely a matter of
form. He has an idea in mind and it is not going to be
easy to persuade him to change it. If you tell him something he doesn't want to hear, he simply doesn't hear it.
And he uses the same tone as before, but kindly, as if it
were his fault if he has forgotten what you just said to
him a moment before. Money was mentioned, but all he
said was: 'Yes, yes thanks'. [. . .] I showed him your
report on the planned contracts, the photocopies of the
letters; Franqui spoke to him about Frankfurt and of the
good job we had done; I insisted on my plan to add
things and said that the most important part is the part
between 1961 and 1963. But Fidel wouldn't be persuaded: he made it very clear: 'I don't want to touch it. If
I touch it, I'll ruin it. At most, I shall limit myself to
writing a preface in which I tell the story of the book,
because I want people to know that this is your work,
and that I don't come into it.' It was the most dangerous
position you could imagine. [. . .]Then I had a brain-
wave: in New York I had had Mike Bessie write me a
letter. I ran to my briefcase, took out the letter, I showed
it to Fidel and began talking to him about America and
of the interest that his book would arouse there. He read
the letter carefully and said: 'Obviously these gentlemen
see the matter from a commercial point of view. They are
thinking of the money they can make, because it is obvious that I am well known in America and a lot of people
will buy my book. However, it might be a great trick, you
see, to use this means to let them know how things really
are and that I am not the ogre the newspapers make me
out to be.' He began to wax enthusiastic: his eyes glit-
tered for a moment, and he raised his left fist: 'It would

really be a fine jest. To use this book to take them from
the rear,' and he made a gesture with his outstretched
hand, energetically, as if he were sticking something into
someone. 'Because, at bottom, the people of the capitalist
world don't know me at all. [. . .] Let them find out, let
them read: something will stick. And not just what the
newspapers say. They can take this book home and keep
it. Now it is decided: I must throw myself into this.' And
I began to insist once more on the need for a fresh work.
'But I don't have the time,' said he, 'you have no idea
how many things I have to do all blessed day.' I know
that he also does pointless things, that he wastes hours
and hours trying out tractors, kids' bicycles, new types of
rifle, seeing how much milk can be squeezed by hand
from a cow's udder [. . .]. 'We can use a tape-recorder,' I
suggested. The idea struck him. 'Right,' he said, 'that
wouldn't be so complicated.' Franqui explained to him
that, often, the tape-recorder gives unexpectedly good
results: more liveliness, more immediacy.

Well played, Riva, you've done it. But the author was left
with a last doubt:
'So, how does this tape-recorder work?'

In those same hours, a Soviet delegation led by Nikolay
Podgorny was arriving in Havana. Preparations had to be made
for Castro's imminent journey to the Soviet Union, where he was
to make a long-term trade agreement. It was about sugar. Cuba
was going to supply millions of tons of it to the Soviet Union: a
permanent (and well-paid) market for the national product.

Riva has another anecdote: as soon as Podgorny got off the
plane, the first thing he apparently asked Castro was: 'Can we
have the rights to your book of memoirs?' Castro, with shrewd
candour, replied that he would ask the publisher Feltrinelli.

But what was the publisher Feltrinelli up to?

Here is his schedule: departure for New York with Inge on 30

January 1964, one day in the Big Apple, then Washington, for a two- or three-day stopover, and then on to Havana via Mexico. The planned stopover: ten nights. Feltrinelli explained all this himself to the American consul when he went to ask for the State Department waiver. He also told the diplomat about Castro's memoirs: the draft text written by the ghostwriters contained a lot of propaganda and not much analysis of the facts, more work was still necessary, especially for the period 1959–63. Feltrinelli seemed to attach much importance to his time in the United States: 'to get to know from first-hand sources about US policy with regard to Latin America and to Cuba in particular'. He stated that he wanted to get a 'balanced' idea of the situation.

On 22 January, the US embassy in Rome telegraphed its opinion to Washington:

We believe that [Feltrinelli] will in any case want to publish Castro's memoirs; and he can get to Cuba without having to pass through the United States. The information and the points of view that he could obtain during his brief visit to the United States could favorably influence the way he handles the memoirs, while denying him entry could give rise to a negative judgement of the US position on Cuba and Castro. In short, we see nothing to gain and a lot to lose by refusing to give him a transit pass.

Riva was highly perplexed by Feltrinelli's plans. In Latin America, you are well received if you come as a European who is offering a new opening; but you will be detested if you arrive as a friend of the United States. He urged:

Always travel as if you were a normal tourist and not like some jittery international conspirator. [. . .] As I have already told you, foreign news can have peculiar repercussions here: if you make particular statements, I cannot answer for the welcome you will find in Cuba. Despite everything, we are still on the razor's edge, since everything always depends on Castro's mood. So be very careful. There is no mediation, it is impossible. At present the United States have taken a hard knock, their hands are tied for the imminent elections, but it is hidebound types like Goldwater who are calling the tune. The Americans will be making no pro-Cuban statements, at least not until the President has been elected. [. . .] So it's a waste of time. What's more, in Cuba they just don't want to know as far as America is concerned.

In New York, Giangiacomo and Inge spent the day with Sanford Greenburger, the agent who spotted talent for the publishing house. In Washington, the principal contact was Henry Brandon, the correspondent of the *Sunday Times*. But the programme also included meetings with Charles Murphy, the senior editor of *Fortune*, and with Ben Bradlee of *Newsweek*, as well as a visit to the physicist Leo Szilard. Szilard had spent a long time in Italy and he knew Inge, who had introduced him to Giangiacomo. He was the man who, together with Einstein, had written to Roosevelt warning him that the Nazis were on the verge of acquiring atomic power.

On the night of 5 February, a plane landed, a sweetish scent wafted in through the open door, and Mr and Mrs Feltrinelli were in Havana.

* * *

For a long time, the charm of Havana lay in the fact that it always resembled itself. (This is no longer the case.)

In early February 1964, my parents experienced all that the capital can offer interested and important tourists: Tropicana & Bodeguita; Hemingway's house (old Renée set the table); the heroes of the Revolution (Haydée Santamaría); Bola de Nieve, the most amazing voice in the Caribbean; and the city's intellectuals. I imagine a lot of crushed ice beneath the palm trees, sunbathing and the moon hanging over the famous horizon. The Feltrinellis were lodged in a government villa with garden and pool.

In the meantime, Italo Calvino, who had just married
Chiquita, was treading the threadbare amaranth carpet of the
Habana Libre, a hotel straight out of great cinema and a
symbol of the time when Havana really was the navel of the
world. The writer was making his first return to the country
where he had been born. He had been invited by La Casa de
las Américas, on the suggestion of Julio Cortázar. On the
evening of 10 February he was scheduled to give a public
reading from *The Road to San Giovanni*. Amused for some
reason by Calvino's presence, Feltrinelli could not attend the
soirée because at nine-thirty Fidel arrived at the government
villa.

The first meeting was inevitably an exploratory affair. Castro
was expecting someone with the aplomb of an old millionaire,
a powerful international publisher. So much so that he began to
talk 'business', sounding out the possibilities of mediation for
the import of chemical and industrial products, agricultural
machinery, taxis, all in exchange for sugar. He said with great
confidence that in 1970 Cuba would produce 8–10 million tons
of it and that the island would also be able to export cattle.

He did not notice right away that the Italian could have been
the same age as he and was not wearing spats. The same Italian
also asked non-pertinent questions: when were the elections
going to be held?, Was mediation possible with the USA? What
was happening in Latin America? He pronounced Spanish
well, but made grammatical mistakes with every sentence.
Castro slowly began to catch on, he stiffened and asked a couple
of times: 'Is this really the millionaire?' Reassured, he decided
that it would be better to show his hand. To impress those
present, he replied to some question or other with a quotation
from Machiavelli: a lengthy lucubration that took even Riva –
who was present at the meeting – by surprise. Machiavelli,
maintained Fidel, had often been misinterpreted.

As they talked, the atmosphere grew more relaxed and the
initial coolness was transformed into liking. Castro laughed,
joked, talked, and backslapped. Feltrinelli was almost

embarrassed by so much cordiality. 'Unspoiled' (in English) was the word Inge chose to define him in her journal.

The conversation freewheeled: the October crisis, agricultural production, the clichés and the tedium of the official documents produced by the Communist parties of Latin America ('Socialism must not be boring but joyous'), relations with the States and, also, *Doctor Zhivago*. Castro said that he had read it, in installments, in the *Diario de la Marina*, in Batista's time. Feltrinelli turned to Riva: 'Those rats! They published a pirate edition!'

At the end of the visit, Feltrinelli noted down his first impressions:*

In my opinion, F. C. is not a Communist or Marxist because the role of 26 July contradicts all Marxist orthodox procedure, because the role of the peasants contradicts in procedure [sic], because his attitude to organization does not reflect the traditional Communist definition or practice. He is a middle-class Utopian and idealist (whose Utopia once came true). He runs this country as if it was his company, his corporation (poor application of the American executive philosophy). He has to be idealist because, as in all countries in Africa or Latin America, there is no bourgeoisie.

Castro's words of farewell to everyone were 'See you soon'. Naturally, no one could say when. Patience was required. Then something changed. On 19 February, Feltrinelli wrote to the collaborators of the publishing house:

Dear Friends,
Here is the situation: after having waited for two weeks, in which we have had only one interview with the Supreme Beard,† we had made up our minds to leave and

---

* English in the text.
† Play on words: in Italian, *barba* can mean both beard and bore.

let things take their rather indefinite course. The days
passed like this (in a magnificent villa with park, palm
trees and revolutionary guards armed with sub-machine-
guns): Riva was supposed to arrive at our place every
morning at eight, but then he would arrive at eleven-
thirty. Numerous telephone calls were made at eight,
nine and ten-thirty, looking for him in his hotel, but to
no avail. Then Franqui would arrive. The stenographer
was the only one to arrive at the agreed time. At eleven-
thirty, therefore, we would have our general meeting to
go over the latest news. Almost every day, we would
receive advance warning to the effect that Fidel would be
coming on the following morning without fail. The night
before he had been watching the pelota, then he had to
go to interview a fisherman who had arrived from
Florida, at four in the morning he had been seen at the
Habana Libre talking with Liza Howard (US television),
and he had gone to bed at 6; at 9 he had been seen visiting chickens (he is a great fan of chickens, cows, etc.),
then, yes, there had been a brief cabinet meeting to
decide whether to cut off the water supplies to the base
at Guantanamo and so on. But tomorrow morning the
thing was sure to come off. Come the following
morning . . . After two weeks of this life, we decided to
leave. But on the day of our departure, we received word
from several quarters of a new evening visit, so OK,
we'll put off our departure. And that evening, in fact, he
arrived [. . .] in a good mood and said, good, come to my
house tomorrow at 9 and we'll get down to work
together. We went, and we found him wearing slippers
and pajama jacket and pants and naturally his beard and
for two hours we got in some good work. He told us to
come back tomorrow (that is today) but today he was
sleeping, he had been obliged to get up twice during the
night on important affairs of state and had had almost no
rest. OK, we'll come back tomorrow. The most important fact is that we are authorized to show up every

morning at 9 at his house and we no longer have to wait
for him. A decisive step. When he is in a good mood, he
talks willingly and a lot. But you have to keep him off his
favourite subject. Which is cows. He dreams of bound-
less cattle farms and, with a certain sexual satisfaction, of
the artificial insemination of one hundred thousand cows
that in 1965 would give him one hundred thousand
calves, of which 50,000 would be females that could be
made pregnant in their turn (artificial insemination) in
1967 and would give birth in 1968 to another 50,000
calves of which 25,000 would be females, and in the
meantime the 100,000 original cows would have become
pregnant once more . . . and so on, for ever and ever,
amen. Our hero talks all the time, to interrupt him you
have to shout. He talks about everything. When he talks
about politics, for example about the role of the party
and of the state of Cuba, you can see that he is improvis-
ing, that is to say, he develops his ideas as he talks (it
gives one a certain pleasure to think that certain questions stimulate him to have new thoughts that tomorrow
(literally) can determine his political stance). . .

So, starting from a certain day, they could knock on the
Comandante's door every morning. On the roof of the house
there was a small chicken coop and a basketball hoop. In the
breaks, Giangiacomo and Fidel would take a few shots at the
basket while Inge photographed their one-on-one matches. 'He
has taken, damn and blast him, a certain liking for me, with the
result that he will work, that is, dictate, only if I am there,'
Feltrinelli wrote to Milan.
    They worked on the basis of a question and answer system.
The topics were extremely varied. On the great political figures: Castro had a poor view of Truman; he had even read his
memoirs, badly written and presumptuous. He admired De
Gaulle's rebellious spirit, but found his memoirs laughable.
That man never made mistakes, he had foreseen everything,
never a doubt, 'a born genius'. Churchill, as far as memoirs

went, was the best of all. On the Communist nature of the revolution: 'The revolution would have been made and would have
been the same even if there had not been one single
Communist. Most of the middle class, and the petit bourgeoisie, are for the revolution: the party must not become a
part of the state.' But, right after that, on the distinction
between party and state: 'We expect party functionaries to be
state functionaries and administrators too.' On the contradictions inherent to his being a man of government and a
professional revolutionary Castro responded with an evasive
smile: 'Yes, there are [contradictions], but in the final analysis
each country must make the revolution with the men at its disposal.'

These were followed by more questions on Cuba, on the
'dogmatic' wing of the party, freedom in the arts, the roles of
science and culture, small private enterprises, the failure to
hold elections in 1959, Latin America, the characteristics of
revolutionary movements, relations with the United States, the
USSR, the different applications of the socialist model, the
agricultural crisis in Eastern Europe, Khruschev, and why did
those socialist states that consolidated themselves become conservative?

Finally, personal questions: his adolescence, the first struggles for peace, the visa for a trip to the United States in 1949: 'I
still can't understand it.' And women too. Feltrinelli noted:
'His sly expression when I asked him what kind of woman he
liked': 'Refined, spiritual, sweet,' came the reply.

On Cuban–American relations, Feltrinelli made an interesting note after the meeting of 24 February, which went on until
four in the morning:

Was present during a long telephone call – about 35–40
minutes – with Liza Howard, who had been to see
Johnson. Liza said that opinions and orientation are
changing in Washington. [. . .] She asked (in Johnson's
name) the Cubans to find a way of making a conciliatory
gesture. Fidel replied that they had saved the life of an

American pilot who had ditched his plane into the sea, they had returned an aeroplane and a fishing boat. Liza suggested – asked for a statement to the effect that in September 1964 all Russian soldiers had left the island. Fidel said that there were only technical advisers, never had the Cuban government recognized the existence of Soviet military personnel on the island: in any case, he would think it over, but there was no hurry. Impression: highly satisfied, but in no hurry to close the deal (as he has already said on other occasions), but has, as I foresaw, an interest in normalization.

During his stay in Cuba, Feltrinelli kept an eye on the publishing house in Milan. Suggestions, orders, advice: on the campaign for the launch of Luigi Meneghello's book, on the organization of James Baldwin's visit, on advance orders for scientific books, on buying. 'Be careful not to order reprints when they are not necessary, but for Christ's sake do so when they are necessary.' Moreover, he was angry with Del Bo, Filippini, Pozzi, Spagnol and Morino: 'I detest your benevolent protectiveness, your phoney paternalism, and the psychological ignorance that leads you to believe that keeping me in ignorance will make me easier in my mind: my ears are ringing with your chatter: 'Uh-oh . . . look what happened today . . . but for goodness' sake let's not tell him because he'll get mad.' Spagnol wrote to him from Milan: 'I knew that the Caribbean was a hurricane zone, but I wasn't aware that they were powerful enough to disturb even the quiet waters of via Andegari . . .' For his part, Filippini sent him a gem: Einaudi wanted to publish a miscellany of Khruschev's speeches. 'An insider at Einaudi told me the reason for this: "Oh really?" (pronounced in the tones of a capricious child) "So Feltrinelli has gone to Cuba? Right. Then I'm going to Khruschev!"'

After a month of work with the stenographer, Feltrinelli went back home. He left Riva to carry on.

At the airport, he and Inge were told that the return flight

was going to be three or four hours late. In the end, it turned
out to be six hours. To kill the time, Feltrinelli dashed off a
note:*

> I have very mixed up feelings about this man: he is a sort
> of Garibaldi, utterly inapt to government work, inca-
> pable of working, reasoning and hard thinking.
> Impulsive, rhetorical. High-pitched. Ideologically con-
> fused. For example on the question of party and State
> (and in practice I don't think things are the way he says
> they are). I think he is poorly informed, he confuses his
> polemical denunciations with reality. He never asks for
> news, he seems to me a person so convinced of himself,
> of the things learned at random and stuck in his mind, of
> the clichés he has picked up, that talking to him is use-
> less. He doesn't listen (one gets the impression that two
> men might really count in the country and are danger-
> ous: Raul Castro and Che).

After the publisher's departure, work on the Castro book
came to a standstill almost immediately. Riva, who stayed on
for another two months, struggled to maintain his concentration. For his part, the author lost it altogether. Castro was
enthusiastic about the project but always had something else to
do. Everything depended on his dangerous mood swings.

To make matters worse, just when Castro was up and running, Franqui would make him lose the thread with pointless
questions that obliged him to launch into endless philosophical
lucubrations. In April, Riva wrote to Feltrinelli:

> For his own squalid little reasons, Franqui would love to
> get proof of Fidel's 'cultural liberalism' from this book,
> and he mistakes a set of superficial schoolboy notions for
> 'cultural liberalism' [. . .] Fidel has no original ideas: no
> one asks them of him, nor does he expect to dish them

---

* The first three lines are English in the text.

up. He has said this himself very well: his gift is political cunning, or, to put this more kindly, revolutionary sagacity. That is, again, a set of practical facts that the memory can reproduce in all their nuances. Let's put it this way, our man is an intellectual of action – not a philosopher or a thinker.

Riva was inundated with documents; he could not manage to persuade the people he was working with that it was possible to make a proper historical book simply by narrating facts: 'Their most frequent key is pomposity (a negative characteristic of South American writers) and ornateness (alas, a recurrent characteristic of the Cuban spirit).' In short, they couldn't 'wrap things up', as they say in the trade when things drag on and on. Franqui wanted to return to Paris; Riva, his liver and brain reduced to mush, was recalled to his homeland. The publishers Athenaeum of New York, Heinemann of London and Hachette of Paris, with whom agreements had already been made, were told that the work was going to take longer to produce than planned. The matter would be dealt with later.

* * *

The Cuban contacts continued throughout 1964 and on into May 1965. Feltrinelli went back to Havana, again with Riva. The situation appeared to have changed radically. The American provocation of 5 August 1964 in the Gulf of Tonkin had shown the Cubans that any form of conciliation between the United States and the Third World was out of the question. Fidel Castro protested over the aggression, and called for aid for Vietnam. The USSR, which had reached an agreement with the USA on the suspension of nuclear testing, moved with caution, and while the Soviets described the American attack as a 'foolhardy action', they preferred to go no farther than that. In October, Khruschev was ousted.

Castro had wanted to see his opponent's hand and now he had seen it: there was no longer any question of normalizing relations, his key themes became the condemnation of North American imperialism, solidarity among Third World countries and the various national liberation movements. Who supported this challenge?

In October 1964, Cuba took part in the conference of 'non-aligned' countries in Cairo and, with Nasser's help, managed to persuade the conference to lend its resolutions a more combative edge. A Cuban delegation visited the new bosses in Moscow and Ernesto Che Guevara went to Beijing to meet Mao Zedong. They wanted to assess the solidarity and the aims of the socialist camp, but the results were disappointing. Their initiative rejected, the Cuban leaders made an effort to forge a new unity: that of the three continents.

It was a key moment. Cuba was showing signs of breaking ranks with the creation of a 'tricontinental' platform uniting the tradition of the socialist revolution with the new energy of national liberation movements. Castro made contact with the Indonesian President Sukarno, with the leader of the Moroccan opposition Ben Barka, with Lumumba's successors, with the Kenyan Mondlane and with most of the Latin American movements. In Havana, preparations were under way for the Conference of the Asian, African and Latin American peoples (January 1966), which was to give rise to the Organization for Latin American Solidarity (OLAS): Cuba was the launching pad for all the aspirations of a restless world.

On 25 February 1965, Ernesto Che Guevara gave a speech in Algiers. He made a tough attack on the Soviet bloc for its fence-sitting attitude to the liberation movements. In April, his military mission left for the Congo. Che wanted 'two, three, many Vietnams' to counter the 'imperialist giant with the feet of clay'. Che had slipped the leash; it was time for him to go it alone.

Feltrinelli returned to Cuba in the middle of these transformations, and God only knows what impact they were to have on him. In Spain, he had ten copies printed of Castro's memoirs. Only as a demo: the work was not yet finished. But by that time, the book was only a pretext for talking about politics.

On arriving in Havana, he found that at least one thing was unchanged: waiting to meet the Comandante. He decided to speed things up. He prepared a card and hung it on the door of his room at the Habana Libre. Passers-by read: 'Hunger strike'. Within half an hour, reassuring functionaries rushed to make amends, and he was invited to Castro's home the following evening. This was when Fidel suggested a contest to see who made the best spaghetti. His recipe: two hens, 500 grams of pasta to be cooked in the chicken broth, with slivers of fresh cheese.

Of this evening, and of the subsequent meetings, Feltrinelli made notes and wrote down a detailed memorandum:

SUMMARY OF CONVERSATIONS WITH F. C. 1965
10 May, eight p.m., in Calle 11 to dine with Fidel (with spaghetti à la Fidel Castro). Conversation lasted from eight until 1.30.

As soon as we arrived – a cordial welcome – I began to talk of the book: Fidel said how well it had been done and that it was fine but much had to be added, especially for the post-revolutionary period, that for the next three months he was going to do nothing else, that he wanted to make an important book; he felt the need to talk about the post-revolutionary Cuban experience because it might be of use to others. He came back to this point several times during the discourse that followed when he mentioned the guidance that had not been forthcoming from the Russians and the Chinese and of how much he had done for the Algerians and the Venezuelans.

After a brief digression on the Cuban situation, on the prospects for agriculture (10 thousand tons of sugar for 1970, then the production of molasses for cattle fodder; of the other crops: fruit, etc.; of the gradual formation of an industry complementary to agriculture with a view to

developing an autonomous industry by 1980; of the 8
million head of cattle that Cuba would have in 1975), the
talk moved on to more general political problems.

1. The new Soviet leaders are capable, sensible.
Even though Khruschev had, especially for the Cubans,
many merits (he supported Cuba and then involved the
USSR in the Cuban and the Latin American revolutions,
which Stalin certainly would never have done). These
new leaders, however, brag less. Relations between Cuba
and the USSR, which in recent times had been politically very tense (he acknowledges that the USSR has
never had recourse to economic blackmail in an attempt
to get its own way on a political level), are now very
good. The tension with Khruschev sprang from the
Caribbean crisis and was now centred on the withdrawal
of the Soviet troops that Cuba finally agreed to as long as
they left all their armaments in Cuba.

2. Relations with Khruschev and the Caribbean crisis.
Khruschev, as has already been said, generously supported the Cuban revolution, which otherwise would
have been unable to stand up to the Americans. In fact,
this was a revolutionary tactic devised by the USSR to
counter American imperialism (see later).
    The missile question. Fidel says that, in a conversation
with a Soviet emissary, the latter asked him what he
thought the Soviets could do for Cuba. Fidel replied:
arrange things so that an attack on Cuba is seen as an
attack on the USSR – but *de facto*, not in words. In order
to ensure that these were not just generic assurances, it
was necessary to install medium-range missiles in Cuba.
Fidel's impression was that his interlocutor had been
sent specifically to agree on this, because the missiles
were then installed.
    Fidel saw the problem of the missile installations as a
strategic matter of the greatest importance and also as a

political matter inasmuch as it would have led to Cuba's becoming a *de facto* member of the nuclear club.

According to Fidel, Khruschev was perfectly aware of the strategic importance of such a decision.

At this point, three criticisms of the Soviets:

a) on a military level. The missiles were installed in the light of day in a very vulnerable position with insufficient anti-aircraft protection, especially against low-level flight. The Soviet ground-to-air anti-aircraft missiles were inefficient below three thousand feet (the ones left in Cuba have now been modified to be efficient from fifteen hundred feet upwards), while the protection offered by the anti-aircraft guns was also insufficient.

b) international politics. Khruschev made a mistake in telling Kennedy that these were only defensive missiles: in fact, he deceived the American president without solving anything because at the end of the day the photographs demonstrated that they were anything but defensive. He ought to have said frankly that these were armaments that fell within the framework of a Soviet–Cuban accord.

c) relations with Cuba: 1) ordering the removal of the missiles without consulting the Cubans, who were *de facto* partners in a bilateral agreement; 2) even accepting UN inspections. It would have been sufficient to add whether or not the Cubans were in agreement.

The Caribbean crisis and the withdrawal of the missiles, followed by that of the Soviet troops, could have had terrible psychological consequences for the Cuban people, who would have felt completely unprotected.

Fidel's impression was that, in the Caribbean crisis too, Khruschev was still among the most courageous of Soviet leaders. The others were still more worried about the possible consequences.

3. The Chinese. Sino-Soviet dissension and Vietnam. Much of Castro's original liking for the Chinese had

dissipated. The Chinese revolutionary attitude in which
he had once believed in fact concealed: a) exclusively
Chinese power politics; b) a continuous, systematic, stubborn and irrational smear campaign against the USSR.

Once they used to say: the intentions are good, it is
only the means employed (illegal propaganda in socialist
countries, factionalism and accusations against the
Soviets) that are bad. In fact, now, it is known that the
means correspond to a politics that is certainly not revolutionary politics but exclusively Chinese power politics.
For example, during the Caribbean crisis the Chinese did
nothing: no advice for either the Cubans or the Soviets.
Only later – and it is a pity that that later did not coincide with the end of socialist Cuba, an end that they
could have blamed on the Soviets – did they stage a
protest. But it was very much a demonstration for
demonstration's sake.

For example, with regard to Vietnam, the Chinese attitude was equivocal, it put a brake on Soviet aid, and
tended to alienate Vietnam from the Vietcong: their
grudge against the Soviets was stronger than their revolutionary zeal.
They ought to set aside their disagreements: the Soviets
are prepared to help Vietnam and union with the USSR
would make them safe from American attack.

For example, the factionalism of the Latin American
parties leads to complete inactivity. The Cubans, at
times, help the revolutionary movements outside the
Communist parties, but they never try to divide a party.

Mao is an arteriosclerotic old fool who talks with the
gods (see reference to recent interview). He is a shit. As
long as he is alive, you cannot count on any changes in
Chinese policies. The absurdity of Mao's attitude and
his senility emerge clearly from some documents in
Fidel's possession. What's more, the verbal account of
the recent Kosygin–Mao meeting, about the Vietcong,
shows that the Chinese stance is absurd. With the

Soviets, you can talk, you can get them to understand things and, gradually, induce them to support the revolutionary movements.

4. Africa and Latin America.
The revolution in Latin America is certainly under way. Currently in Colombia, in Paraguay and in Chile the situation is developing fairly rapidly.
In Venezuela the guerrilla war is still developing. Cuba's support of this movement is quasi-official. But the Cubans could not do this if they didn't have Soviet backing in their turn. The Cubans give and do what they can. Santo Domingo: the attitude of the Americans is really absurd. Bosch was certainly not a Communist and at first the movement was no more than a military putsch. But the panic of the Americans has transformed the Santo Domingo case into a popular revolt. It has created a rift within the OSA. Caamaño was an unknown officer but many young Latin American officers could well follow the example he set by giving the people arms.

The Cubans have pushed the USSR into the United Nations debate. The most explosive situation, however, is in Africa: the Congo, Angola, South Africa and some east African countries are on the brink of revolution. More Soviet support – perhaps indirect – is required and large quantities of arms ought to be sent to Nasser and Ben Bella. This revolutionary spirit of international aid needs developing. When there was tension between Algeria and Morocco, the Cubans didn't think twice before sending a fully equipped battalion to Algeria within eight days.

5. American imperialism.
While Fidel never spoke against capitalism in general or in particular against the European version, his stance with regard to the Americans is extremely tough and absolutely intransigent. You get the impression that,

come what may: a) it is not possible either to come to
terms or coexist with American imperialism; b) it must
be fought with steadfast determination. You always have
to shoot. If the Cubans at the time of the Caribbean
crisis had not shot at the American aircraft that flew low
over Cuba, if they had not shot then (counter to the
opinion of the Soviets), today you couldn't even play
football in Cuba without the risk of hitting some
American plane. It is not a matter of defence but of staying forever on the attack.

Perhaps when the Cuban revolution is forty years old,
the Cubans will begin to think of the risk of compromising what they have constructed, but not today.

In my view, this is not hate for Americans in general,
even though it is not clear what [Castro] would like to
happen in America, what the turning-point should be
and how it should be brought about.

6. The Cuban military situation.
The defences are well organized, articulated and distributed throughout the whole country. The system does not
offer concentrations of men and means open to easy
attack by the enemy.

The anti-aircraft defences against low-level flight are
very well organized. The ground-to-air missiles are
installed in well-defended, hard-to-hit positions.

7. Various. Plaja Giron.
Judging by their information and the manuals, the
Americans rightly foresaw that the recently delivered
armaments were not yet efficient. In fact, the time scales
of the training courses run by the Czechs suggest that it
would have taken one or two years before the Cubans
would have been in a position to repel an attack. Luckily,
the Czechs intervened, telling their Cuban pupils this:
what you have learned by day, you must teach rapidly to
your comrades at night.

Only by doing this were they able to organize almost a hundred batteries as well as the battalions needed to repel an attack.

In case of an American attack, their brief was to resist so stubbornly and for so long that an alarmed international public opinion would have mobilized. In particular, the USSR was expected to react. The Soviets are slow and often clumsy, but when they get going they are unstoppable.

Stalin: a madman who liquidated the flower of the Soviet general staff and of the party and who allowed the mobilization of a German army three million strong without taking counter-measures, a coward and an idiot. What we now need – says Fidel – is for the USSR, calmly and firmly, to put a stop to the effrontery of the Americans in Vietnam and in Germany.

My personal considerations:

a) Fidel looks as if he has put on a little weight but he is in very good health;

b) the country is still run like a large company: steering committees elected from above but functional none the less. So, as it is in a large company, you have to take public opinion into account, and even here they take public opinion into account;

c) the Che Guevara crisis. After Che's speech in Algiers, there was a full-blown crisis determined by: 1) the speech itself; 2) contrasting views on industrialization. More specifically, whether it was necessary to give priority to agriculture and the industry complementary to agriculture, or whether it was necessary to proceed to the more general industrialization that Che probably saw within the frame of reference of the particular interchange between socialist countries. The fact remains that for two months now Che has been living in the country and no longer shows up at the Industry Ministry.

Today, 19 May, in giving the news of his mother's
death, he made no reference to the fact that, at
bottom, he is still officially the Minister for
Industry.

But the dissension between Fidel and Che goes
back a long way. In fact, even in the days in the
Sierra Maestra, Che would go his own way and
practically eluded the control of the high command,
so much so that he was frequently reprimanded.

d) The Cuban economic situation is much improved. In
any restaurant, you get three times more for the same
price than you would have received last year. The
shops seem to be well stocked with clothing. Trucks
run on good tyres. Yogurt is abundant and cheap.
The agricultural industry is aiming for diversifica-
tion: fruit, pine trees and vegetables, while, naturally,
an intense effort is being made to develop the cattle
farms, which give an overall impression of being well
looked after and in good order.

Considerable results have also been made in the
rearing of chickens and in egg production – 92 million in March. The price of eggs on the black
market has fallen from $0.30 to $0.05 and, in April,
for the first time, they exported 17 million eggs.

e) The internal political situation seems good (for
example, less soldiers around – less weapons). The
CIA is concentrating on attempts to organize an
internal plot calculated to overthrow the regime
from within.

These efforts lead to petty plotting and, consequently, to increased political vigilance.

Every now and then, these little plots are discovered. News of them is not given to the press.
Internal vigilance is, I think, more intense now than
it was before. The army and the police are without a
doubt the best-organized and most efficient sectors
in the country.

f) But the screw has been tightened a little, especially in the cultural field. Some cliques have been gaining in strength and power. For example, the hold of the Writers' Union on the publishing houses. Writers' unions should never have control over publishing houses, which should instead be run by officials or even by individual writers but without answering to or depending on the Writers' Union.

[. . .]

21 MAY – QUESTIONS TO ASK FIDEL

a) Why is he so against homosexual intellectuals?
b) Refer to the news of the deaths among Tschombé's mercenaries and get him back on the subject of Africa.
c) Which other personalities does he think it might be interesting to have write a book like his?
d) Santo Domingo: what can be done to help Caamaño's forces? Non-intervention is not a form of realpolitik. Isn't a more effective and consistent solidarity required?
e) First Hungary, perhaps to a lesser extent, and then Santo Domingo have demonstrated the inefficiency of the United Nations when one of the two superpowers is involved. What does he think the effect of this will be on the United Nations?

[. . .]

21 MAY, 8 P.M. – dinner with Fidel in the government villa. He arrived at 9.40 and stayed until 12.10.

The topic of conversation: the homosexual problem. With unbridled and disturbing spontaneity and violence, he said: at this time we must extol the finest qualities of our people. There is no place for parasites (as if there were no parasites apart from homosexuals) that concentrate in certain areas and influence youth. Pathetic individual cases. Predictably the target of his railings was extended from pederasts to cover intellectuals: architects, writers (e.g. Del Puente), theatre folk, etc., as he developed a heroic conception – already expounded with regard to the struggle, and discrimination against pederasty – against the (traditional) Cuban intellectuals. Ay! ay! ay! I spy dangerous clouds of intolerance!!

[. . .]

On the personalities that might be asked to write: Nasser, Peron (?).(A brief discussion about Peron, who from this continent certainly looks like a demagogue but not a Fascist), Ho Chi Min, and Che. In this regard, he [Castro] was very gallant. He said that Che was cutting sugar cane in the west. He joked about the problem of Che but didn't say anything. Yes, he did say that Che's Algerian speech was not very political, and that the problems he brought up (but which ones?) ought not to have been brought up in public.

But the conversation hinged above all on intellectuals and homosexuals. Great consideration for Alejo Carpentier but none for the others, all of whom he considers to be parasites. The problems of the intellectuals are more complex than recruiting 1,000 people to cut s. cane or raising 10,000 cows, and cannot be tackled with the same drive, with the same energy, with the same infallible certainty of results. And this is why F.C. basically considers them to be pointless problems.

Fidel Castro – It is hard both to make revolutions and to maintain them. You have to avoid what happened in the French Revolution, using the guillotine until there are no more revolutionaries, or what happened during the Soviet Revolution.

It is necessary to combine intellectual and manual work (*sic!*)

These and other simplistic statements of the kind, about literature, and the arts, oozing with the machismo of a well-nigh intolerable puritanism allied to a profound ignorance of the sexual and psychological, ethnological and sociological problems that determine sexual mores and the development of the arts, confirm the impression that there has been a turn of the screw in respect to cultural and moral problems alike.

Fidel is still more interested in military problems (books on the history of battles, war movies) with an enthusiasm and an interest that is almost juvenile.

It is true that Cuba's military problems are of the maximum importance; however, it seems to me, they interest him and arouse his enthusiasm more this year than they did last year.

I don't know which of the two got carried away, but Fidel and Feltrinelli were talking less and less about the memoirs and Feltrinelli's notes no longer seem like working notes. The project for the autobiography was beginning to come apart at the seams. That this was so was also Riva's fault. From Cuba, Feltrinelli suggested that he be replaced:

The mess he has made here is indescribable and typical. He has worked a bit on the papers they have given us, and he has drawn up a memorandum that says nothing. When Fidel is around, he doesn't say a word (true, it's hard to talk to Fidel, he always does the talking). Apart from that, Riva runs about Havana on his own business, as if he were alone, taking the car and seldom saying if or when he will return. He is a smart aleck, a child prodigy. Not that he hasn't grown up, he has grown up all right, but he has remained a child prodigy who has got too big for his boots.

By then, the business of the book had become merely a contest of ideas between an impolitical politician (Giangiacomo)

and an ultra-political politician (Fidel). Feltrinelli wanted
something from Castro that might be transformed into public,
official decisions. He was expecting an exchange among equals
that he was, of course, unable to obtain but that he sometimes
felt he was about to achieve. At a certain point in their talks,
without mincing his words, Feltrinelli attacked the anti-gay
obsession of the Cuban authorities (and of Fidel in person).
Two days later, the prison authorities released a group of students listed in police files under 'P' for pederast. Coincidence
or consequence?

The two visits of 1964 and 1965 had a very powerful impact
on Feltrinelli. He talked of this himself in a semi-serious but
sincere, interview with Gianfranco Venè in a glossy magazine.
It was in 1967:

> In 1964, when I became Castro's friend, I no longer
> believed in anything. No type of commitment, either
> ideological or political. Then . . .'
> 'Castroism?'
> 'No, but the fact of finding yourself talking about
> world politics face to face with a head of state, and being
> in direct contact with a concrete environment like the
> Cuban one, can change something in your life.'
> 'For example?'
> 'I speak for myself, naturally. We are living in times in
> which we do not know how to give a content, a perspec-
> tive to our anxieties. We talk of politics and we talk of it
> in an abstract way. [. . .]
> 'But not Cuba. Cuba is there, and politics is con-
> structed day by day with immediate effects. And, more
> importantly, it is constructed outside the usual frame-
> work: capitalism, Soviet socialism . . .'

In April 1967, Feltrinelli was back in Cuba for a two-week
visit. Castro took him along on a trip to Camagüey. They travelled by car at night. Riva was also with them. Although still
formally with the publishing house, he was there to write a

newspaper article. The famous autobiography was no longer mentioned.

In Havana, Feltrinelli made friends with the photographer Alberto Korda. They talked at length about Che. Korda gave him the negative of a photo taken seven years before, during the funeral for the victims of the La Coubre disaster (a cargo ship full of weapons that had exploded at its moorings). His Leica had scanned the tribune draped in the colours of mourning that was reserved for local dignitaries: it was a windy day, and two chance shots immortalized a strange expression on Guevara's face.

Korda said that Feltrinelli was pessimistic about Che's fate. No one knew that he had been in hiding in Bolivia for five months.

* * *

On 1 June 1967, Giangiacomo Feltrinelli wrote, in English, to Lyndon B. Johnson, the President of the United States of America:

Dear Mr President,
I am a leading Italian publisher.

From time to time, my authors, because of their writings, incur the wrath of governments: as a publisher, it is my duty to do whatever I can to guarantee their freedom and to help them be heard.

Ten years ago, it was the case of Boris Pasternak, who was attacked by the Soviet Writers Association and by the League of Communist Youth. I was Mr Pasternak's publisher at that time. Today, it is the case of Régis Debray, a young French philosopher who is the author of *A Revolution Within The Revolution*. Debray was arrested by the Bolivian police at the end of April, 1967 mainly because he wrote this book. Since his arrest, little has been heard of him and he has been held incommunicado. There are rumours that he has been brought to

Panama to be questioned by United States officials.
Official reports from Bolivia refer to a trial which will
soon be held. But this trial will be a farce since the
President of Bolivia, General Barrientos, has said that (a)
'the adventures of Mr Debray will end in Bolivia' and
that (b) he will ask his government to pass a law reinstat-
ing the death penalty in Bolivia.

The fact that the US strongly supports General
Barrientos is known throughout the world. American
influence in Bolivian politics, in the Bolivian economy, is
a determining element, demonstrated by the presence of
US military personnel and military aid. The responsibility for Régis Debray's fate is therefore directly in the
hands of the US government. [. . .] As the publisher of
Mr Debray, I ask you, Mr President, to exert all your
powerful influence for the immediate release of Régis
Debray, and as a representative of a large section of
Italian culture, I respectfully suggest that you fully
acknowledge all the implications of Mr Debray's prolonged detention and, worse still, his possible execution
or imprisonment.

Washington did not make a prompt reply. By way of compensation, in early July there was a call from Rome: it was Luis
Hernandez, the first secretary of the Cuban embassy. He was
little more than twenty years old and had a beaten up old Fiat
600 that just made it to Milan. Hernandez needed to talk to
Feltrinelli face to face. He was sent by Manuel 'Barbarroja'
Piñeiro, the head of the secret 'Liberación' department and the
chief of Cuban counterespionage service. His internal enemies
called him 'James Bongo'.

When I went to Cuba in 1992, I went to visit him.
Barbarroja's beard was white, he ought to have retired long
ago, but with characters like him, you never know. Would he
tell me everything? He wouldn't. But we did talk, for a long
time, on the veranda of his house. He also summoned
Hernandez and another man connected with the affair.

Piñeiro had a good memory, which he used intermittently, and Hernandez also had clear recollections of his trip to Milan in the summer of 1967. He had never seen Feltrinelli before. On arriving in the guest apartments in via Andegari, he immediately noted Feltrinelli's brightly-coloured tie and the hundreds of magazines and documents lying all over the place: 'Can this be the millionaire publisher?'. Feltrinelli was sitting on the floor. Hernandez joined him on the carpet and they began to chat.

Apart from a few short articles in *Le Monde*, in Europe generally and in Italy, not much was known about Bolivia, the guerrilla war, or of Debray. On 19 April 1967, on coming down unarmed and in civilian clothes from the Camiri hills, Debray had been arrested with the Argentinean Ciro Bustos and the Anglo-Chilean photographer George Roth. Their capture gave the Bolivian military proof that Che was in Bolivia. Debray had been sent to maintain connections with Cuba. In 1966 he had already made a reconnaissance mission to Bolivia on behalf of the Cubans. When they arrested him, he said he was a journalist, but he was tortured.

Hernandez, in other words, Piñeiro, in other words, Fidel, felt that a campaign of solidarity was urgently required to draw international attention to the Debray case. The Cubans proposed that my father personally follow the trial scheduled to be held in the coming weeks. (Debray's French publisher, François Maspéro, was already about to leave.) Five minutes later, the decision was made. ('He has millions of defects but he is a man who makes quick decisions,' Goffredo Parise once said of Feltrinelli.) Feltrinelli also offered to contact possible travelling companions, but to no avail. He had in mind Lelio Basso, Vittorio Foa,* and Antonio Giolitti. Giolitti, an erstwhile minister of the centre-left, was left dumbfounded with the telephone in his hand when my father called him: 'But Giangiacomo! I'm just about to leave for Cogne . . .'

---

* (1910–). Politician, member of the Partito d'Azione, he joined the Partito Socialista di Unità Proletaria (PSIUP). He was elected to parliament with the PCI in 1987.

'The only instructions we gave him were to go to La Paz.' According to Piñeiro and Hérnandez, there was no prearranged plan.

On his arrival in Bolivia on 9 August, Feltrinelli checked in to one of the two grand hotels of the capital, the La Paz, room 311. The city was swarming with journalists who were not journalists, informers who were informing God knows whom, observers who were observing heaven knows what, tourists who were not real tourists, Anglo-Chileans, Franco-Argentineans, German-Bolivians, Cuban-Americans and Guatemalan-Danes. All bustling about, but keeping a low profile. The Italian mingled with the crowd. He frequented the lobby of the Hotel Copacabana, tried to buy a map and a copy of the Bolivian constitution, booked an excursion to Lake Titicaca, and inquired about the permits required to get to Camiri: this was why he was here. Camiri was the prison in which Debray was waiting to stand trial. In his first hours in La Paz, Feltrinelli tried to get in touch with Humberto Vázquez Viana to find out about his brother Jorge, known as 'El Loro'. He was a guerrilla. Captured and wounded by the rangers, while still alive he had been thrown out of a helicopter flying over the jungle.

According to the reconstruction of the Cubans Adys Cupull and Froilán González, the authors of the investigative book *La Cia contra el Che* ('The CIA versus Che'), Feltrinelli apparently also met Colonel Carlos Vargas Velarde of the Ministry of Defence, who allegedly offered to provide him with proof of a CIA presence in Bolivia and of the American plan to infiltrate mercenaries and Cuban counter-revolutionaries into the country. Their brief was to carry out spoiling missions in the hot zones, in order to lay the blame on Che's 'gang'. A few months later, Colonel Velarde, suspected of being hand-in-glove with Havana, was found dead in his office. (His presumed meeting with Feltrinelli has never been confirmed by any other source.)

In *La Cia contra el Che*, it is also said that the Italian publisher was approached by George Roth, the photographer arrested with Debray and suspected of being a CIA collaborator. Roth wanted to offer Feltrinelli a report on the Camiri episode.

Around mid-August, Sibilla Melega landed at La Paz airport. Twenty years old, from Merano in northern Italy, she was the beautiful blonde who sold beatnik trinkets in her boutique in Brera. She had been on vacation on Stromboli when Feltrinelli had sent her a ticket for her first transatlantic trip.

On the morning of 17 August, Feltrinelli realized that he was being tailed, and the following afternoon, at 5.30 p.m., two plain-clothes officers presented themselves at his hotel and escorted him to the offices of the DIC (the Bolivian criminal investigations department). A long interrogation and then straight off to prison. The news of his arrest caused an immediate international stir. 'The impact was enormous,' recall Hernández and Piñeiro.

Antonio Arguedas, then the Minister of the Interior, speaking of these matters thirty years later with the journalist Antonio Peredo, in the autumn of 1997, recalled that the tip-off regarding Feltrinelli's presence in Bolivia had come from the CIA. His arrest was the work of the head of the intelligence service Roberto Quintanilla and the American agent Julio García, who was on the ministry staff. The interrogation was conducted directly by the CIA, but produced no results.

There was no shortage of reasons for arresting him, but the pretexts were risible: the 4,000 dollars they found in his pocket, the hundreds of photos he had taken (but they were of Lake Titicaca!), the maps (but they were printed by the Istituto geografico De Agostini of Novara, Italy), the contacts with the Vázquez Viana family (but the father of 'El Loro' was a famous historian: the family was very well known). The suspect clung to the sound rule of saying nothing. His interrogators lost patience: 'You're a Russian spy! You're an agent of Soviet Communism!'.

Sibilla was in the hotel when they took him away. She was stunned. Finding herself catapulted into a drama she could never have imagined, she dashed to the Hotel Copacabana,

where she ran into Jan Stage, a thirty-year-old Dane who had
been hired by the Cubans to send the news from la Paz via
Paris. We shall be coming across him again later. He destroyed
Feltrinelli's contacts book and notes that Sibilla had in her possession. Some days before, my father had asked Stage to see if
he could do something about hiring a plane, a small cargo
plane, a DC3, anything, as long as it flew. (According to Stage,
it wasn't clear why Feltrinelli needed a plane. Perhaps to fly
someone out of Bolivia. Whom?)

On 19 August, Sibilla too was arrested and questioned.

That afternoon, all the Italian popular press ran the story. *La
Notte* of Milan: 'Publisher Feltrinelli vanishes in Bolivia'; the
same headline for the *Carlino Sera* of Bologna and for *Telestar*
of Palermo.

The following day, the headline of the *Gazzetta di Vigevano*
read: 'Feltrinelli arrested in Bolivia', the same headline
appeared in *France Soir*; *Le Monde* was more cautious: 'Regis
Débray's Italian publisher apparently held by police'. The feeling was that the press was responding well. Some
commentators provided detailed lists of the accusations levelled at Feltrinelli: he had contravened clause C of the decree of
28 January 1937 whereby foreigners were forbidden to interfere
with the internal affairs of the country. Minister Arguedas
issued a statement: 'Bolivia is faced by the serious problem of
the guerrillas and can have no respect for those who work
openly with them.'

In Italy, President Saragat and the Foreign Minister Fanfani
intervened immediately. Thanks to them, the Bolivian authorities expelled Giangiacomo Feltrinelli, after one day and two
nights in jail.

On 20 August, at 2 p.m., they took him to the airport. To
return to Europe, he had to stop over in Lima. Just enough
time for them to declare him persona non grata there too.

On the 21st, from the *Times* to the *Glasgow Herald*, there was
a single headline: 'Publisher expelled from Bolivia'. The *Kölner
Stadtanzeiger* was slightly behind with the news but ventured
the most accurate headline: '*Zhivago* publisher arrested'. More

up to date was the *Corriere d'informazione*: 'Feltrinelli also expelled from Peru'. Minister Arguedas issued a press communiqué: 'If freedom and justice did not exist in Bolivia, Giangiacomo Feltrinelli would not have left the country alive.'

As he was escorting Sibilla to the airport, Colonel Roberto Quintanilla took an image of the Virgin Mary from his pocket. He gave it to her. His voice carried above the noise of the jeep as he advised her to light a votive candle to the Madonna.

The political objective had been attained. The publisher was shaken by his narrow escape, but euphoric at the same time. When he arrived at Linate airport in Milan (via Lima and Madrid), he was wearing a blue pullover and carrying an attaché case. A Senior Service in his mouth, he was whisked away by a black Citroen DS, avoiding the assault of the journalists.

In Italy, there was no shortage of declarations of solidarity, but there were also those who protested against him. Some papers launched furious attacks; the neo-Fascists of the MSI party made their opinions clear in parliament, and in the Feltrinelli bookshops in Rome and Milan they did the same, but with sticks and cudgels. Their war cry was 'Down with Feltrinelli, the agitprop millionaire'.

A few days after his return from La Paz, Giangiacomo offered Sibilla a new vacation. They left for Malaga and rented a two-master to sail to Oran and from there to Algiers. The sea was pretty rough, the helmsman got lost a few times and, when they reached their destination, because they did get there in the end, the sails were ruined. Feltrinelli met Colonel Boumédienne and told him he was planning to go to Rhodesia. There was some guerrilla action going on in the border regions. An ever more perturbed Sibilla persuaded him to drop the idea and to go back to Italy, this time by plane.

During his North African trip, Feltrinelli found the time to write two long articles on his Bolivian adventure, which were published in Italy in early September. More than a factual account, it was a hallucination. The tone was emphatic. In his piece for *Espresso*, he denounced the slaughters perpetrated by the Barrientos regime, the wretched conditions of the peasantry, and American interference. His report ended on a note of certainty: 'There is no doubt about it: another Vietnam has already begun.' But, a few weeks later it all came to an end at the village of La Higuera. Colonel Quintanilla had Che's hands amputated and preserved in formaldehyde: they were the proof that he no longer existed.

In May 1972, Minister Arguedas (who in the meantime had abandoned the CIA for the Cubans) was to issue a surprising statement. He said that, in August 1967, Feltrinelli had offered the Bolivians a ransom of 50 million dollars for Che, in the event of his capture. The CIA said that the deal was out of the question. True or false?

'The only instructions we gave him were to go to La Paz.' According to Piñeiro and Hérnandez, there was no prearranged plan.

* * *

In January 1968, Feltrinelli returned to Cuba once more, for a three-week stay. This time he was accompanied by Enrico Filippini who was to recall the trip in an article for *La Repubblica*:

> I went with him to Havana for the 'Cultural Congress', which was the last episode in cordial relations between Castro's regime and the European intelligentsia. On the plane he did nothing but write. 'What are you writing?' I asked him. 'Articles for *La sinistra*.' *La sinistra* was the monthly founded by Lucio Colletti,* bought and later scuppered by Feltrinelli. In Havana they gave us adjoining rooms. He asked me never to close the door, and said

---

* Lucio Colletti: An Italian intellectual and a former Trotskyist (in the 60s), he now holds a seat in the Italian parliament for the centre-right party 'Forza Italia'.

that he would do likewise: that way we could go in and
out whenever we wanted to. Once I went in his room. He
was sleeping on the floor, on a pallet made of newspapers
next to the bed. I had gone in to suggest that he make a
few publishing contracts: one with a really old anthropol-
ogist called Ortiz, who had written a fantastic book called
Africanía de la musica cubana, and another two with certain young sociologists from the Cuban Institute of
Books. 'You sign them,' he said. 'But my signature has no
legal value,' I said. 'It doesn't matter.' I observed him
wandering the corridors of the Habana Libre. I heard
him make a speech in Spanish that only an Italian could
have understood. I grasped a few comments. I had
understood: he wanted to let the Cubans know that his
function as a European publisher had ceased, that he
thought of himself only as 'a fighter against imperialism'.

During his stay on the island, Feltrinelli worked on an essay
on the Italian situation called 'Guerrilla warfare and revolutionary politics'. When he returned to Milan, the Italian secret
services obtained a photocopy of the document: 'we managed
to get hold of the original for a few hours' (3 March 1968).
How did they do that? Microfilm at customs or a 'mole' in via
Andegari? In his text, Feltrinelli offers a few examples of the
'vanguard strategies', with examples from South Vietnam and
Venezuela, that were needed to orientate the future struggles of
the Italian working class. The language swings from catatonia
to obsession.

There are three possible strategies, he said, two wrong ones
and a right one. The incorrect strategies were grouped under
the 'revisionist' concept, inspired by the PCI, and the
Trotskyist concept of an 'armed revolutionary insurrection in
the future (which opposed the PCI's cautious strategy in
appearance only). The correct line instead involved 'the use of
systematic and progressive counter-violence'. 'Political guerrilla warfare must develop as the fundamental strategic element
in this current phase of the struggle of the Italian proletariat':

against class power, and against the authoritarian involution of the system. Resistance against coup attempts from the right, an application of 'foquismo'* and the internationalist character of the struggle, were all a necessary contribution to the strategy of the Italian radical left.

The Italian secret services considered Feltrinelli's ideas rather unoriginal if not downright comical. But from then on, their surveillance became even more obsessive.

Late that spring, an urgent invitation arrived from Havana. They didn't say what for, but it must have been something important. When Feltrinelli landed, he learned that Castro wanted to give him and Maspĕro a copy of Che's Bolivian diary, which had been smuggled out of La Paz by Minister Antonio Arguedas: this was Operation 'Aunt Victoria'. Holed up in a little villa in Vedado, Feltrinelli translated the text in a couple of nights.

The diary was to come out in Italy in 1968 (before Maspĕro's version), and the rights were sold for no charge to the publishers of half the world. At that time, the Dutch publisher Rob Van Gennep resembled Che a lot: 'I read the news of the diary's publication in the international press and I sent a telegram to Milan to find out if I could have a copy of the manuscript. Within forty-eight hours, I don't know how, I received it, without an accompanying letter. I rounded up ten journalists and, in one night, the translation was ready. Ten days later, we had sixty thousand copies of the book in the bookshops. It was a huge success.'

The same thing happened in Italy. The cover of the Italian edition bore the legend: 'The proceeds of this publication will be donated entirely to the revolutionary movements of Latin America.' Questions were asked in Parliament. Feltrinelli printed thousands of posters from the negative of the famous

---

* Reference to guerrilla warfare tactic. Sporadic hit-and-run attacks are seen as the metaphoric equivalent of lots of 'little fires' that, theoretically, will one day unite to form the big blaze that is revolution.

photo by Alberto Korda ('Che in the sky with jacket') and had them hung in his bookshops. The image flew over every city square on the planet. Much later, a victim of lean times, Korda was to say that if he had asked for a percentage on that photo, he would have become a millionaire.

An embassy colleague of Luis Hernández, Andrés Del Río, was bemused when Feltrinelli handed him a suitcase full of banknotes: 'The proceeds of this publication will be donated entirely to the revolutionary movements of Latin America.' Perhaps because something like this had never happened to him before, Andrés Del Río did not know what to do with all that money, and so the suitcase was transformed into a bank deposit amounting to over half a million Swiss francs. The name of the account? The functionary still remembers it: 'Río Verde'.

8

When the signs came, they came as a surprise to everyone. The 'golden age' of post-war prosperity was losing its lustre in the year 1968: the crisis facing De Gaulle, the 'Prague Spring', the 'Little Red Book', the *White Album*, Tommy Smith and John Carlos raising black fists to the sky, *Butch Cassidy and the Sundance Kid* in the cinema, an explosion of wage demands around the world, further cracks in Sino-Soviet relations, guerrilla warfare in the southern part of the globe, and the struggle at Nanterre, 22 March 1968. For the first time, you could count for something at the age of twenty, and sixty-eight meant the student revolt that was almost never limited to the schools and colleges. And, above all, there was Vietnam: the inelegant swaggering of defeated imperialism. Vaster and more indefinite questions were emerging, a new anti-capitalist aware-ness in a West already in the toils of its third general crisis, a dry run for what would later be called globalization.

What is certain is that the world had never before witnessed events like those of Paris in May 1968, when an alliance of stu-dents and workers brought both the city and industrial production to a standstill for almost a month.

In Italy, things got off to a slower start: the watchword of power was still 'national reconstruction', the third Moro administration was in government, and the centre-left was finally eclipsed. But from the end of 1967 (student unrest in Turin, but not only there) to the autumn of 1969 (labour unrest in Turin and everywhere else) there was a crescendo of unrest. The right to study for the children of migrant workers; no more piecework for arrogant factory bosses; and the need to understand, finally, that this was a Struggle that could be engaged, if only with the chick next door: it all merged into one single wave. The thrust of this chaotic movement was liberating, prepolitical, almost precultural, and it unleashed its energies by striving toward something indeterminate: it was the ultimate Rabelaisian banquet of Utopias, and at times it was a bumpy ride.

Within the ranks of the traditional Left, the two non-Communist socialist parties united, and while the PCI condemned Russian intervention in Prague, its opposition was about as dynamic as that of a sleepwalker. The real point was to get into government maybe in three thousand years' time, then the final surge, history's ultimate strategy, would usher in socialism. This was basically a pacifist standpoint: revolution does not mean war, the crowds of militants were told of an evening at the various Feste dell'Unità.*

Just like their counterparts at the Sorbonne, the Italian students waved red flags and sang the 'Internationale'. But the idea of Revolution was intensified because of the nature of Power in Italy: absentee, corrupt, complicit, and repressive. By the time 1968 was already over the nature of the 'revolutionary party' became the focus of debate, and old doctrines were brought out and dusted off. There was no gap between doing and saying; even though there were some people who saw things from a gradualist point of view (to make as much revolution as is possible within their expected lifespan) others fell victim to the principal shortcoming of all revolutionaries: impatience. If it was to be, let it be now or never.

* Regular fund raising events organized by the Italian Communist Party.

The stairway to heaven stopped well before the threshold. The rights of employees were established by the Workers' Statute; conventions and habits begun to change. These were years of ardent hope, which is already a good coefficient for a generation. 'A great festival of democracy' or 'the anti-modern involution of an excessively modern decade', as the historians now argue it. With benefit of hindsight, some of them talk of a class revolution, and of the emergence of a new awareness within the Italian middle classes. I'm sure they are right.

'In the beginning was action.' The thinking of the sixties was dominated by the problem of action. 'I realized that Feltrinelli was going off the rails, that he had fallen in love with an analogy,' wrote Enrico Filippini, 'that he no longer understood the value of cultural mediation, that he had exceeded his own role, that his impatience had won. He became hasty, slapdash, and headstrong . . .' This is what happens when history becomes religion.

When 1968 came along, Feltrinelli was ready for it. In fact he was a precursor whose ideas were shared by many. He knew the world and had travelled extensively; he was not insular, and he had a global strategy. Shortly before this great historical moment, he had become convinced that the taking up of arms, perhaps by way of a response to the enemy, had become inevitable. Some people were amazed by this. The most generous interpretations maintained that his decision was 'tactically' mistaken. His attack strategy was that of a guerrilla: against the atomic bomb even a tin of beans might come in handy. From a certain point of view, Feltrinelli was not wrong: the Revolution was in danger, but who could rescue it?

Feltrinelli's 1968 began a few months early, that is to say after the Bolivian adventure (August 1967). On his return, he found numerous messages of solidarity (there was even a Marxist movement in the Valle d'Aosta), and he received invitations to speak in public from all over: Florence, Lugano, Livomo, Novara, Palermo, Catania, Rome . . . In Modica, in the province of Ragusa, he was denied the use of the assembly rooms in the city hall and the conference was held in a seedy motel.

Plain-clothes police attended every meeting, and their reports were transmitted to the Ministry of the Interior.

In Genoa, Feltrinelli was approached by Giovanbattista Lazagna, who had been awarded a silver medal for his work with the wartime underground movement. Lazagna was a member of the PCI who felt frustrated by the party's soft line, or perhaps he was just frustrated by life. He was a sanguine, slightly bitter fifty-year-old. He had written to Feltrinelli to tell him about a series of meetings to be held in the Anpi (National Association of Italian Partisans) club of Novi Ligure. The idea was to invite Feltrinelli to talk about Latin America. They met in Genoa, where Feltrinelli was scheduled to speak. Lazagna gave Feltrinelli a book of memoirs of his experience with the Resistance and invited him to a meeting in a farmhouse complete with a meal of spit-roasted goat. Around the fire sat about thirty comrades with long memories.

The meetings in Novi Ligure soon became an important date, and not only for ex-partisans or young radicals from the area. The topics changed from time to time, but in the debates that followed the same questions would always crop up. How to give the Italian left a revolutionary strategy once more? What was the lesson of the struggles in the Third World? Feltrinelli talked of Cuba, Bolivia and Latin America; Romano Ledda of Guinea Bissau; Lelio Basso of Vietnam, which he had visited. Before every meeting, cars with a variety of out-of-town numberplates were seen in the valley. Some faces were well known. There was the Sienese Viro Avanzati, the commandant of the 'Spartaco Lavagnini' partisan division; there were the Cattaneos, father and son, from the Piacenza area. In the end, it was Pietro Secchia's turn. Although the debate had been fixed for nine in the evening, at ten in the morning he was already on the platform of Alessandria railway station. Lazagna, who went to pick Secchia up, gave him a military salute and announced that he wanted to show him what activities were going on locally. 'There's no need, I know all about you,' said Secchia cutting him off. According to Lazagna, Feltrinelli had already told him all he needed to know.

Before his death, the PCI member and Shadow Minister of the Interior Ugo Pecchioli mentioned the Ligurian affair in a book: 'I talk of some of these people with respect, because they believed in what they were doing and stuck their necks out in full awareness of the serious risks they were running. [. . .] Lazagna and Feltrinelli were neither provocateurs nor adventurers in anyone's service, but comrades who felt that the time had come to take up arms once more. There was not merely dissent between them and us, but complete and outright opposition.'

Feltrinelli accepted many invitations in the autumn of 1967 as he shuttled to and fro, talking to groups of one to three hundred people. I can see him, impassioned, too much so, but he was about to boil over and there he was talking away, maybe swearing a little, making rambling speeches in which he nearly lost the thread. But he found it again for the grand finale: 'I haven't come here to talk in geographical or historical or ethnical terms, which is perhaps what many people expected of me.' The subjects were the death of Che and the Debray affair but, above all, 'political action'. When 'the Italian road to socialism no longer exists, peaceful solutions no longer exist, and the space for mediation no longer exists', the only chances of combatting Fascism and imperialism were reduced to a 'head-on clash' with them.

On 13 November 1967, Feltrinelli gave a talk on South America at the San Saba club on the Aventine, Rome. 'He attracted a large audience composed mostly of all the so-called "left-wing groups" in the capital,' says a political police report* dated 25 November. An informer maintained that, in the course of the evening, Feltrinelli had announced to the audience the fundamental planks of the revolutionary platform sanctioned by the Tricontinental Conference in Havana. As far as the

* This document and the police reports that follow all come from the Confidential Affairs office of the Ministry of the Interior.

speaker was concerned, the death of Che was a grave loss that would not slow down the struggle, but would lend it new vigour. But, while this was true, it had become more important to take an active part rather than to indulge in disquisitions on the various Marxist–Leninist debates. Cuban empiricism had achieved more results than all the doctrines elaborated by the various Communist parties faithful to Moscow, and the PCI had also become a tool of conservatism. The concept of 'political guerrilla warfare' held good not only for Latin America but for the entire Third World and even for many advanced capitalist countries – especially where the shadow of an authoritarian regime loomed.

According to the report drawn up by the political police, Feltrinelli's public activism was a source of disappointment at various levels of the PCI, which was basically neutral regarding the strategies employed by non-European revolutionary movements: the use of PCI-owned premises and associations for such conferences was not appreciated. The Rome Federation opened an inquiry into Feltrinelli's presence in the area.

In fact, there was reason to be on the alert. 'There is great ferment in the circles of the so-called Roman left concerning Giangiacomo Feltrinelli,' stated the latest report to end up on Minister Taviani's desk. On the fringes of the San Saba conference, Feltrinelli apparently contacted some representatives of the local radical left to inform them of his plans and to ask for their political support. He spoke of *La sinistra*, the revolutionary Trotskyist magazine that he was trying to relaunch with the aid of its founders. Transformed into a weekly, *La sinistra* could serve as a forum for those whose stance was to the left of the PCI. Feltrinelli asked the Romans to get their forces on to the streets and to take part in the nationwide co-ordination of the 'revolutionary fragments'. As he wrote at the time to Professor Toni Negri* of Padua University, the point was not

---

* (1933–). A university professor, he was one of the founders of Potere Operaio. He fled Italy for Paris, where he taught at the Ecole Normale. After spending some years in a Rome prison, Negri is now on day release.

unification: what was needed was to link up in the interests of common action.

In Rome, the police reports tell us, the various extra-parliamentarian political groups in the city found themselves obliged to decide whether or not to meet with Feltrinelli. A 'Deep Throat' was always present at the meetings. On 15 December, seven or eight people met in the home of a member of a group known as the Revolutionary Tendency of the Fourth International. Some spoke for the Maoist faction, others for the League of Marxist–Leninists, there was a Trotskyist who was a former member of the PSIUP, another person representing his own magazine, *Classe e Stato*, and a pro-Castro journalist formerly with *l'Unità*. The Maoist faction said right away that they would refuse any intercourse with those who would not accept a clear declaration of support for the leadership of the Chinese Communist Party. The others emphasized that no agreement could prejudice the ideological autonomy of each faction. In the end, however, they decided that something could indeed be done. But, at least while things were in the exploratory phase, some trust was necessary. Some harboured doubts about Feltrinelli, but at least he had the means: they decided to go along with him and see what happened.

Five days later, they met with him in the back room of his bookshop in via del Babbuino. As well as those already mentioned, the meeting was attended by people from *La sinistra* and another two magazines that came out somewhat irregularly, *Quaderni rossi* and *Classe operaia*. And of course there was Deep Throat. Feltrinelli chaired the meeting and explained his ideas, talking of the role the new weekly could play, avoiding those arguments that were the subject of ideological polemics between the diverse factions, and saying that 'liaison committees' were taking shape in Milan, Naples and Palermo. He maintained that it was time to make a move.

I don't really know how those present reacted. Probably at least one of them got to his feet to call someone else an *agent provocateur*: the psychological drama had already surpassed their powers of argument. The great clash was knocking at the

door: everyone was expecting it, but it did not look like anything they had expected.

The Roman 'liaison committee' soon went up in smoke. As
did the idea of relaunching *La sinistra*. Almost immediately, the
willingness to work with Feltrinelli became an attempt to iso-
late him: he was seen as useful to the movement but already
seemed too distant from it. For his part, he began to see the
'mechanical' nature of their internationalism, the 'rhetorical'
quality of their anti-imperialism, and, when it came to their
concept of the class struggle, he thought they were simply far,
far too traditionalist.

In late 1967, Feltrinelli's mind had turned to Sicily (where he
sent the journalist Saverio Tutino to make a reconnaissance)
and to Sardinia (where he went in person). On 8 December, a
local newspaper ran a small article about this:

FELTRINELLI BOOED IN CAGLIARI
After receiving a warm and enthusiastic welcome from
the large audience that had come to the 'Winter Garden'
rooms in Cagliari to hear his talk on Latin America, the
publisher Giangiacomo Feltrinelli was later the target of
a show of hostility in the vicinity of his hotel on the part
of groups of youths. The protest ended with the well-
known publisher, at the centre of a heated row over his
visit to Bolivia, being subjected to a real barrage of
booing and whistling. It seems that this hostile protest
was organized by elements belonging to extreme right-
wing youth groups. However, everything went off
without further incident and as Feltrinelli left Cagliari he
made a good-natured comment on the episode stating
that he had become a 'political figure' and so, as such, he
was destined to receive not only displays of approval, but
also the attacks and insults of his opponents.

After the speech, Feltrinelli stayed on in Sardinia for a few
days and accepted an invitation to go hunting. A couple of

friends took him to Tronco del Sole, at the foot of the Setti Fradis hills. It is a great natural terrace overlooking the sea, 900 to 1,000 metres above sea level, where the eye is drawn to the remains of the *nuraghe*, small prehistoric forts, on the mountainside, below. As for the hunting, they returned empty-handed. They roasted some meat brought from home and washed it down with the violet-coloured local wine. The party ended with a shooting contest using the empty bottles as a target. The only person to score a hit was Carla Frontini. I know about her thanks to a piece published in a Sardinian magazine in which she recalled:

We invited him [Feltrinelli] to hold a conference. This was done in agreement with the other comrades, some left-wing intellectuals whose relations with the PCI were already critically strained, the group that formed the nucleus of the future *Manifesto*, *Potere operaio*, and lots of 'mavericks', as they used to call them at the time. We rented the Winter Gardens in via Manno and we organized the conference. But the first attempt came to nothing. Feltrinelli had missed his plane. There followed a series of frantic phone calls. He tried desperately to find an air-taxi. Nothing doing. At the second attempt, the conference went off with no problems. He left us all somewhat puzzled, if not downright flabbergasted: 'Sardinia as the Cuba of the Mediterranean'? But despite certain incongruities in his talk, we were captivated by his charm. He was a strange man, so different from us ordinary people! He came across as decidedly brilliant (and powerful), with a touch of folly. On that occasion, a deep and strong friendship grew up between us. He came to our house and slept on the settee in the study. And so, our little house at the foot of Monte Urpinu became his '*pied-è-terre*' for the whole time he frequented Sardinia: 1967–8 and a part of 1969. He was a good, kind, and very generous man. He told us his story, which we found pretty amazing [. . .].

There were many good reasons for Feltrinelli's interest in Sardinia. Perhaps they begin with the invasion by Carthage in the sixth century BC: the native Sardinians fled into the mountains. Split in two, with 'colonized' coastal areas and plains, and Indian reservations in the centre (partisans, 'resistance fighters'), the island bred that stubborn spirit of resistance and courage, known locally as *balentia*, that lives on today in the rugged folk of Sardinia's equally rugged Barbagia district. In more recent times, the royal House of Savoy and the various governments of the Italian Republic have looked after the business of pillaging and exploiting.

In Sardinia, things began to move at the end of 1967. And it was not a matter of a handful of intellectuals goaded into action by the inequality of relations with the metropolis but whole towns like Orgosolo that revolted against everything, students who rejected a future as specialized migrants, militants repressed by the police, bandits who fled and never got caught. Is there a connection between banditry and politics? The first to wonder about this were the Rome-based offices of the underground political movements. Armed shepherds and guerrillas are not the same thing. But they both inhabit the same impervious terrain and a rebel always enjoys popular respect or support .

Feltrinelli's trips to Sardinia produced six pamphlets for the 'Edizioni della libreria' series. Youth clubs protesting against the national park in Gennargentu, the agro-pastoral economy, an emigrants' 'charter', the grounds for separatism, and notes on the 'police state' and ostantatious military exercises were the topics of these small best-sellers. Naturally, Feltrinelli met everyone and even went so far as to contact the bandit Graziano Mesina, a legendary figure at the time. All very mysterious. Did Feltrinelli really offer Mesina 'rehabilitation' in exchange for 'insurrection'? The bandit did not need this, as he did not need money or weapons, which he took whenever he wanted. But the slogan 'the Cuba of the Mediterranean' appealed to many people. Feltrinelli realized this during his first visit to the Supramonte area. After having gone through a normal police roadblock, a young national serviceman inexplicably ran after him and said: 'You're Feltrinelli, aren't you? Don't be surprised if one day you find that many people see things the way you do.'

Sardinia and the south of Italy in a Third World light: like Vietnam and Korea, Guatemala and Venezuela, Laos and the Philippines, Mozambique and Guinea; for a class war on an international scale! All you had to do was glance at a newspaper: armies of liberation were in action everywhere, half of Guinea had been liberated, the same held for Guatemala, while the Têt offensive was to show that guerrilla forces can strike at any time, in any place. Guerrilla warfare seen as the absolute synthesis of political struggle and military conflict, a third world war against imperialism, waged from trenches of a new kind dug in the cities and the countryside, in the schools and neighbourhoods. Through this application of the Debrayan theory of 'foquismo', you could hope to win the sympathies of the masses.

These were theories that updated the partisan war to whose memory they appealed, unconsciously or otherwise, because of all the things that that experience had represented. Feltrinelli remodelled this material, only conceptually at the time, in order to tackle what he believed was the imminent danger: an Italian-style *coup d'état*.

Sometimes you forget just how long Italy is. If you make a diagonal cut across it, north of Sardinia, you come to the area known as the Trentino. Feltrinelli went there to talk at some point in 1967, still on the subject of Latin America. This was useful for him in so far as he could get to know the place. 'The problem of the South Tyrol', he maintained, 'is exactly the same as that of Sardinia.' He met Sandro Canestrini, the lawyer, who had always been a local celebrity. An ex-partisan of radical-libertarian principles, he had defended goodness knows how many left-wing extremists during the hard years, not to mention the Schützen (a South Tyrolean separatist group inspired by memories of the peasants' resistance against Napoleon), the Jehovah's Witnesses and an assortment of poachers.

Canestrini and Feltrinelli were friends: 'Feltrinelli would often arrive without warning. If my wife and I were out, he would climb over the fence and stretch out in the garden, smoking and gazing at the moon. When we came back, if there was a shadowy figure lurking somewhere, it was Giangiacomo.' According to Canestrini, the South Tyrol had a special significance for Feltrinelli: his family came from there, the Valle dei Cervi is not far away and Sibilla, his new girlfriend, was from nearby Merano. But Feltrinelli was also struck by the pride of these frontier folk and by the particular social relations and rules of the peasant communities: if the values that traditionally underpinned the defence of local independence continued to be upheld, then perhaps it might be possible to link up with a new socialist ethic that would serve to weld the ideals of the new world on to a pre-proletarian culture. In other words, the bells of the country churches might ring out one day in the name of an anti-Fascist independence movement inspired not so much by Lenin but by the 'peasants' war', by the battles against Napoleon, or by the Anabaptist traditions of the Bauernkrieg.

The South Tyrol was also a part of the Triveneto, a happy hunting ground for secret services, various branches of military intelligence, and clandestine organizations that are ready for anything. This area was the stronghold of the Balena Bianca,* of the main NATO Atlantic Command centres, of the key units of the army, of Fascist subversive networks and also of that shadowy operation known as 'Stay Behind'.† It was the experimental laboratory of the invisible war against all Red Flags.

* * *

* The 'White Whale', the nickname for the Christian Democratic party.
† A clandestine structure created during the Cold War whose brief was to oppose any attempts by the Communist party to seize power in Italy. Supported by certain groups within NATO and by the Italian secret services, it was also set up to resist in the event of a Soviet invasion.

'The truth is, I repeat, that no one believed us. "What interest could they possibly have", our people thought, "in carrying out such a sensational act? This is Europe, not Latin America after all!"'

This is how Vassilis Vassilikos described the atmosphere in Athens before the spring of 1967.

The Solo plan seems like an old sci-fi movie, from the days when man dreamed of going into space and invented strange tin cans to do it with. Was the *coup d'état* only the madman Giangiacomo's nightmare?

The end of 1967 witnessed a sensational political scandal. In the course of a libel suit against *Espresso* brought by General Giovanni De Lorenzo (the former head of the SIFAR intelligence unit), top-ranking carabinieri and army officers confirmed that in July 1964 De Lorenzo was plotting to lead a coup in Italy: one night carabinieri units were to have arrested labour union and left-wing political leaders. The General's armoured brigade and the Folgore regiment of paratroops were standing by. Perhaps it was only a plan to respond to street agitators in the event of a new authoritarian centrist coalition government, in order to prevent another July 1960, when unrest in Genoa obliged Minister of the Interior Tambroni to resign.

The point of reference for an analysis of those events was a series of articles written by Nenni* for *Avanti!*. Nenni maintained that the socialists had to accept the mediocre compromise that was the reconstitution of the 1964 Moro government in order to prevent a shift to the right of such dimensions that 'the memory of July 1960 would have paled into insignificance' by comparison. Basically, the rest of the

* (1891–1979). Lived in exile in France from 1926 to 1942. A great tribune of the people, he played a key role within the socialist movement during the Spanish Civil War. Nenni was the architect of the rapprochement with the Catholic right that took concrete form when the Socialists were invited to become a part of a right-wing government in which he was deputy prime minister.

left interpreted these events as the yielding, the weakness and the capitulation of the socialists, who were internally divided, moreover, and saw the theory of an authoritarian threat as a pretext with which to justify their decision to join the government. This is a rough summary of how people on the left saw matters until 1967.

The articles on the De Lorenzo case printed by *Espresso* caused a scandal. The inquiry modified previous interpretations, and the risk of a near-coup in 1964 was recognized.

Now, in 1967, the world was in the grip of political fever and this made the fear of sensational events more plausible. If the right (in the broadest sense of the term) had been plotting to stage a putsch for fear of the socialists in 1964, who knew what they were up to now; so people thought three years later, with the Americans bogged down in Vietnam, the coup in Greece, an Arab–Israeli war, and more besides. The events of May 1968 in France were already imminent and in Italy elections were planned; the usual elections, of course, but also the last elections that would be held upon due termination of mandate in the history of the republic.

The squares and the streets of Italy were embellished with new slogans: leftists favoured things like 'The university is our Vietnam', and 'Agnelli, The shop floor is our Indochina!,' and rightists chanted 'Let's cut the crap / Bring in the Colonels' or 'First Athens, then Rome!'. Of course, the Fascist MSI was easily identifiable and the monarchists were thin on the ground, but there were creeping symptoms of an authoritarian 'silent majority', and you never knew what the Christian Democrats might do. Fears of a *coup* were very widespread. Militants of the PCI and PSI were advised to act with circumspection, party branch offices were kept on an emergency footing, and banners were made ready with slogans about the repression, while activists were advised to sleep away from home and to have a 'safe' address.

The parliamentary inquiry into the abortive *coup* of July 1964 soon ran aground, as usual, but Nenni declared that the investigation, which had not been supported by his party,

'would have taken on some disquieting aspects for the country'.
'He couldn't have put it more clearly than that,' commented
Feltrinelli. The historian Santarelli wrote 'that silence was to
provide protection in future for those "bodies separated from
the state" and for that "crypto-dictatorship" within the state
apparatus, which Ferruccio Parri* was to denounce in 1968'.

The Italian system was a petrified system, which had not
developed to the point of allowing tensions to be expressed
and controlled: this was 'imperfect' democracy. But the Italian
situation was unlike the Greek one: the old PCI was a great
mass party (as was the DC) and so the theory propounded by
Giorgio Galli in an essay written in 1986 seems well grounded:
'The real instrument of pressure on the left was never the
preparation of a *coup d'état* (with or without American assistance), but the likelihood of one (without the capacity to carry
out the threat) that was constantly dangled before the leaders of
the left.' Feltrinelli did not grasp the difference. 'The threat of
a *coup d'état* in Italy still remains!' he wrote in late 1967.

Less and less a publisher, more and more a political figure,
Feltrinelli split Italian society in two. He became a kind of
lodestone.

As far as the (die-hard Fascist) right was concerned, he was
the symbol of all the corruption of the reds, the 'eau de cologne
revolutionary' who printed subversive pamphlets. If he so
much as stuck his hands in his pockets and strolled out to the
theatre of an evening, the matter could not pass unobserved.
And an indignant letter to the right-wing weekly magazine
Borghese was inevitable:

2 Nov. 1967

Sir,
Some weeks ago, I went to a well-known theatre in Milan
to see a show called *My Name Is Abel*, a collection of

* (1890–1981). An anti-Fascist and democrat, he was prime minister of the
first coalition government after the war.

popular songs. Four young Communists sang songs
protesting against the military, the capitalist Agnelli, the
monarchists and the war in Vietnam: in short, against
everyone, except the Communists, of course. The whole
thing was alternated with an allegorical commentary
delivered by some fellow standing behind the curtain,
while pictures of Johnson and other personalities were
projected as the four youngsters sang 'The Red Flag' and
'Bella Ciao'. After the show, the foursome proposed a
public debate. Among the persons present there was a
moustachioed long-hair and a young woman wearing an
audacious miniskirt; this person was Giangiacomo
Feltrinelli in the company of a girlfriend. Having drawn
attention to himself, our Giangiacomo could hardly forgo
talking. With theatrical emphasis, he talked of the
wartime Resistance movement, of world revolution, and
of the 'profound emotion' that he and the audience had
felt on listening to these songs, but he was disappointed
because people are content to be moved emotionally and
do not come together as a united whole to acclaim 'freedom'. This was the speech made by Giangiacomo
Feltrinelli, rather carried away, the poor soul, together
with his miniskirted friend, who was carried away altogether. Yours sincerely,

(signed letter)

There comes at least one moment in life when you don't give
a damn what other people say. The more Feltrinelli's antics
were ridiculed in some circles, the more he enjoyed them.

And when he posed for two photographs for *Vogue Uomo*,
wearing an otter-skin cape and a busby, the bewilderment was
complete. 'From the heights of his bristling moustache, the
publisher turned male model invites us to throw caution to the
winds, to claim our rights, to face up to the need for the last
consumer good that we men have neglected: male fashion.'
This was the benevolent comment of a centrist newspaper.

This time, even his own people were up in arms. After the

photos were published in *Vogue*, Alba Morino Laricchiuta, the spokeswoman of the 'Feltrinelli collective', withdrew into that silence typical of Southern Italian women. 'We all tried to cover his back, we were really in the trenches, but Feltrinelli permitted the publication of those photos . . . Only later I was led to think that the photo feature was merely a way of throwing people off the scent, he had other things in mind.'

In January 1968, in fact, the man with the busby was already on his way to Cuba, immersed in his restless thoughts.

* * *

1968. Family chronology. (February 1998. Mingus at full blast every evening, *New Tijuana Moods*, fog over the columns of San Lorenzo.)

4 January. At Omi's place in Gottingen. Omi was my maternal grandmother. Christmas 1945 seemed eons ago. Inge, who was agitated, seemed to be thinking of that time. On that occasion a feast was half a chicken and two potatoes bartered for a couple of pieces of cutlery. Her recollections of girlhood: 'we were always hungry'. This time, Omi had to cater to other appetites (and my bronchitis too). Gg ought to have been in Oberhof with S.

Early in the New Year, Giangiacomo left for Cuba.

20 January. Gaia's [Servadio] book was launched in Turin. Inge introduced Italo Calvino to Gianni Agnelli. The same launch featured Ernest Nagel's *The Structure of Science*.

23 January. A letter arrived from Venezuela; but wasn't he supposed to be in Cuba? 'How far is he gone?' noted Inge in her diary.

1 February. Back in the office. Calm, with no bees in his bonnet, Feltrinelli had not seen Fidel. During the journey he wrote down the rough draft of an essay. The intelligence services mention this.

2 February. He was in via Andegari, lunch in Gaia's honour.

He told someone to take note that the new book by Max Frisch was on the way, and advised someone else to read the first biography of Kim Philby. Then he headed off to via del Carmine. By then, he was living with S on a regular basis.

3 February was a Saturday, with my parents at Villadeati.

6 February was my sixth birthday. Family lunch. Dad took a nap. In the afternoon a little party with my friends in Primary 1. Dad brought a cake, *Mama's in the fact'ry (she ain't got no shoes)*.

7 February. Gg wasn't around, no one knew where he was. Not even Tina. Chaos in the office.

9 February. Gg dropped in briefly.

14 February. He asked Inge if she would like to take over the foreign literature series from Riva, who might be leaving. She turned the offer down.

16 February. Gg in Berlin, where he gave a speech at the Technische Universität during the Vietnam Congress (a key moment for the local movement). He spoke, in German, as a representative of the foreign delegations, and on the subject of Vietnam he found a way of mentioning the chemical workers' strike in Hesse. 'We were all amazed that he knew something about the chemical workers' strike in Hesse,' recalls Günter Amendt, one of the strike leaders.

16 February. Feltrinelli published a paperback edition of the writings of Ho Chi Minh. Inge went to the cinema: *Blow Up*. Alberto Arbasino and Mario Schifano went with her. Gg called: he asked her to send greetings telegrams to the Berlin Congress: from Moravia, Monica Vitti, the mayor of Reggio Emilia, the usual names.

21 February. Gg back in Milan. Rather cantankerous in the office, nice at home. He told Inge about the situation in Berlin. Inge had dinner with Arnaldo Pomodoro.

22 February. Inge heard Brega saying: 'He is convinced that he wants to go all the way. It's not the best idea, but I understand him.'

26 February. Editorial staff meeting. On the way out, my parents linked arms: 'I have become what I am thanks to you, but as far as politics goes, I have to go it alone.'

29 February. Bad dreams, I talked about them with I. The

editor of the *Corriere* to lunch in via Andegari. Giorgio Bocca called the writer Alfredo Todisco a Fascist to his face. No one left the room.

1 March. Gg was ill, according to Tina.

On 4 March he showed up again, in a good mood; he turned down an offer from Rowohlt to produce a series together.

7 March. Gg in a bad mood. Misunderstandings with the *La sinistra* people; he had trusted them, now he felt he had been ripped off. That evening Inge and Montale were invited to Vittorini's place. Vittorini had always been nice to her, with or without Gg.

Mid March (?). An informal meeting at the Institute with four or five youngsters from the Milanese movement, a couple of Germans, two members of Gauche prolétarienne, a Portuguese and a student from Trent. Half of Italy's universities 'occupied' at least once a year. Trent was in the vanguard of the movement. The ritual discussion called for 'themes for analysis and recognition'. The student from Trent was Renato Curcio:* 'Feltrinelli asked me for a detailed report on what was going on in Trent. Nothing more. That first meeting was only an exchange of ideas.'

8 March. Everybody in Villadeati. Dad and I cleared the Bermuda grass from the English lawn. That same day, the intelligence service of the Interior Ministry sent out a circular in which they showed they were doing their duty. They knew all about the 'liaison committees' promoted in Milan, Rome, Perugia and Palermo. They had read in secret what the publisher Feltrinelli had written during his trip to Cuba. They knew about his theories of guerrilla politics and his desire to pull Italy out of NATO.

20 March. Inge suggested that Gg use a pseudonym for the new pamphlet he wanted to publish. He talked about this with the editorial staff. He made up his own mind: no pseudonym.

---

* (1941–). A sociology graduate from the University of Trent, he founded the Red Brigades. Curcio's revolutionary activities cost him almost twenty years in prison.

The next weekend, Villadeati again. On Sunday a party for Iris Murdoch, visiting with her husband. Lots of guests, Dad arrived on Saturday night.

27 March. Pasolini to lunch in via Andegari.

28 March. Carlos Fuente's turn. Gg never shows up any more.

4 April. Memphis. Martin Luther King killed. This should be noted because the housepainter Josef Bachmann was soon to say that he had been inspired by this event.

5 April. Friday: Gg went to Bologna in the evening.

6 April. Toward midday, he dropped in on the bookshop in piazza Ravegnana, tried to call mayor Fanti, ate a sandwich in Toby's bar in via dei Giudei (with Romano Montroni), had a rest in his hotel. At 6 p.m. he met some young people from the Marxist Centre, a Maoist association. That evening, a brief visit to the Arci club and dinner in company at the San Donato restaurant in via Zamboni.

7 April. Back to Milan on the 6.45 express. The police did not miss a second of his Bologna visit. Telephone calls, photofits of all the people he met, his movements, it was all noted. They filmed him on his way to Toby's with the book-seller Montroni: the camera was mounted on the Asinelli* tower.

11 April, toward evening. Inge was in the garden at Villadeati when the housekeeper Piera arrived, out of breath. She said they had called from Germany and that she had understood that Mr Huffzky was dead. Three bullet wounds. Hans Huffzky was from Hamburg, fifty-four, a self-made man and a thoroughbred journalist since he was eighteen (with the *Frankfurter Allgemeine*); a friend of both my parents and my friend too. Inge met him when Hans was creating the first women's magazines in Germany (with *Gruner und Jahr*) and she was a photo reporter. Hans was a cheeky Saxon who had always loved us. Generous, and an excellent chess player, he was

* One of two renowned medieval towers in Bologna. An emblem of the city.

an ironically scurrilous gentleman. But on 11 April 1968 they had not shot him (Piera was a little confused) but Rudi Dutschke, who was cycling through the streets of Berlin. With a bullet in the head and one in the body, Rudi was in a serious condition. His attacker was called Bachmann, a house painter and a fanatical devotee of Hitler. Months and months of campaigning in the 'bourgeois' press had borne fruit. Militant students launched a furious campaign against the Springer* newspaper group. Clashes with the police.

12 April. Milan. Filippini recalls Gg taking an Einaudi publicity poster, turning it over, and writing in felt tip on the back: 'Berlin, 11 April, Rudi Dutschke has been shot, Fascism will not overcome!.' He hung it up outside the bookshop in via Manzoni. (The publishing house was about to come out with a book on the German students' revolt with a contribution by Dutschke.) The German student leader's condition seemed hopeless. In Milan, too, meetings were held to decide on what to do. On one of these occasions, some wise guy took the floor and wondered if it might not be better to wait for Dutschke to die before demonstrating: it would make for more impact. Gg, they say, almost gutted him.

13 April. A group of extra-parliamentarian activists, students, most of them Maoists, assembled in front of the German consulate in via Solferino and headed for the nearby head offices of the *Corriere*. They considered the paper the equivalent of Springer's press. Stones were thrown at the windows. Feltrinelli, who had gone to see what was happening, was charged with having organized the demonstration: delight and attacks on the part of the more rabid press, followed by his being cleared of all charges. Dutschke did not die.

16 April. Gg regularly in the office, very affectionate. He and Inge called Hans, who has prepared an open letter attacking Axel Springer. 'Too weak,' maintained my father.

17 April. Roberto Olivetti to lunch. He had the knack of

---

* Axel Springer (Altona 1912–85), founder of Germany's biggest publishing group and the owner of various magazines.

talking about intimate matters without embarrassing people: 'How goes your ménage?' he asked my parents. 'Very well,' replied my father, 'we even flirt.' Gg received a letter from Giulia Maria Crespi, the owner of the *Corriere*. When he read it, he was infuriated.

In April, all the most important Italian universities were in turmoil. After the riots at Valle Giulia (1 March)* at the University of Rome, it was said that the students were not running away any more. The character of the movement changed. The PCI's newspapers backed the struggle.

Oreste Scalzone[†] was a student leader with all the necessary characteristics, apart from the physique: he knew all about the workers but was not identifiable with any particular group; he had read all the books and seemed ready for anything. In early April, he found himself in a Roman hospital with his neck in traction following a raid carried out by right-wing MSI supporters on the University of Rome on 16 March. On the national scene, the political elections were in the offing: the Maoist factions came up with the idea of annulling the ballot papers or leaving them blank. Scalzone, who kept himself up to date thanks to the constant flow of hospital visitors, thought up an appeal aimed at preventing an elementary blunder; no vote was to be handed on a plate to the reactionaries; better to vote for what left-wing groups there were: 'You don't write long live Mao on the ballot paper, you write long live Mao in the struggle!' The appeal became a pamphlet for the Feltrinelli bookshops. When Scalzone met Feltrinelli, the publisher struck him as a South American. A few insignificant changes were made to the student leader's text.

Just for the record, again in April, PCI leader Pietro Longo overcame all his diffidence and met with Scalzone, while by the

* 146 police officers were injured, as well as an unspecified number of students. The disturbances marked the advent of violent tactics within the student movement.*
† Founder of the Via Volsci Collective, one of the leaders of Potere operaio, he is currently in hiding in France.

25th the first Molotovs had already exploded, at a plant owned by a subsidiary of the Boston Chemical Corporation.

1 May. Gg took part in the Berlin demonstration; I know, because there are newspaper library pictures. The Italian intelligence services contacted the Germans to inform them of this. They warned the Germans that Feltrinelli was a dangerous individual with a 'frenetically subversive personality'. The Germans sent their thanks.

4 May. Weekend at Villadeati. The guests were one of Inge's schoolmates and her husband who was an astrophysicist with NASA. They lived near Berne. Gg made a surprise visit. Everything OK, it seemed as if nothing had ever happened.

7 May. Gg asked I. to send money to Venezuela through a well-known German industrialist who was to be kept in the dark. The twelfth volume of the works of Gaetano Salvemini was ready.

8 May. A party for the writer Antonio Barolini: his book had come out. Gg came from Brescia. Guests included the banker Cingano and Roberto Olivetti. Roberto would have liked to tell Gg not to do anything crazy.

Two days later, my parents saw the painter Renato Guttuso on the street and they ran away laughing.

12 May. Gg asked if he could sleep for a few nights in the guest apartments (problems with S. too?). Inge told him that he didn't have to ask: 'You own the whole building.'

That same evening, Gg bumped into a group of students in front of La Scala theatre. They attacked him verbally; he was not one of them.

13 May. He read me a book before taking the sleeping car for Paris.

18 May: the *aula magna* of the University of Rome, an assembly of the student movement. Gg was present. The students asked him for a concrete contribution in support of their cause. Very much on edge, Gg stepped up to the microphone to be met with shouts and wisecracks, *the cash, give us the cash . . .* 'I don't think that indulging in public tomfoolery, like signing a cheque here and now, would be dignified either for me or for

you.' Howls, whistles, catcalls, and the publisher left, vastly disappointed. Rome was already basking in summery heat, but the tourists hadn't arrived yet.

The same evening found him in Pisa: dinner at Da Antonio with Luciano Della Mea and Giorgio Pietrostefani (both of the Pisan branch of Potere operaio), and Aldo Brandirali (of the Falcemartello, or Hammer and Sickle group). The argument continued on a patch of grass outside. The headlamps of the cars were on; Brandirali and Pietrostefani nearly came to blows.

On the 19th and 20th of the same month, elections were held all over Italy. The unified Socialist Party lost ground, the PCI gained some and the DC was up 1.8 percent in the Senate and 0.8 percent in the Chamber of Deputies.

20 May. Fidel called about the *Bolivian Diary*; Gg was probably in Madrid.

26 May. Brega and Del Bo conferred in the presence of I.: 'As a friend, he no longer gives anything. He is on a downhill slope with no return.'

End of May. At the Warsaw fair, the books on the Feltrinelli stand were confiscated.

End of May. France, the Ministry of the Interior. Gg was on the list of foreigners deemed *persona non grata*. The French maintained that he had financed half of the extra-parliamentary left-wing groups of Paris. President Pompidou was to say more or less the same thing in the course of a state dinner attended by Marella Agnelli and Lord Weidenfeld.

1 June. Inge attended a soirée in Milan in honour of Arthur Schlesinger, jr, formerly adviser to John Kennedy.

3 June. Gg sent a telegram to Tina from Havana.

(On 5 June the presidential candidate Robert Kennedy was assassinated. Andy Warhol was shot and wounded.)

6 June. Gg returned. Inge was in Holland for an international publishers' conference.

12 June. Gg sent an unsigned telegram to I. Two days later, they were both in the office and in Villadeati for the weekend. One talked of Cuba, the other of Amsterdam. They drank something strong.

16 June. Paul Léautaud's *Private Sector* was in Italian book-shops for the first time. A marvellous book, worth reprinting.

20 June. Inge left for the Venice Biennial with Furio Colombo.* Gg said he was in Rome, Paris, Sardinia, no one knew for sure.

24 June. Family lunch in via Andegari with Morino of the press office. The news of the day was that the person in charge of the science series had resigned. Gg reacted badly when Inge told him that his publishing house was falling apart.

26 June Fritz Raddatz, who was with Rowohlt, phoned to propose that he publish Daniel Cohn-Bendit, the leader of the French student movement. Cohn-Bendit's book would certainly be a success, but Gg's response was cool: 'I don't publish books by anarchists.'

The following day, he left for Hamburg.

28 June. Inge got a good report on my behaviour in kindergarten. Gabriel García Márquez to dinner in via Andegari.

Surprisingly, someone recalled having seen Gg on 29 June in Val di Chiana, in Cortona, decidedly very far from Hamburg. According to the witness, Feltrinelli's Citroen DS picked up a Florentine youth who was wanted after striking a policeman with a shovel during the election campaign. The cop was in hospital and the youngster wanted to go to South America. Gg parked him in Switzerland for a while.

2 July. Letter to Olga Ivinskaya. Talks with the Soviet State legal advisory office were dragging on: 'I assure you, dear Olga, that it almost drives me crazy when I think of the lack of understanding I have to deal with: I find it incredible that people try to prevent me from fulfilling what I consider to be a moral obligation toward the persons dear to the Poet and thereby obtaining, at the same time, the full and very well deserved rehabilitation of his noble memory.' Gg sent her five thousand dollars.

3 July. Cohn-Bendit phoned five times: 'Why don't you want my book?.'

* (1931–). A journalist and writer, he is currently the editor of *l'Unità*.

A good deal of sex at the publisher's: *Love and Orgasm* by Alexander Lowen, a reprint of the Masters and Johnson report, Malinowski's *The Sex Life of Savages in North-West Melanesia* and Lely's biography of the Marquis De Sade (in paperback).

6 July. Everybody off to Gargnano, on the lake, Gg included. There were Hans Huffzky, the writer William Samson, and Anna and Roberto (whose marriage was heading for the rocks). I could hear them talking late into the night on the verandah. There was talk of my first school (not private); I was to go after the summer. My father would have willingly sent me to a kibbutz.

7 July. A present of a real bicycle. Pea-green, beautiful, with a high saddle. Dad had to put blocks on the pedals so I could reach them. First attempts on the avenue lined with linden trees. Hans was allergic to Samson's aftershave. We stayed on Lake Garda all week, without my father. Brega called Inge and told her: 'Save your energy, you'll need it soon.'

13 July. Gg arrived unexpectedly. He spent the night playing chess with Hans. Guests included the actor Klaus Grüber and Marianne Feilchenfeldt with her sister, Edith. Hans was a touch allergic to women who were no longer young. Inge met Marianne (née Breslauer) in Paris in 1955. Born into a Jewish family from Berlin, Marianne was a photographer who had studied under Man Ray. A friend of Marlene Dietrich, she had been exiled to Holland in 1936, and had recently lost her husband, Walter Feilchenfeldt, one of Europe's most brilliant art dealers. Marianne now lived in Zurich and we had all got to know her, grateful and admiring. Gg showed up in the morning wearing orange-coloured pants. He was nice to everyone.

16 July. Valerio Riva left the publishing house.

On 20 and 21 July, the constitutional congress of the Marxist–Leninist Falcemartello group was held near Brescia. The Milan contingent proposed a unity strategy for the forces of the revolutionary left. 'Giangiacomo Feltrinelli, who reached Sulzano in his own Citroen motor vehicle, registration number MI-D12981, left around 23 hundred hours of Sunday 21, presumably for Milan.'

By the time a further 'confidential' note described Gg's movements in Parma, we had already been off the Corsican coast for two days, on board the *Eskimosa*. It was 28 July, and we returned to Porto Ercole on 3 August.

6 August. According to Cuccia's diary, the publisher Feltrinelli went to see him at his Milan office early in the morning.

7 August. Gg sent a telegram saying something like 'I'm deeply in love with Bo.'* 'Bo' was the code name for his son.

19 August. Inge and Gg meet in Rome and have lunch together.

27 August. Gg, expected, failed to show, not even for a quick hello and a game of chess.

7 September. Inge: 'This is really the end.'

9 September. Gg sent a telegram, a disagreement with Balestrini.

10 September. Parise felt misunderstood and neglected, all the authors were complaining.

11 September. Much aloofness. Del Bo said: 'The Giangiacomo we knew no longer exists.' Inge was worried about me.

16 September. Gg was in Milan but did not go to the office. He came home late and found Nanda Pivano[†] and Ettore Sottsass at dinner.

18 September. An evening for Saul Bellow. Gg behaved badly, and left early with Anna.

End of September. The Buchmesse was unlike all the others, Frankfurt was completely militarized. Gg serene with I. ('That's already something'). During the 1967 book fair, Gg was seen protesting outside the Greek consulate wearing a shocking-pink jacket (so the papers say). That year, at the head of a tiny delegation of publishers, he descended on the mayor's home to protest about police repression. Inge was thrown out

* English in the text.
† A writer, she translated Hemingway into Italian. Also known for her translations of the writers of the Beat generation.

of the best hotel in town because she had met the leader of the students in the hall. A new generation of European publishers: friendship with Klaus Wagenbach, and with Dominique and Christian Bourgois.

2 October. Gg came home to find out about my first day at school. We played chess. The bell rang: it was Giannalisa. Gg did not let her in.

3 October. Gg visited his mother. He told her not to torment I. When she was in Italy, Giannalisa spent a good part of her time seeking information on him, on I., and on S. I have her notes.

4 October and following days. A new clash between Giannalisa and Gg. Hans arrived. Dinner at Don Lisander. Weekend at Villadeati.

8 October. First real day of school.

10 October. Chess match. Advance copy of *Bacacay*, the new Gombrowicz.

13 October. Gg with me at judo lessons.

16 October. Even Arbasino was fed up, all the authors were fed up.

22 October. Calm lunch, all the family together. Inge had been to London and talked about her trip.

24 October. They forgot me at school. I watched the janitors eating.

29 October. Afternoon and evening with Gg. We played.

7 November. He was in the office. Frigid with Inge, then affable again.

Evening of 11 November: ruckus at Milan Central Station, 'Red Rudi' had arrived with his family. He was met by Gg. Too many photographers, some shoving and police intervention required; the Citroen drove off with a screech of tires. Public protests on the part of citizens 'indignant' over the police escort. Rudi had come to convalesce, he needed looking after. He was *persona non grata* in half of Europe and at home in Germany the climate was intolerable. At first, he stayed in our house.

14 November. Strike at Feltrinelli.

19 November. Rudi was very agitated. He got mad because lunch was served ten minutes late. Gg in a foul mood. Peter Schneider arrived. Giovanni Pesce sent one of his men to protect Rudi.

26 November. Rudi almost fainted on the street as they were taking him to the dentist's.

27 November. Our guest was still rather ill, afraid, anxious, hypersensitive to noise, but he changed and became more likeable. His visitors included Fritz Raddatz (who wanted to write a book with him), Bahman Nirumand (who had written a book on Persia for us), Rolf Hochhuth and Gerhard Amendt.

28 November. Gg was in the office. He seemed kind but totally uninterested. With Rudi, things went better.

29 November. Tax inspectors visited the publishing house.

2 December. Gg was in Sardinia. The responsibility for everything was on Inge's shoulders, including looking after Rudi. A new volume on the Sumerians in the 'Il mondo della figura' series.

5 December. St Nicholas Day party with thirty children. The police showed up to ask if Rudi had a permit to stay in Italy. Rudi played with me, taking off his shirt to show me the holes made by Josef Bachmann's bullets: 'So now you go back to Germany, you get yourself a sub-machine-gun, and you knock him off. Ta-ta-ta.' This is what I apparently said to him. The remark was printed in the 'Famous words' feature in *Stern* magazine (12.1.69).

6 December. Lunch with Gg and Inge. He talked a lot about politics and I didn't understand much.

9 December. Row between Gg and I. She threatened to take me to live in New York. He said that within six months I would have to know the truth. What truth? That evening, a party in town for Eco. Inge went with Bocca, Arbasino and Camilla Cederna. Milan was still a beautiful city.

14 December. Inge in Paris. On 17 December, Gg arrived and took a room in the hotel.

18 December. Giannalisa gave Inge a stupid spoon as a present. Christmas gifts in the publishing house. Tina refused hers

because it was not a politically correct gesture. 'They don't appreciate the simple things any more,' murmured Brega.

21 December. Pre-Christmas lunch with Benedetta, Giannalisa and the director Franco Parenti. Grandmother talked only with him. She did not know he was her daughter's fiancé.

23 December. With Inge first to Frankfurt and then to Gottingen. Mamma was not well, she had a fever. But we went just the same to the Schillerwiese, to Cron und Lanz for cheese-cake, and to the theatre for the Christmas show. Gg did not call. I only asked once where he was. We checked out our horoscopes with *Fatevi il vostro oroscopo!*, which had just come out in the 'Universale Economica' series. Düstere Eichenweg 27 was still a great place to stay.

* * *

Another emblematic event was what befell the magazine *Quindici*, which had sprung from the rib of Group 63, distributed and financed – but not published – by Feltrinelli. Not that it sold much, only one of the first issues (with a free poster of Guevara) exceeded *n* thousands of copies. Suddenly the editorial committee realized that more broadly based contributions were required: it was Furio Colombo who sounded the alarm: 'In Turin, it's getting like Berkeley.' And Umberto Eco added: 'Look, from now on we're no longer the last in line.' The students, or others in their name, set to writing and, at a certain point, the group of Roman activists showed up in the editorial offices. 'Shit, it's taken us fifteen years to change this way of talking,' yelled Valerio Riva; 'I'll talk any way I want,' Scalzone calmly replied. The split was inevitable: the radical wing of the 'movement' was out of synch with the cultural horizons of the previous generation, of people like Pagliarini, the editor Giuliani and Guglielmi. Staff and contributors got their wires definitively crossed.

Feltrinelli took notes, observed matters and was probably in contact with everybody. Together with Scalzone and the

professor of theoretical physics Franco Piperno, he had a reciprocal interest in confrontation. Natural opponents of the
traditional labour union structure, Scalzone and Piperno were
'Marx in Detroit'-types, metropolitans who felt the revolution
had to start in the cities, the epicentres of capital. Feltrinelli, a
third worlder who felt left-wing factions should present a
united front, thought that radical political discourse had to
have its feet firmly on the ground. And he did not understand
those who dismissed the importance of geopolitics, and of war.
And the PCI? It wasn't possible to pretend that the PCI did not
exist. It was a time of great ferment. 'For the first time I saw
the "plan", during a meeting held in Ginevra's* home in Lerici.
I think it was on that occasion that Feltrinelli asked me if I
could find him some ink-remover. According to me, he had
some already, but it was a way of sounding out the ground.
The matter shocked me.' Professor Piperno (who is the source
of the story about the ink-remover, a compound used to dis-
solve and erase typewritten characters or rubber stamp ink)
and Feltrinelli had been locking horns since the second half of
1968: pressure from certain sections of Southern Italian society,
the forces to be reunited between Milan, Rome and Genoa, the
weekly *La classe* to be launched in support of the political
struggle inside the Fiat workshops, the houses to be rented for
comrades who went to Turin, the advance sales of *Potere
operaio*, the new newspaper planned for the hot autumn of
1968. 'Feltrinelli used to criticize us for excessive economism.'

January 1969. Feltrinelli was disappointed by the news from
the PCI: the 12th Congress was in the offing. The left inside
the PCI, he maintained, might as well have not existed: 'non-
existent men'. Things were not much better in the branch
offices: 'There have been some vain battles.' The Federation
congresses went badly, a débâcle. 'According to the forecasts,
the congress will be very hard on the old guard and the left.
Government offers to hold out a hand to the PCI are multiplying:

* Ginevra Bompiani.

after twenty-four years of Togliatti's politics, we shall see the PCI return to government. Shit.' And again: 'Almost all my efforts with regard to the official left come to nothing. All the efforts made to marshal the real left in the country, or almost all of them, hit the target. The objective situation is ahead of the subjective situation.' These were considerations disclosed to Saverio Tutinio, the correspondent of *L'Unità,* who Gg felt had been 'talking too much' from Havana again.

* * *

E. R. first migrated from Bari to Milan, then he played his last, desperate card. On 21 January 1969 he found himself in Cologne in search of a job. He found one (as a hand in the Ford plant): a tough start, heavy work, and absolutely no rapport with the local community. He decided almost immediately that he would do better to go back to Italy. His round-trip rail ticket in his pocket, he went off to the Immigration Office only to discover that the ticket became valid only after spending a year in Germany: E. R. could not leave.

One day at Ford, E. R. met a comrade from the old days in Bari, where they had both been members of the PCI, to whom he described his disappointment. The friend said 'Come see us, we have an Italian club'. The club, Circolo Italia, was run by the PCI but in practice it served as a working men's club. Most of the members were Sardinians. They had set up a canteen, offered a help service and had begun to distribute flyers. Then came the first contacts with the Red Falcons (the local youth movement) or with analogous associations run by the Spanish, Turkish and Greek communities.

At the club, E. R. met a very young worker from Nuoro (Sardinia), Giuseppe Saba, who worked as a maintenance man at the Bauer printing works. A taciturn young man who kept a low profile, Saba was the type who would not open up unless he knew you. They became friends.

The political objective of the Circolo Italia, in that phase, was the preparation for 1 May 1969. The Italians were in the midst of a row with the German labour unions: 'Struggle against the German bosses, for the return to Italy' might have been their slogan. They circulated their documents widely, in Italy too.

The workers responded well. On 29 March, eighty of them went to Bonn for a demonstration outside the Spanish embassy. Clashes with the police, a few arrests. Two days later, the target was Radio Cologne and its Italian-language programmes. They occupied the radio station in order to transmit a communiqué. A red flag and an anarchist flag fluttered above the radio station's offices.

In early April, an undersecretary from the Italian Foreign Office visited Cologne for a conference on emigration. Invited guests included various dignitaries, diplomats and the wives of Tom, Dick, and Harry, but there were no invitations for Circolo Italia or for any other grass-roots structures run by the two hundred thousand Italians living in the area. Five down-at-heel characters, including E. R. and Giuseppe Saba, promptly showed up at the consulate for the conference: 'You can't get in without an invitation!' But the five forcibly occupied the stage, said their piece without mincing their words, and created a certain commotion. The following day, even *Bild Zeitung* ran the story.

One of Circolo Italia's projects was to create a small library. Requests went out to numerous Italian publishers, but only one replied: 'I'll give you two hundred thousand lire's worth of books, send me a list.'

In Battipaglia, on 9 April, the police fired on demonstrators during the general strike: two people died and two hundred were injured in the clashes. For the first time, a German factory took industrial action in protest against events in Italy. 'Giuseppe, shall we go to Milan for the demonstration?' E. R. asked his pal. 'We set off. In Milan, I thought of going to see Feltrinelli: it was 10 or 12 April 1969. I went to via Andegari 6: "I'd like to speak to Giangiacomo Feltrinelli, I'm an Italian emigrant come from Germany". "Come on in, come in". I told him the story of my life, my political curriculum . . . When I received a telegram signed Fabrizio, making a date to meet in front of Cologne Cathedral, I knew it was from him.'

In Cagliari, there were plans for a conference to be held by the Sardinian Emigrants' Front for early May. E. R. and Saba were the delegates from Cologne and again they stopped over in Milan. 'There, on 4 May, I introduced Saba to Feltrinelli.' The two workers wanted to publish an open letter on emigration: Feltrinelli's pamphlet series suited their purpose perfectly. They sought inspiration in Bolotona, half an hour from Saba's hometown of Nuoro. E. R. wrote the text in the sacristy of a church: it was the only place with a typewriter.

From the end of May to July 1969, E. R. and Saba, armed with a publishing contract to cover their expenses, roamed all over the Federal Republic of Germany under assumed names. They sent off to Milan political documents from grass-roots emigrant organizations and made contact with the eighteen committees that had sprung up in the meantime. From Milan, Feltrinelli warned: 'The situation here is coming to a head, we are on the verge of a *coup d'état*, a mass response is required, and our emigrants have to be reorganized.' On 4 and 5 July, arrangements were made for a broadly based meeting to be held in Ulm. Forty representatives came from several cities and an Italian journalist, or at least that's what he said he was, also showed up. He had a moustache, took notes, talked little and never made any explicit reference to things like guerrilla warfare or clandestine cells. At the end of the meeting, he made agreements with five or six of those present. E. R. did not seem to agree with the set-up, and he dissociated himself. He did not want to play the 'revolutionary functionary'.

His account is enhanced by an anecdote: during his wanderings through West Germany in search of contacts, E. R. used an address supplied to him by 'Fabrizio'. He was put up for the night by a man who claimed to be a writer in his free time. He was to recognize the man later, in a newspaper report on the Baader–Meinhof group.

* * *

The problem facing the Americans was how to stop Aldo Moro. After the PCI had distanced itself from Moscow over intervention in Prague, Moro suggested a 'strategy of attention' towards the Communists. The concept was put before the leadership of the DC in November 1968 and was reiterated in February 1969, around the time of Nixon's visit to Rome. Kissinger talks of this in his memoirs: Aldo Moro was the advocate of 'new openings in domestic politics'. Faced with serious social strife, in order to guarantee the democratic system he might have asked for the support of the PCI, thus legitimizing it. In order to avert the risk of this happening, the Americans wanted the 'assumption of specific decisions' that unstable Italian coalitions could not easily take.

In early 1969, a strategy for institutional change in Italy got under way (this was later stated by Gian Adelio Maletti, the ex-number-two of the SID, when questioned in 1996 by the Commission enquiring into bombing atrocities). As the political scene was in a state of high excitement over the behind-the-scenes clash between Moro and his right wing colleague Rumor,* the British press was the first to talk of destabilization.

In the April of 1969, there were forty-five episodes of violence in Milan. Activists beat one another up in the streets, the offices of the PCI were torched, as were the offices of left-wing newspapers, partisan associations and even the student-occupied Albergo Commercio, a former hotel. There were also many other terrorist attacks in cities all over Italy. Apart from the hospitals, there was no place safe from the risk of a little bomb (as the fascists used to put it).

On 25 April, a bomb exploded on the Fiat stand at the Milan Trade Fair. Five people injured. Another explosive device was found in the Central Station. Three days later, a parliamentary debate was scheduled on the matter of police violence in

---

* Mariano Rumor (1915–1990). A Christian Democrat and one of the *dorotei*, he was prime minister on five occasions.

Battipaglia, but the issue was struck off the agenda because of the stir caused by the events in Milan. As far as the bomb at the trade fair was concerned, the investigation pointed to the anarchists.

In Milan though, 'anarchist' means some well-known associations: the 'Sacco and Vanzetti' club in via Murillo and the more recent 'Ponte della Ghisolfa' and 'Scaldasole' clubs. Heterogeneous membership, a few small bombs put down to the more adventurous fringe groups, and a fair number of shady characters. At that time, in Brera, there lived two long-standing libertarians, Eliane and Giovanni Corradini, who had been in contact with the Spanish anarchist movement for years. The Corradinis (she owned a shop that sold artists' materials, he was an architect) were not involved with the up-and-coming anarchists, but had their own circle of people who were more or less crazy (in Brera, it's hard to find someone who isn't). The investigations into the bomb outrage of 25 April were centred on them. The police arrested the architect and his friends. According to Corradini, there was a kind of feud going on among the Milanese anarchists: perhaps someone had fed the police a tip-off.

The alibi of one of the principal suspects was that he had spent Sunday 25 April with the Corradinis in their apartment in via del Carmine. The occupant of the apartment on the floor below came to his aid: Giangiacomo lived there with Sibilla and he confirmed the story. He was questioned on suspicion of perjury. The publisher was a friend of the Corradinis (they had edited a book on Bakunin for the publishing house): had the authorities picked on them in order to get to him? A young police inspector, Luigi Calabresi,* dropped in from the political office. His was almost a courtesy visit, and Feltrinelli made him a present of a book.

---

* (1937–72). In charge of the political section of the Milan police when the left-wing activist Pinelli fell (or was thrown) from a fourth-floor window of police headquarters in December 1969, Calabresi was assassinated in May 1972.

The legal wrangling over the trade fair bomb dragged on painfully for the whole of 1969 and a part of 1970 (arrests included). Then, everyone was cleared. A new investigation led to a definitive conclusion that right-wing subversives had been responsible.

In July 1969, the 'Edizioni della libreria' published a brief text (of fourteen pages) by Giangiacomo Feltrinelli. The title: *Estate 1969* ('Summer 1969'). Subtitle: *La minaccia incombente di una svolta radicale e autoritaria di destra, di un colpo di stato all'italiana* ('The looming threat of a radical and authoritarian swing to the right, and an Italian-style coup d'état'). An appendix by the Greek writer Vassilikos eliminated any doubts about the basic thesis. It began: 'We didn't think this could happen in Greece either.'

The political scene. The schism within the socialist movement was imminent, as was the crisis of the Rumor administration. The reconstituted Social Democratic Party, with the support of the *dorotei** and the approval of the head of state, called for the premature dissolution of parliament. In the pamphlet *Estate 1969*, it was announced that something serious might happen during the summer or autumn. The information came from the old Communist Pietro Secchia, but the soft-core weeklies also talked about it in their pre-summer editions (the June number of *ABC* featured a photo of ladies accompanied by an unequivocal headline: 'August Bank Holiday With The Colonels'!).

The intensification of military operations (in Sardinia), some 'dress rehearsals' of telecommunications blackouts (Rome and Pisa, in spring) and the blatantly intimidatory tactics of police and carabinieri were specific signals. And even though the Christian Democrats denied suggestions of an authoritarian trend, their words confirmed that there was a risk of one.

In the economic field, the government's anti-inflationary

---

* The majority, centrist group within the DC, which provided numerous ministers and whose members were appointed to powerful posts in finance and administration.

measures led to stagnation. The effects added to those of infla-tion, without curbing it. A crisis was looming for the great monopolistic industries, which chose that very 1969 to plan changes in the top echelons of the General Confederation of Italian Industry (*Confindustria*). *Estate 1969* had no doubts: this was no reformist neo-capitalism! The line advocating clear-cut opposition to the workers' movement would win out among the bosses. Among its supporters lurked the hard core of those who were in search of order.

But what form was this *coup d'état* to take? *Estate 1969* imag-ined the application of a new, 'Italian-style' model, a cross between a (French-style) bloodless *coup* and the Greek version (complete with the suppression of democratic liberties). The model was flexible, and could be modified as necessity dic-tated. If the unvarnished Greek version seemed improbable, there was the eventuality of a *coup* in two phases, a political phase followed by a repressive phase, without neglecting the possibility of some agreement with the opposition calculated to preserve the institutional window-dressing. In this case, the authoritarian turn could present itself in the form of a 'state of emergency' supported by the right, by the military, and natu-rally by the Americans; foreign diplomats could be fobbed off with a story to the effect that it was a stop-gap measure, dic-tated by a situation of exceptional gravity, with a promise to restore democratic legality. As in Greece.

According to the reasoning of the author of *Estate 1969*, the imminent threat of a radical shift to the right made it necessary to adopt a specific political and military stance. The plans coin-cided: in fact, when faced by a *coup de main*, it is of decisive importance to prevent the regime from stabilizing itself and to offer armed resistance. To do this, you need a clandestine net-work able to withstand the first wave of repression.

With hindsight, the subversive imagination and criminal capacities of those behind the 'cold civil war' (the definition is Carl Schmidt's) were to outstrip the imagination of the author of *Estate 1969*. Some politico-military lobbies had already linked up on a transnational scale by the early sixties, the 'strategy of tension' was all the rage between 1969 and 1974, but it continued to be said of Feltrinelli that he was 'obsessed' by a *coup*. Why? In the August of 1969, Italy was in the middle of a NATO alarm (*l'Unità* of 7 September ran a banner headline proclaiming this) and the chief of police Angelo Vicari was to say that subversive activity was at its height in that very month; from his exile–retirement in Johannesburg, Gian Adelio Maletti testified to the presence of NATO officers in Italian barracks in the Triveneto area . . . So why?

In August 1969, taking a train in Italy was very becoming risky and it was not the fault of the state railroads. On the night of 8–9 August a spate of explosions rocked about ten trains and stations. Others were found unexploded. Was this the dress rehearsal? Police first looked for South Tyrolean separatists, then for the wretched anarchists. Some years after, the courts indicted the extremist right-wing group Ordine Nuovo (New Order), headed by Franco Freda and Giovanni Ventura. It was indeed the dress-rehearsal.

In the early days of that month, Feltrinelli was preparing to face the *coup*. In the Apennines above Genoa, he rented a farmhouse procured for him by Lazagna through a butcher living in Rocchetta Ligure. The ex-partisan functioned as an adviser and secretary, especially in the disbursement of cash. No, he was not a samurai. For about twenty days the farmhouse was occupied by Giuseppe Saba, the Sardinian, with a couple of his compatriots who had been recruited during the meeting in Ulm. One evening 'Fabrizio' swept in and unloaded two radio transmitters from his grey Citroën. He had a good relationship with Saba, but spoke little with the other two. The message was to stand ready for guerrilla action in the event of a *coup d'état*. In the farmhouse there appeared three sealed crates, a Winchester carbine and a Colt Cobra revolver.

At the end of the month, the second Rumor administration having been installed (without a *coup d'état*), Giangiacomo left for Cuba with Sibilla. By that time, his relationship with the Cubans was the stuff of legend, like the story about his having delivered them a cargo of seeds, powdered milk and medicines – not to mention turkeys and breeding hens from Arkansas.

His welcome was as friendly as ever, with a couple of one-on-one meetings with Fidel, and all amid the usual feverish atmosphere. One evening, he noticed that the black lift operator in the Habana Libre was weeping: '*Que pasa?*'. 'Ho Chi Minh has died.'

After Havana, a meeting was scheduled in Caracas with the bookseller Valerio Bertini. Bertini had been sent for a three-month trip to Uruguay, Brazil and Argentina. The official purpose: a reconnaissance of the (legal and otherwise) left-wing organizations there. But the Venezuelan appointment fell through and, on his return to Milan, Feltrinelli conducted a tape-recorded interview with Bertini: he had done a good job. (We have to ask ourselves why a sophisticated Florentine bookseller, accustomed to meditating with Henry Miller in the squares of San Gimignano, and politically a right-wing social democrat, ended up in South America playing a secret agent. The power of 1968 plus Giangiacomo Feltrinelli?)

The Hot Autumn began in Turin at the end of the summer, when Fiat suspended 35,000 workers after a long series of strikes. At the Mirafiori plant, they were protesting about the company's non-compliance with agreements on salary scales. But there was much more than that in the air. The renewal of the contracts for engineering, construction and chemical workers (which had been approved without any problems only three years before) created an explosive fusion of industrial strife throughout the peninsula. The labour unions' struggle now seemed to need basic political objectives. The mediocrity of the new Rumor administration, from which the socialists had also been excluded, made it seem a mockery. The attitude of big business (especially Fiat), often one step away from a lockout, became provocative. 'The autumn may well prove a "hot" one,' said the socialist newspaper *Avanti!*, 'and not because of a handful of extremists, but as a consequence of the enduringly

purblind attitude of the bosses towards the changing balance of
power that is evident at all levels of society.' Preparations were
made for a hundred days of agitation, 520 million hours of
strike action, and huge demonstrations.

On 19 November, ten million Italians joined the housing strike
called for by the labour unions. In Milan, the streets were full of
families with children. Outside the Teatro Lirico, there was an
encounter between supporters of the same strike, 'proud adver-
saries' in dialectical opposition to one another. The inevitable
scuffles followed. The police supervising the situation were jittery. Then someone ordered them to move in, the nightsticks
came out and the jeeps gave chase to the demonstrators. The
circumstances surrounding the death of officer Antonio
Annarumma are not clear: the police maintained he died from a
blow with a metal bar; maybe he struck his head as the jeeps
were bouncing up at high speed on to the sidewalk. It was the
first of a long series of funerals that rainy autumn in Milan.

The Annarumma killing caused an uproar: one of the leading
members of the DC, Giulio Andreotti, stated that any weakness on the part of the state towards violent minorities could
lead to an uncontrollable situation. President Saragat let it be
understood that the moral authors of such crimes lurked in
certain newspapers and called for 'criminals, whose purpose is
to destroy life, to be put where they can do no harm'. His
spokesman let it be known that no progress could be made if
matters continued like this: rumours of immediate elections, of
a strong executive, of a revision of the constitution . . . The
atmosphere was that of a last stand, of imminent cataclysm.
Federico Umberto D'Amato, the head of the office in the
Interior Ministry concerned with confidential matters, moved
to Milan, which was apparently swarming with fascists from
the Veneto and Greek soldiers inspired by the Aginter Press of
Lisbon. The British press was very alert to the perilous nature
of this moment. (The Labour Party was in power there and did
not want Italy to become like Portugal, Spain and Greece.)

*

On 4 December, at 11 a.m., the accused replied: 'I am Giangiacomo Feltrinelli, that is my name.' He arrived at the law courts in Milan wearing a polka-dot tie, a dark jacket and an even darker expression. Judge Amati questioned him about his 'perjury': the April episode again; Giovanni Corradini was still in jail. But it was merely a pretext: the views of the publisher, 'known for his revolutionary oddities', had been subjected to extremely thorough investigation: they wanted to link him with some embarrassing acquaintance, some compromising pamphlet. Inspector Calabresi had done his damnedest, and had not always played fair. Today, the attorney Canestrini recalls that Feltrinelli was aware of this escalation, of a larger scheme involving him. He seemed shaken. Then came piazza Fontana.

Milan, 12 December, 4.37 p.m.: sixteen dead and eighty-four injured in the explosion at the Banca Nazionale dell'Agricultura. A second bomb failed to detonate in the premises of the Banca Commerciale, in nearby piazza della Scala. In Rome, three synchronized explosions caused slight injuries. It was a composite operation (perhaps more bombs were planned). Antonino Allegra, the chief of the police political squad, had a name in mind. That night, a hail of dispatches arrived in Milan from the Ministry of the Interior and from counterespionage centres in Cagliari, Genoa and Livorno. That name cropped up every time.

On the morning of 13 December, the name rang out for the first time during the packed press conference in Milan police headquarters. Some journalists asked police chief Guida if it was true that the publisher Feltrinelli had been arrested. He paused before replying, and all present were left free to speculate as they wished. 'For the present,' another pause, 'the publisher has not been arrested.' 'Is he wanted?' pressed the journalist. 'I cannot answer that,' and the chief cut him short.

Feltrinelli could not be arrested because he wasn't around. Anonymous phone calls came in: 'Where is the rat?' Well-known journalists like Zicari, Spadolini, Ronchey, Pansa and

Tortora called at all hours. Newspapermen in search of a scoop rushed to Villadeati. The police wondered: is he in Cuba? In the south of Italy? In Algiers? In the Far East?

The last time we saw him at home was in early December. Inge could give herself no rest, 'I wouldn't like him to be framed', was all she could say. At a party, the famous literary agent, Erich Linder, gave the impression he knew a lot about things: 'Inge will desert the sinking ship.'

On 14 December, inspector Allegra requested a warrant to search the offices and home of Giangiacomo Feltrinelli: 'There is reason to believe that in his domicile and in the offices of the publishing house there is evidence pertinent to the bombing.' Ugo Paolillo, the judge who received the request, turned it down. The mechanism had jammed somehow. For want of anything better, the tax inspectors checked out the publishing house; judge Amati signed a warrant permitting the carabinieri to inspect the Feltrinelli Library, ordered the withdrawal of the publisher's passport and signed a prevention order forbidding him to leave the country. Theoretically, Judge Amati's initiative was not related to the events of 12 December, but to an extremely convoluted affair in connection with an anarchist pamphlet dated February 1969. The forty-something mistress of a young anarchist confessed to having sent a flyer to the Feltrinelli Library after a very minor terrorist episode in the city. The witness, who had been primed by Inspector Calabresi, was later declared unreliable by the judges. It is not clear whether the flyer had really arrived: sending communiqués to the 'library of the workers' movement' was in any case common practice in ultra-left-wing circles).

The 'hunt' for Feltrinelli looked like a crucial moment in the aftermath of piazza Fontana. Or, rather, it was an ideal way to try to drag the PCI into the kind of 1948-style, under-the-threat-of-terrorism election campaign that Saragat wanted. Thanks to Feltrinelli, whose political career had begun in the Duomo branch office of the PCI, who visited Castro, financed *Potere operaio*, and did not finance the anarchists but had friends among them, it would be possible to show that the PCI was fomenting 'red thuggery'.

On 15 December, around midnight, the railway worker and anarchist Giuseppe Pinelli, illegally held in custody since the evening of 12 December, fell from the fourth floor of police headquarters in Milan. Chief Guida made a new statement: 'His alibi had fallen apart. He thought all was lost. It was a desperate gesture, a kind of self-accusation.' That same day, Pietro Valpreda, also an anarchist, was greeted by a question from Judge Amati that resounded throughout the entire courthouse: 'Who are you anarchists? What do you want? Why are you so fond of blood?' They arrested him for the bombing. Outside, in piazza Duomo, they were holding the funeral service for the victims.

The anarchists were no more than a stopgap and Operation Piazza Fontana was not over. This was all still within the ambit of an Italian-style *coup d'état*. After the bombs, there was contention among the various Italian intelligence agencies regarding the 'management of the dead', as well as much passing of the buck; the secret plan was also revealed abroad (the *Observer* brought the Greeks into things right away with a headline, 'The Strategy of Tension'); the DC backpedalled about the proclamation of a State of Emergency, and the PCI (which knew a lot) gritted its teeth and remained vigilant day and night.

Bringing the piazza Fontana affair to a conclusion became an obsession of the coming years. In 1973, some extreme rightists thought of planting the same timers as were used on 12 December 1969 in the basement of a belvedere. In the castle of Villadeati.

9

Milan, June 1996, an ordinary afternoon. There are countless reasons (and I know them all) for sending
Giangiacomo Feltrinelli to the devil and going off for a pizza,
or for a drink, just to put the whole thing out of mind. Perhaps
it would be worth cutting loose, taking a step back from the situation, awarding myself an end-of-century amnesty for
disagreeable thoughts, and just enjoying the sultry heat of an
ordinary afternoon.

In 1969, some of Feltrinelli's analyses no longer seemed to
make sense; factors in play included impatience ('political', personal), adventure, fanaticism, the allure of arms, the unnatural
desire for justice, vanity (is there audacity without vanity?),
order and not disorder. Nor is there any need for posthumous
justifications (moral, historical, or political); the words of Leo
Valiani,* one of the founding fathers of the Republic, should
suffice: 'Feltrinelli acted in perfect good faith and in a spirit of
total disinterest, which deserve the maximum respect, in the
course of his political and conspiratorial development, which

* (1909–99). Politician, journalist, writer, senator and historian.

led to the personal sacrifice of a man who believed in the immi-
nence of a fascist reaction in Italy.' So, it's all clear. But what is
it about all this that just doesn't add up to me?

Forty-three years old, a several-times world champion publisher, a diary chock-full of internationally known names, four
languages, a son to raise, a twenty-year old 'fiancée' and a life
partner hoping for a return match, an economic position of the
first order: complete abdication. No one has done what he did.
'Because we had nothing to lose, he had everything to lose,' said
Augusto Viel, who before following Feltrinelli's lead (because
others made the same choice) had been a part-time painter
and decorator.

My father heard about piazza Fontana from a radio news
broadcast. It was in the chalet in Oberhof, which Sibilla (officially fourth wife since early 1969, with a wedding in Lugano)
was transforming into a real home. They would have liked to
stay there until Christmas ('He wanted to write an essay'). His
reaction, as he listened to the news in the Stube, was immediate: 'It's like the burning of the Reichstag, I must go back to
Milan and call a press conference at the publishing house!'

The Citroën shot across the Brenner Pass on 13 or 14
December, heading for Milan. But in those very hours, something changed. Perhaps they warned him: 'The papers have
mentioned your name.' He came to know that via Andegari
was staked out by plain-clothes policemen. He could not know,
but perhaps imagined, that they were constructing a case
against him (the scheming of the carabinieri and their stool
pigeons emerges from the records of the Milan courts).

He had to make up his mind. To go back to Milan, place
himself at the disposal of the police and defend himself against
the accusations that he saw (and he wrote this without thinking
of himself) as inspired and directed by one great repressive
design; or to go the other way, into clandestinity, for which he
was already prepared (and the events of 12 December merely
confirmed his theory).

The Citroën ate up the foggy miles (was it the 13th or the
14th?) and he turned off towards Borgosesia. It was already late

when he knocked at the door of 'Cino' Moscatelli, perhaps Italy's most celebrated partisan commander. Cino listened to him, but he was in a quandary over what the party might think. A couple of hours later, the shark-like snout of Feltrinelli's car slipped into the first of the tunnels and Genoa spread out before him in the tenuous wintry dawn. It wasn't a random decision; Genoa is the 'red' city by definition, and is home to many people who fought in the resistance movement. He hid in Giovanbattista Lazagna's house. Here, he collected his thoughts and sent off a letter to the staff of the publishing house, to the bookshops and to the institute. He said he had opted for 'untraceability':

> It is the only condition that allows me to serve the cause of Socialism, the cause I chose 28 years ago, when in 1942, at sixteen years of age, I used to write 'death to Fascism' on the walls of Milan, when in the February of 1945 I joined the communist party, when I created the Feltrinelli Institute and the publishing house in 1948 and 1954, and finally when we used that organization to develop political and cultural themes that were ever more bound up with, and ever more the direct expression of, the working classes in Italy and in the world. [. . .]
>
> My predictions were not unfounded. At the first opportunity, taking its cue from the criminal attacks of the Fascists, the campaign of hatred, denigration, slander and persecution launched by the right against the publishing house, the bookshops and myself has exploded with the fury and violence of a hatred bottled up for over twenty years. Hired journalists, police and judges are now hand-in-glove and are trying, by resorting to all kinds of iniquity, to involve me in events and situations that not only have nothing to do with me, but are also a far cry from the revolutionary strategy that some, for reasons that are not very clear, have honoured me with championing.

All very emphatic: rhetorical but clear. The first public

response – in the form of an interview for the new magazine *Compagni* ('Comrades') edited by Nanni Balestrini after *Quindici* – was much in the same vein. It came out a few months later.

What do you think of the recent terrorist attacks and the Milan bomb outrage?

It seems clear to me that the attacks of 12 December, for that matter like those of 25 April in Milan and those on the trains this summer, are the work of right-wing extremists, people under the control of a right-wing command organization that has a specific political plan, which is implementing a specific conspiracy against both the institutions of parliamentary democracy and especially against the Italian working classes. The plan underpinning this conspiracy, the intermediate objective, is that of providing a series of pretexts that will enable the forces of repression of the Italian state apparatus to unleash a violent attack in Italy, to create a political climate that might justify a reactionary inversion and a violent suffocation of the claims of industrial and agricultural workers. These attacks are not the result of an offensive launched by the political vanguard of the Italian proletariat.

And the Italian situation?

It is extremely grave and serious. The coalition of the Italian and foreign right is far from being beaten, on the contrary it is stronger and more united than ever. [. . .] The centre-left, and the DC in particular, has shown itself incapable of implementing decisions suited to the needs of the country. They cannot opt for the left, because of the strongly right-wing leanings of both the social democratic movement and of broad strata of the DC, and out of a cold calculation of their own strength: Rumor recently stated that the government no longer controls either the army or the police, both of which are forces of determinant political importance in the current situation. There is consequently nothing surprising about the fact that the government is incapable of defending institutions and citizens against the threat of the right, and that the perpetrators and instigators of the carnage in Milan and the terrorist attacks in Rome go unpunished: the government and the DC are forced to grant these forces virtual impunity and immunity in exchange for the crumbs of power that are left them.

What can the traditional left do in a mass battle against the right?

It's hard to say, but I very much doubt whether the traditional political organizations, the ones that would have the strength [to fight] today, are contemplating such a strategy. For twenty years now, they have been working on the basis of a different, Labourite standpoint; cells were selected with prospects of a parliamentary, electoral path to socialism in mind. Let's not forget that the strife of last autumn was forced on the labour unions by the working class, which would otherwise have ousted them, and so, today, faced with a dimension of the struggle that was neither foreseen nor desired, perhaps the political organization, in many places at least, would be unfit to play the kind of role in the struggle that such a strategy involves. But above all I believe that the leaders of these traditional political organizations cannot or do not wish to give due consideration to the situation, to the possibilities it offers, or to the responsibilities that it obliges them to accept.

Why would anyone want to frame Feltrinelli, harm him, or have him liquidated?

In my capacity as publisher, I have been found guilty of

thinking and therefore of having conspired, of publishing and therefore of having instigated the defence of liberty, of having denounced the intriguing and plotting of the right-wing coalition and its plans for an authoritarian involution, for a *coup d'état*; of having conspired towards and fomented the defence of the political and economic freedoms of our country. In the eyes of the right-wing coalition, I am guilty of having conspired to publish pamphlets in defence of the cause of the freedom and independence of the Sardinian people and of having supported the cause of the political and economic emancipation of the Italian proletariat, of the population of the underdeveloped regions, of the migrant workers forced by the violence of hunger and poverty to leave their homes and their lands. In the eyes of the Italian and the international right, I am finally guilty of having sustained and supported the struggles for independence and socialism of the peoples who, arms in hand, are struggling against imperialism. With the aggravating circumstance of having used the means at my disposal to publish books, pamphlets and messages that might spread the idea of freedom, progress and socialism among the Italian working classes. These, in the eyes of the right, are crimes that should be punished. But I take full responsibility for these things that the right sees as crimes: if they are crimes, then I am proud of having committed them.

Come on, Giangiacomo, come back, don't play the martyr, defend yourself properly, call the press, mobilize people publicly, reply in your own way, but come back. . .

That way, I would show faith in the rules of the game in our society, in the impartiality of the law, in the order and institutions of the state. This is what a good part of public opinion wants, because this would allay the doubts, fears and uncertainties that those same people harbour toward the impartiality of the law, the rules of the game in our society and the order and institutions of the state. The same doubts, fears and uncertainties that gnaw at the conscience of the majority of citizens but that many, too many, do not want to admit. But these doubts, these fears, must not be allayed and calmed; on the contrary, they must be enhanced, because that is the only way to attain a first level of political awareness, the indispensable premise for the renewal of society. Everyone must know what the workers, the farm workers, the unemployed and the shepherds know: that we live in a country where not everyone is equal before the law, in a society in which, to quote a remark made by Petrella [Generoso Petrella, a judge] in a recent interview with the *Corriere della Sera*, 'the crisis of law is not only a crisis of inefficiency but it is a crisis of values and content'. And so, if I don't show up in my office, it is because, faced as I am with the ongoing conspiracy of the coalition of the Italian and the foreign right, I have no confidence that the truth will triumph. Against a press that systematically carries out terrorist acts, I feel, the way all citizens do, defenceless. Against the intrigues and the provocation of the right and of certain forces within the executive, I feel defenceless in a country where, at the end of a 'normal' interrogation, you can fall to your death from the fourth-floor window of police headquarters. [. . .] But above all, if I choose not to give battle on this issue today, it is because I do not feel that this personal battle of mine is the personal battle that needs fighting. Democracy, justice and liberty cannot be measured by the 'Feltrinelli case'. They cannot be measured by safeguarding the political and civil rights of a Feltrinelli. [. . .] Until the rights of the working classes of the Italian proletariat are recognized and safeguarded, I refuse both the convictions and the acquittals of a system that discriminates between citizens, dividing them into those who have friends, money and lawyers and therefore rights and power, and those who have no money and are therefore exposed daily to the ugliest forms of harassment and the most atrocious abuses.

The publishing house, in the days following 12 December, was under siege. There was still no news of the publisher, but plenty of insinuations in the press. From via Andegari, appeals went out for statements of solidarity from the intellectual world. Some sent generic telegrams ('I share in contempt for neo-Fascist speculation. Lalla Romano'); others opted to talk of the publishing house ('I willingly declare that the Feltrinelli publishing house has published morally praiseworthy books. Giuseppe Ungaretti'); or made distinctions ('Despite ideological differences I express full solidarity against continued defamation of institute and publishing house. Davide Lajolo'); while others again offered wholehearted support ('Outraged by shocking libel campaign against your person and publishing activities. Ludovico Geymonat'). Prompt replies were received from Luigi Nono, Alberto Arbasino, Luciano Anceschi, Cesare Musatti,* Lelio Basso,[†] Eugenio Scalfari, Giorgio Manganelli, Lucio Lombardo Radice,[‡] Cesare Zavattini,** Giulio Carlo Argan,[††] and Norberto Bobbio:[‡‡] 'I add my feeble voice, weak as it may be, to the chorus of protest against the gradual – but not imperceptible – transformation of a vaunted constitutional state into a police state'.

---

* (1892–1988). The father of psychoanalysis in Italy. He published the complete works of Freud.
† (1903–78). An attorney and a left-wing socialist.
‡ (1916–82). Mathematician, member of the PCI.
** (1902–89). A writer who was one of the most important members of the Italian neo-realist movement.
†† (1909–92). A famed art historian close to the PCI, he also served as mayor of Rome between 1975 and 1980.
‡‡ (1909–). Philosopher, professor of the philosophy of law, writer of juridical texts, a theorist of political science and one of the most important advocates of the cultural renewal of the left.

A guest in the Lazagna home for two weeks around Christmas time, Feltrinelli contacted the Roman group of Potere operaio. They fixed a meeting. A little car took the Aurelia highway in the direction of Genoa. Oreste Scalzone brought along Carlo Fioroni. They went to Genoa to talk, and maybe to lend a hand. Not that there was any real need for it, but sometimes it's a good thing to assess the authenticity of one's relationships. Feltrinelli told them he was thinking of leaving the country. That can be done without attracting attention, said the two guests. We know who to contact.

A few days later, a second meeting was set up, again in Genoa, again with the ex-partisan Lazagna guarding the door, and thanks again to the good offices of the inscrutable Balestrini in his corduroy jacket. This meeting was also attended by Franco Piperno, the national leader of Potere operaio and Professor Toni Negri. During the meeting, the embryonic organization that Feltrinelli had already conceived emerged clearly. Psychologically, he accepted that he would have to live in clandestinity. Before winding up the meeting, they decided to use pseudonyms for greater security. Lazagna's apartment, a kind of *pied-à-terre* just outside Genoa, overlooked a small factory with the sign 'Fratelli Ivaldi' (Ivaldi Brothers). Feltrinelli said: 'I'm going to call myself Osvaldo.' Scalzone recalls that he later realized that 'Osvaldo Ivaldi' was the false name used by Giovanni Pesce during the Resistance. He never asked Feltrinelli if 'Osvaldo' had come to him by chance or whether it had been a deliberate choice.

Cocco Bill, a comrade with the network in the Como area, was told to be ready for the evening of 30 December: 'We need to cross [the border] at the safest point there is.' It was a bad time because of strict anti-smuggling surveillance. Cocco Bill did not know who he was to take out of the country: 'I thought it was a comrade with Potere operaio, there had been a few dragnets at the time and there were a lot of wanted people about.' But on the 30th so much snow fell that the crossing was postponed for forty-eight hours. On 1 January 1970, Cocco Bill met with 'Cinto', the most expert and famous 'mule' in the area. They waited. Three men got out of the car down on the valley floor: two were leaders of Potere operaio, and the third was a stranger to Cocco Bill. The crossing into Switzerland, through snow over a metre deep, took little more than hour. On the other side they were supposed to meet up again with the two Potere operaio men, who had passed through customs in the car in the meantime. But they did not show, as they were lost in the maze of small local roads. So Cocco Bill left the stranger at the railroad station, where he asked the smuggler what he could do for him in exchange for his help. It turned out that Cinto had a son who would have liked an encyclopedia. Cocco Bill glimpsed a quick wink: 'Catch you later . . .' Only after the train had already left did the two comrades from Potere operaio arrive with a screech of tyres. 'They came up to me, all worked up, saying "Did you figure out who he was or not?" Until then, all Feltrinelli had meant to me was a publishing company that produced books I was interested in.'

Some made ironic comments about the publisher's 'untraceability', while others came up with good arguments, as in an article run by *Espresso* (January 1979): 'We have to express strong disapproval of Feltrinelli's recent behaviour. The police have been searching for him for 26 days. His duty is to present himself before a magistrate or the chief of police in Milan, thus clarifying his position. There are some who say that Feltrinelli is rejecting this solution out of an overwhelming desire to play the revolutionary. This would be an absurd and dangerous inclination.' The reply (in a letter to the editor): 'I believe that these events mark – with or without a *coup d'état* in the short term or in the distant future – the end of the delusions and hopes that go by the name of the Italian road to socialism [. . .]. From this time on, everyone has been invested with new responsibilities, foremost among which is that of grasping and judging with clarity the real terms of the question and of not deceiving themselves or others.' *L'Unità* took issue with these statements in polemical vein.

* * *

Paul Ginsborg has written that 1969 was 'the most subversive year in the recent history of the workers' movement', while Feltrinelli defined it as 'the year of destiny' (in an interview with *Die Zeit*, January 1970). On a subliminal level at least, everyone accepted the logic of conflict. The stuff of heavy-weight sermonizing and sophistry in debate, words were not used to define but to evoke, or 'pierce' reality, shattering it. There were plots of every kind and colour, authentic impulses and insincere schemes, criminal tendencies and staunch enthusiasms. It was a climate typical of revolutionary times: suspicion and intrigue predominated at every step of the way.

When Feltrinelli decided to go away, to be untraceable or clandestine as the case may be, his personal commitment ruled out any possibility of return. Usually this is a mistake: it is salutary for the intelligence not to believe blindly in what one does. But in this case the decision was total, and Feltrinelli let this be known irrevocably. He wrote to the companies that he ran, saying that he was becoming more and more absorbed by 'publishing commitments' and since these commitments clashed with the interests of the companies themselves, he asked them to accept his resignation. His representatives were given spoken and written instructions to keep the assets liquid, to safeguard some positions, to realize others, but, above all, to make no more investments: the objective was liquidity.

On 1 February 1970, Feltrinelli expressed the wish to transform the institute and the library into a foundation bearing his name ('Forgive my impudence or my vanity').

The situation was less clear regarding the publishing house and the bookshops. On the one hand, they were a source of problems and conflict, and there was never enough money. Feltrinelli no longer had the time or the desire to run them.

'Now you're going to have to shift for yourselves!' was the most frequent message. On the other hand, financing had to be guaranteed as long as there were assets to cover it. The publishing house's continued existence was dependent on a political battle that put it in jeopardy. 'I know that the DC and the government have plans to close it down, as does the Italian Office of the Greek general staff,' wrote Feltrinelli to his attorney Tesone. In the hypothetical event of a compulsory closure, the idea was to honour all commitments to employees, suppliers and authors, but the claims of the banks were to be resisted at all costs. Inge became vice president of the company, Professor Giuseppe Del Bo was nominated managing director and Giampiero Brega became the editorial manager. All had the widest possible powers. The representatives nominated to run the other companies within the group were also given *carte blanche*. They did not agree with Feltrinelli, and in fact they all tried to stop him (but who agreed with him and who could stop him?), except perhaps for Filippo Carpi, the lawyer. Carpi lived in Rome, in contact with the equestrian circus that was the capital city, but he was an anti-Fascist who had marched side by side with Pertini* in 1945. In February 1970 he wrote to my father:

The alternative seems simple to me: either you come back, and personally accept your responsibilities, or you keep faith with those in whom you placed your trust at the time and who when put to the test have given ample proof of their having deserved it. As for coming back, my (fraternal) advice is to stay out of circulation for a while. Over these last few days leaks from authoritative sources suggest that your recent activities in the country have been subject to close surveillance (what kind of people are close to you?). So don't add any fuel to the flames.

* (1896–1990). Great resistance leader and highly popular President of the Republic from 1978 to 1985.

My father replied to everyone with a metaphor: 'When the weather turns nasty, take in the sails, head into the wind, and wait for it to blow over. It's an old rule of the sea that holds for the land too.'

At this difficult point in his life, my father wrote me a letter for my eighth birthday.

29 January 1970

Dear Carlino, first of all, may you have a very, very happy birthday. I hope that Mummy has organized a nice party for you. I'm sorry and I'm sad about not being able to be there too. Unfortunately I am far away and, in all probability, I shall have to stay far away for some time to come. I had tried to explain to you, some time ago, how the world, and Italy too, is divided into two kinds of persons, into two classes: those who have money, lands, factories and houses, and those who have no money, and have to work like dogs to earn some money, only a little, and often not even enough for them to live on. Those who have money, who have factories and land, become richer and richer by making others work and by profiting from the labour of the workers. It is obvious that between bosses and workers there has always been a struggle that sometimes becomes particularly tough and violent. Then the bosses recruit the Fascists, common delinquents, and they call in the police and the carabinieri. And this is exactly what is happening today. As you know, your dad is on the workers' side, and he finds it unfair that a worker must work to make the boss rich. And since your dad is on the workers' side, even though he has money, and in fact he uses that money to print and publish books that defend the cause of the workers, the bosses, the wealthy people, have organized a violent campaign against him. All this is part of a bigger battle between the bosses and the rich people on the one side, and the workers and farm labourers on the other. In Italy

today, this battle has become particularly keen, tough
and violent. And your dad is in this battle, in this struggle, up to his neck. It is a battle for freedom and against
the injustices of the bosses, so that the poor people, the
workers, may finally have a decent life, and so that they
may send their children to school. How long will this
battle, this struggle, last? I don't know, Carlino. Let's
hope it doesn't last long, let's hope that tomorrow you
may live in a society, in a country where all these injustices no longer exist. And this is also why, so that one day
you may live in tranquillity, studying, working for yourself and for others, and not just to make money, I and
many other friends and comrades are fighting against the
bosses, against Fascism, and against injustice. I hope I
haven't bored you with this explanation, but I would like
you to know why I had to go away, why and for what we
are fighting. But I began this letter by sending you my
good wishes for your birthday. Have a very, very happy
birthday, Carlino. It's not going to be an easy year for
you either. Mummy wrote me to say that you got really
excellent marks at school: I am very happy and proud of
you. I know you really like the school where you are now,
your friends, and your teacher. It is right that you study
and learn many things. That way, you will always be able
to think using your own head. If over the coming
months I find a little time, I shall try to write you a history of Italy. The history they teach you at school is all
wrong and specially made to confuse your ideas. I am
well. Over these recent weeks I have been studying and
working very hard: in the evenings I am always dead
tired. Well, Carlino: a big hug and lots and lots of love,
your daddy

* * *

After the bombs of December 1969, the climate had become
chaotic: everyone was talking about the need to take action,

the readiness of the 'movement' was growing to an almost exaggerated extent. Add to this ingredients with state reprisals and a dash of Mafia, then pour on petrol instead of ice: this is the futurist cocktail that was the Italy of the Molotovs, launched by state-sponsored massacres into the space–time of the seventies. People weren't even clear about which organization they belonged to, it was a situation marked by fluidity, changes of heart, and by bizarre happenings great and small.

Above ground, in Milan the student protest movement was in full cry. In Turin, Pisa and Marghera, Lotta Continua was doing its bit. On a theoretically more sophisticated level stood *Potere Operaio*, particularly strong in Rome and the Veneto. Less visible, the Red Brigades were still linked with Sinistra Proletaria but the so-called Gruppi di Azione Partigiana (the GAP, or Partisan Action Groups) were also forming. Who were they? The name comes from the wartime Gruppi di Azione Patriottica, or patriotic action groups, organized by Pesce during the Resistance. 'We feel a commitment toward these comrades to carry on and definitively win the second phase, which has already begun, of the war of Liberation,' said one of the first documents from the new formation. According to Lazagna, GAP was a universal acronym used by Feltrinelli for the clandestine groups with which he had connections. These were based in Genoa, Milan and in the Trentino. There was some activity in Piedmont and in the Veneto too. '*Progetto memoria*', a study carried out by Renato Curcio, lists sixty-five persons under police investigation, 70 per cent of whom were aged between twenty and thirty. Their number included professionals (sixteen), workers (eleven), teachers (six), and military personnel (one) . . . But the core must have numbered about thirty, including two or three migrants and a couple of Sardinians, real desperados or denizens of the anonymous housing estates in the suburbs.

In Genoa, another group was already active, on its own account. 'An unknown clandestine commando, unlike the usual left-wing extra-parliamentary movements, not students,' the local press was to say. 'Yes, Tupamaros, that's what you can call them . . .' said the men of the political office of police head-quarters. The members of this group were almost all slum kids, with ex-partisan fathers, almost all ex-Pioneers,* a movement of which some were still members. Mario Rossi was a former taxidermist, the others worked in the naval dockyards or at the Ansaldo steelworks. For these men, the piazza Fontana bomb outrage had come like a sabre blow to the legs and they set out to 'get things done'. They thought that a couple of terrorist attacks (destined to fail) might serve the purpose. Probably they got in touch with some of Feltrinelli's Genoan circles: acquaintances, names written down on slips of paper, furtive meetings in alleyways.

In the pamphlet titled *Against Imperialism and the Right-wing Coalition* (published in March 1970) Feltrinelli drew on Gramsci and Marx in order to reveal the limitations of parliamentary democracy, and on Lenin in order to explain how strikes are immediate instruments in the class struggle but also a useful phase in the dynamics of revolution. The text went on to present a complete political platform: demands for economic rights for factory and office workers (working hours, good salary policies, decent free housing for all, the development of workers' committees); economic rights for poor agricultural workers and shepherds (guaranteed salaries and free seed, the suppression of landed income, the assignment of expropriated lands); the reform of the education system (free schooling until eighteen years of age, real student grants for adolescent students, the elimination of report cards, free housing for those living over fifty kilometres from the university, a teacher assessment system on the part of family members and students); important changes in the criminal code (no preventive custody, a general reduction of sentences, and the abolition of life imprisonment). Naturally, Italy would have to leave NATO and cease producing arms, which were earmarked for the

---

* A left-wing Scout-type organization.

workers' committees that would disarm the military forces (whose budget ought consequently to be reduced by 80 per cent). As far as the question of the recovery of economic independence was concerned, it was easy to imagine the fate reserved for RAI-TV or for foreign companies, but this was only part of a long list that added nothing to a crude representation of socialism, realized or unrealized or unrealizable. It seems mere whimsy therefore, trash, an old phone book found in the cellar. Nor is there any point in taking a scalpel to separate the words, because too much time, more time than the calender would indicate, separates us from them.

28.2.70

Dear Carlino, I am sending you, a bit late, a present for your birthday: a small collection of stamps from various countries. Each stamp has a drawing of a typical fruit from that country. With Mummy and a big atlas, you can find the countries whose stamps I am sending you. Dear Carlino, thank you for your letters, which always make me so very happy. I am glad that you're doing well at school and that you have taken up judo again (are you already a champion?). A big, big hug. Your dad

* * *

The radios certainly came from West Germany. According to Feltrinelli's concept of subversion, the tools that were to hand had to suffice, but he was attracted by technology. I remember the bulky electrical apparatus he had bought before leaving Milan. It transformed a sheet of paper into thousands of tiny little strips. He advised me never to trust to fire when destroying documents: you have to reduce all the ashes to dust after the flames are extinguished, otherwise the material can be read in relief.

The radios were big, fairly sophisticated for the period and came in handy when it was announced that MSI leader Giorgio

Almirante* was to visit Genoa. A public meeting was scheduled for mid-April. This was unheard of; MSI leaders did not, could not, speak in Genoa. On the national political scene, a government crisis had just been overcome and sensitive regional elections were coming up. The only really unusual thing was the rising temperature of the conflict. Even the pope was afraid when the anarchists from Cagliari took to the streets.

At television news time, while the talking head Tito Stagno was commenting on the third manned moon mission, a small compact car was wandering through the outskirts of Genoa. The prerecorded tape was ready, and the antenna was tuned to a nicety: 'Attention please, attention please, this is radio GAP, *gruppi di azione partigiana*, this is radio GAP, *gruppi di azione partigiana*, stay tuned . . .' In the bars, people's gaze shifted from their playing cards to the television, and I have somewhere a small collection of press cuttings: the typical item read 'Mysterious television interference in the Genoa Voltri area'.

The mobile radio station was a Morris Mini. The message was recorded on a small tape recorder. The equipment was the car radio antenna, a hook-up to the car battery, and details of the frequencies passed on by some comrades who worked at RAI's headquarters in Genoa.

Feltrinelli did not take an active part in the operation, but the lunar voice talking over Tito Stagno's commentary was his.

MUSIC . . . Attention please, attention please, this is radio GAP, *gruppi di azione partigiana*, this is radio GAP, *gruppi di azione partigiana*. Workers of Genoa, stay tuned . . . MUSIC . . . Attention please, a Fascist demonstration is to be held in Genoa on Saturday afternoon. Fascist action squads from all over Italy will be massing in Genoa to hear a speech by Almirante. As happened in Milan and Rome, the Fascist action squads will employ all forms of violence. Workers, comrades, young people, citizens, let us all rally in order to strike at and destroy

* (1914–88). Leader of the MSI, the neo-Fascist party.

the Fascist action squads, to drive the Fascists out of
Genoa . . . Let us get ready for a great day of struggle,
against the bosses, against the Fascists, let us strengthen
the unity of the working class . . . MUSIC (The Red
Flag) . . . Attention please, attention please, this is radio
GAP, *gruppi di azione partigiana*, this is radio GAP,
gruppi di azione partigiana, Transmission over . . .
MUSIC (The Red Flag) . . .

Soon after, more cases of television interference occurred in
the Genoa area, then in the Trent area, and also in Milan. A
young Milanese militant with the GAP recalls an attempt [to
make an illegal broadcast] in the city's historic Porta Ticinese
area. Years later, he had done and seen it all, but that trip over
the cobbles in the little runabout, with Feltrinelli at the wheel
and the radio in the boot behind them, lingered in his memory
as a really dream-like scene.

On 12 March 1970, my parents met in Nice. Inge was shat-
tered. She had come by car and had had the feeling she was
being tailed the whole way. My father had another face; there is
something curiously obscene about the face of a man who usually wears a moustache when he shaves it off. My father also
had new metal spectacle frames. He told her to follow him, and
they went into a beachfront restaurant, where they sat down
without eating. The conversation was harrowing. From my
mother's diary: 'No one can understand him, neither Brega
nor Del Bo, he's lost.'

Although he had been untraceable since December 1969,
Feltrinelli kept in periodic touch with the 'old guard', mainly
Del Bo and Brega.

Both were extremely puzzled by his decision not to reappear
in public.

'Uncle Sergio' was not made for adventure. One look at him
and you could tell, he looked like some reserved monsignor.
'Forget it Giangiacomo, don't run risks,' he would say every
time he saw him. An outburst that was first and foremost

emotive, like that of a big brother. One evening, near Cormano, on the outskirts of Milan, they met to talk over some publishing business. The meeting was also attended by the accountant Pozzi, the former dispatch rider with the partisans. The three men came across a roadblock. Feltrinelli had false papers and everything went smoothly. 'The next time we'll have him arrested,' murmured a desperate Del Bo to Pozzi. All the commotion led to his first heart attack: I saw him collapse over the table at dinner in via Andegari.

With Brega, it was different: Feltrinelli and he were the same age, they were on different, more intimate terms. Brega, the pragmatist, saw that there were few ways out of the situation. He tried to make his case to Feltrinelli on a logical level, but the boss is the boss and above all there was a publishing house to be run (Brega was an authentic titan in the service of books). One night, while Brega was waiting for Feltrinelli near a park in Milan, a car drove by at speed and a pistol shot rang out. The bullet buried itself in the door of his old Volkswagen. He never discovered whether this had to do with some underworld feud or whether it was a warning.

Sergio and Giampiero usually met with Feltrinelli in Milan, in Switzerland, or in Oberhof, in Carinthia. Whenever he called, they would show up. The dates were fixed in writing: 'We'll meet in front of your house at 5.30 p.m., that way you can accompany me out of Milan to chat for a bit', or: 'I propose that we meet in Zurich at the usual railway station restaurant'. If Feltrinelli did not show, the date was automatically replicated the following week, same time, same place. Otherwise they kept in touch through letters addressed to the house of a friend of a friend.

The most important topic discussed at their meetings, and dealt with in their correspondence, was the publishing house. While in via Andegari they were still trying to maintain a delicate balance in the way things were planned and managed, for Feltrinelli the party was over: it was no longer possible to develop the publishing house in a conventional way, everything had to be subordinated to political ends. Basically, the house's offerings had to be 'very aggressive', bypassing even legal copy-right conventions. Feltrinelli came to attach more importance to a text on the costs of motorization than to an essay on literary criticism; a report establishing the responsibility for pollution, province by province, was to be preferred to any poetic work; and an atlas on accident prevention in Italy or a pamphlet on the phenomenon of commuting were certainly better than any essay on the Risorgimento. Money was well spent on publiciz-ing a book on the military machine and not on the 'basically rather ugly' prose of a Balestrini. And, in any case, Brega was told to read the articles in *Punto Final* for the pamphlets on Latin America; 'you absolutely must' publish the speech made by Fidel on the centenary of Lenin's birth; and as for the rights to Arghiri Emmanuel (*Unequal Exchange*), even though Einaudi had bought them, 'it may be that they are not that much interested in publishing this fundamental text for the understanding of modern mechanisms of colonial exploitation. Try to persuade them to sell you the rights and speed up pub-lication as much as possible. I don't give a damn whether it comes out with Feltrinelli or Einaudi: as long as it comes out fast.'

Apart from that, it was all one big argument, about the pos-sibility of reorganization, an increase in capital, distribution problems, or the money for the pamphlets. But here the pub-lisher in Feltrinelli would often emerge: 'Dear Sergio, it is precisely because I am fond of you that I tell you, face to face, man to man, cut out the childish stuff, the false questions of pride, etc. I know more than you do about financial and eco-nomic questions. There's no time to argue or throw tantrums. Have faith in your old Gg.'

I have reason to believe that on the night of 29 March 1970 my father visited Villadeati. Maybe he was crying for the moon, or perhaps he made the detour as he was travelling between Milan and Genoa. No one saw him as he emerged from the shadow of the great cedar of Lebanon. Behind the house, on the lawn, gleamed clumps of primulas, narcissus and snowdrops, even the first tulips. Probably he lingered for a few minutes before going back down through the woods and disappearing. A continuous series of new roads, new journeys awaited him.

Two weeks later, on 11 or 12 April, Feltrinelli was in Rome. He gave advance notice of this in writing to Pietro Secchia. 'I would be very glad to see you again and to have a chat with you. Let me know, through the comrade that will bring you this letter of mine, where and when. You choose the time and the place while bearing in mind the appropriate precautions. I embrace you with affection. Yours, Giangiacomo.' What they were to say to each other face to face was not mentioned.

Relations between Feltrinelli and Secchia (who was by that time isolated from the bureaucracy of the PCI) have been the subject of much conjecture. Even the former Israeli Prime Minister Benjamin Netanyahu has offered a crazed version in a book called *Fighting Terrorism*. Secchia is represented as the head of a terrorist structure connected to Soviet military intelligence, and Feltrinelli, 'another product of the GRU', was one of his affiliates.

I would put things differently: Secchia was a natural reference point for the strategy of the new GAP movement in Italy, and he was one hundred per cent in agreement with their worries about the risk of a *coup*. He had written about this in *Colpo di stato e legge di pubblica sicurezza* ('Edizioni della libreria', 1967). But Secchia was getting old, and he was a bit out of touch, even though he was very much in the public eye (as vice president of the Senate of the Italian Republic). And so, certainly, he offered suggestions, analyses, maybe even a few trusted addresses, but the world was changing and Secchia could no longer change. All this is admirably expressed in a letter to Del Bo, again in the spring of 1970, in which Secchia comments on the experience of the monthly, *Compagni*. He did not understand those youngsters that wrote for the magazine, they spoke an incomprehensible language, full of empty, maximalist expressions; they were inconsistent, they attacked (instead of criticizing) the PCI and the Soviets. In short: thumbs down. But in Secchia's opinion, the interview with

Feltrinelli, in the first issue, was 'the most thoughtful piece,
clear and intelligible'. Some of Feltrinelli's statements were
debatable, but he was 'a diamond among potsherds'. Secchia
was not sure what to make of some of Feltrinelli's decisions: 'I
don't know, I don't criticize, and I don't judge,' he wrote to Del
Bo, but as for those youngsters, well, an old military leader
could not hold them in much esteem.

He and Feltrinelli kept in touch, but perhaps they met just
one more time in Rome.

On 15 April, Giangiacomo was expected in Chiasso by Inge,
Brega and Roberto Olivetti. It was Inge's idea that Roberto
come: perhaps he could talk to Feltrinelli or make him talk. My
father did not appear.

Twenty-four hours later, my mother and I were waiting on a
platform at Innsbruck station. Inge very nearly failed to recognize him when he came up to us. They had taken their first
train from here, twelve years before, and now she thought he
looked like a tramp. We went to eat something at the Gasthaus.
I was all over my father, playing with him. I was after all
responding to an invitation he had made.

                                                       1.4.70
Dear Carlino, I'm sorry I didn't manage to send my
Easter greetings in time. I hope you had a good time in
Villadeati. I know the weather was good and certainly the
primulas, the narcissus and the snowdrops behind the
house must have been in bloom. And maybe even the
first tulips. Dear Carlino, I'd like it if you were in
Innsbruck on 18 April. If you take the TEE* from
Milan, I'll wait for you at the station and so we can spend
a week together in Austria. Would you like that? You
can't imagine how much I want to see you again. I know
that I'll be making you miss school for a week but maybe
that's not so serious. What do you say? Give Mummy a

* Trans-European Express.

hug and tell her to be happy and not to worry. Ciao
Carlino, your dad

For those days in Oberhof there were also Nanni Balestrini
and Cesare Milanese, as well as Sibilla, of course. Milanese
had worked for *Quindici* and was writing a book on Clausewitz
for the publishing house. He had been the one who had taken
the letter to Secchia and it was he that Giangiacomo asked to
keep in touch with some of the old guard of the partisan
movement. Mildly irritated, Milanese refused; it was the failure
of an attempt at persuasion. 'Better men than you have tried to
tell me that,' replied Feltrinelli, high-handedly, when Milanese
vainly tried to explain that guerrillas didn't usually win real
wars.

For a couple of months now, the press had been talking less
of Feltrinelli. Investigators inquiring into the piazza Fontana
bomb outrage were firmly convinced that it had been the work
of the anarchists, but his name no longer cropped up. Nothing
was known about the GAP groups, nor did anyone know where
Feltrinelli was. The odd journalist ventured into Carinthia but
without getting much done. The Italian consulate in
Klagenfurt let it be known that they had no specific information. Feltrinelli is known to have made a brief visit to Paris (in
January), where he was interviewed by a German journalist.
The French police maintained that he had left for Pyongyang,
North Korea. The Italian secret services did not rule out the
possibility that he was still in Italy, perhaps in Sardinia: 'The
publisher's hiding place is apparently in open countryside near
the home of a trusted friend.' Finally, according to Netanyahu's
reconstruction, Feltrinelli allegedly stayed in Prague every
other week.

In this phase at least, it was probable that he was moving
between Austria, Switzerland and northern Italy. And Paris,
because he signed up under a false name to follow a course in
forgery held by Joseph, a fifty-year-old of Armenian origins
with an Argentinian passport, a black beard and slippery ways,
hundreds of *faux papiers* under his belt and, for the future, a

dream of inundating France with counterfeit francs. Joseph
was wanted by the police but enjoyed certain privileges because
he had collaborated with the Maquis against the Nazis.
Feltrinelli spent about ten nights in his studio, until the forger
said: 'You wouldn't be Feltrinelli, by any chance?' He dropped
the forger: after all, he already had some passports and plenty of
blank identity cards sent to him by a 'mole' who worked in the
offices of the town council of Novi Ligure.

6 June

Dear Carlino, round about now you will be finishing
your second year of school: I'm sure you will finish it
brilliantly, with excellent marks. Good boy. It has been a
hard year for you too, just as, unfortunately, the years to
come will be difficult too. That's why I am telling you
this: enjoy your holiday now, because you have earned it.
Where are you going this summer? To Villadeati, of
course, but after that? To Porto Ercole? I really hope we
shall be able to spend at least a week together, but I still
can't tell you what my trips and movements will be for
this summer. But I shall try to keep in touch, in some
way, with you and Mummy. For now a big hug. Your
dad

In August, I went to Oberhof for two weeks. I took along my
dog, a shaggy-haired basset hound called Enzi. My father and
I did simple things: reading the papers, putting on records,
'*Arbeiter, bauern nehmt die Gewehre* . . .', strolling through the
village talking about our own business. And pineapple
Caribbean-style, North African-style fried bananas,
Palatschinken. Lots of fun with him, and playing tricks. I was
inventing a new trick every minute: I wouldn't let him sleep, I
hid things, and I followed him everywhere; all a bit obsessive. I
began to understand the life he was living, I found the drawer
with the pistol. And, furtively, I sprayed myself with his blind-
ing self-defence spray. It hurt.
    One afternoon, I went with the dog to a dell I knew in the

woods. You follow a dirt trail for a bit, with the Windwurf*
standing in orderly piles on either side, then the trail swings up
toward the wood. The objective was a place where bilberries
grew. But I also saw golden-yellow mushrooms and specimens
of every tree in the world, including the Serbian pine, birch and
sycamore. The incident occurred on the way back: we came to
a bend and I realized we were no longer alone, I don't recall the
type of horns, but I recall a pair of eyes as surprised as ours.
The animal ran off and the dog chased after it. And so it got
dark and I had lost the dog I had dragged on the train all the
way from Milan: dear Lord, dear Lord, let him come back! In
a flash, nature had become a cavern, and I ran home to get
help. My father didn't believe the story about the animal
encountered on the path, or perhaps he was pretending to make
the adventure even greater for me. When he came back, it was
already night, and the dog was lolloping along behind him.

On 28 August, I stepped off the train in Stuttgart. Inge came
to pick me up.

* * *

In the autumn of 1970, Italy was rocked by the riots in Reggio
Calabria. The first phase of the revolt had already exploded in
July, when the city's application to be recognized as the regional
capital was turned down. A railway worker and member of the
CGIL labour union died, the police injured a hundred or so
people, and crowds stormed the police headquarters. Reggio, a
right-wing city, was in bad shape: in September, the MSI's
rabble-rousers urged the people to take to the barricades. The
police response to this was brutal. Another death. Four bomb
attacks on trains. Through Lazagna, the leader of Lotta
Continua, Adriano Sofri,† asked for thirty million lira in order

---

* Trees felled by the wind and then sawn up and stacked.
† A leader of Lotta Continua and a journalist, Sofri was recently imprisoned
for his part in the murder of Inspector Luigi Calabresi. Many Italian intellectuals have repeatedly appealed for his release claiming that he is innocent.

to move men into Calabria. The intention was to take a protest that had been taken over by the neo-Fascists and shift it to the left. Giangiacomo was not crazy about Sofri.

In northern Italy, on the other hand, the clandestine organization known as GAP had been active since spring 1970. Their main objective was to root the Italian struggle in the vigour of partisan action, by staying on the offensive against the ever more ruthless attack of the 'imperialist right'.

In May, the Genoa-based group known as '22 October' had organized two (unsuccessful) bomb attacks against the offices of the PSU in viale Teano and the US consulate in Genoa. It is very hard to say who was who; the sobriquet '22 October' had been coined in the courts and newspapers. Perhaps it might be better to talk of a third, Genoa-based column of GAP (the other two were in Milan and Trent). Of course there was collaboration, if not a 'federation', with the 'real' GAP. In particular, for the campaign of interference organized by Radio GAP, which was resumed that very September during Richard Nixon's visit to Italy. Contacts with the Genoan GAP group were maintained by Lazagna or some of his people. But such contacts were reduced to a minimum: the group's lack of compartmentalization was too risky, and their recruiting was too lax.

On the other hand, the 22 October group (or the GAP Third Column) lived its own life and prepared autonomous fund-raising activities, like the kidnapping of Sergio Gadolla (5 October 1970), a scion of one of the wealthiest families in Genoa. They kept him for five days in exchange for a haul of 200 million lira. It was probable that the group had the support of the Milanese GAP, but 'we did not want bosses of any kind', as one of the former members of that nucleus recalls today. Indeed, a couple of them did not trust any support that came from people 'who had no first-hand knowledge of material suffering'.

The only self-financing operation that the 'real' GAP planned meticulously, but without putting it into action, was a plan to rob the casino at St Vincent, in Val d'Aosta. But it is

clear that the logic was purely symbolic. In this case the rob-
bery was inspired by a similar operation carried out in Latin
America. See 'Operazione San Rafael', Carnival at the casino in
Punta del Este, from *I Tupamaros in azione*, page 87, Feltrinelli
Editore.

In the meantime, the Milan-based GAP was trying to make its
presence felt with a series of operations intended to shift the
idea of sabotage on to a 'mass level'. The target was the sector
with the highest percentage of fatal accidents and injuries in the
workplace. Between 28 August and 17 September, in
Lombardy alone, ten construction workers had died.

The requirements were two or three bottles of petrol, a few
tins of tomatoes stuffed with explosives, and some adhesive
tape and lime as a sealant. During the night, when no one was
around, the fuses were lit underneath the cement mixers. On 22
September, explosions occurred in the Fratelli Proverbio and
Socogen building yards; on 24 September in the Torno yard;
and on the 26th of the same month in the Stefi yard. Who were
the bombers? 'At present,' replied Milan police chief Antonino
Allegra, 'we are unable to give a name to the bombers.
Investigations have only just begun.'

Comrade 'Osvaldo' played a direct part in the nocturnal raids
on the building yards. I asked Giuseppe Saba: 'What was he
like?' 'He inspired confidence in everyone.' Sardinians know
how to keep their mouths shut.

Giambellino is one of the sprawling proletarian reservoirs on
the west side of Milan. You breathe politics with the air here.
The PCI, historically very strong, was struggling to contain
the new thrust that united fathers, mothers and children. In
Giambellino, if they felt like it, they could take over the whole
quarter.

Following Tambroni's* attempt to establish a repressive
regime, one of the first Maoist groups had sprung up within

---

* (1901–63). Minister of the Interior during the public disturbances that
occurred during the MSI Party Congress in the summer of 1960.

the local branch office of the PCI. This group was known as 'July 60'. A couple of its members invented a delegation, went to Beijing, shook hands with Chairman Mao and wound up on the front page of the local newspapers. A typical sixties anecdote. In the seventies, Piero Morlacchi, who frequented a local working men's club called La Bersagliera, helped to found the Red Brigades.

The heart of Giambellino is piazza Tirana, a handsome Albanian square with a secondary railway station. The meeting place was La Bersagliera, frequented by a very mixed bag, underworld types included. The gangsters of those days had agreeably left-wing sympathies, even in the spaghetti westerns.

Piazza Tirana witnessed the birth of the 'Valentino Canossi' brigade of the GAP, which claimed responsibility for the building yard bombings. It was made up of four or five members. The journalists went through the yearbooks of the Resistance in an attempt to identify this Canossi, but they did not find him. Valentino Canossi was a worker who had been killed in an industrial accident on 2 September 1970, a few days before his retirement. On 24 October, the third number of *Il partigiano gappista*, four sheets stapled together, issued an ultimatum to the association of the construction industry threatening new reprisals. 'Every new death in the yards, every worker murdered, will be revenged!'

On 1 November 1970, my parents were once more outside Italy. 'I love you very much Ingelein . . .' but she was heartbroken: she thought it was a never-ending tragedy, she hated to see him in that state, and thought he was completely lost. He said that the publishing house was bringing out inaccurate books on the Tupamaros and he asked her to take me a letter.

> Dear Carlino, I haven't written to you for a long time
> and I haven't heard how you are doing. In any case, I
> hope that you are well and that, in these first days of
> school, you are among those at the top of the class. How
> the did the grape harvest go at Villadeati? Did you pick

the grapes before the rain came? Have you been doing your homework? And are you managing to control your outbursts of rage (*Wutanfälle*) the way you promised? I had to go to Oberhof for four days and I really missed you (and even Enzi, even though finally it was possible to get some sleep). It had already begun to snow when I left. Sibilla sends you a big hello. I'd like to know all your news. Write me a long letter. And be close to Mummy, who is really on the ball. Dear Carlino: I send you a big hug and hope to see you again soon, your dad

Operation Tora-Tora, on the night of 7 December 1970, was for a long time considered a parody of Luciano Salce's film *Colpo di stato*, a blend of cabaret and *cinema verité* which had been shown at cinemas the year before. It was a *coup* attempt organized by Prince Junio Valerio Borghese, a former commander of the Decima Mas, a crack Italian naval unit (something like the British SBS or US Seals) but it came to an abortive end and the public did not hear about it for several months. His Fronte Nazionale troops managed to occupy one wing of the Ministry of the Interior, the armoury, and the archives. But the ex-paras, the forest rangers, the neo-Fascist action squads, the Mafia commando groups and the army divisions massed in the barracks that were allegedly ready for action were all suddenly stopped by a telephone call. In that moment, Licio Gelli,* a mattress dealer, ought to have been in a lift in the Quirinal Palace on his way to get President Saragat (whom he knew and with whom he socialized, though no one knows for what reason) in order to hand him over to the conspirators.

'It emerges clearly that the Borghese *coup* attempt was not the joke some people have tried to suggest it was.' This comment, made twenty-five years later, is a typical product of the

---

* Founder and Grand Master of the masonic lodge P2, at the heart of the subversive events that rocked Italy in the seventies. Today under house arrest.

parliamentary committee inquiring into the bombings. Scalzone added something to this when he said he vaguely recalled that Feltrinelli had talked of a plan to kidnap Borghese. He talked to me about this from Paris, in 1995.

For Christmas 1970 I went back to Oberhof to see my father. As well as the majolica stoves, the stalactites of ice hanging from the eaves and the usual dog I had taken with me on the train, there were a few guests with us. Valerio Morucci of Potere operaio was one of the group and he joined in our snowball fights. My father built a real igloo in front of the house, perfect, inhabitable. He equipped it with one of those metallized plastic covers that astronauts use. It weighed twenty grams and protected you from the cold. As a matter of fact, if you wrapped it around your body you could survive at any temperature. We also went for long walks and come the evening I would be staggering with tiredness. The dog, sitting at the top of the stairs, would bark at anyone who came near the bedroom. Benevolently, my father tried to quiet him: '*Aber Enzi . . .*'

On 10 January 1971, I went back to Milan.

* * *

My father's 'foreign policy'. True or false? Contacts with Habash, the most intransigent of the Palestinian leaders, with Algerian circles, with the Germans of the Rote Armée Fraktion, with the American Black Panthers, with the Tupamaros in Uruguay, with eastern European intelligence services. Through a group of businessmen with offices in Geneva, Feltrinelli was supposed to have plotted in favour of Arabs and Palestinians, supported the Bolivian and Venezuelan guerrillas as well as the Irish irredentists, procured weapons for the Greek resistance movement and for those fighting Franco in Spain. CIA documents describe him as 'the most important Castrist agent in Europe', while the ultra-American journalist Claire Sterling did not mince her words: 'No matter which way you judge him, unbalanced, sexually disturbed, vain, weak, arrogant, fanatical, frustrated, reckless, regrettably eager for adulation, and inclined toward irrational dreams and unbridled ambition, Feltrinelli conditioned the history of a decade.'*

True or false? The motto of the Tricontinental (1966), 'a global strategy to counter the global strategy of imperialism', is unambiguous. But in 1970 this strategy was in poor shape in the countries it had sprung from: some key figures (like Che) had died and the forces of reaction were in the ascendant ('covert recolonization'?). But 1968 in Europe had rekindled the idea of linking up revolutionary vanguards wherever they might be and, in Giangiacomo's mind, of building an organizational bridge between Europe and the Tricontinental.

'He wasn't one of our agents, there was never anything coordinated about his activities in Europe. He kept us informed, and we knew we could count on him. But Europe wasn't a priority for us. With Italy we had only normal relations, and we weren't even that close to the PCI.' This is what Manuel Piñeiro had to say from Havana (in December 1992).

To interpret the Feltrinelli of 1970–1 as an independent figure who looked to the Authentic Revolutions to smash all frontiers in the portent–prodigy of the final counterattack, fits in with his previous biography. Conceptually, he was still convinced that the socialist camp, obtuse as it was, was for all that a set of 'progressive' systems, the principal bastion against imperialism. The Cubans had something to do with his 'one-man-show', while for contacts farther east one example-metaphor should serve the purpose: the instructors in Punto Cero (Cuba) were certainly from the DDR, but Markus Wolff, the intelligence boss in East Berlin, could say nothing about Feltrinelli's activities in Europe.

Feltrinelli was said to be shuttling continuously between Italy, Austria, Switzerland and France, with a network of contacts in which, however, it was not always clear who represented what. Jan Stage, the Danish journalist in the service of the

---

* It ought to be added that Claire Sterling was a combative neo-conservative who wrote on many other issues (with *Newsweek*, especially).

Cubans until the early seventies, was often with Feltrinelli. They had met at the Copacabana in La Paz in August 1967. Now Stage called himself 'Camillo'. Stage thought that Feltrinelli's plan to set himself up as the European depository of the world's revolutions was purely Utopian. Very little had been done in concrete terms. As for the eastern European countries, Stage denied that there were direct contacts of any kind, while Sibilla, who at the time was on standby in the silent valley of Oberhof, also dismisses Netanyahu's assertion of the twenty-two trips to Czechoslovakia. (In fact, it seems that Feltrinelli did not make so much as one trip there, until the end of 1970 at least.) Nothing has really been proven: but when the circulars of the European intelligence services said Feltrinelli was in Beirut, he was with me, I swear, on an asthmatic old train between Villach and Klagenfurt.

11 January 1971. Feltrinelli met Giampiero Brega. A catastrophe, the two men no longer understood each other. Del Bo was also upset about a rather cold letter he had received. Sergio no longer wanted to see to the running of the publishing house: 'Either he comes to get us out of this mess, or he gives us the cash as promised.' But he carried on, despite the fact that the house was in the middle of a heated dispute at the time. The managerial situation was not good, only the seven bookshops were breaking even: everything else was going badly, very badly, and the banks were piling on the pressure. The men in via Andegari proposed a staggered financing programme. In order to manage the downsizing operation, they fixed a budget and proposed to cut costs and titles. Nothing doing. As far as the publisher who was no longer a publisher was concerned, downsizing was out of the question: 'The publishing house is an instrument of the class struggle!' No more petit-bourgeois idealism! The publishing house had to carry on its political battle against the hostility of the capitalist groups and of the PCI. At the end of January, he asked his men to make a decision: conform, collaborate or take their leave. He also had other ideas: a collective could control the house's line and some carefully selected political figures would agree to form

a supervisory committee and even become shareholders. In the pursuit of these objectives, Feltrinelli proposed a final, massive financing operation with a compensation fund to be used to protect those earning the lowest salaries. Then the publishing house would have to stand on its own two feet. During the secret meetings with the staff from via Andegari, Giangiacomo talked tough. Inge thought he looked awful and that even his teeth were going to pot.

Dear Carlino, happy birthday! I would be glad if at this time you could feel all the friendship (you're not a baby any more, but a big boy, and you know what friendship means) and, naturally, all the affection and love I bear you. I have no great gift for you, at present: only a seashell. I haven't been able to find anything else, for the time being. But perhaps the best present I can give you is to struggle for a better world, for a fairer world. Now that the Fascists are filling the newspapers with the stories of their exploits (and unfortunately the hospitals with the injured), you will begin to understand that, outside the tranquillity of your home, of Villadeati, and of Oberhof, a ruthless life-or-death battle is going on, a battle for justice and freedom against the terrorism of the Fascists and the bosses, against injustice, poverty and hunger. And the greatest wish I can make you, Carlino, is that by the time you grow up, all these struggles and all this suffering will be only a distant memory, something that you read about in books and study, but not the way it is today, a reality against which, believe me, every honest man must fight. Dear Carlino, I haven't heard from you for a long time. But I am sure you are well (even though this January Villadeati must have been submerged by snow and rain). How's school going? Write to me some time. A big hug and loads of birthday wishes, your dad.

In the first half of February 1971, the Genoa-based column of the GAP struck at the factories owned by industrialists believed to be financing the MSI: the Borghi family's Ignis plant in Sestri Levante and the Garrone refinery in Arquata Scrivia. The group later interrupted television broadcasts to claim responsibility for the bombings. In Milan, Trent and surrounding areas, attempts were made to take the initiative once more. 'More than anything else, these were demonstrative actions, made to gain experience. We had no military training, apart from some lessons given by a few ex-partisans.' These ranged from the diffusion of propaganda to the placing of incendiary devices that could not explode to rudimentary bombs that could. This is Giuseppe Saba's recollection. The GAP's raids caught the newspapers unprepared. Was this political terrorism or what?

The organization was strictly divided into watertight compartments and if one thing was indispensable it was discretion. At that time a 'how-to' handbook for subversives was circulating among the most extreme fragments of the left. Things like: be sure no one is tailing you (every militant always had to feel he was being followed); be careful with correspondence and notes (write down as little as possible) and be wary of the telephone (always mistrust it, and use public phone boxes only). Militants were always to keep silent, were always to feign ignorance, and had to keep cool under questioning (explaining oneself is dangerous, better to deny things, always). Under the heading 'equipment' there were other warnings: militants always had to be ingenious and their instruments had to be 'mass instruments', in other words, easy to make with cheap and commonly available materials. The paragraph on improvised explosive devices counselled a blend of potassium chlorate tablets (available in pharmacies) and caster sugar, the kind they use for cakes. Or: mix paraffin or tar with sawdust, adding thin flakes of Marseilles soap and kerosene. Valerio Morucci* put it like this: 'One time, at a house in Rome, Feltrinelli made a

---

* (1949–). He was one of the leaders of the BR at the time of the Moro kidnapping. He conducted the interrogation of the prisoner.

demonstration. He mixed up two really improbable ingredients, but he managed to make them explode.' Morucci saw the flames reflected in the lenses of Feltrinelli's glasses. The publisher's face was thin, bony and almost ascetic, with a short beard streaked with white. The face of an Italian anarchist or a Cuban Communist, but it also reminded Morucci of the face of a man 'committed to the study of the Talmud'. 'I listened to him, aware that everything he said, no matter how strange it was, was backed up by a world of life experience that demanded respect.'

For the timing devices and for the electrical circuits, they could exploit the principle of the dilation of dry seeds. Peas, beans, or other desiccated seeds increase their volume by 50 per cent after soaking in water, and as they swell, they push a blade upwards, thereby triggering the contact device.

The handbook, around thirty pages in all, was later duplicated and adopted by the Red Brigades, who were about to make their début. One of the founders, Alberto Franceschini, suspected that the handbook was of NATO origin, and had somehow fallen into the hands of the 'reds'. Others maintained that it was the translation of a Swiss pamphlet, prepared to instruct the population in the event of a Soviet invasion. It would do.

On 7 January 1971, there was a case of arson in the Milan warehouse of the Pirelli–Bicocca plant in via Sarca. This caused a disastrous fire and a thirty-year-old worker who was trying to extinguish the blaze died in a sudden burst of incandescent flame. The newspaper blamed left-wing extremists. Many years later, it became known that the action was the work of the MAR, or Movimento di Azione Rivoluzionaria (Movement for Revolutionary Action), a neo-Gaullist paramilitary outfit with presidentialist and putschist ambitions of whom the GAP had talked in alarmed tones in one of their first official documents. Such camouflaged bombings, like the one at the Pirelli plant, served to provoke extreme left-wing groups. A few weeks later, in fact, the Red Brigades organized their own attack on Pirelli. They burned a series of trucks at

Linate. It has yet to be established whether the BR (or the GAP) and the MAR had used the same military handbook. It is possible.

March 1971 witnessed the issuing of the first arrest warrant for the Red Brigades. It was in the name of Enrico Castellani. In his house, in via Castelfidardo, they found fuses and explosives.

Not far away, in via Andegari, unaware of all this, Professor Del Bo was wringing his hands in panic. The situation was taking an apocalyptic turn. Who was paying these Red Brigades? Every hint in the media became a suspicion, every suspicion an added source of anxiety.

It was to get even worse a few weeks later, when a murder was given massive newspaper coverage.

On 26 March, the former Genoan taxidermist Mario Rossi killed the deliveryman Alessandro Floris during an armed robbery in the offices of the city's institute of council housing. The plan, with which some members of the 22 October group disagreed, seemed to be rather straightforward. An accomplice, a clerk with the institute, had supplied them with accurate information about the arrival of the bags containing the pay packets. But something was not right: the loot was two hours late in arriving, and Mario Rossi and Augusto Viel, who were lying in wait, began to get jumpy. Then the delivery arrived. In a flash, Mario saw that it was time to move, that the mission could still be accomplished. 'Handsuuuup!,' the bag, the shot aimed at the ground to make sure no one would follow, long strides towards the road, another shot at the ground, Christ! . . . Someone was coming after them. Augusto was a few metres away, waiting aboard the scooter, but the scooter wouldn't start. Desperate jabs at the kick-starter until the engine finally caught and Mario jumped on, first bounce. But Alessandro Floris, the deliveryman, was still following them, and he was closing the gap. At that precise moment, Ilio Galletta, a twenty-five-year-old student, was on the terrace of his house, trying out his brand-new Pentax automatic. He immortalized the scene in eighteen shots. The police gave only three photos to the papers. In one of these, Rossi is seen in the saddle, the bag between his belly and Viel's back, his head turned with his right arm beyond the line of his shoulders. He shot at the tarmac but hit Floris in the abdomen as he dived to stop them. The images shocked Italy. To emphasize the homicidal intentions, the sequence shown in the press was mounted upside-down and incomplete.

Rossi 'the Tupamaro' was arrested a few minutes later. Thus ended the last operation carried out by the Genoan group. Viel managed to get away, but the other members of the band were soon captured. Viel made contact with the Milan-based GAP and a hiding place was found for him in the city. In the hours following the events of 26 March, in a warehouse rented in Rossi's name, investigators found Carlos Marighella's* manual of urban guerrilla warfare, some radio transmitters for the television interference campaign, sticks of dynamite and banknotes from the Gadolla ransom. It was not hard to work out the political motives behind the attempted robbery and to reconstruct the activities of the Ligurian group over the previous months. But, in the press at any rate, no connection was made between 22 October and the GAP.

From prison, Rossi wrote a letter to the judges, confirming that expropriation was good revolutionary practice, and that famous anarchists and Communists had done the same thing in the past. He declared that he was a militant in good faith, an 'unknown Communist', and an actor in an operation that, by chance, had cost the life of a worker. 'But doesn't it often happen that men of the same class find themselves on opposite sides of the barricade? Floris sacrificed his life to defend what I am fighting against. It is saddening that the capitalists never pay in person . . .' Feltrinelli, visibly shaken, apparently said more or less the same words to the omnipresent Scalzone when

---

*Carlos Marighella: ex-leader of the Brazilian Communist Party and a guerrilla fighter with the ALN, he was murdered in 1970.

they met in Milan on the bridge in Via Farina on 28 or 29
March.

Five days after Floris, Roberto 'Toto' Quintanilla, the
Bolivian consul, was killed in Hamburg.

10

Bolivian machinations. Quintanilla was a cop, says Régis Debray today, holed up in his little apartment in the 6me arrondissement. Numerous first-hand accounts of the period describe Quintanilla as a pitiless torturer. Osvaldo 'Chato' Peredo has never forgotten the three mock executions prepared for him. On the third, the colonel popped up like a saviour ('What are you doing to this boy?'), stopped the firing squad a split second before they pulled the trigger and tried to soft-soap him into talking. But Chato knew very well who he was up against. He knew of Quintanilla's special status as a CIA man, and of his role as an organizer of repression. He knew these things thanks to a photo in which the colonel can be seen standing over the corpse of Chato's brother Inti. The photo is almost identical to the one showing the colonel standing over the lifeless body of Che. Inti was the second brother Chato had lost: Roberto 'Coco' Peredo had died with Che.

When government police captured and killed Inti (9 September 1969), the National Liberation Army (ELN) was on the ropes, decapitated. Some militants maintained that it would have been better to hide in Chile, others were determined to stay. At this point 'la gringa' enters the story, Inti's girlfriend, who later became Chato's girl.

'La gringa' was Monika, born in Germany in 1937 and brought to Bolivia by her father after the war. The father was Hans Ertl, a celebrated documentarist. Rommel had wanted him at his side and Ertl had portrayed the war according to the dictates of propaganda. On his arrival in Bolivia, Ertl settled in the countryside near Santa Cruz, but he still went out on photo safaris. He ventured into the Peruvian jungle in search of the lost city of Paititi. According to the legend, eighty thousand Incas had hidden there in order to ensure that the Spaniards did not get their hands on the gold. Monika accompanied her father on his trips and in the meantime she grew up: tall, beautiful, blonde and spiritual. She had a strong character. 'She was more masculine than the men,' recalls Debray, who met her in Cuba in 1971. 'She wasn't afraid.'

From the end of 1969, the Bolivian political scene was rocked by one sensation after another. General Barrientos died when his helicopter fell out of the sky. Perhaps it was an accident, perhaps it was a question of army officers feuding over some gun-running deal (with Israel? with Iraq?). Two journalists who enquired into the crash lost their lives. Deciding who was going to be the next president of Bolivia became a tormented process. They managed to elect six different ones in a single day. After a popular uprising, in October 1970, the populist army officer Juan José Torres won the day. He was almost a democrat, and the Americans had him ousted a year later.

Quintanilla's star began to wane during the chaotic events of 1970. He had handled the Barrientos crash inquiry in an ambiguous manner, and there were too many skeletons in his photo album. Better to send him away, as consul in Hamburg. 'But for us he was still a target, and we were on his trail,' recalled Chato twenty-seven years later. Following Inti's death, Monika Ertl wrote a poem ('Christ in September') invoking the colonel's death: 'Quintanilla, Quintanilla, no more shall your nights know peace . . .'

On 1 April 1971 the new consul in Hamburg agreed to see a young Australian woman who needed a visa for a folk group. When he went to greet her, the last thing he saw was a pistol. So ended Colonel Quintanilla. In her flight, the girl dropped her wig, her handbag, her Colt Cobra .38 Special, and a slip of paper with the words 'Victory or death. ELN'. Australia had nothing to do with it, and Monika was identified almost immediately.

Chato Peredo never had particularly close relations with the Cubans. Today he maintains that the Hamburg operation was decided autonomously. 'It was our idea, I had no relations with Havana. The decision to send Monika was inevitable, she was German, and she knew the language. We claimed responsibility for the operation right away.' The killing was the only operation of its kind carried out by Latin Americans in Europe.

It is not clear how the ELN came into contact with Feltrinelli, but Jan Stage had given Chato Peredo a Kleenex box stuffed full of dollars in a park near the University of Santiago. The cash was needed for Monika's trip to Europe, because the ELN was broke. Before Monika, in January 1971, a couple of Venezuelans (brother and sister) had gone to Europe to kill Quintanilla. On their way through Carinthia, they decided that the enterprise was too risky. The sister was friendly with a promising Cuban army officer, Arnaldo Ochoa, who was looking after Venezuelan affairs at that time.

The Cubans probably knew all about the trip planned by Monika, who landed in France in the early spring of 1971. In a harbour on the French Riviera, aboard a second-hand motor yacht, Feltrinelli handed the pistol over to her and an accomplice: 'It may come in handy as a reserve,' he said to them. At the last moment, before the shooting, Ertl decided that the Colt was more reliable than the Browning she had originally intended to use.

According to one important source, Monika and Feltrinelli barely knew each other. According to others, they were well acquainted. Finding the truth is about as easy as finding the lost city of Paitití. Monika fled Hamburg for Chile, via

Switzerland and Italy. In Santiago she gave Chato a Dunlop cigarette lighter, a present for him from Feltrinelli.

(Further ramifications: after Chile, Monika went to Cuba, where she saw Régis Debray. Together, they plotted to kidnap the accountant of a lumber firm in La Paz, a German named Klaus Altman. By pure coincidence, it had been Monika's father who had found the job for Altman after the two men had met in a downtown bar called the Café La Paz. But what Hans Ertl did not know was that Altman was none other than Klaus Barbie, the war criminal known as the 'butcher of Lyon'. According to Debray, Monika had a score to settle with the Germans and wanted to denounce the cooperation between the CIA, the Nazis and the military régimes. And cooperation there was. Especially when the hunt was on for Monika, who was living in Bolivia under the odd name of Nancy Fanny. She was killed on the outskirts of La Paz in May 1973.)

On 17 April 1971, the information on the pistol used to kill Quintanilla had still not been made public. Inge, Del Bo and Brega met with Feltrinelli in Paris. After the row of the previous winter over the publishing house, they were ready for anything. But Feltrinelli was calm and thoughtful, he listened, asked questions and gave advice. 'He's still the boss . . .' Brega and Del Bo took notes. The day before, my father had written me a message about the seven young fir trees he had sent me.

> Dear Carlino, for the firs you have planted: remember to buy some peat and put plenty of it around the roots. Then, especially in summer, you have to see that the trees are watered: not too much, but enough. Bye, a big hug, and see you soon, dad

In the space of a few days, the news began to leak out: the pistol had been bought in the armoury near the Capitol cinema in via Croce Rossa, Milan. The national and foreign press speculated about the involvement of Feltrinelli, the legal purchaser. He had not appeared in public for almost a year and a half.

The evening papers ran a headline: 'Feltrinelli arrested in Paris?' (26 April). Interpol was investigating, but no request was made for an international arrest warrant. Feltrinelli was not directly involved with the Hamburg operation. But the Colt was the one Valerio Morucci had seen in Feltrinelli's shoulder holster a few months before. He recalled it decades later with considerable pathos: 'Sewn on to the strip of leather that ran up from the holster to the shoulder there was a cartridge-belt with six extra bullets. I had never seen bullets like them before. They had shiny, chrome-plated shell cases and noses of a dense, bright colour. I begged him to make me a present of one'.

When the furore over the Colt became insistent, Feltrinelli disappeared completely. Inge shut herself up at home and would not answer the telephone. One evening, she told me everything, even about the consul and the pistol. By that time, Inge was in the trenches full time and the publishing house was ploughing ahead blindly, but life somehow went on. New books included *Silence* by John Cage and Nigel Calder's *Violent Universe* (*Eyewitness Testimony to the Astronomic Revolution of 1968/69*). One day, Umberto Eco would drop in; the next day, the editor of the mathematics series. Why didn't we ask Salvador Allende for an exclusive interview about Chile? He had just been elected head of a democratic government. Régis Debray, back in Paris after a long prison term in Bolivia, was the right person to do it. We could ask for world rights, and so the absent publisher would be proud of us (a good way of showing him that it was still possible to make books).

At the end of April, Inge received a message: it was an invitation to Madrid to meet someone who would have told her something about Feltrinelli. She went, but no one showed up. The situation was heating up. A leader of the Milan Federation of the PCI looked up Tina at the office of the publishing house. He informed her that he had heard from Rome that someone was planning to kill Feltrinelli. Many years later, Armando Cossutta, with some slight imprecision regarding events and dates, made this matter known: 'One day, Longo called me and said, "It has come to our attention that someone wants to kill

Feltrinelli. Contact him and put him on his guard. It's a very serious matter."' I asked Cossutta if he could remember who had given him the word: 'Maybe it was the Soviets, or maybe our channels inside Italian intelligence . . .'

Not even the functionary of the Cuban embassy, Andrés Del Río, knows for sure when his government told him to contact Feltrinelli. They met in the vicinity of the Stazione Termini railway station in Rome. It was their last meeting. The message that Del Río had to give Feltrinelli was exactly the same as the message forwarded by Longo and Cossutta. Perhaps even the dates coincided.

What is certain is that Roberto Zangrandi wrote to Brega in April 1971 about an 'important and delicate' matter. 'It would be very much in Giangiacomo's interest if I could manage to meet with him. It is essential that he learn about the news I have concerning him in time. You understand that I cannot say any more.' Zangrandi, a former Feltrinelli author with *Lungo viaggio attraverso il fascismo*, was working for *Paese sera* at the time. A few weeks previously, his newspaper had published an inquiry into the degeneration of Sifar, the army intelligence service. Zangrandi had procured confidential documents thanks to discreet sources. Perhaps he had fresh news, perhaps he wanted to warn Feltrinelli as the PCI and the Cubans had done.

* * *

On 17 May, Debray arrived in Milan to talk about the book–interview with Salvador Allende. He was courteous, liked the idea, and asked for a lot of money. Outside, it was raining heavily, and Debray's mood was unstable. Inge asked Debray if he had any news of Giangiacomo, and she questioned him to see if he saw any way out for him: 'It's too late now,' he replied. They both left for Villadeati, where they were to pass a week-end that neither would forget. The first guest to arrive was Alberto Moravia. The writer had just come back from a long visit to Latin America, where he had written a series of reports.

He put his things in his room, installed himself in the lounge and started talking. His sole topic of conversation was incest.

The rain was pelting down, it was thundering and the gravel of the drive ran with rivulets of water. Around nine o'clock, someone rang at the door to say that Feltrinelli was at the foot of the hill. Inge had let him know that Debray was coming. After so much time it's hard to say, but it seems to me that letting him know about that weekend at Villadeati, with such famous guests, was a way of offering him a pretext, a stimulus to measure himself against people who were not 'Red-eye' or 'Sickle-tongue'. When he appeared in the living-room, Moravia did not recognize him (though they had never been close): Feltrinelli was not sporting the famous moustache, and Moravia was quite unaware of his possible arrival. Then he suddenly understood, he was annoyed, and fearful that he had been lured into a trap. He asked my father if he was still living in Paris and went back to his conversation with Debray, as if nothing had happened. They were still going on about incest. That was when Giangiacomo got impatient. Moravia noticed, slowed down and turned toward him. The alcohol slowly helped create a more favourable atmosphere. When everyone retired, I was supposed to have been in bed some time before. I hadn't seen my father arrive, and in fact I wasn't even supposed to know he was coming. But I knew, because Inge had not concealed her anxiety very well. So, when he came in silently without switching on the light, I was already on my feet for a surprise hug. In the late morning, from the stairs, Moravia's snoring was clearly audible. The weather was slightly better but my mother was upset, she had realized that we had not been all together here for three years. Tomás Maldonado arrived before lunch. (Tomás had only recently settled in Milan, after wanderings that took in Argentina, his homeland, the Hochschule für Gestaltung in Ulm and Princeton University. From the early seventies, he was to take an active interest in Carlo Feltrinelli, who knew he could always count on him.)

At Villadeati the hours passed in an atmosphere of unreality.

At lunch, the talk was about Padilla, the Cuban writer imprisoned by Castro. Moravia: 'He is mediocre, but he is an artist, he
must be defended. But I'm not an anti-Castroist.' Moravia
talked diffusely with Giangiacomo, and in the end he decided
the publisher looked better without his moustache: its absence
made him look 'more vulnerable'. But he did not trust Debray,
so much so that he whispered into my mother's ear in the overly
loud voice of the hard of hearing: 'Is this Debray a man of
action, a man of letters, or a pederast?' Giangiacomo withdrew,
first with Tomás to talk about politics and about me, then with
Inge: 'If something happens to me, you must carry on fighting . . .' She was dying inside and she wondered against whom,
against what? Before the sky turned pink, Giangiacomo went
off across the lawn beneath the great cedar. We went back to
Milan. Monday was a school day.

> Dear Carlino, hurray for the holidays!!!! Right? How did
> school go? Did you pass the exams? Sure, but with what
> marks? Do you know who was behind me, in the wood
> half-way down the hill, when I left Villadeati the other
> day? Enzi, naturally. I had to give him a real lecture to
> get him to go back. Are the strawberries ripe yet? With
> all this rain, the fruit won't be up to much this year. Pity.
> Get that ceiling that is falling down fixed, the one that is
> held up by that really thin post. Remember to tell
> Mummy about that. As for your hideaways, you've made
> some nice ones but they ought to be better equipped and
> better camouflaged. Dear Carlino, I hope you have a
> good June, and a good holiday. I hope to see you soon.
> Look after yourself and stay on the ball. Your dad

* * *

In the first six months of 1971, Francesco De Martino was
nominated as leader of the PSI, Minister Restivo made revela-
tions about Junio Valerio Borghese (the investigation into the
coup attempt was subjected to a cover-up), and there was a

general strike called over housing reform. *Il Manifesto*, the new left-Communist daily, appeared on the newsstands. When it was still a mere journal, it had led to the expulsion from the PCI of its founders. A PCI delegation took part in the 24th Congress of the CPSU. The leader of the group was Enrico Berlinguer, the deputy leader of the party under Longo. *L'Unità* dealt at length with the William Calley case, Calley being the officer that Nixon had pardoned after he had been imprisoned for the My Lai massacre. Erich Honecker's election as secretary of the East German Communist Party was front-page news.

Giorgio Galli wrote: 'On a social level, the first half of 1971 was characterized by widespread agitation, with endemic episodes of petty violence both in the schools and in the factories. But neither the political nor the economic classes thought that a revolutionary process was under way.' If anything, public opinion, major newspapers, and the political leaders were all paying more attention to the rumblings of forthcoming *coup* attempts from inside and outside the corridors of power. The DC had become inward-looking, worried about all those votes straying to the right.

'The state must be smashed, not replaced!' Each of the extreme left-wing groups pranced around the squares, each with its own recipe for revolution. Potere operaio and their first cousins Lotta Continua continued to gain ground in various cities. Both organizations wavered between an overt and a covert political strategy while the security forces emphasized the military character of their mobilization. They confronted the police, the Fascists and even the students of the protest movement who, in Milan, were the only ones in the world to chant 'Beria, Stalin, GPU!' (with the blessing of the old Stalinist Alberganti).

In June, in the clandestine world, the Red Brigades had caught up with the GAP. It was still really small beer, but in terms of attacks, sabotage or demonstrations, their tactics seemed equivalent; both counted on an organized underground structure. The Red Brigades were making converts, the first

factory-based cells were being created, above all in the Pirelli
and Siemens plants. The PCI had already entered that phase in
which it did not see, or did not want to see what was going on.
After the arson attack at Linate, *L'Unità* wrote: 'Those who
carried out the attack, while sheltering behind anonymous
pamphlets containing revolutionary expressions, are acting on
behalf of those, like Pirelli itself, who have an interest in
making the workers' responsible struggle for contract renewal
look like a series of acts of vandalism in the eyes of public
opinion.'

While the papers were still talking about Quintanilla,
Feltrinelli was in hiding somewhere, writing a long letter to
the Red Brigades (20 May 1971). He 'congratulated' them on
their initiative, and expressed a hope for collaboration and
political cooperation in the broadest sense of the term. He proposed that they work together on a political, strategic and
tactical platform, with the aim of specifying what they were
fighting for and how it was to be done. He sent off a rough
draft for discussion, emendation and diffusion. While main-
taining the specific character of each organization, his objective
was the creation of a People's Liberation Army ('PLA-
Communism and freedom – Victory or death'), intended as the
fighting arm of a Popular Liberation Front. A definitive version of his idea was circulated that summer: 'For Communism
and freedom, a preparatory document for a political platform'.
As well as the unified command, they needed to create a legal
aid structure, as well as a Red Help lifeline for comrades who
might find themselves in trouble. Feltrinelli financed the idea
with quite a lot of money, which was diverted elsewhere. He
would have liked to involve people like Umberto Terracini*
and Lelio Basso, who had led many legal battles in favour of the
workers over the last few decades.

In the spring of 1971 there were the first meetings with the

---

* (1895–1983). President of the Constituent Assembly, one of the most
intransigent fathers of the Constitution and a senator (PCI) from 1948 until
his death, he was a dissident who none the less remained a party member.

leaders of the Red Brigades, in particular with Renato Curcio and Alberto Franceschini. The latter, a twenty-year-old Young Communist from Emilia and a newcomer to subversion, usually met Feltrinelli in the gardens of the Castle in Milan. 'I was well aware that Feltrinelli was much more than the GAP, because he travelled, because of the people he knew, and because of the publishing house. I always had the feeling that he knew something more than we did. He was not the kind to react spontaneously, he had a plan for insurrection, a global project . . .'

On 25 April, the Red Brigades printed the newssheet *New resistance*, two numbers in all, in which the GAP communiqués appeared. It was a concerted move. Perhaps there was enough space in which to march together. But it was not yet quite clear who was to play what role, even though the members of the Canossi column of the GAP drank coffee and brandy together with their cousins of the Red Brigades in the same bar in Giambellino. To seal these good intentions, on 15 July, the Red Brigades and the GAP sent out a leaflet – and a radio message on Radio GAP – in which they claimed responsibility for a bombing carried out the previous day in the Quarto Oggiaro district of Milan. They had blown up the Morris Mini owned by a Fascist who in his turn had blown up the automobile of a PCI militant.

But perhaps the differences emerged right from the start: subtle, impalpable, ridiculous but substantial. A former member of the Canossi brigade, who was never arrested, tried to explain this to me. He went straight to the point: 'Competition had a deleterious effect at all levels. The prevalent logic was to do more than the others and to do it before them, and the BR showed they were good at this right from the start.' But if Feltrinelli's platform was never agreed to, it was because the differences were more than trivial. As Prospero Gallinari* put it, there were 'two concepts of the class struggle then under

---

* A Red Brigades member involved in the Moro kidnapping. Imprisoned, he is now on day release.

way': one offensive, and the other defensive. The model was apparently like this: according to the Red Brigades, the constitution of an armed party presupposed a long-term struggle, a gradual process (as in China?) in order to reach the heart of the state. In the meantime, the idea was to accumulate support with the 'propaganda of the deed', while demonizing the enemy.

From the standpoint of Feltrinelli's 'Third Worldism', the situation invited a different analysis: the involution of Italian democracy suggested a prospect of revolution in the short term that ought to unite the forces in the field, especially if a part of the PCI were to join in. The military branch would then launch a hit-and-run guerrilla campaign.

According to the Red Brigades member Franceschini, the real difference between the BR and the GAP was precisely a question of timing: 'Feltrinelli was the only one to think of the revolution in contextual terms, now or never.' Victory or death: the Revolution was in danger, who could rescue it?

* * *

According to the Italian secret services, Feltrinelli was in Prague from 30 May to 1 June and from 30 July to 4 August of 1971. Aided and abetted by the Czech authorities, he allegedly entered the country with a passport in the name of Giancarlo Scotti, a resident of Florence. On the first trip (again according to Italian intelligence) he accompanied Mario Rossi's former partner Augusto Viel, the one who got away after the Floris killing in Genoa, and who remained in hiding there for six months. All of this is allegedly proven by a postcard of Wenceslas Square received by Viel's mother.

I traced Viel to a bar in the harbour of Genoa. Over twenty-five years had gone by since his presumed journey to Prague, two thirds of them spent in Italian prisons, very far from the pages of the newspapers. He was getting by on the strength of odd jobs, and plenty of alcohol before evening. He still had the look of an old-style conspirator. He told me he had never really been to Prague, and that he had signed the postcards for his mother while he was in Milan. Someone else had then posted them from the Czech capital in a bid to trick investigators into calling off the search for him in Italy. Some doubt remains (displacement? amnesia? in Prague only for the weekend?), but I think that substantially he was telling the truth.

Just to put everyone's mind at rest, Feltrinelli did in fact go to Prague at least three times in 1971. Prague is a magnificent city with an important Cuban embassy and an intercontinental airport. One trip there perhaps coincided with a journey to Latin America. This was the expedition to the Tupamaros of Montevideo that everybody has talked about, but no one – not even Sibilla – remembers exactly when it took place. It could have been July or September, and on one leg of the journey there was a stopover in Cuba. According to Debray's recollections, Feltrinelli was with him when they were training at Punto Cero.

What is certain is that I met my father again on 9 August. From the pier in Nice harbour, I saw him bustling about the *Sharopp*, a big Scottish boat that was hard to control. He was very nervous. In the course of a manœuvre, he collided with the yacht owned by David Niven as the actor looked on from the deck, one eyebrow raised in eloquent disapproval. But the *Sharopp* was a real sea-going craft that could carry crates of arms across the Mediterranean (I don't know if this really happened) or be used for sensational projects (which never came off).

My father put me to bed in a corner of the prow, near the forepeak. The swash of the harbour water made me feel really nauseous and in the bistro facing the *Sharopp* they served *salade niçoise* with hard eggs and old anchovies: on the second night, I got up and vomited. I vomited for the past and the future, I vomited for all the anticipation of our far too condensed meetings, and I vomited from the porthole on to the beautiful people I didn't give a damn for. I don't know how, and I don't know when, but I explained to my father that I didn't feel well. He made up his mind quickly: the next day we shut everything up and left for Austria. I travelled with Sibilla, who understood less than I did but she was nice. On the plane, a pockmarked American wearing a Stetson sent her a *billet doux* from the row behind us. Jacques Fischer, an engineer born in Liège, was flying the same route aboard another plane. When he got to the Valle dei Cervi, he returned to his real identity and climbed up with me to Lago Verde. It's so high up, you sometimes feel you are on the moon.

At the end of September, Rome was the venue for the 3rd Organizational Conference of Potere Operaio. Almost a thousand delegates came from 57 sections and 108 cells (there was even one in Zurich). The preparatory theses were a remarkable reinterpretation of Karl Marx's *Grundrisse*, and the conference centre in Rome's Eur district was the perfect frame for 'political canonization'. The conference tackled what had been described as the Crisis of the Planner-State* and gave its blessing to the 'Leninist' shift in the group's orientation: it was the birth of the 'party of insurrection' and the defeat of those who looked to the *Manifesto*, with its more gradualist line. But there were still more than two party lines and at the end of the day the victor was Franco Piperno,† who mediated between a moderate stance and the call to arm the masses by resorting to the usual *doppio binario* (double track) strategy, a particularly Italian form of fence-sitting.

At the Congress, all concerned had their say amid the usual feverish atmosphere of those years. Two militants in a little room above the auditorium recorded and transcribed the speeches. Behind them, a strange character without a moustache was taking notes. When he went away, discontented, he did so without being noticed. In theory, Potere operaio had declared a shift farther to the left, but Osvaldo was not convinced about the equation between the masses in revolt and an

---

* From the title of an essay by Toni Negri.
† (1945–). Professor of Physics at the University of Cosenza, he was the co-founder of Potere Operaio in Rome in the late sixties.

army. Where was the plan? It was all too reliant on spontaneity. Behind the words there were no concrete facts, there was little or nothing. They seemed to be creating a structure that was strongly centralized, oligarchic and deeply bureaucratic. It was also marked by strong personalism: 'Many of them are still petty bourgeois Marxist ideologists.' His idea for a common strategy uniting the fighting forces could not but fall on stony ground. And he realized this: with Potere operaio we can talk tactics, and there could be some cooperation in the Milan area, but as far as other things are concerned, it would be better if everyone resigned themselves to relying on their own resources. What was more, relations were not good, especially with Negri. According to Piperno, the two men really distrusted each other. Negri saw Feltrinelli as the wealthy publisher steeped in the archaic myth of the Resistance betrayed. For his part, Feltrinelli harboured doubts about the ideological myth of the endlessly contentious professor's astuteness.

Albeit without much hope, Osvaldo wrote to Piperno on 27 October. It was the famous letter to 'Saetta' in which he reiterated his idea of bringing the revolutionary forces under a 'unified command' that would eliminate 'old boundary lines or particularisms'. The alternative, wrote Feltrinelli, was to carry on as at present, every man for himself. Saetta–Piperno's reply was again disappointing.

In October 1971, Feltrinelli prepared a new text, entitled '*Lotta di classe o guerra di classe?*' ('Class Struggle or Class War?') This fifteen-page collection of warmongering solipsisms written with cheerful disregard for syntax was handed to Cesare Milanese so that he could read it and find someone to publish it (under a pseudonym) in some magazine. Feltrinelli and Milanese met in front of Parma cathedral and took a stroll through the old city centre. Milanese says that Feltrinelli had realized that the situation was not as good as he had imagined. He was disappointed with the failure to apply what everyone was loudly declaring theoretically and politically. He had written the text out of a desire to think things over. (Or a need for revocation, suspension, verification?) 'I had the impression that he wanted to get out from under,' said Milanese. Giampiero Brega thought the same thing in the winter of 1971. Was it still possible to break his fall?

'*Lotta di classe or guerra di classe?*' is a text that unfolds in large elementary categories, seen as fundamental: the state, power, class and the class struggle. At the time, each document was drawn up with a list of definitions within the reach of those who intended to think, talk and act as a 'class'. Every definition in this regard became important because it provided a more accurate definition of the revolution, which was the final measure of both party and state. Feltrinelli was no longer the 'rural' GAP member with an obsession about the *coup d'état*: half-measures were not admissible; indeed, away with all half-measures. A spade is a spade, revolution is (class) struggle, and struggle is war: the revolution is war. And it was in this way that class could become the equal of the state in terms of strength: war is the form of struggle through which class reveals its own power as real political power, not merely as opposition. Failing to recognize this means failing to understand that revolutionary war demands general rules; it means pursuing partial, compromise solutions devoid of that world perspective that revolution requires if it is to be true revolution; it means becoming the other side of that reformist coin that leads to deadlock, and to the neutralization–negation of the struggle.

These are statements of principle that reveal the thinking behind an attitude: Feltrinelli went underground to be more visible, a move that was at once ingenuous and functional, a shift from the implicit to the explicit to avoid making the conflict seem what it was not. At least until the winter of 1971, he did not realize that he was out of step with the events going on all around him. Until then, he had tried to explain the reasons for his design but others had already outlined alternative plans. In '*Lotta di classe o guerra di classe?*', the thing that he feared most was the failure to follow up in a revolutionary sense the events unleashed by the movement of 1968: 'No appreciable progress has been made [. . .] Why this spectacle, this rather negative result? Why?' The revolutionary movement, he explained, lacked 'strategic strength, a political, military and revolutionary counter-power that might confront, wear down and disarm the political and military power of its adversary.' Feltrinelli was afraid that history would decree a no-contest, the dissolution of the revolutionary opportunity. Hence the obsessive need to define the revolution in very high terms. But the non-revolution in store for Italy (1974–81) was to unfold in terms that were neither high nor low, but simply different. It ended in a squalid no-contest fought with sawn-off shotguns.

* * *

A hideout is a hideout. A one-room apartment, kitchen plus bathroom, in a side-street on the edge of Milan. You arrive warily, enter the light-green neon of the stairwell, go up to the first or second floor, a plywood door. Inside there is a plastic cupboard and two bunks, Italian brandy on the shelf, and a clamp mounted on the table holding a thin steel blade in its jaws: duplicating 'spadini'* for the purposes of car theft. Life in the hideouts was not exactly great, nothing particularly romantic about it. A crate with Marlboro written on it held stripped-down firearms bought in Switzerland and imported in the bodywork of an NSU Prinz. Or maybe they were from Liechtenstein: in the armoury in Vaduz, all they require is an identity document (but as you may purchase only one item per day, the 'Blond' and 'Pepito' had to stay on for a week).

In via California, in October 1971, there were four pistols and a sub-machine-gun. A radio transmitter with a low-frequency feeder stood in place of the television, and there was some canned food beside the cooker. For food and company there were the neighbourhood eating-houses out in the frost and the fog and the wind. Other typical hideout materials: newspapers, magazines, pamphlets, bunches of keys, false

* Literally 'small sword': a tool for forcing car door locks.

rubber stamps, document blanks and clothing. In the cupboard there were explosives, plastic explosive in cigarette packs, a Vietnamese anti-tank grenade (!), detonators, electrical circuits and watches. Osvaldo had developed a kind of mania for explosives. 'Günter' said he had bought the watches in a bar for three thousand five hundred lire for three pairs. Next to nothing.

In Milan, the GAP had at least four hideouts (and the BR were preparing the same number). In 1970, a friend of Lazagna's from Canton Ticino had bought the apartments on Feltrinelli's behalf. 'They are not for the revolution, they are for defending ourselves,' Feltrinelli had told him. They were rented in the names of 'fronts', who paid the bills regularly by mail. The Milan hideouts were frequented by two groups: the Giambellino crowd (that is, 'Praga', the only one who lived in the hideout, the 'Blond' and his cousin, 'Pepito', 'Red-eye' and 'Sickle-tongue') and another group from the north side of town ('Günter', 'Rooster', 'Bruno', 'Napoli', plus a few mavericks from the Italian Maoist outfit, the PCI-ML). Not everyone in the two groups knew one another. Just as not everyone knew the two or three comrades on secondment from Potere operaio and co-opted by the GAP, so it was no longer clear which outfit they were really from. 'You couldn't understand what the fuck was going on': thus Cocco Bill, who was one of them. The situation was confused. The suburban housing schemes turned out a stream of lumpen proletarian-individualist-rebel-misfits who declared they were ready for anything. In the bars of piazza Napoli and piazza Bolivar it wasn't hard to find men ready for an attack on the state police barracks or, if it was getting late, maybe a quick (armed) anti-Fascist patrol in Brianza. On the fringes of the clandestine structures there appeared characters like Marco Pisetta, a small-time smuggler from Trent imported to Milan by Renato Curcio after a few terrorist attacks in his home area. By the time Curcio introduced Pisetta to his friends at the Bersagliera, Pisetta was already a police informer (he became one officially in the spring of 1972). And he wasn't the only one. It was all very labyrinthine.

Osvaldo trusted four or five of his men, but the others were not allowed to know who he was (and even if they knew, no personal questions). As for recruitment, there was always the worry of finding new people; there were too many cowboys around who wanted only to raise Cain. They asked too many questions, talked too much, and were prone to indulging in theoretical debates about as subtle as the walls of Jericho.

Giangiacomo got on better with that mixed bag that was the old PCI: in the fall of 1971, in Milan, he dropped in on Pesce a couple of times in the dead of night; in Rome, he talked with Aldo Natoli (the only journalist with the *Manifesto* that he appreciated); one of Moscatelli's lieutenants was glad to put him up in Romagnano Sesia; Arnaldo Bera had two hideouts ready near Cremona, and Lazagna, who was working for the national social security service, had moved to Turin. Feltrinelli could talk openly with all of them, and all of them thought he resembled a hunted animal. Lazagna told a friend: 'His fate is sealed. They will put up with everything, even subversion in your own backyard, but when you supply arms to others you sign your own death sentence.' Who would not tolerate what? The intelligence services of America, France, Germany and Israel (the Israelis were very enterprising in Italy) were concerning themselves with the 'chief agent of Castroism in Europe' on a weekly basis.

At least four people heard Feltrinelli say 'if they find a dead man under a bridge, that man will be me'. When he said this to Inge, he had the gaunt face of a man in bad shape. They met in the Navigli* in Milan in early October 1971: it was their first encounter in the city in two years. The street was dark, and he was dressed too lightly. The talk was again about the publishing house and the last financing operation: after that, you'll have to get by on your own. But we were already getting by on our own.

---

*Old working-class area in Milan.

November '71

Dear Carlino, So Mummy tells me you have to wear glasses? Damn, you're getting just like your dad, who can't see the hand in front of his face! Thanks for your photographs and for your note. Unfortunately the Fascists are to be feared (never underestimate your opponent – that's a good rule). They are people who want to rule by force and to use force to defend the interests of the bosses. I'm glad you went to the demonstration. I heard that Enzi got better – you don't know how happy that made me. I've grown a bit of a beard and you'd hardly recognize me now! You with glasses and I with a beard! But there's no helping it: if we met on the street, we would recognize each other right away. Bye Carlino, bye son. Grow well, grow strong. A big hug and, to the cry of hooray for raising hell! I send you a thousand kisses. Your dad. I really hope we will be able to see each other around Christmas. Bye

One of the GAP bases, near piazzale Loreto, had a large box-room soundproofed with mattresses propped up against the walls.

In the winter of 1971, all the Milanese underground militants were talking about 'attacking the lackeys of power', namely bosses, factory overseers, spies, policemen, and Fascists. The usual routine was to burn their cars. The pamphlets said that such acts need not necessarily be barbaric: in order to mock the oppressive structure of power (and to inject the masses with fresh confidence), a little irony was required. The Red Brigades were thinking in terms of symbolic kidnappings, like a quick gagging, a photo and off you go, and even the GAP was looking at possible kidnappings: the Blond stalked the German consul for two weeks, Pepito kept tabs on an executive with the Autobianchi car firm, and Sickle-tongue knew every move made by Michele Sindona, then involved in a take-over bid for the Bastogi corporation. Sindona was to lose out to Cefis-Montedison and Cuccia-Mediobanca but the event marked his arrival on the scene. The diminutive Sardinian kept an eye on him in the street and noted down his routine movements (but the BR were after Sindona too, and one night they tried to plant a Molotov cocktail under his car).

It was only thanks to an entirely fortuitous circumstance that Feltrinelli did not become a kidnap victim himself.

* * *

Martino Siciliano often dined at Endo, the first Japanese restaurant in Milan and the only one in Italy in 1969. Siciliano, a telephonist by trade, was a cog in the very right-wing wheel of Ordine Nuovo between Milan and his hometown of Mestre, near Venice. He had become known in that area by sticking up 'Mao–Nazi' proclamations under fake left-wing acronyms in order to sow confusion (ploys that tickled Federico Umberto D'Amato of the Office of Confidential Affairs, the Italian intelligence service). At Endo, Siciliano tackled chopsticks and tempura in the company of his gang leader, also from Mestre, who was holding forth on the chosen race (Scandinavian male with Japanese female?) or on the use of dishwasher timers for bombs. Siciliano listened and learned.

The gelignite he had seen prepared for two missions on Italy's eastern frontier (Gorizia and Trieste, October 1969) failed to detonate, but that December the bomb went off in piazza Fontana and twenty-five years later Siciliano sang: sure, he said, his group of former street thugs had something to do with it; the 'Japanese' gang leader was Delfo Zorzi, here are the names of the CIA connections . . . A Milanese judge, Guido Salvini, set to work in an attempt to unravel the mysteries of the great Italian garbage dump.

'The name Feltrinelli was a target right from the start.' Siciliano recalled having taken part in the assault on the Feltrinelli bookshop in Milan's corso Europa in 1968, as part of a group that had set out from the Federation offices of the MSI. In 1971, the target was even more of a target.

It is not clear who had the idea, but one of the worthies of the right-wing network in the Veneto area, a person who owns a castle in Carinthia, had something to do with it. Oberhof is not far from the castle in question. Marco Foscari took along his gamekeeper, who was a former SS member, and Siciliano. The trio had no problems finding the house; Oberhof is not exactly Tokyo. They had two cars, rifles, binoculars, ether, ropes and a trunk for Giangiacomo Feltrinelli once he was tied up. The plan was to go back into Italy and have him found by the police. (Alive? Dead? The aim is not clear.) From the wood, they spied for long enough to understand that there was no one in the chalet, not even Sibilla. Doors bolted, mission postponed. This episode occurred in the first half of 1971, but, said Siciliano, it could have been the autumn.

Inside Ordine Nuovo – and the groups close to it – the talk was often of Feltrinelli. Nico Azzi has mentioned a sniper's rifle that was left for him at an Austrian airport. The order came from the intelligence services, which had the railway station in Klagenfurt under surveillance.

Feltrinelli was now to Italian intelligence what Castro was to the CIA. The equation is logical and is easy to explain. But Federico Umberto D'Amato added something more to it. For him, it was a personal matter, it had something to do with a kind of anti-intellectual hatred, or a different interpretation of literature, something toxic. Feltrinelli was the one who sold books that were the stuff of dreams; D'Amato had made a career for himself without any need for culture vultures; he was the Italian functionary who had made it to the control room of the mysteries, a bon viveur and a gourmand.

The Office for Confidential Affairs commissioned the book: who lives by the book shall die by the book, is that what they thought? *Feltrinelli guerrigliero impotente* (Feltrinelli the Impotent Guerrilla) came out with a khaki-coloured dust-jacket, publisher unheard of, 'printed in April 1971'. Perhaps the date is not correct. Giangiacomo bought the booklet in Porta Nuova railway station in Turin in November, after Lazagna had told him about it. He went to see Lazagna, who had moved to Turin from Genoa after his promotion. Of late, the two had seen less of each other. In the station bar, Lazagna watched Feltrinelli leaf through the pages with great detachment.

Feltrinelli guerrigliero impotente aimed at showing the world that the man was mentally unstable, a complex-ridden personality with a dash of radical chic. The (anonymous) author had pillaged a bundle of press cuttings, the divorce decrees and a few other news items scraped together here and there. The actual biography is almost deliberately neglected.

Years later, the former Feltrinelli editor Valerio Riva was to publish with Rizzoli the only book by Federico Umberto D'Amato: *Menù e dossier* (1984). The two men had known each other for a long time. Apropos of Feltrinelli, in November 1997, Riva recalled the secret revealed to him by the spymaster D'Amato on the subject of the khaki-coloured biography: the author of the book was one of the founders of 'Bagaglino', the favourite cabaret of the Roman right.

* * *

From the newspapers: on 3 December 1971 Castro was at the stadium in Santiago, Chile, with Allende and another hundred thousand people. The crowd responded warmly to appeals for the defeat of the creeping right-wing military plot. On Saturday, 28 November, three hundred thousand people assembled in Rome to hear speeches on the same theme, 'Stamp out the Fascist action squads and prevent all reactionary moves'. On the front page of *l'Unità*, Luigi Longo: 'All efforts to revive Fascism in our country can and must be crushed . . .'; 'The commitment of the PCI today, as it has always been, is a commitment to non-stop vigilance and struggle . . .' And Aldo Tortotella: 'The boldness of the subversive forces has been dented, even though the situation is still extremely serious and dangerous from many points of view . . .' Never had so many people been seen in piazza del Popolo.

In December, balloting began for the election of the Italian head of state. Amintore Fanfani, the DC's sole candidate, fell immediately by the hand of the *franchi tiratori*, those politicians who secretly voted against the party line. Then it began to look like the next possible candidate might be Aldo Moro, but this did not appeal to the smaller conservative parties and, in particular, it was viewed unfavourably by some currents within Moro's own party. Berlinguer offered to support Moro late in the day and it looked as if in the home straight the winner might turn out to be Giovanni Leone, a Neapolitan lawyer who lacked the *physique du rôle*.

On the second anniversary of the carnage in piazza Fontana, the extra-parliamentary left also commemorated the death of the young extremist Saverio Saltarelli, killed by the security forces during the demonstration held on the first anniversary. Four or five unauthorized assemblies were announced in town, and the police were on standby all the way to the motorway toll-booths. Potere Operaio, led by Negri, were planning a pitched battle. Preparations made on the evening before included the making of three hundred Molotov cocktails in a small apartment in the city's university quarter. But it was the subversives' tough luck that a passing patrol car spotted them loading the petrol bombs into a car and arrested almost all of them. A communiqué from Potere operaio talked of victory all the same and attacked those far leftists (such as the *Il Manifesto* group) that had dissociated themselves from the plan to fight in the streets.

Three years after the bombing, the inquiry into piazza Fontana was still at sea. Valpreda, the anarchist, was still in jail, and legends began to surface about the nine witnesses who had died in obscure circumstances. Like in Oliver Stone's *JFK*. Milan police arrested Giovanni Ventura and Franco Freda, inexplicably ignored by the investigators (the first reports on them date from shortly after the bombing). This was the start of a legal saga known particularly for its denouement: Valpreda's acquittal.

In the other Italy, the year ended with Giovanni Agnelli's confirmation as head of Fiat, while a contender on the television quiz show *Rischiattutto*, an expert on the paranormal, won thirty million lire, and Mafia boss Tommaso Buscetta broke probation in New York: according to the *New York Times*, the real danger in Italy was 'spaghetti with Chile sauce', in other words, a PCI ever more closely aligned with the government

At Christmas, I was in Gottingen until the 29th. In Düstere Eichenweg, everything was fine as usual: white berries hanging over the fence, old verandas with merrymaking students, the Max Planck Institute, my grandmother's kindness, and Hans Huffzky, who had come from Hamburg to take me to Austria. With Hans, we set off by train. Apart from my father and Sibilla, we found 'Camillo', the little blond Dane Jan Stage. At New Year, the fireworks were reflected by the branches of the trees sagging under their burden of snow. We also launched a mini-rocket with a parachute (my father always kept an eye on the toyshops). For 1972 I received a real steel wristwatch, not a toy. The first days of the New Year were one chess match after another. Hans said that when it came to chess my father and I both shared the same defect: a good attack but a poor defence. He maintained that the challenge in Reykjavik between Bobby Fischer and Boris Spassky would have decided the Cold War. Giangiacomo talked politics; you could see that he hadn't changed his mind, but he seemed less obsessed. In the end, they elected Giovanni Leone: I showed my father my home-work assignment, an essay on the new head of state. He said that Leone had been 'elected with the votes of the Fascists', but he let me get on with it. When seven years later a Feltrinelli book was to lead to the resignation of the President,* he was no longer with us.

* * *

Again in January 1972, CIA and FBI dispatches (available under the Freedom of Information Act) pointed the finger at

---

* See note on Camilla Cederna p. 270.

Feltrinelli, 'Castro's principal agent in Europe'. But it would be
better to say that he moved alone or in the name of vanguards
he thought he could count on. There were direct relations with
Venezuela, Bolivia, Uruguay, but the Cubans were not much
interested in adventures in the old continent. 'They did to him
what they did with Che, they ditched him,' was the rather
sweeping theory advanced by Giuseppe Saba, the ex-lieutenant
of a man called Osvaldo, and today a pizza chef in a town near
Nuoro.

   In early 1972, Feltrinelli confided in those who met him that
he had been obliged to step up his vigilance. He no longer used
the car or the plane but travelled exclusively by train, in second
class. From his movements it can be deduced that he was
spending most of his time between Oberhof, Switzerland (was
there a base near Chur?) and Milan. But he never let himself be
seen in Milan. For three years he had been checking out the
barbed wire between himself and the world and it would have
been an elementary blunder to emerge from a crowd and say
'hi' to me from underneath a blond wig. Our sole contact was in
the Engadine, shortly after my tenth birthday. He had taken a
room in a small hotel. I don't have a precise recollection, but I
have a vague memory of his coughing so badly that the other
tourists steered well clear of our table. Fear of tuberculosis. He
was ill at that time, plenty of people remember this ('He had
lost weight', 'He was smoking too much'). Sibilla, who lived in
Oberhof, mentioned the onset of bronchitis during a hurried
visit. This became pneumonia in one of the GAP bases in
Milan. Six days in bed. Tina secretly returned to duty to bring
him medicines. She was the only person in the world to know
he was there, completely alone.

Two GAP regulars, never identified, just to give an idea of the
milieu: Günter and Rooster from the same neighbourhood, lived
there until a few years ago. Günter died in 1977. Giangiacomo
had invented the nickname; Günter Grass came into it because
the men's surnames sounded similar. Typical. Born in 1927, at
seventeen Günter had seen Filippo Beltrami fall in action in Val

d'Ossola. Beltrami had been covering the retreat of Günter's partisan group. Twelve men died, including one of the Pajetta brothers. Before receiving his mortal wound, Beltrami, wounded in the legs and clutching his sub-machine-gun, turned toward Günter to tell him to run for it. After that, Günter's biography doesn't say much, apart from the fact that things weren't going so well for him. He spent what he earned too fast. By the end of the sixties, he was frequenting the bars of the neighbourhood, rubbing shoulders with underworld types (the notorious armed robber Renato Vallanzasca) and the extremist splinter groups of the far left (like the pro-Chinese factions). Officially, he did odd jobs as a plumber–electrician and even as a street vendor. When he entered the orbit of the GAP, he offered to serve as the boss's trusted factotum. He often had money problems and Osvaldo would occasionally slip him fairly large sums so that he could have his teeth fixed. As well as relays and faucets, Günter knew his way around explosive devices.

Rooster was younger than Günter. Born after the Resistance, he was twenty-five in 1972. A man who has always been an office worker, you would never guess that he has travelled the world. The first trip was in 1971, by ship to South America. He had known South American songs since boyhood, having learned them from compatriots who had come home to die in the poor country area where he was born. But the real Buenos Aires was another matter. In his pocket he had a letter of introduction from the Milanese student protest movement; his contact should have been an architect on friendly terms with the Montoneros. The contact did not come off, but Rooster wandered around the country, crossing the border into Chile and Bolivia. In Santiago he managed to shake hands with Salvador Allende during the inauguration of the academic year. He lived with a family of peasants in the Cochabamba area of Bolivia. He came back to Italy after six months (October 1971). He found the faceless suburban apartment blocks once more, the Maoist comrades of the PCD'I* on the verge of the umpteenth

* The Maoists.

schism and the desire to do something here too. He noticed new faces in the bar: a Sardinian and another man who spoke in the dialect of Genoa. It was these two who took him to Osvaldo, one evening in November 1971. Osvaldo was a spontaneous character, matter-of-fact and simply dressed: he seemed one of them. Only after a few weeks did Rooster realize that Osvaldo was not simply Osvaldo, and he was surprised: 'Why are you exposing yourself like this?' 'I want to be the first among the first but also the last of the last.' Another time, he came out with 'I'm doing all this for my son.' The enormity of the expression still gives me pleasure. But Rooster did not like it, the revolutionary struggle does not encourage private emotions.

Around 24 February 1972 Giangiacomo was in Oberhof. His lungs were a little better; he was eating salt for his blood pressure and drinking hot water for his liver trouble. Robert Amhof, his attorney in Vienna, saw him for an afternoon and found him 'normal'. They discussed a few divisions to be made among the Austrian properties and talked about some other administrative matters. 'Then we took a stroll in the woods' (From *ABC*, 7 April 1972). 'He was worried. "You know," he said to me, "every time I have my back to the woods, I get the feeling that someone might shoot me. Let's get this business done quickly. I am afraid that I won't live much longer."'

On 27 February, Feltrinelli left Oberhof, leaning out of the train window to the last minute, waving to Sibilla. He probably stopped in Switzerland for at least a week. On 4 March he met someone in the House of the People in Lugano. On 6 March he wrote: 'Dear Ingelein, I suggest that we meet at 1 p.m., Wednesday March the 15th in Caffè Bar Lugano . . .'* The rest of the letter talks of an appointment with a Swiss notary in order to sort out some dispositions by will regarding his son's inheritance. Strange. 'Why do you not bring Carlino along with you or is it too complicated?' the message ends. On 7 March, Feltrinelli entered Italy by train via Ponte Chiasso, mingling with a group of commuters.

* English in text.

Milan confirmed to him that the climate was getting very tense. Four days previously, the Red Brigades had kidnapped an executive with the Sit–Siemens group for a few hours in order to question him about plans for the restructuring of the plant. It was their first sensational operation. The episode aroused much comment within the far left: Avanguardia Operaia thought it was a ploy engineered by the intelligence services, Manifesto said nothing, while Potere operaio and Lotta Continua exulted as they wanted to emphasize the link between such commando operations and mass armed struggle. There was a call for a general mobilization of the extra-parliamentary left on 11 March to prevent MSI leader Giorgio Almirante from speaking in piazza Castello. Clashes and aggressive policing were predicted.

On 8 and 9 March, meetings were set up in the suburbs, seven in all. Osvaldo sent Rooster and 'Bruno', a young worker with the Marelli corporation, to measure the distances between the girders of an electricity pylon in the countryside near Lecco. The two men carried out their task correctly.

On 9 March, Osvaldo met Oreste Scalzone to talk about the demonstration planned for the 11th. Scalzone recalls: 'He asked me if, in my opinion, the movement might have accepted it if he and some of his comrades came armed to the demonstration, with a brief to defend themselves if necessary. It was the first time I had heard the expression "combat groups".' Scalzone replied by opening hundreds of parentheses: at present, such a thing was politically untenable. Perhaps Osvaldo was disappointed. Scalzone later said (in *Frigidaire*, October 1988): 'For the umpteenth time, [Feltrinelli] used an image that was dear to him: we extra-parliamentarians were like ping-pong balls kept dancing in the air by the jets of a fountain. The jets of water were the social struggles; when (inevitably, since the struggle is cyclic) they sank back, we would have fallen.'

The demonstration of 11 March resulted in fierce clashes between marchers and police. In via Verdi, alongside La Scala, a passing pensioner was killed when he was struck by one of the tear-gas canisters fired at eye level by the riot police. Osvaldo had summoned his men to a little villa in San Siro. They listened to the radio news and made ready.

On 12 and 13 March, there were more evening meetings in seedy eating-houses far from the usual haunts. Who did Feltrinelli see? Perhaps someone who came from Trent.

On the afternoon of the 14th, after 5 p.m., Günter's brother met Feltrinelli in the hideout just outside Milan. He seemed in a good mood. At 7.30 p.m. Osvaldo had an appointment with Rooster and Bruno in front of the Vox cinema in via Farini.

The idea was a real but relaxed operation, almost a rehearsal. It had nothing to do with competition with other groups ('Don't let's talk crap,' says Saba). Osvaldo had already carried out similar missions, but Rooster and Bruno got to the Vox three minutes late. Too much. But for them it was the first time.

Bruno had flatly refused to go, but Rooster had insisted. First he had asked him as a friend ('Come on, you come too'), then came the confession: 'Look, Osvaldo is Feltrinelli!' 'Then I'll come, if we get busted, someone will look after us.' Bruno was euphoric; he had met Osvaldo on various occasions, but he hadn't realized who he was. At 7.35 p.m. on the 14th, they set off with the aim of sabotaging two power pylons along the via Cassanese, near Segrate, a suburb just outside Milan. They were travelling in a Volkswagen minibus. Another three GAP effectives, Günter, Praga, and Sickle-Tongue, had similar targets along the canal leading to the town of Abbiategrasso. San Vito di Gaggiano. There was a pylon there too.

The weather forecast was for weak and intermittent showers in various areas of the city.

What mattered was that on Wednesday 15, at 1 p.m., we were waiting in the Caffè Bar Lugano, but no one showed. I was in a hurry to get back; at 5 o'clock I had a basketball game.

The chronicle of the hours that followed is the chronicle of another world intruding on mine. Here we must mention Twist, a dog found wagging its tail frenetically in front of 'a corpse of the male sex, lying on the ground, under a power pylon'. It was around 3.30 p.m. 'A dead man? Are you sure? Couldn't it just be a tramp lying there asleep?' Luigi Stringhetti, Twist's master, who rented a field in the hamlet of Cascina Nuova (Segrate), had to repeat his story to the commander of the local police station. Sure he was sure: he had seen him under the four stanchions of the pylon, among the stones, lying on his back with his arms spread-eagled, as if on the cross . . . At 4 p.m. they informed the carabinieri station at Pioltello, while in central headquarters in Milan, in via Moscova, the new shift had just come on duty. It had been a quiet day, and lots of men were out for the National Congress of the PCI at the Palalido, a large sports complex. The assembly that had witnessed the crowning of Enrico Berlinguer* as party leader had opened two days before, with greetings from the foreign delegations. When the station at Pioltello informed headquarters, they sent out the nearest police car: 'Fox to Fox 63, on the Nuova Cassanese highway they have found . . .' By 4.30 the situation was accelerating fast, and soon Stringhetti and Twist were to become the two most photographed mammals in Italy: portraits with beret, on the bike, with the dog jumping to catch a piece of bread, and the index finger pointing to the misshapen pyramid of the pylon. 'Power pylons will never seem the same to me again,' the writer Vassilikos was to say later. Beneath the pylon in Segrate, at 4.30 on Thursday 15 March 1972, the troops of the bomb squad gathered, along with the 'political' squad, the carabinieri, the forensic team, the Domestic Incident Service,† the gravediggers, the journalists (first to arrive were those from *Il Giorno*), the photographers and the rubbernecks. An army of ghouls beat a path to the scene. Investigators ascertained that the 'terrorist without a name' had used fifteen sticks of dynamite for the charges at the base of the pylon, but it was impossible to estimate the power of the charge that had

---

* (1922–84). Politician, member of parliament from 1968, and from 1972 to 1984 secretary general of the PCI. He promoted the independence of the PCI from the policy lines of the CPSU and advocated the 'historic compromise'.

† A play on the acronym DIS (Defence Intelligence Service), a branch of the Italian secret services.

exploded on the cross-member four metres up and that was presumably the cause of his death. On the edge of a side road, two hundred metres from the bedlam, they decided to break into the sand-coloured Volkswagen minibus with the yellow drapes over the rear window.

Toward evening, after the heat of the moment had passed, the investigators examined the evidence in their offices. They had left an electrical generator at Segrate to illuminate the pylon and to enable the search for further evidence. The surrounding darkness and the fog seemed ever deeper. The body was in the morgue. It was the corpse of Vincenzo Maggioni, said the identity card they found in his pocket; born in Novi Ligure on 19 June 1926. The photo – what can I say about the photo? – was of a face without a moustache. In the wallet were another couple of photographs, the size of stamps: a young blonde woman running and a portrait of a kid of about ten. They opened the minibus. There were millions of clues (the insurance was made out in the name of Carlo Fioroni) and a packet of Senior Service on the dashboard.

I don't know whether it was one of the 'political' squad or a Carabinieri officer who was first to say, 'It's him!'

(That evening Inge came home early after a dinner in honour of Paolo Grassi, the newly appointed superintendent of La Scala. Roberto Olivetti was also there. She said she had had 'a horrible premonition'.)

As about a million Milanesi slept, the presses were rolling: 'Terrorist dies near Milan while trying to blow up a pylon'. This was the headline in the early edition of the *Corriere*. Below, there was a photo taken from a distance: the man with the beard, lying among the weeds, seemed to have lost a leg.

At 7.30 on the morning of the 16th, Inspector Calabresi had asked the doorman in via Andegari make him a coffee. Calabresi used to drop by now and then. He waited until Giovanni, the doorman, had finished shaving. Then he took him down to the morgue. Giovanni did not make an identification. But in reality he had recognized him.

At least thirty people who had nothing to do with the

underground political struggle started with surprise when they saw the photo of Vincenzo Maggioni in the papers. The most incredulous tried drawing a moustache on the face. They folded up the papers and then called or dashed off to via Andegari in person.

Around one, I went into the living room to find the 'old guard' all present: Sergio, Giampiero, Silvio and Filippo. They were making phone calls and their expressions were grim. My mother gave me the news. Memories of hugs rose up from deep down inside, but these were no more than my lacerated memories: the main thing was that Inge was not going to weaken, and neither would the 'old guard'.

(On the night of the 16th, my mother had to identify the body. It was Sibilla's turn the following day. The papers were already chorusing 'It's Feltrinelli!')

On the morning of 17 March, before the radio news, Rooster spotted a certain amount of activity in the yard. From the window he saw three characters in uniform; they were making straight for his balcony. He got out of bed, limping, and approached his mother: 'Mum, nothing's happened, I swear it. Just a little accident in the car, the other evening . . . with my friends on the way to the lake . . .' The police arrived at the door. They conferred, but, surprisingly, they knocked at the apartment next door. It was about some banal heroin deal. Rooster's state of mind in those moments became a lifetime condition. He got out of politics, and no one ever looked for him in connection with the night of 14 March 1972.

* * *

Milan, September 1999. How's it going? Fine.

If it weren't forbidden, I'd talk about my sons, Francesca, my friends, rock'n'roll, my life as a publisher in via Andegari, of www.feltrinelli.it, of the new bookshops in southern Italy, and of the Feltrinelli Foundation. Then there are the lousy moments, the pointless things, the filth in the lungs and the incomprehensibility of the world: but if anyone asks me how it's going, I say fine. Everything's fine.

I don't think about it, after all these years it would be too much, yet no one knows that frightful death on 14 March 1972 better than I do. To die for your ideas, the most radical of fairy-tales. But it was a death that did not unleash the power of symbol, it triggered displacement or caricature on both left and right, a life swallowed up by a fortuitous contact in a watch that cost no more than a can of beans.

Handling explosives in the night at Segrate was not easy: a brusque movement, a hole in the adhesive tape, and the pin would make contact with the base of the watch casing. Who prepared the timers? The off-the-record versions are discordant. The case was filed away as an 'accident'; 'but as far as I am concerned Feltrinelli's death remains a mystery', the magistrate who declared the case closed at the time still says.

Bruno died in a car smash in the early nineties. I tracked down Rooster last spring; it wasn't easy. Pathos is a bubble of hot air and standing in front of the newsstand in the railway station is no place for pathos: he had been holding a story for me for twenty-seven years. He's OK, but to this day he is still brooding over a terrible memory. As far as explosives go, he told me, he didn't know anything about them and, as for the missions, that was his first and last. He did not take part in the preparations. All he had to do was to lash a wooden platform to the pylon to support the dynamite. Osvaldo had climbed up, and he asked Bruno to come up and help him: the charge on the central cross-member was to make sure that the pylon would fall in the right direction. An act of sabotage to create a blackout seventeen years before the Fall of the Berlin Wall, one year before the Chilean coup, and one month before the ferocious political elections in Italy.

In San Vito di Gaggiano, the other commando unit decked out its pylon with sticks of dynamite. Nothing happened. The police experts later concluded that the charges 'would never, but never, have exploded'. But, in Segrate, Rooster was hurled

several metres backwards by the shock wave. Before he noticed
the splinter buried in his leg, he was overtaken by the classic
split second in which he saw his whole life going by. He could
see nothing around him, then he saw Bruno running for the
road, one hand clamped over his ear. He had a perforated
eardrum and he was in a state of panic.

One was in shock, the other didn't know how to drive, and
the keys to the minibus were in Osvaldo's pocket. They ran for
it. First on foot, then aboard a local bus.

They could have done nothing to save Feltrinelli.

'Feltrinelli has been murdered' was the immediate conviction in
via Andegari. Because, on top of the desperation and the not
knowing, there came the first slogans from the right:
'Feltrinelli, piazza Fontana, urban guerrilla warfare, and now
prison for the accomplices!' (For the next ten years, there was
scorched earth all around us.)

The foreign press entertained the suspicion that the publisher had been taken to Segrate while unconscious. (Poison? A
karate blow?) And the suspicion of a 'terrible set-up' also
resounded in Berlinguer's report to the 13th party congress. In
reality, the presence of the CIA and geopolitical considerations
was at once far subtler or far more blatant than could ever be
admitted by Oreste Scalzone, the author, with Piperno, of the
most exact headline: 'A revolutionary has fallen' (*Potere
Operaio*, 26 March).

On the morning of the 15th, around 10 a.m., as soon as the
fog began to lift, two GAP members went to Segrate and saw a
car parked on the Cassanese road alongside the Volkswagen
minibus: well before Stringhetti on his bicycle and Twist the
dog, someone was already under pylon 71 of the AEM. Who?

Experts' reports and counteranalyses followed (like looking
for the dopamine gene using a butcher's knives), accompanied
by inquiries and counterinquiries, white books and tape record-
ings: all that was missing was a Zapruder-type videotape.

L'Unità of 17 March 1972 offered a portrait with an explicit
headline: 'Tragic Symbol of Failure'. The PCI's daily was

aiming at the big target: 'heir to a colossal fortune, he had had a varied career. From the prisons of Bolivia to an appearance in *Vogue* . . .' They dwelt on the business of the four wives. But the PCI's secret investigation into Feltrinelli's death did not confirm the 'accident' theory.

On 15 March 1972, Pietro Secchia was into his second month in a clinic. He had felt unwell on his return from a trip to Chile, where he had spent a week with the democratic, national, revolutionary and popular government. His people talked of a potent poison in the food served aboard the plane. They alleged that the CIA was behind this. Secchia was delirious for a month. He did not have long to live, but on 15 March he recognized Vincenzo Maggioni and thought that they had murdered him. On seeing the comments in the party newspaper he wrote to Cossutta so that the new secretary general might reconsider things: instead of echoing the pulp magazines, the left ought to 'inform millions of Italians, especially the workers, what Feltrinelli had done since 1946 for the development of Italian culture and the knowledge of Marxism'. As I said, he was delirious.

There are times when the flux of things goes in the wrong direction and it is impossible to reverse or modify the trend.

The Monumental cemetery with the pharaonic family chapel is not the place where I would have liked them to take my father. It is my only regret. Uwe Johnson and Alberto Arbasino have written about his funeral. Some original sequences are preserved in Bellocchio's film *Sbatti il mostro in prima pagina.* Milan was completely militarized: one police officer for every participant. Eight thousand altogether. Helicopters in the crystal-clear light. The coffin was carried on the shoulders of Feltrinelli booksellers.

There were clenched fists and red flags and cries of 'Comrade Feltrinelli, you shall be avenged!' Régis Debray used a megaphone to explain that Feltrinelli had friends all over the world. Sibilla was at the cemetery all morning. For her, too, it was a very tough time, then and afterwards. Shielded by dark glasses and a black veil, Giannalisa issued her statement: 'Finally my suffering is over.' The student movement leader Mario Capanna* (a PCI flunkey, Giangiacomo would have said) made a speech. Giulio Einaudi came. There were Feltrinelli's German colleagues Heinrich Maria Ledig Rowohlt and Klaus Wagenbach (who made a brief speech), students bunking school for political reasons for the first time, and the tears of those who had shared important moments with him or even just a plate of *risotto al salto*.

Several years later, a traffic policeman stopped me to give me a ticket. He felt he had to tell me that he had been on duty at the cemetery that day. And he recalled seeing the cortège passing by with the red flags and the flowers from Oberhof and Villadeati. He, too, had raised a clenched fist, and his superiors had made him pay dearly for that. Communism, one of the great themes of the last century, was more than just Ceauşescu overthrown by a crowd in a dreary cement square.

The father is the father and I am the son. What remains, remains. Without nostalgia. He taught me how to get hooks out of fish and how to roast meat, how to walk in the snow and how to drive fast, and to consider that there are not just apples and pears but fruits that provide nectar in the desert, to understand the story of the poet who died in his cage and many other things I still don't know, or are part of our secret language.

A father must know when to be strict and he must write letters, that is how I'd like to be. I saw him overturn tables when they should have remained where they were, 'because everything and I mean everything must and will change', and I saw him endure the fury of the fever that makes man weak because man is weak. He warned me that life is punctuated by sudden heartbreak, but I didn't see him grow old with the 'historic compromise' or bilateral cataracts. Did the explosion happen

* (1945–). A leader of the 1968 student protest movement who took a philosophy degree while in prison. A writer, he was elected to parliament with Democrazia Proletaria in 1979.

because of a brusque movement up on the cross-member (the fabric of the pocket pressing against the watch-case, the pin making contact) or did someone set the timer with minutes instead of hours? The answer would serve to end the story, but it would not establish what really matters.

The private papers of Giangiacomo Feltrinelli, including the correspondence with Boris Pasternak, are kept in the foundation that bears his name. The Secchia Archives are also there. (Any reproduction, even in part, of documents, letters and articles is forbidden. All rights relating to materials that are not part of public archives are reserved by the publisher.)

The documents from the Office of Confidential Affairs of the Ministry of the Interior come from the files on investigations into right-wing subversion in Lombardy and the Veneto conducted by the investigating magistrate Guido Salvini.

The internal documents of the Italian Communist Party are kept in the Fondazione Istituto Gramsci in Rome.

The papers on my grandfather, Carlo Feltrinelli, are in the state archives.

Archives in Washington, Moscow, Berlin, and Athens were consulted for the purposes of this book.

I wish to thank all the people who gave me their accounts. Many others have not been mentioned in the book but are fully entitled to be a part of it: I am thinking, for example, of Irene

Panatero, Stella Bossi, Aureliano Casati, Eliseo Campari and Beniamino Triches.

An affectionate embrace goes to the 'old guard': Silvio Pozzi, Romano Montroni, Valerio Bertini, Carlo Conticelli and Tina Ricaldone. Sadly, Giuseppe Del Bo, Giampiero Brega, Filippo Carpi and Gaetano Lazzati are no longer with us.

Duccio Bigazzi, who died recently, gave me the courage to finish this book; Bettina Cristiani, Cesare Milanese, Adriano Aldomoreschi, Cecco Bellosi, Oreste Scalzone, Gianfranco Petrillo, Aldo Giannuli, Alastair McEwen, Gianluigi Melega, Luciano Segreto, Chiara Daniele, Peppino Zigaina, Angelo Verga, Alberto Cavallari, Giandomenico Piluso, Giuseppe Saba, Juan C., Margherita Belardetti and Salvatore Veca were all extremely helpful. None of them is responsible for any shortcomings or errors contained in the text.

Senior Service owes much to many other people, especially in via Andegari: every one of them deserves my gratitude.

Finally, the support and encouragement I received from Rodolfo Montuoro was of fundamental importance; and then there is Francesca. Francesca did more than anyone.

.